Holding On to the Air

Florida A&M University, Tallahassee
Florida Atlantic University, Boca Raton
Florida Gulf Coast University, Ft. Myers
Florida International University, Miami
Florida State University, Tallahassee
University of Central Florida, Orlando
University of Florida, Gainesville
University of North Florida, Jacksonville
University of South Florida, Tampa
University of West Florida, Pensacola

Holding On to the Air

To Kat

AN AUTOBIOGRAPHY BY

Suzanne Farrell

with Toni Bentley

University Press of Florida
GAINESVILLE/TALLAHASSEE/TAMPA/BOCA RATON
PENSACOLA/ORLANDO/MIAMI/JACKSONVILLE/FT. MYERS

Copyright 1990 by Suzanne Farrell
Preface to 2002 edition copyright 2002 by Suzanne Farrell
Letters by George Balanchine copyright 1990 by the George Balanchine Trust
First published 1990 by Summit Books, Simon & Schuster
Published 2002 by University Press of Florida
Printed in the United States of America on acid-free paper
All rights reserved

07 06 05   6 5 4 3 2

PHOTO CREDITS
4, Lewis J. O'Brien
5, 11, 14, 15, 16, 17, Martha Swope
6, 7, 10, Fred Fehl
8, Cecil Beaton photograph courtesy of Sotheby's, London
9, copyright Time, Inc., reprinted with permission
21, W. Reilly
22, 23, 25, 26, Paul Mejia
24, 34, 35, Lloyd Fonvielle
27, Costas
28, 29, 30, 32, 33, 37, Paul Kolnik
31, Keystone
36, Elliott Erwitt
38, Steven Caras

LIBRARY OF CONGRESS CATALOGING-IN-PUBLICATION DATA
Farrell, Suzanne, 1945–
Holding on to the air: an autobiography / Suzanne Farrell with Toni Bentley.
p. cm.
Includes bibliographical references and index.
ISBN 0-8130-2593-1 (pbk.: alk. paper)
1. Farrell, Suzanne, 1945– . 2. Ballet dancers—United States—Biography. 3.
Ballerinas—United States—Biography. I. Bentley, Toni. II. Title.
GV1785.F37 A3 2002   2002020448

The University Press of Florida is the scholarly publishing agency for the
State University System of Florida, comprising Florida A&M University,
Florida Atlantic University, Florida Gulf Coast University, Florida Interna-
tional University, Florida State University, University of Central Florida,
University of Florida, University of North Florida, University of South
Florida, and University of West Florida.

University Press of Florida
15 Northwest 15th Street
Gainesville, FL 32611–2079
http://www.upf.com

Contents

Preface to the 2002 Edition

"Belief: Conviction of the truth of some statement or the reality of
some being or phenomenon esp. when based on examination of evidence."
—*Merriam Webster's Collegiate Dictionary*

GEORGE BALANCHINE was the most influential person in my life—and I
believed in him. Ideally, my performing career would have ended before
his death. My reason for writing this autobiography was that I hoped
it would help me to survive his death and the unspeakable loss of my
soulmate. Working on the book and revisiting my life kept me busy and
grounded for a year after my retirement.

Of the enormous legacy Balanchine has left to thousands, the most crucial for me was his philosophy of "Now . . . Don't save!" Though I always
danced this philosophy, it became the single most important factor in helping me live not only in his absence but also with my retirement. "Now" it
seemed obvious that the next step would be to impart all those lessons,
stories, ballets, teachings, and osmotic understandings that were shared by
George and me to the dancers of the New York City Ballet. It was not to be.

In July 1993, I was fired by Peter Martins, co–ballet master of the company. He spoke through the company manager, who called me and said
that Peter questioned my ability to teach and therefore could not justify my
salary. I was devastated and desolate. Now what? My home, family, company, and employment had been abruptly taken away.

However, Balanchine could never be taken away from me. He had
called me his muse. If I could inspire him in his lifetime, I believed he
would conspire with me in his afterlife. Still—how, when, and where that
would happen were unknown. Balanchine often said to us in class, "You
will all open ballet schools one day and teach!" We all giggled because
when you are a dancer those thoughts are so far from your mind.

Serendipitously, in 1993 James D. Wolfensohn, chairman of the John F.
Kennedy Center for the Performing Arts, invited me to conduct a series of
master classes for students of my choosing from the Washington, D.C., and
surrounding Maryland and Virginia areas. The initiative was sponsored by
Wolfensohn, and the students' only responsibility was to attend all eight
classes. This modest project proved so successful that in 1995 the Kennedy

Center enlarged the program to the national level. The intensive three-week program, "Exploring Ballet with Suzanne Farrell," takes place every summer.

Largely through the efforts of Barbara Horgan, Balanchine's personal assistant, the Balanchine Trust had been founded in 1987. This independent organization was created by his heirs to oversee the worldwide licensing and production of his ballets. I became one of the Trust's *répétiteurs,* and by 1995 had staged sixteen of his ballets throughout the world. This work culminated in an invitation to stage a week-long season of Balanchine for the Kennedy Center's twenty-fifth anniversary in October 1995.

I engaged soloists from the American and international companies I'd worked with before, as well as local dancers. The resulting ensemble had the appearance of a refreshing new company, and the press deemed it a triumph. I relished the work-all-day/little-sleep-nights, reminiscent of my performing days with Mr. B.

Ever since the first publication of *Holding On to the Air,* Hollywood has expressed interest in my book. Certainly my life had celebrations and catastrophes big enough for the big screen, but I was not about to consign it to a movie makeover. I did, however, work with the independent filmmakers Anne Belle and Deborah Dickson on a documentary, *Suzanne Farrell—Elusive Muse,* which was nominated for an Academy Award in 1997.

When my husband and I divorced in 1998, it was again work that would balance my life. I got as far away as possible and worked in Moscow with the Bolshoi Ballet. During 1998 and 1999, I staged *Mozartiana,* the last ballet Balanchine choreographed, and *Agon,* the 1957 masterpiece of collaboration between Stravinsky and Mr. B. For some reason, it was important to me that the dancers from George's birthplace have the good fortune to dance his ballets and to realize his genius before the end of his century.

Although I had not consciously calculated a strategy for having my own company, it seemed as though I might be destined for one. Certainly, Balanchine had shown me how a company should be run, artistically and successfully. I had sat for many hours in the dark auditorium of the New York State Theater listening to conversations Mr. B was having with the costume designer, with the lighting designer about trying new effects, and with management about programming and touring schedules. Listening and learning and remembering.

All this came into play when the Suzanne Farrell Ballet became a full-fledged company in association with the Kennedy Center in the fall of 2000. Our first two seasons included appearances in Washington, D.C., New York City, and regional tours, with a repertory of ballets by Balanchine, Maurice Béjart, and Jerome Robbins.

During my performing life I was a person who spoke the language of music and dance—and few words. But the farther away I've come from my dancing days, the more I have had to use words in order to make myself understood as a teacher. Not merely to explain ballet steps, but to make those steps come alive visually and musically. A musical picture. It's as if you had loose bits of colored glass, two mirrors, and a cylinder. When these components are placed together correctly, a kaleidoscope will be formed and the movements of the bits of glass will reflect a variety of patterns and dynamics. So too with a ballet. Except with a ballet, in addition to the physical components you must reflect the heart and soul of the choreographer.

In August of 2000 I joined the dance faculty of Florida State University in Tallahassee as a Francis Eppes Professor. Every time I teach—whether students or my company—I inwardly giggle as I hear George's voice long ago: "You will all teach one day!"

A dancer's life onstage is short. Teaching extends my dance life. I am the beneficiary of every dancer who came before me and I am grateful. I am happy being a conduit to, through, and beyond each dancer I work with. I have learned so much and have exciting ideas for the future. And, perhaps, that will be another book.

Suzanne Farrell

Avant Scène

T he stage is dark, but in one corner, in the shadows, kneels the curved, still body of a man. His silhouette shows his face buried in his palms, as if in anguish, as if remembering . . . or as if dreaming. Out of the darkness behind him, in a single shaft of light, steps the figure of a young girl. Her hair is loose, her white gown is flowing and translucent. She reaches toward the man, but he cannot see her until she stands over him and peels his hands from his face. The stage brightens as the man rises, and it is revealed that his hair is graying at the temples and his movement is not as elastic as it once might have been.

The two figures begin to move together, quietly at first, then with such passion, tenderness, and reckless desire that if this were fiction it might endure, but if it were life it could not. She appears to lead, and he to follow, desperately trying to catch up with and seize her youth, her beauty. She is his destiny, he is hers, but fate intervenes and separates them. They end as they began; he kneels, and she replaces each hand and then each finger across his eyes. He cannot see her now, but she is yearning, reaching for him even as she backs away into the shaft of light, into the shadows. The curtain falls.

.   .   .

Meditation, danced to the sad heightened strains of a Tschaikovsky violin, was the first ballet George Balanchine made on me. I was eighteen, Balanchine was fifty-nine. Critics were shocked that the "cool," "calculating" master choreographer of Stravinsky's neoclassical chords could be so blatantly emotional, so romantic, so tragic, so vulnerable. They even accused him of "Russian" sentimentality. But those who knew him weren't surprised; he didn't stop being Russian when he became American. I certainly wasn't surprised that my boss had feelings, even the need to love and be loved. I was, however, very much surprised to learn that it was I who inspired these feelings—onstage and off.

I was very backward. All my energies had gone into dancing. By the time I turned eighteen, my love life consisted of one date with my best friend's brother when I was fourteen; but as I towered over him by several inches, there was little room for romance. There were, a few years later, two kisses, but I felt little for either of the men. My first love affair began when I was barely eighteen and was the longest, most complex, most productive, and most important of my life. It was also the most passionate and tumultuous, although it did not begin with a kiss but with a ballet. Kisses came several years later, but they signified little that was not already apparent. Within a few months it seemed as if the whole world was talking, guessing about, predicting, and lamenting our alliance, and they seemed to know a great deal more about it than I, one of the principal players. But Balanchine made his feelings about me public long before he declared them in private. The precedent was set for the next twenty years of our lives.

Meditation was the beginning of our relationship, and more than twenty ballets later, *Mozartiana* was the climax, the distillation of all that had preceded it. Again Tschaikovsky was our music, but this time the open emotion was tempered by the spiritual purity of Mozart. But *Mozartiana* was not the end, just as Balanchine's death a few years later was not. For me it will never end; Mr. B is as much a part of my life and my soul as my own self. He always said, "You are the other half of my apple." He also said that he was, in the words of the Russian poet Mayakovsky, "a cloud in trousers," and so it is not surprising that our attachment existed in a time and place that was not always here and now as most people define "reality." And yet two people were never more in the moment, the present moment, than he and I. In fact, the importance of the moment was perhaps his most vital lesson, and he could not have had a more willing disciple than myself.

But when I received his first letter I was still, while far from re-
bellious, unconvinced and confused. It was the beginning of many
years during which I would remain confused. At least when I danced
everything was crystal-clear, to myself, to the audience, and to him.
Thus dancing became my sanity and my salvation, while life remained
life with all its ups and downs, twists and turns.

In October of 1963 Mr. B told me he was going to do "something"
on Jacques d'Amboise and myself. Jacques, who had been a principal
dancer with the company for ten years, was my childhood idol; I had
danced with him, in the form of an armchair, when I was a star-
struck twelve-year-old ballet student in Cincinnati. Already one
dream was coming true. It was the first of many, and it did not take
me long to realize that having your dreams come true can be dangerous.

I was excited, nervous, and curious at the idea of having a ballet
made on me and presumed that the "something" would entail choreography using what I thought I could do best, which was being
what I was. And what I was, to me, was an inexperienced, unde-
veloped, eager, energetic girl from Ohio, who had been in the corps
de ballet of the great New York City Ballet for exactly two years. I
had always wanted to be sophisticated, and I had the courage to
pretend I was on occasion, simply because I knew I wasn't—in my
family I was the baby, and they called me "Bean," short for string
bean. So when Mr. B's letter outlined a romantic situation, a dilemma
of sorts, it threw me for a loop. It also threw me in the deep end, but
as I was soon to learn, he knew who could swim and who couldn't,
and he knew it long before they did. The letter was mailed from
Hamburg, Germany, where he was directing a production of Gluck's
Orpheus and Eurydice for the Hamburg Opera.

Dear Suzanne!
Here is the poem I promise to you before I went to Hamburg.
That is how Jacques should feel when he is dancing pas de deux
with you. Show to him and to Diana [Adams]. She is your guar-
DIANA-angel! but not to anyone else.

I CAN'T FORGET THIS BLESSED VISION,
IN FRONT OF ME YOU STOOD MY LOVE,
LIKE INSTANT MOMENT OF DECISION,
LIKE SPIRIT BEAUTEOUS FROM ABOVE.

THROUGH LANGUOR, THROUGH DESPAIR AND SORROW,
THROUGH CLAMOR AND THROUGH RESTLESS SPACE,

I HEARD YOUR VOICE FROM NIGHT TILL MORROW
AND DREAMT AND DREAMT OF DARLING FACE.

THE YEARS OF STORM COMPEL SURRENDER,
DISPEL AND SCATTERED DREAM OF MINE,
AND I HAVE LOST YOUR VOICE SO TENDER
AND FACE SO HEAVENLY DIVINE.

P.S. I hope by now you are thin and beautiful and light to lift.

See you soon,
Your G.B.

It was my first love letter, but at the time I was too distracted by the P.S. to realize this with any sort of intelligence. I took it all at face value: the poem described the two abstract characters that Jacques and I were supposed to be. I was far too naive to presume that Balanchine might be interested in me in any way but on the stage, as that character, in that pas de deux. I was right: this was, after all, work—but if I was not yet that woman, I was to become her. To say Balanchine's steps and Tschaikovsky's music made me her is to simplify, and yet in a way they did. I don't know if I became her because she was really me and Balanchine saw that long before I did, or if I became her because Balanchine wanted her, needed her, and in me found a body and a mind willing to risk being her. The question does not have an answer, like one of Mr. B's favorite queries for young dancers, "Which comes first, the chicken or the egg?" What is indisputable is that in *Meditation* Balanchine prophesied the future. I don't know how he could have known so much of what was to happen. Since I was the story, I couldn't see it; I just danced it. It was only an eight-minute pas de deux, and it was everything.

All this is clear only in retrospect. At the time I had several more immediate worries than what life would have in store for me. Before Mr. B left for Europe, we had a few preliminary rehearsals. We began at the beginning of the ballet, which was not always to be the case, but for me it threatened to be the end. Jacques was kneeling center stage with his face in his hands. I was to enter from the back corner behind him with three simple steps—full step on my right foot, up to pointe on my left and then pointe on my right, stopping in fourth position. There were four of us in Studio 1 at the School of American Ballet on Broadway and 82nd Street that afternoon—Balanchine, Jacques, myself, and Gordon Boelzner, the pianist—and I was acutely embarrassed.

Mr. B, of course, didn't mention any story line; he described only what he wanted physically. It was to be as if I were parting an invisible curtain, parting clouds, with my arms out to the side. "You just hold on to the air when you're up there [on pointe]," he said. "You're riding on the air." It sounded so simple, and I tried to envision what he wanted, but every time I stepped up there I'd teeter and wobble and keel over. Finally he said, "Well, we can't stay here forever. Let's pretend you're already in and take it from there."

Far from being relieved, I felt awful. It was no secret that Balanchine had many beautiful and accomplished dancers in his company, established ballerinas, as well as a considerable quantity of young talent, and every single one was vying for his attention. I saw him joking with Suki Schorer and Patricia Neary; I saw him making ballets on Patricia McBride, Diana Adams, and Allegra Kent. He clearly didn't need me, and here he was showing a little interest, and I couldn't do the first thing he asked. Over the next few months I did learn how to do that entrance, but every time I did, a feeling of inadequacy flashed through me. I was humbled, as I was to be so many times, to learn that being motionless on stage is far more difficult than the more obvious tricks of the dancing trade.

While Balanchine was in Hamburg, I practiced and practiced the entrance, and then his letter arrived and threw me off balance again. I was sitting on a red vinyl bench at the School of American Ballet when Nathalie Gleboff, one of the School's kind but severe Russian directors, handed me a white parchment envelope and said, "Here's a letter for you from Mr. Balanchine. He never writes letters." I knew that was true, we all knew that. I've little doubt that for people like Mrs. Gleboff, who had been associated with Balanchine for many years and had seen him through many ballets, many wives, and many love affairs, the signs of trouble were already clear. I saw trouble, but not for the same reasons. I was flustered even before I opened the letter to know that he was thinking about me at all. I curled up alone in a corner of the bench and read the letter for the first and—until recently—last time.

The beginning and ending were written in blue ink, the poem in red. I was really frightened by it, and I was hurt by the P.S. If I needed to lose a little weight, I should have known it, I shouldn't have had to be told. Again I felt stupid and inadequate, and I was so upset that I proceeded to try to lose weight right there, sitting on the bench. Thus my life was now hinging on two big problems—getting my entrance right and losing weight.

After recovering from the P.S., I had yet more decisions to make. "Show to him [Jacques] and Diana." What did that mean? Diana

Adams was one of Balanchine's most favored and esteemed ballerinas at the time, and he had created many great ballets using her long lean line and cool elegance. She had also discovered me as a fourteen-year-old in Cincinnati and been instrumental in getting me to where I was; thus she was my "guar-DIANA-angel." But she was by no means a pal or even a close friend. Nevertheless, Mr. B said to show her the letter, and so I did. I folded the P.S. so she wouldn't see it. I don't recall what she said, probably not much, but whatever it was, it didn't lead me to worry about the implications of the poem; it did not occur to me that I was entering into an emotional abyss so deep that perhaps I should decide if I thought it might be worth it. It *was* worth it, but I never once stopped to consider that question.

Perhaps Balanchine was sending a message to Diana also, although considering that they had their own past together and that she was a good friend of Tanaquil Le Clercq, Balanchine's wife, it would seem strange. But people in the theater have different understandings; their closeness is bound and sealed by work above and beyond and after personal emotions have entered the picture and done their damage. Or perhaps Balanchine thought it would scare me less if he said to show it to someone else, that a witness would attest to his good intentions.

I did not, however, have the courage to show the letter to Jacques. I didn't show it to my mother either; Mr. B hadn't said that I could. I sensed that it was incriminating evidence, and yet I didn't know quite why. It was far too special to destroy, so I hid it away in the back of my dresser drawer. I hid it from myself as well as everyone else; just the fact of receiving it made me feel as deeply as I had ever felt. I didn't even reread it; it was too staggering to unfold, and when Mr. B returned from his trip, it was never mentioned between us, ever. The letter remained hidden for twenty-six years.

Analyzing underlying meanings in poetry had never been my strong point in school, and to me the poem was "lovey-dovey" stuff, like something in the movies. I came from parents who did not love each other, so my idea of love between a man and a woman was Hollywood's. I cried desperately at *Love Is a Many Splendored Thing*, thought falling in love was wonderful, and hoped one day it would happen to me. But I was also raised in the Catholic church, where being in love was a very serious affair; it meant marriage—without divorce. I believed this, even though my mother, my grandmother, my great-aunt, and eventually one sister were all divorced. I wasn't going to be.

I always, however, imagined myself in love. It was with someone specific, but he didn't have a face. I wouldn't have known real passion if it had knocked on my door, so I proceeded to believe that this poem was about how I was supposed to feel in *Meditation* toward my partner. I had great difficulty seeing myself in the picture. I didn't know how I was going to do it; I had never been in love. But I could always pretend, that was something I knew how to do all too well.

I didn't stop to give much thought to the significance of the ending of the poem, which became in turn the ending of the ballet. If there was a sense of futility about this great love, a sense of it being an impossible vision, I didn't feel it. When I danced, the romance, the tenderness, the embraces, and the caresses were full-blown, full-blooded passion. They were, after all, the first time I had ever been embraced, caressed, needed, wanted, and loved as a woman, and nothing could have been more real to me. It was only in my coming and going that I was elusive, while together our love was unquestionable.

Over time it became clear that the man in the pas de deux was Balanchine; he even told Jacques to put gray in his hair and I can't help feeling that if he had been younger he would have danced it himself. Never, though, did he say it, never would he have said it, but never was anything more apparent. I didn't have an understudy for *Meditation*, then or ever. No one else has ever danced it.

We finished the ballet in November, and it premièred in New York City on December 10, 1963. Balanchine had not only choreographed a ballet; he had choreographed our lives.

Part

I

———— �£ ————

CHAPTER ONE

Cincinnati

I always thought I'd be a clown. I did not dream of being a famous dancer or any other kind of dancer, I was too involved imitating Marilyn Monroe and Martha Raye. My performances were usually in the kitchen or the living room, and if someone saw me I would run away, embarrassed. But I wasn't so embarrassed that I couldn't be cajoled into numerous public appearances at various back-yard carnivals and later at school recitals. Daily life in Mt. Healthy, Ohio, was fine—but pretending was finer.

My grandmother and her sister, Aunt Helen, lived around the corner from us. That was as far as my mother moved when she married my father, but at the time I guess it was far enough to qualify as a typical adolescent escape from parental authority. Mother married eight days after she graduated from high school, and my father, who was twenty-one, was the only date she'd ever had. She wasn't allowed to go to downtown Cincinnati alone until after she married. Mother has always said that her marriage was a mistake from the start, but I think they must have once loved each other in some fashion and she has forgotten. As time went on, being a mother held more promise for her than being a wife.

My sister Donna—we called her Sug (for Sugar)—was born just

over a year later, and Beverly two years after that. Sixteen months later, on August 16, 1945, when I came along, I was wanted but unplanned. They called me Roberta Sue after my father, Robert. Since there were already two beautiful blond, blue-eyed little girls at home, everyone was shocked to see that I had a full head of straight, coal-black hair. When it grew, I had platinum-blond roots, and it looked as if I'd had a bad dye job. But everyone was satisfied with the explanation that in addition to our German–Irish ancestry we were direct descendants of Pocahontas. Mother called me her little papoose.

Mt. Healthy is now part of Cincinnati, but forty-five years ago it was a quiet little residential town, and going into Cincinnati was going to the Big City. Our four-room house was small but comfortable with the requisite white picket fence and backyard with sandbox and rabbits. But grandmother's house was where the fun began. It had a long driveway, two tall pine trees, and a little patio porch. Sug, Bev, and I thought this was the height of chic and elegance. A pinball machine from a local bowling alley had been installed in the basement, and I spent many hours zapping the lever and watching the ball fly around in the maze. I played to win.

My great-grandfather's family had worked in a tannery in Cincinnati and had left in the garage a workbench with leather odds and ends. There was only a single step up to the bench, but that was all we needed to call it a stage, and my sisters and I hung a few sheets as curtains, laid out a couple of chairs for the audience, and proceeded to produce, write, rehearse, and perform our variety shows. It's where the ham in me was born.

We would drop off invitations—"You are invited to a Carnival at 1508 St. Claire Avenue given by Donna, Beverly and Roberta Ficker and Joyce Dryer"—in mailboxes, and eventually people began to cringe when they saw me: another weekend, another show by those Ficker girls.

We were very serious about our productions. At six I was an elf (one of Santa's); at seven, a clover (we pantomimed "I'm Looking Over a Four Leaf Clover," and I lay flat on the stage until the end when my friend would say, "Shall I pick it?" and up I popped); at eight I was Nat "King" Cole (lip-synching "Just One of Those Things"). My big inspiration was a television show called "Dotty Mack's Pantomime Hour." Dotty Mack, who looked like a young Elizabeth Taylor, Bob Braun, and Colin Mail were the three regulars, and they pantomimed hit songs of the day. Watching them, I saw no reason why I couldn't imitate Marilyn Monroe. I lowered my voice, wrapped my arms around my shoulders, hugged myself, and rocked my hips.

Teresa Brewer's high-pitched, country-western style and Martha

Raye's loud, wide mouth and rolling eyes provided other challenges. To me this wasn't just playing. I didn't want anybody to watch me; I was performing for people who didn't exist, for an eventual audience. I would be conned into an imitation, and then, when everybody laughed, I would run away, hurt. When they said they weren't laughing at me but with me, I'd staunchly reply, "Well, I'm not laughing at all." These various performers had a certain something that impressed me, and yet I never imitated anyone that I eventually became like. Or else I missed my calling.

My first public display, however, was as a dancer. I had taken a few ballet classes by the age of nine, but there was little that was classical about my number at the local public school performance. The newspaper advertised the event: "Donna Ficker, well-known Hilltop dancer, will be featured in tap and ballet numbers, Beverly on the piano and Roberta doing a 'special dance.' " Mother had spied me doing some very wiggly choreography to the current hit song, "Cherry Pink and Apple Blossom White," and she suggested I do this dance for the occasion. I wore a black leotard and a wonderful multicolored mambo skirt that was short in front with a train of ruffles behind. With bare feet and a big red flower behind one ear, I improvised—shaking my shoulders, swaying my hips, knocking my knees, and I suppose generally being pretty risqué. The music really got to me, all the trumpet rolls, the deep muffler draw-outs, the bongo drumbeat.

I remember two things from that performance. I realized that when I was alone and the music was on the record player nobody would know if I was doing the correct "choreography" or not, and that the song seemed an awful lot longer than I had expected. When it was over I wished I hadn't done it; it was not taken seriously and I was dead serious.

Mother was very theater-minded. Though she claims to have had no ambitions of her own, she could have been a producer or a set designer. She would scrimp and pinch pennies all year long to have an elaborate Christmas; the whole house became one huge decoration, and we always got everything we asked for. She would lock us in our bedroom Christmas morning until everything was perfect and she had the movie camera loaded, ready to record our entrance. Everything was just slightly rehearsed and then carefully preserved on film even though we had no projector to show the movies. Mother was a forward-thinking woman, and she knew that one day there would be a projector somewhere.

Mother was our greatest conspirator, and she thought she had the three most talented daughters anyone could have. In spite of being a working mother, she sewed many of our frilly dresses, carefully ironing every ruffle and curling and braiding our long blond hair. There was nothing in my childhood to show me that I couldn't be someone other than who I was. Even the rigors of going to school and learning history, math, and science didn't make make-believe any less real. It probably made it more necessary.

Mother came from an exclusively female family, which was made possible by divorce. She was an only child. Her parents were divorced when she was six months old, and her mother moved back to the family house and never remarried. Mother met her father only twice, once when she was eight and he came back saying he still loved her mother, and again when she was grown and divorced herself. Mother was brought up mainly by her grandmother because her mother was often bedridden, unable to walk for an entire year at one time, with what they called "tuberculosis of the groin." Later on, when I knew her, she was considerably stronger and had made a living over the years by hand-tinting cards for the Gibson Card Company and various photographers. In time her only sister, also divorced, came to live with her. There were no men to be found anywhere near my family. Except my father.

I have never known much about my father, and I don't remember much, except that his parents were first-generation German-Americans. Father was a tall, good-looking man, and my parents were a handsome couple. He had studied briefly for the priesthood but did not pursue it.

During World War II, Father was exempted from military service because he was employed as a shipping foreman for J & F Schroth Packing Company, which supplied the Army and the Navy with all the prime cuts of meat while sending the surplus cuts to our Allies in Europe. Only 5 percent of their produce was left for the general public and this was dispensed through strict food rationing. For the last year of the war Father worked for Crosley Motors, which was engineering small landing-craft motors for the planned invasion of Japan. When Japan surrendered—and I was born—the demand for the motors ceased and Father went to work for another meat-packing company, which proceeded to close within a few years, buckling under the pressure to unionize. By the time I was four, he was working for Kluener's Meat Packing Company.

Because he delivered meat to various nearby districts, my father was away from home several nights a week, which was fine with my mother and became normal for us. She always told us that if he hadn't been absent so much their marriage wouldn't have lasted as long as it did. I'd like not to believe that. She also told us that if it hadn't been for us, her daughters, she would have divorced him sooner. I have always been very uncomfortable with that responsibility and think it unfair.

On occasion, Father would take each of us in turn on an overnight delivery. First we would go to the market to stock up and walk through the huge refrigerator rooms with sides of beef hanging overhead dripping blood. Everyone would make a big fuss over "Bob's girls" and give us wieners to eat. As soon as he had all his orders filled, we would climb way up into the cab part of the truck and drive to the small country stores where he made his deliveries. It was fun at the time, but later I developed an aversion to meat.

Father did not approve of Mother's vigilant efforts to offer her daughters artistic outlets, and it became a major point of tension between them. But no man in Mt. Healthy in the early 1950s would have thought that any kind of career in the arts was a possibility for his children; no one, including my mother, had ever seen the real thing. Father was right, except Mother didn't agree. Lessons cost money that we simply didn't have. Sug, Bev, and I soon realized that if we wanted to have piano or dance lessons, we had to be able to get scholarships. Mother never told us this in so many words; she didn't need to.

Mother came from a self-supporting family, where work was work and play was work. If any of us weren't good at what we were being taught (as I wasn't at painting), those lessons ended. Her overwhelming belief in us didn't blind her. She was pursuing rather impractical interests in a practical manner, and that's probably one very good reason why I was able to become what I became.

Ballet lessons for Sug began, indirectly, because of me. I was less than a year old when my sisters and I contracted terrible colds; mine turned into pneumonia. I was rushed to the hospital, and my mother was given the choice of me not surviving or a fifty-fifty chance if they gave me penicillin, the new wonder drug; they didn't have time to test whether or not I was allergic. After a month in the hospital under an oxygen tent and the tender care of our family doctor, Charles Keifer, the penicillin worked, and I was able to go home. But I had a spot on one lung for several months. Mother was twenty-five at the time, and my illness was the most terrifying event in her life up to that point. Perhaps it was the beginning of the little bit of spoiling, of overconcern and extra attachment to me that has influenced the course of my life ever since—for better and for worse.

Mother was advised that if Sug went to school, she could bring home various germs that I was not yet strong enough to fight off, so to compensate Sug for being delayed a year from starting first grade, she sent her to private dance lessons.

Mother had never seen a ballet performance. She grew up watching vaudeville, but like most little girls, she had had her eye on a pair of pink toe shoes. She was not allowed to have them. After Sug began lessons, Mother went to see the Ballet Russe when it came to town, but she didn't think much of it.

For several years Mother paid for Sug's lessons by cleaning and baby-sitting for the teacher, an austere German woman, who tried to talk Mother into letting me take class as she watched me bouncing around the place, waiting for Sug. Mother became suspicious when the teacher kept saying that we were very talented, and yet no scholarships were forthcoming, only more and more housecleaning. This prompted her to do a little research; she wanted only the best for her girls, and she suspected by now that this wasn't it. Marian La Cour was.

Miss La Cour taught at the Conservatory of Music in Cincinnati, so several times a week we'd all pile into our old Pontiac after school and drive downtown for Sug's ballet classes and Beverly's piano lessons. It was a forty-five-minute drive, and I went along because mother couldn't afford a baby-sitter to stay home with me. It was a natural progression under these circumstances that I should eventually end up in a ballet class too.

Despite my frilly dresses, I was the tomboy of the family, always dirty, always up a tree, always walking in circles. Physical foolery extended to roller skating, dodge ball, and even an occasional fist fight. Not far from our neighborhood there were construction sites for what they called "subdivisions," the skeletons of the identical houses in a new residential development. My girlfriend and I spent hours swinging from the rafters and balancing on the beams around rooms that didn't yet have a floor and walking through the new giant sewer pipes.

I was unafraid of physical damage to myself and spent my first nine or ten years with scabby knees, scabby elbows, and frequent bloody noses. Mother thought ballet lessons might channel a little of this energy. They did. Since both parents worked, there was very little discipline at home; yet when it was offered as part of an occupation, all three of us took to it like fish to water. No doubt the various fights and harsh words we overheard late at night at home were emotionally confusing, and discipline offered a much needed stability and sense of control. I sucked my thumb until I went to first grade and was shamed out of it. But discipline didn't squelch my more reckless side, and I didn't outgrow pranks for many years. I never outgrew the resolve to win at a game that was winnable.

One game that wasn't in this category was "Ballet." I don't know why, but my sisters and I thought of ballet as a familiar scenario, not a profession. The three of us shared a bedroom, and the bed was our stage. Sug was the Teacher, Beverly was the Mother, and I was the Student, Daisy. Sug would lie flat on the bed and hold me up in the air with her feet on my stomach, and I would pretend to fly and dance, waving my arms around wildly. Bev would watch and offer corrections, "That's not very good," "Straighten your leg." Sug would respond philosophically, "She has talent," or, "She didn't do too well in class today." Eventually we became pretty elaborate in our experiments, and my head went through the wall on several occasions.

Acrobatics, wild, risky, and reckless, were in fact what I liked about ballet classes at the conservatory. Mother would pick us up from school at three o'clock and drive as fast as she could into town. We'd change into our leotards and tights in the car and run straight into class at four o'clock. The first fifteen minutes were allocated to acrobatics on big, thick mats. The next hour was for ballet, which in the beginning I found a little constraining because it required a certain amount of conformity, precision, and concentration. The last fifteen minutes of tap were more fun; I loved the way the clicks and the rhythms overtook my body and made it move. Within a few years all this changed, as I realized that ballet used both acrobatics and musical pulses but with a much broader range of movement.

The beating of drums provided another kind of rhythm that entered my system and filled me with feelings of importance. During the years after World War II, Mt. Healthy, like the rest of the nation, took full advantage of the chance to display its patriotism with parades; I don't think we missed one of them. Later when I danced Balanchine's *Stars and Stripes* and *Union Jack*, the marching days of my childhood came back to me; I felt I had been marching all my life. I took clarinet lessons because I wanted to be in the band, but it was a futile experiment that left me with puffy, round cheeks and no breath. Then I thought the drums would be my instrument; they are, after all, the heartbeat of the parade, but they were already claimed. Eventually I settled for baton-twirling classes, and this led to my first unrehearsed solo performance.

The girl who was supposed to lead the Memorial Day parade got sick, and my teacher picked me to replace her. My original blue costume was changed to a white pleated skirt and jacket with gold braid and buttons and bare legs with white anklets and white-and-black saddle shoes. I thought it was grand, but because it was cold and wet outside, Mother's ever-present fear of my catching pneumonia again surfaced, and she insisted that I wear tights. "Mother, I'll be the *only* one wearing tights!" I wailed. And then it dawned on me: "I'll be the *only* one wearing tights . . . maybe that's not so bad. . . ." And so I went, proudly wearing my pink ballet tights.

I grew up wearing uniforms because we attended parochial school. I can't help thinking that this was the perfect preparation for a life onstage where clothes are not an attempt at personal expression but part of the work.

School was of only intermittent interest; spelling bees were fun, a chance to stand up and compete, and I liked quizzes and tests, anything with a challenge. I wasn't stupid, but I had a hard time sitting still in class and was always being reprimanded for fidgeting. Nonphysical concentration was simply boring.

Spiritual contemplation on the other hand was not boring; it involved ceremony, pageantry, and singing, rather like a good parade. Mother had converted to Catholicism when she married my father, and while neither of them was particularly pious, we had services and catechism at school. The church we attended was very old and had a beautiful dome of gold stars on a dark blue sky. Painted in the center was the Holy Trinity with God the Father, holding the Greek letters alpha and omega, one in each hand.

Every May, the month of Mary, a girl would be chosen to crown the statue of the Virgin as the Queen of Heaven. It was a simple ceremony—the chosen girl, wearing a long white lace dress with a veil, walked up a wooden staircase (the statue was on a big pedestal in the school courtyard) and laid a crown of roses and baby's breath on Mary's head. I always wanted to be chosen for this special privilege. I never was. I was probably too rambunctious.

Years later this came back to me when Balanchine choreographed *Don Quixote* and I portrayed the Virgin Mary. I had certainly not been "practicing" for this all my life, but I did know the meaning of her beauty, her serenity, her importance.

In high school we were taught Latin, and we read many Greek myths. My favorite was the story of Pyrrha. There was a small pastel picture in our Latin book of this maiden with very pretty long hair, wearing a stola. Walking along the edge of the sea, she held a rock in one hand, about to throw it over her shoulder. Across the seam of the page, behind Pyrrha, were people emerging from all the rocks she had thrown. Some had shoulders and heads, some torsos, all were in different stages of development; trying to become whole, they were reborn. The oracle had destroyed everyone except Pyrrha because of their baseness, and she had gone to the oracle crying, "I'm so lonely, I'm so lonely." The oracle told her to go to the river, pick up the rocks and throw them over her shoulder, but never look back. Pyrrha obeyed, and that image of faith and courage impressed me.

It must have been so hard not to look around, and yet if she did they would all die. I didn't want to believe that people died. This difficulty with death has never left me despite my religion and the promise of the glories in Heaven.

In 1955 the Ballet Russe came to town. It was the first time I saw a professional ballet company, but even then I saw it from the stage, not the audience. They needed a little girl to play Clara in a performance of *The Nutcracker*. It was the first time I had been on a real stage, the beautiful big stage of Cincinnati's Music Hall. In the first act Clara was danced by a member of the company, but they needed a little girl to replace her in the second act. They telephoned Marian La Cour, and she suggested me. Arriving just before the performance, Mother and I climbed the big creaking stairs to the backstage area. We didn't know where to go, so we went into a dressing room to ask someone. I saw rows of costumes hanging on the rack and beside them a bunch of stark naked girls smoking. I didn't know where to look. With eyes on the floor I said, "I'm supposed to be Clara," and a very nice girl said, "Well, let's put some makeup on you." She used a little eyeshadow, rouge, and lipstick and pulled my hair away from my face, fastening it with a ribbon. I was escorted to the wardrobe woman who put me into a beautiful white dress with an Empire waist and blue sash, white, ruffled pantaloons, and the little white ballet slippers that I had brought with me. By now I was thoroughly enjoying myself.

I was taken down to the stage, where a ballet master told me what I had to do. Aside from greeting the Sugar Plum Fairy and her cavalier when they arrived onstage, I was to sit quietly on a little red velvet bench on the side for the whole act. The curtain went up, and I was in heaven. The Sugar Plum Fairy and her cavalier (Alicia Alonso and Igor Youskevitch) came in on a little wheeled boat, but as he stepped elegantly out of the boat there was a huge noise, and all the scenery shook. Youskevitch had tripped. He nonetheless retained his noble bearing, and I was very much impressed.

The ballet proceeded, and as each divertissement ended I did a little silent applause. The ham in me took over, and I applauded differently for each dance, turning my head, smiling, opening my eyes wide, "oohing" and "ahing" everything. Now I was really participating and helping the show along. I loved the responsibility. At the end of the ballet there were numerous bows as all the dancers lined up and walked toward the footlights to receive applause. No one had told me what to do now, so I remained in character on my bench with my feet tucked neatly underneath me. After what seemed like an eternity, I decided I'd better bow too. I stood up in front of the bench, held the edges of my gown, and curtsied. Suddenly I heard a deep voice next to me growl, "I don't know what in hell she thinks she did!" I was horrified to hear someone cursing and felt humiliated at having done the wrong thing. Neither Deni Lamont (the growler), who later joined the New York City Ballet, nor I could have known that this was only the first of many bows we would take together.

After the performance I asked Alicia Alonso for her autograph, and she was very kind. She sat me down and, holding a silk stage lily, told me the story of *Giselle* while my mother took photographs. Except for my *faux pas* I was delighted with the whole evening, but not enough to declare that I wanted to be a ballerina. That didn't happen until I felt the need in my own body; I couldn't feel that from watching someone else dance.

Several years after the Ballet Russe visit, the Royal Ballet came to the Music Hall. In their production of *The Sleeping Beauty* they needed four mice to pull the wagon of the wicked fairy Carabosse. It didn't occur to me that wearing gray tights, a gray leotard with a long tail, and a big menacing mouse mask was not as glamorous a role as Clara had been.

Once we had fulfilled our main purpose, pulling on the wrought-iron wagon, our duties consisted of running around in a threatening manner, pawing our whiskers. I wanted the company to hire me. I thought that if I was the best mouse they ever saw they would be forced to take me along with them on tour, so I proceeded to do some very intricate improvised choreography enhanced by some verbal mouse behavior. While I was squealing, "Eek, eek, eek," someone pulled my tail; I had missed my cue to leave the stage. Again, I had overdone it.

One day in the summer just before my tenth birthday I was rocking in the hammock in the yard when Mother came through the back door. She said, "I have something to tell you." "Okay," I said, swinging my legs back and forth. "I'd like to get divorced. I can't live with your father anymore." He was always "your father," never "my husband." I asked, "Have you told anyone else?" She said she hadn't. I was the first one she told, perhaps because I was the youngest and she wanted to see if I could handle it. I said that if that's what she wanted, it was all right with me.

We all knew Mother was unhappy, and we had seen our parents fighting. I had walked into the living room one night, and he had his hand raised against her. I screamed, and they stopped. They tried not to involve us, but in a four-room house with walls you could put your hand through, there wasn't much we didn't know. When Mother cried, she did it in private, but we knew. I remember coming home after dark from playing in the street and seeing my mother in her rocking chair listening to Nat "King" Cole. I could tell that she was drinking, and I could see the red end of her cigarette. I tiptoed into my room and went to bed.

The worst part about the divorce was having to tell our friends, especially since we were Catholic. We were always very conscious of appearances and what other people would think. There was little harmony in the house, and with my father being away all the time anyway we weren't really going to miss him. On occasion I would think how nice it would be to have the perfect little family sitting around a Duncan Phyfe dining table at six o'clock every evening. But it was easier to imagine the Duncan Phyfe than to visualize us as that happy family.

The process of separation and divorce wasn't traumatic, thanks to Mother, who arranged to have all the proceedings during the summer holidays, when she sent us off to my grandmother's cottage in upstate New York in the Adirondack Mountains. (Grandmother was forced to spend time in the mountains because she suffered from chronic hay fever.) We didn't see or hear anything, and when we came home in late August, my father was gone. Mother now had what she wanted: her three girls to herself. She made a superhuman effort to not interrupt our lives more than necessary, and I admire her for that. Being good little girls, we accepted what had happened, and the fact that we had our ballet and music lessons helped to divert our attention. I was still not devoted to dancing, but at least I came home exhausted.

The divorce was finalized a year later, and things began to change. Although Mother was to receive some child support, it wasn't enough, and she had to get a second job. Most people in town worked locally, with regular hours, but for my mother that was impossible. She wanted to be available to her daughters, so she worked at night as a nurse's aide at several hospitals. She came home in the early morning, got us out of bed, fed us breakfast, and sent us off to school before she went to bed. In the afternoon she picked us up at school to drive us to and from the conservatory before she went back to work. Eventually she signed up to study for a nursing degree, even though she was technically too old for the course.

Mother's full schedule led to our one and only experience with household help. Omie, a very large, gray-haired woman, arrived as a sort of live-in nanny to cook our meals, clean the house, and check on our comings and goings. Perhaps it was a delayed reaction to the divorce, but we saw her as a cackling witch and proceeded to make her life a living hell. Whatever she cooked, we wouldn't eat; whatever she said, we wouldn't do. Our rebellion worked. One day poor Omie packed her bags and left. Mother came home to a house of three self-sufficient girls, and never again did anyone else take care of us.

Shortly afterward Mother told us that she was putting the house up for sale, and when we returned from our summer sojourn in the Adirondacks she was living in a dingy one-room apartment in the seediest part of town, with furnishings from the Salvation Army. We were shocked that she had been there all summer by herself. Suddenly we saw reality: we had gone from a nice little house with a white picket fence and a father supporting us to a single mother living in a virtual slum.

We became adaptable at an early age because we had to be. I have never felt a victim of circumstances, my parents' divorce included. We were poor, but we always had food on the table. Mother was very thrifty, and while we may not have received as many presents as other kids or as many as we used to, we still had nice Christmases. I have never been frightened by having the bottom drop out of my life, which it has on several occasions, perhaps because the first time it did, I survived. I learned early.

I never resented my father for this; after all, it had always been Mother doing everything, and in some ways life wasn't any different. I'm not sure whether or not I felt that he loved me. He looks as if he does on my baby films. Maybe he was as loving as he could be at that time, in that place, in those circumstances. I can't say I was unhappy. Life went on, and dancing and music became more and more the center of it, and that was a world my father had never been a part of.

Mother's tiny, shabby apartment was only temporary. Soon we moved into Cincinnati, directly across the street from the conservatory. Our priorities were being set. Mother had a plan. Just down the street from our new apartment was Cincinnati's most prestigious Catholic girls' school. Ursuline Academy was located in a beautiful old stone mansion. It attracted all the richest girls in town and had a reputation of being very exclusive. It also cost a small fortune. But Mother trooped off down the street to talk to the nuns. When she came home she told us that we would all attend the academy free in exchange for teaching ballet classes for the students several times a week. Sug taught the class, Bev accompanied on the piano, and when I was old enough, I demonstrated. Our old game of "Ballet" became real. I also modeled for the art class and still feel personally responsible for those girls' proficiency in drawing a long scrawny ponytail attached to a little head with not much of a profile. The ponytail was my trademark.

Now that we lived so close to the conservatory I began to hang around there even when I didn't have a class. I would sit next to the pianist when he played. His name was John Iden, and he was a rather eccentric man who lived on Coca-Colas that I would fetch for him at frequent intervals. I became one of the fixtures, and I felt highly privileged when I was allowed to open the blinds in the studio before class and let in the light. While class was going on we could hear someone across the hall practicing voice exercises or piano scales. Everyone was very mature, dedication was in the air, and I absorbed it by osmosis. I didn't want to be anywhere else.

Marian La Cour was a very dignified lady, always beautifully dressed in tailored suits, with her black hair in a high chignon. When she taught class she wore a black leotard, tights, and ballet shoes. She believed in discipline and had a wonderful method of teaching us the names of the steps. She would demonstrate a tendu; we'd all tendu; then she would have the whole class pronounce what we were doing, "tandooo." "No, not 'tandooo,' *tendu.*" And again we'd all chorus, "tandooo" and point a foot in the proper direction.

After two years of study, she allowed us to go on pointe, rather earlier than is now considered wise, but for many mothers and daughters a pair of toe shoes was the reward, the point of all that training. I got my shoes, complete with suede tips for longevity, and up I went. It was a revelation. I loved it up there. I felt so important. I don't recall any pain, any bloody blisters, though no doubt there were some; I was fearless. At first we weren't allowed off the barre with our shoes, just little relevés and piqué perches, holding on for support, but eventually we could be kept back no longer and piquéed around the studio and down the hall. To this day I think there is nothing more beautiful than the look and smell of a new pair of toe shoes, and I thought of that every time I sewed ribbons on a new pair.

Eventually Miss La Cour suggested I take the older girls' class that Sug was in, as well as my own, probably to keep me out of trouble. I thought the girls were all wonderful, and even though I couldn't always keep up, I loved the struggle. Each spring there were two school performances, the junior and the senior recitals. Because there were so few boys and I was always tall for my age, I usually ended up in the boy's role, the prince, partnering one of my classmates. It was not until March of 1958 that it all changed.

I was not supposed to be in the performance at all. It was for the senior girls, but when one became ill, I was thrown on, a move that was to become a pattern in my life. Marian La Cour was giving a demonstration with the Cincinnati Orchestra entitled "Introduction to the Art of Ballet." We danced on the apron of the Music Hall stage, where the Ballet Russe had performed, while the orchestra played behind us. We danced Miss La Cour's choreography to Chopin's *Les Sylphides* in short tutus, with sparkling little crowns on our heads. Sug had a solo, and I was one of ten corps girls.

I do not remember the performance, only the rehearsal. There I was on that huge old stage, looking out into the theater with its chandeliers and tiers and boxes. I thought of all the famous people who must have stood where I was standing, and I felt as if some of their dust, their feelings, their excitement had been sprinkled on me. I decided that I wanted to dance. I wrote in my scrapbook, "Being on the big and beautiful Music Hall stage convinced me that I want to make ballet my career!"

I kneeled down and peeled a large splinter off the old wooden stage to remember that moment; I still have it. So at the age of twelve I decided that dance would be my life.

Mother was not a typical stage mother. She made lessons available to us, but she never watched class, never hung around commenting on our progress. She had been lonely as a child, and perhaps she knew that if you have the arts in your life you will never be lonely. I have often been alone, but I have never felt lonely when I was dancing, even dancing by myself.

My father did not come to our recitals. It mattered to me that he didn't seem to care. I thought it strange and not very kind; lack of interest can be more hurtful than outright hatred. Once a year Ursuline had father/daughter night, when all the girls dressed up and attended the festivities on the arms of their dads. I never attended, but I was able to be there—as part of the entertainment. I did a little dance number on the stage for all the other fathers and daughters.

Father still lived in Cincinnati, and as part of the settlement, so that Mother could receive child support, he had visiting days—Sundays from eleven until six and Wednesdays after school from three until five. He would take us out to eat at the drive-in, to the movies, bowling, or a baseball game. This was fine with us, because with so many activities we didn't have to talk much. It wasn't awful, but we didn't mind when he canceled visits, which he did more frequently as the years went by. The bottom line was that we needed the money, so we were acquiescent, but I can't say we looked forward to Sundays. There were times when I felt a little sympathy for him, but I always thought Mother had done the right thing.

I had rarely visited the local library before I made the decision to dance, but now I haunted the halls of the dance section. I couldn't bring the big picture books home, so I sat there for hours looking at them and memorizing names and poses that I would go home and reproduce in the living room. The history of dance didn't interest me; its visual impact did. I wasn't intellectual about what to me was physical, and I have never changed in that respect. For every birthday and Christmas I asked for ballet books, but as yet I had seen almost no live performances. Eventually I saw a film of Ulanova doing *Giselle*, and a few of the various companies traveling through Cincinnati. I thought everything was wonderful; I was undiscriminating. Though I knew about the classic ballets—*Swan Lake, The Sleeping Beauty, Les Sylphides*—they were not my inspiration. I had no ballerinas as role models, and I had no image that I wanted to be like. Although I loved stories, it was not the trappings or lavish productions that excited me; it was the music and the moving.

I had a partner in this ballet business, Kate Kahn, Miss La Cour's niece. Kate was one of five children of rather wealthy parents, and it was a great treat to spend the night at her big house. She had her own bedroom and a maid who braided our hair and made us dinner. We would climb into our practice clothes, put on the record of *Swan Lake*, and dance for each other. Big glass windows provided a reflection like a mirror, and two armchairs served as our partners. We knew, from our books and magazines, two male dancers that we liked—Michael Somes of the Royal Ballet and Jacques d'Amboise of the New York City Ballet—and we named an armchair after each. One of us had to improvise through an entire band on the record while the other watched, and we alternated dances until the entire four-act ballet was over. I've always thought my capacity for endurance was born in Kate's living room.

When we couldn't spend the night together, we would tie up the phone for hours giving each other ballet combinations to do. First we'd write them down in the dark, using a flashlight: "Glissade, jeté, glissade, jeté, pirouette . . ." and then we'd both put the receiver down and get up and slide, jump, slide, jump, turn before reconvening on the phone to discuss the difficulties and changes necessary. We also figured out our stage names. I was to be Roberta Ellohnov or Suzanne Vonne, some inversion of my mother's maiden name, von Holle, and Kate was going to be Katherine Page in honor of Moira Shearer's character in *The Red Shoes*.

When we were not in class or counting fouetté turns, Kate and I became the pranksters of the conservatory. When no one was around, we would stick a hand up the Coke machine, pull down the cup, and set the whole machine running for free. We charged down the slick corridors to see how far we could skid on our heels, went into the empty dormitory halls and left miscellaneous notes on girls' slates:

"I love you, I love you," or "Phone 765-9832." We got great satisfaction from standing on the fifth-floor fire escape and spitting water on people walking up the stairs. After class our favorite pastime, while waiting for Kate's mother to pick her up, was to get a pint of ice cream each, sit on the lawn outside, and devour the whole thing!

A week after the recital at the Music Hall I made a debut of a different sort, as an actress. Eva Parnell, a very imposing woman who spoke in a throaty voice like Tallulah Bankhead, was head of the drama department. She was producing *Guest in the House* and needed a young girl to play the daughter, Lee Proctor. I wrote in my scrapbook at the time, "I really enjoyed this role. It was a part about an easily and always affected little brat." I imitated the symptoms of the "guest," a neurotic woman prone to numerous physical, amorous, and emotional disorders.

I was thrilled to be involved with older people and had a crush on every boy. One girl taught me how to knit, which I thought a very grown-up hobby, but I never learned how to shape or cast off, so I made scarves that could circle the globe. I did well in the production, and as a result got a more prominent role in a pageant play called *Six Who Pass While the Lentils Boil*. I played the young medieval boy who stirs a caldron of lentils while various different characters wander by. Just before the première I came down with the mumps, and our family doctor forbade me to perform. I lay in bed until he left, and when Mother came back into the room I had my clothes on ready to climb out the window. I was frantic; I had a responsibility and no understudy, and I wasn't going to cancel. Mother became my accomplice, and the show went on.

When the shopping mall in town was opening its new toy store, they called Marian La Cour for a young girl to pantomime in a commercial. A skit was devised which involved the fantasy of a little girl and her giant panda bear friend. Hamming wildly, I enthused over our two-dimensional house and various furry friends. But I only had to mime the part; my lines had been prerecorded by a real actress. They sent me a recording of the scene so I would be familiar with it, but they told me to keep my back to the camera when the lines were spoken so it couldn't be seen that I wasn't saying them—except I was. I had memorized the script, and as I was pantomiming, I mouthed the words exactly on cue. I had absorbed the timing of music and dialogue, and the cameraman and director were thrilled because they didn't have to worry about avoiding my face. In later years, when I was described as a very musical dancer, I often thought of "Toytown U.S.A." I could intuitively synchronize rhythms, but this was inborn, not learned.

Over the next few years I performed a vast range of roles in both recitals and fund-raisers all over Cincinnati—a domino, a Christmas card, a gazelle, a beatnik in a version of *West Side Story*, a gypsy, an Irish lass, and a snowman who partnered all ten snowflakes.

The Ficker sisters were gaining a reputation in the music community of the city. There were articles in the newspaper with headlines like: "Tale of Three Sisters: One to Make Music and Two on Their Toes." Sug and Bev were the first people who really impressed me with their talents. Sug (Donna by now) began helping Marian La Cour as an assistant ballet teacher, and Beverly was something of a child prodigy, having played the Mozart *Piano Concerto in A Major*, K. 414, with the Cincinnati Civic Orchestra at the age of twelve.

After one recital a lady came up to me and said, "You know, you have talent. You should go to New York." I ran to my mother. "She said I have talent and I should go to New York!" We looked at each other in silence. It wasn't the first time the subject had been mentioned. But we couldn't afford to move within Cincinnati; how could we ever get to New York? Nevertheless a seed had been planted, and although nothing was said, Mother started planning.

Bev had learned all she could from her teachers at the conservatory, and Mother was feeling an urgency about my training as well. I had become a big fish in the Cincinnati pond, but Mother knew the real pond was anywhere but in Ohio, so when the National Ballet of Canada came to Louisville and a friend suggested I audition for their school, I did. Toronto, where the company and school were based, wasn't New York, but it was somewhere besides Cincinnati. What was essential was a scholarship. We sent a photo to Louisville and received a telegram on March 19, 1960, to come and audition. A ballet mother, Mrs. Cotrell, drove her daughter, Dana, and me three and a half hours through the snow to Louisville. It was a woeful audition; classroom performance has never been my best showcase, but I didn't expect the letter that followed.

April 1, 1960

Dear Mrs. Ficker,

I was pleased to see your daughter Suzanne in Louisville recently.

In my opinion there is no time to be lost in the furthering of Suzanne's training. Her posture needs immediate attention. For example she has a "sway" back when she dances which can only be corrected by careful basic training. Fortunately, she has good legs and feet, but her arm movements and positions are lacking in quality and line because she hasn't theoretical knowledge of the basic essentials.

Certainly she is talented enough although there is just a chance
that she may grow too tall. . . .
                          Sincerely,
                          Celia Franca, Artistic Director

I was devastated, although I wondered what "theoretical knowledge
of the basic essentials" meant. I still wonder. Despite my "sway" back
and incorrect arms, they did say I could attend their school, but no
scholarship was offered. I had stayed after my audition to see the
performance, and I now took solace in the fact that I had written in
my scrapbook, "The company itself was not so impressive."

The audition had an amusing reverberation nine years later, when
I danced with the National Ballet of Canada as a guest artist with a
very lucrative contract. At a party after the first performance, someone
commented on how nice it was to have me there dancing, and someone else said with wry humor, "We're spending a fortune on having
you here." I turned to Celia Franca and said, "Well, there was a time
when you could have had me for free." "Must you always remind
me of that!" she cried.

I think it probably would not have been the right place for me
to study, although at the time all I saw was rejection and, worst of
all, an official opinion that my ever-increasing height was a very
real problem. That was one thing I could do little to alter, although
after hearing that you grow at night, I tried to sleep curled up in
a ball.

In October 1958 we read in *Dance Magazine,* our major contact with
the ballet world outside Cincinnati city limits, that the New York City
Ballet was to perform in Bloomington, Indiana. We had read about
Balanchine's company, and that was enough for Mother to decide
that we should see it. She wrote sick notes to excuse us from school,
and we set off across the river.

The program opened with *Fanfare,* then Melissa Hayden and André
Eglevsky danced the *Sylvia Pas de Deux,* followed by Patricia Wilde
and Francisco Moncion in *Firebird.* I had read about all these dancers,
and I was thrilled to see that they actually existed. Melissa Hayden's bourrées impressed me enormously—I had never seen such
speed and grace; but it was *Symphony in C* that made me decide. I
don't remember the principal dancers, and it was not the second-
movement adagio, which I later danced so many times, that made
me say to my mother, "I want to be in this company." It was the
finale—what seemed like hundreds of girls in hundreds of white tutus
doing hundreds of hypnotizing fast tendus. I did not dream about
being a leading dancer; I dreamed about dancing, and I saw that

in this company everyone danced. This confirmed what I already seemed to know, that the New York City Ballet was where I might fit in.

About a year before, I had formed my own company, and I called it the New York City Ballet Juniors. There was a photo of Balanchine's ballet *Apollo* imprinted on my memory. It was of Diana Adams and Patricia Wilde in white tunics with Jacques d'Amboise in black tights and a white sash. Until then I had seen mostly photos of British dancers—Margot Fonteyn, Moira Shearer, Beryl Grey—because most ballet books at that time were English. But this photo was different. There seemed to be more energy; the legs looked more interesting, more worked. The British dancers looked posed; these American dancers looked alive, so when I formed my company I named it after theirs.

It consisted of Kate and myself and a number of other girls who were able to stay after ballet class on Saturday afternoons. *Dance Magazine* wrote out the steps each month to various famous variations from *The Sleeping Beauty* or *Swan Lake*, and I reconstructed them for the girls, standing at the front of the studio, leaning on the barre, imitating my teacher: "Knees up, pas de chat, pas de chat." We had no music, so I sang. After the others went home, Kate and I would stay and have turning competitions, 32 fouettés, 64 fouettés. I remember once actually pumping out 128; needless to say, quality didn't count after a while.

I had received a recording of Tschaikovsky's *Serenade in C for Strings* for my birthday, and I found the "Russian Dance" section so beautiful that I decided to choreograph to it. The Cincinnati Opera was performing *Aïda* and had left in the studio four long gold poles with gold stars on top, and I decided to use these as props. Since I was interested in mythology, the ballet was called *The Kingdom of Diana* and had a vague story about the goddess Diana traveling across the sky and her battles with other deities. Mother let me cut up some old sheets, and I made little Greek tunics for the cast. In retrospect I think it is interesting that I didn't have fairies or swans or sylphs or a doomed lakeside scene in the ballet. It was never finished because the girls always had to go home for supper, but I thought of it again when I finally came to New York and saw Balanchine's *Serenade*. It surprised me that Mr. B had done a ballet to the same music.

Nineteen-sixty was the first year of the Ford Foundation scholarship program, the program that eventually changed the face of American dance, and Diana Adams was appointed as one of the program's regional scouts. It was her very difficult job to travel across America to various ballet schools and assess the talent, to award local scholarships, and to recruit young dancers for the School of American Ballet, Balanchine's school in New York City. The territory was uncharted, and Diana felt an enormous responsibility to both the Ford Foundation and the vulnerable young dancers whose lives she could alter.

She arrived at the conservatory a few weeks after I had been rejected by the Canadians, and I had just decided to come out of my self-inflicted "retirement." It wasn't really an audition; she simply watched a regularly scheduled class. But we all knew who she was and why she was there. I was thrilled to see that she was blessedly tall. I don't think I performed particularly well that day, even though I danced as if my life depended on it. And it did—Diana had been told to pay special attention to Elaine, another (much shorter) girl in my class, whom I considered my severest competition.

I had brought my New York City Ballet program from Bloomington and asked Diana for her autograph. "Good Luck!" she wrote and signed her name. She then disappeared to talk with Miss La Cour, and we all went home knowing nothing. Diana had given me hope, not only because she was tall and a successful dancer, but because she suggested a world of elegance I had not seen before. Dressed in a navy-blue-and-white checked wool suit and high-heeled shoes, she appeared refined, calm, and what I wanted to be—sophisticated.

I interpreted what she had written on my program as highly personal and repeated over and over to myself, "Good Luck, Good Luck . . ." as if it were a charm designed especially for me. Maybe Diana thought I would need good luck, or maybe she always wrote "Good Luck," but that didn't matter to me; I can still go a long, long way on even a hint of encouragement. Had I needed tangible proof of hope, improvement, or success, I never would have become a dancer. Dancing is a profession based on belief, like a religion.

All I got from Diana that April was a suggestion. Miss La Cour had told her that my mother was planning to move to New York, so Diana suggested that when we arrived we call the School of American Ballet. Only many years later did I learn what had really happened. Diana had not felt able to award me a scholarship because she saw my attributes as too contradictory. I hadn't had as much formal dance training as other girls my age, and so in the technical category, the one she was supposed to look for, I lost points. But I scored points in two categories she hadn't seen before that were difficult to measure: movement quality and musicality, and she thought there was nothing to lose by getting a second opinion in New York.

So with only the prospect of a phone call and a lot of naive hope, we decided to move. Everyone told my mother she was crazy to go to a big city with two young girls, no job, and no place to stay, but by now Mother was hell-bent on getting out of town. Donna was going to stay in Cincinnati and attend the university. She was eighteen, and since she had grown up not to have the body for ballet, she had switched to studying modern dance. At the university she would major in physical education while teaching ballet on the faculty at the conservatory. She was a wonderful teacher. I had overtaken Donna on the ballet stage, but if there were any hard feelings about it, they were not voiced. Perhaps she did cry at night because I was succeeding where she hadn't, but we loved each other, and no bitterness ever revealed itself.

Mother found Donna a little apartment and installed her in it. The girls at ballet school gave me a *bon voyage* party, and I received my first diary. This is the first entry:

JULY 2, 1960

DEAR DIARY – I went to a party that Judy Murphy gave for me. I was completely surprised. I got you, bath salts and cotton slippers, tights, hose and a case, five dollars and very nice cards.

The diary was to chronicle what I was well aware was my biggest adventure to date. The next day I chose a name for it—"I think I shall name you Diana. Okay?"—and so unknowingly Diana Adams was to be the trusted recipient of all my most important and private thoughts.

At the beginning of August we packed. We sold what furniture Donna couldn't use in her apartment and took an ironing board, Bev's music, my dance clothes, and a hot plate, all stuffed into cardboard boxes. Mother had enlisted a very handsome drama student from the conservatory to drive with us for protection in case we got a flat tire. Jim Smith also wanted to go to New York to pursue a career on the stage. On August 10, our caravan pulled out of town, our old blue Ford with a U-Haul in tow led by Jim in his flashy aquamarine Thunderbird. Even if we failed, we weren't coming back. We didn't formally say goodbye to my father; we had said goodbye to him a long time before. Mother has always said that we would never have gotten to New York if she hadn't divorced him.

Just before departing I received a goodbye telegram from Kate: "I'll be searching the newspapers for you, Balanchine's newest discovery and star."

CHAPTER TWO

Audition

❧

J im's shiny new sports car began the trip leading but ended up crawling to a halt behind our 1952 Ford. We pushed his car into a parking lot just outside of Erie, Pennsylvania. Unable to afford a hotel, we settled down in the two cars for the night, Mother and Jim in the Thunderbird, Bev in the front seat of our car and me on the lumpy floor in the back with the boxes. The car was fixed the next morning, and our caravan proceeded.

We had arranged to stay for a week with some friends of Mother's in Ossining, about an hour north of the city, so my first glimpse of New York came a few days later. We were typical tourists and tried to see as much as we could in one day.

Mother was more nervous than I about the prospect of my audition at Balanchine's school; she had decided by now that Balanchine was the top, and starting at the top seemed like a dangerous thing to do. It was against her midwestern work ethic; if you failed, the only place to go would be down, probably with shattered confidence. Despite the New York City Ballet Juniors and *Symphony in C* in Indiana, I remained realistic about where I might dance. American Ballet Theatre had a school, and Radio City had a ballet company, and both were on our agenda. But Diana had told us to call the School of American Ballet, so we did that first. Afraid that we might not understand New York habits, we enlisted our friend Nelle Fisher, the choreographer for the Cincinnati Summer Opera, to phone for us. I was told to come at eleven-thirty the next day.

Even though everything depended on this audition—and since the Canadian fiasco, auditions seemed to me like tortures designed to break my spirit—I had not taken a ballet class for a month. Frantically, I took a class at American Ballet Theatre's school, but in 1960 teenage dancers were not obsessive, and I didn't worry about being out of shape. Nevertheless, I took the audition very seriously:

I went into the basement of our friends' house and did another barre.

That morning, we took the train into the city and rented a studio at the since demolished Columbus Circle Studios so that Miss Fisher could give me a warm-up. At eleven o'clock Mother and I climbed into a taxi and told the driver the address—2291 Broadway. There was a canopy over the door that said in painted letters "School of American Ballet." Inside was a long, steep stairway—I counted twenty-nine steps. Since then I have always sewn on my toe shoe ribbons with twenty-nine stitches, which is far too many. At the top of the stairs was a fire door that read "School of American Ballet," this time in big black stick-on letters. I turned to my mother and said with quiet gravity, "Here goes."

Inside it was very gray and empty. I heard piano music playing but saw no one, just a long corridor lined with red vinyl couches, like a coffee shop. We found a woman behind a desk and I said, "I'm Suzanne Ficker, and I have an audition." I was usually Suzi Ficker, but we had decided that Suzanne sounded more official; to us it meant the difference between Cincinnati and New York. I was rather surprised when all they said was, "Go and get changed," and pointed to a door. I didn't expect red-carpet treatment or blaring trumpets, but since this was my big moment in the big city, I was a little shaken that they were so matter-of-fact about it. But I obediently went into the dressing room to change. I thought my black scoop-necked leotard with cap sleeves and my pink tights were very chic—at least they were in Cincinnati—and besides they were the only ones I owned. I wore old soft toe shoes instead of leather ballet slippers, because I had seen in pictures that professional dancers always wore toe shoes.

Outside the woman pointed to the end of the corridor and said, "Have a seat." We passed a door with a typewritten note on it saying, "Do not open the door while class is in progress." But I heard music and couldn't resist peeking at what I already considered my competition. I saw girls at the barre doing ronds de jambe on the floor. They all looked terrific, and I turned to Mother and said, "I don't stand a chance."

Now I began to worry. When you're from a small town, you don't know what big time is, you only know big-time small time, and that is a far cry from big-time big time. It was scary, so many tapered turned-out legs, straight knees, and arched feet all in a row. I had been the star in Cincinnati, and here I already knew I was not.

Mother and I sat, as we were told, in the far corner of the hallway, frozen like stone. Still no one else appeared and except for the tinkle of piano music from the studio it was silent. Click, the front door opened, and like marionettes Mother and I turned. There at the far end of the corridor was George Balanchine.

I had never seen him in the flesh, but I knew it was him, and he looked just as I knew he would. That year *Dance Magazine* had run a two-part article on Balanchine and the New York City Ballet, and in one issue was a picture of him, very austere in his embroidered cowboy shirt and black string tie. It was my only vision of him, and it was exactly what came through the door of the School of American Ballet that day—the jacket, the shirt, the tie, everything.

As he came toward us, all I saw was the photo getting bigger and bigger in front of me, only this was in color. Mother and I grabbed each other, and she said, "Oh my God, there he is."

"I'm Suzanne Ficker," I said, "and this is my mother." Mr. Balanchine did not introduce himself. He clasped his hands, did a little bow, and motioned toward a closed door. I jumped up and went with him. My mother says all she could think was, "There goes my baby—with that *man*." It was my fifteenth birthday.

I didn't know at the time how unusual it was for Balanchine to audition me himself, although I knew he was a famous ballet company director and didn't presume that he had time for everything.

We went into an empty studio. I briefly wondered where all the other kids for the audition were but soon resolved the question—this was how they did it in New York. I also expected that he would tell me what to do, as in my previous experience, so when he asked me if I had a routine, a number, to show him, I said, "No." I knew this was not a good beginning, and I didn't want it all to end right there, so, hoping to salvage the situation, I quickly told him that I knew a dance from my June recital. He said, "Oh, all right, do that," leaned on the barre, tilted his head back, and looked down his nose. "I'll sing the music," I explained, hoping to fill the loud silence echoing in the empty room, and proceeded to hum Glazunov's *The Seasons* and dance Miss La Cour's choreography. He just watched.

I don't know what he thought, but as the years went by I often asked him, "What did you ever see in me that day?" He never answered; he only laughed.

It seemed like an eternity that I was there singing and dancing. Finally he held up his arms and said, "Stop, stop, stop. Come over here." He had me sit on the floor and take off my shoes. He wanted to examine my left foot, because, as I found out later, Diana had been concerned about it. It had been kicked by a horse and totally crushed, leaving me flat-footed on one side. It could easily have meant that I would never be a professional dancer, but I think by then Providence had taken over.

The accident had happened exactly two years earlier, on my thirteenth birthday. Everything seems to have happened to me on my birthday. To me feet were feet; I had no sense that my stubborn streak might jeopardize my career. I had no career. And I certainly wasn't going to sit home on my birthday to protect my body from injury.

We were in the Adirondacks with my grandmother, and I wanted to go horseback riding with my friend. Grandma was against the idea, but I insisted, using my birthday as coercion until finally she gave in.

The horses were in line, following each other obediently, but after an hour or so, as we were returning home, they broke rank. My horse saw the stable and began to gallop. My friend's horse, angry that the order was being challenged, wanted to run too, but my friend was scared and pulled on the reins. Her horse reared and kicked my foot as I galloped by. Had I not had western-style stirrups with a big leather guard in front, I wouldn't be a dancer today. My foot was crushed, and it hurt like mad. But worse was the prospect of facing Grandma.

A man came out of the stables with a bucket of cold water, and I hobbled home carrying the bucket with my foot in it. Grandma was on the porch, watching. There was no hospital for sixty miles, and since Grandma couldn't drive anyway, we just went to the nearby village to see the local doctor who was used to treating poison ivy and bee stings. He shook his head skeptically and said to keep the broken foot in ice water. No X rays, no cast, nothing. It is amazing that it healed the way it did. It's not a great foot, but I'm proud of the little arch I have developed in it. But more important, when it finally did heal, it had no weakness—I could hop around the world on it, and often feel that I have.

In Mother's baby films of me I can see that once upon a time my feet were equally arched. It had been a beautiful foot, and I often worried that it wasn't as developed as the other one and would say so to Mr. B. He would only grin and say: "Oh, dear, but you know, if it was a beautiful foot, you'd be perfect."

When Mr. Balanchine held my foot in his hands that day, I felt that he was holding my life. I wasn't sure what he was thinking, but he had strong, warm hands. He asked me to point my right foot and saw that it was nicely arched, and when he asked me to point my left, he saw that it wasn't. Then, still holding my left foot, he tried to bend my toes back in the opposite direction.

I didn't know what he wanted, so my instinct took over and I resisted. I gritted my teeth and wouldn't let him bend my toes. He sniffed in his inimitable way, let go, and said, "Fine." He helped me up from the floor and led me to the door, very much the gentleman. As we went out into the corridor where Mother was waiting, he said, "Thank you," and I said, "Thank you." He disappeared down the hall. It was over.

I changed back into my street clothes, and we left the way we came. No one said a word to us. We walked down the twenty-nine steps and went next door to Schrafft's for ice cream. My diary entry for that day was not hopeful:

DEAR DIANA — Today my audition was terrible. I could hardly understand a word Balanchine said. The school is very nice.

The next day the phone rang, and the lady at the other end said I had a scholarship. Later we received a letter outlining the rules:

August 19, 1960

Dear Mrs. Ficker,

This is to advise you that Suzanne has been awarded a full tuition scholarship for the 1960–61 school year. We are also prepared to give her an additional grant to cover her tuition at the Professional Children's School. The following conditions are attached to our scholarship awards. The students are required to have an excellent attendance and to notify us of the reason for missing any of their classes. They will not go to auditions or perform anywhere without our official permission. They will not study any form of dancing at any other school. Our school reserves the right to discontinue the scholarship of any student whose progress or behavior is unsatisfactory. We suggest that you give Suzanne a medical check-up before she starts classes. We are looking forward with great pleasure to having Suzanne with us next year.

Sincerely yours,
Eugenie Ouroussow,
Executive Director, School of American Ballet

My diary became considerably more effusive:

I auditioned for Mr. Balanchine on my fifteenth birthday and received the scholarship on August 17. It was so exciting. It will always be very vivid in my memory.

We immediately found a doctor and I had a thorough examination. I was healthy, but when we tried to give the report to the School they didn't want it; it was only a suggestion. But to us a suggestion was a mandate, and we lived to the letter of the letter for the next year.

It was not a stipulation of the Ford Foundation that Balanchine himself approve each scholarship; only many years later did it become apparent that I had been the exception to the rule. Diana had obviously said something to Balanchine about me, and he had listened. He trusted her, just as I would come to trust her.

The scholarship was essential to our survival, but the grant to cover my schooling was an unexpected bonus. (Professional Children's School is an institution devoted to providing academic instruction for children in the performing arts who are not always able to attend during regular hours.) Less than a week after leaving Cincinnati, with hope but no promises, I was virtually under contract to New York's most prestigious ballet school.

The Red Shoes was frequently shown on television in Cincinnati. It was always the late, late movie, and I used to stay up to watch it. I would write down all the dance steps I could decipher and practice them during commercials. At the end of the ballet—the ballet within the movie—after the heroine has been danced to death by the magic shoes, Leonide Massine comes out in front of the curtain, does a rather sad, turned-in entrechat-quatre, and holds out the shoes as if to say, "Anybody want these?" I remember one night sitting up alone saying to myself, "I'll take 'em, I'll take 'em!" But I didn't know then where they were. I knew now that they were made in New York, and Balanchine himself had put them on me.

We needed a place to live, but we couldn't afford much. Acquaintances in the Cincinnati arts community had told Mother about the Ansonia, a large prewar apartment hotel on Broadway and 73rd Street. It was famous for housing musicians, opera singers, and other theatrical people, and now it seemed that we qualified. Many of the apartments were huge and spacious, with views over Broadway—but not ours.

We had a one-year lease on a one-room studio on the sixteenth floor, and after the trundle bed and Bev's second-hand baby grand piano were installed, there was very little room for us. There were two small window seats, but we kept the blinds drawn because we faced over the courtyard directly into other apartment windows. There was a little closet in one corner where we installed our hot plate, but we weren't supposed to cook because of the lack of ventilation. More often than not we ate at the Horn & Hardart Automat across the street. The bathroom had a bathtub, but the toilet often didn't work, so we used the one at the Automat. We decided to paint the room what we thought would be a wonderful sky blue, but given the total lack of natural light, it was dreary and oppressive. None of these inconveniences bothered me, however; my home was not at the Ansonia. It was ten blocks uptown.

We moved in on a hot, sticky summer day. We parked the Ford and U-Haul trailer directly in front of the Ansonia entrance on Broadway, and while Mother went inside to finalize things with the manager, Bev was stationed upstairs to guard the apartment; we had been told New York was dangerous and we were wary of everyone. We had unloaded all our boxes onto the sidewalk, and I was to stand guard, ironing board in hand. When a woman came up to me and shoved a five-dollar bill in my hand, I looked at her suspiciously. I was under strict orders not to speak to strangers. I grimaced and handed back the money. "No, no," she said kindly, "take it. Haven't you just been evicted?" I broke my silence and said proudly, "Oh no. We're moving in." She grabbed her five dollars back and walked on. After that, whenever the coffers were low, Mother always threatened to put me out on the street with a rusty ironing board.

Mother had saved only enough money for the security payment and the first month's rent, so she immediately enrolled with a nursing agency that provided her with a steady stream of jobs as a private-duty nurse. She worked, as she always had, at night so that she could be home for Bev and me during the day. This was also practical, since the bed only slept two; she used it during the day, and because the curtain was drawn we had to do our homework by candlelight. Even with the scholarships—Bev got one to the Manhattan School of Music and attended the High School of Performing Arts, which was free—there was very little cash, and Mother often worked twenty-hour shifts, arriving home completely exhausted.

Classes at the School began the first week of September, and I was immediately enthralled. Most of my teachers—Felia Doubrovska, Anatole Oboukhoff, Pierre Vladimiroff, Antonina Tumkovsky, Helene Dudin—were, like Balanchine, Russian émigrés who had fled their country during the decades following the Russian Revolution. For me, it was the beginning of a life influenced not only by Imperial Russian ballet technique as filtered and altered by Balanchine, but also by Russian temperament, its committed dedication and its extreme joy. I would later learn about its melancholy fatalism.

SEPTEMBER 7

DEAR DIANA — My second day in class was much better. Miss Adams, a secretary and another lady watched. Mme. Doubrovska who taught toe yesterday taught ballet today. I was much better and felt they were all watching. There are a few fifteen-year-olds in the class and one fourteen-year-old. I am one of the youngest, however, being the best is my goal.

The next ten months of my life revolved more than ever before around the ballet studio. With one or two ballet classes every day except Sunday and a little academic school sandwiched in between, I led a secular life of rigid routine, hard work, and little else. Looking back now over the rather repetitive and banal diary entries from that time, I see that they could have been written by any fifteen-year-old who wanted to dance. I counted the hours, the pirouettes, and the compliments, but I was either unable or too shy to confess just how desperate I was to be good. It was life or death to me even then, but I realize that only in retrospect. I did, however, know at the time that losing my scholarship would be like losing dancing, and I carried with me, every single day, this fear. Improvement in dancing, therefore, became my sole concern, and I graded and measured and compared my progress.

Dancers from the company often taught class at the School—Jillana, Nicholas Magallanes, Melissa Hayden—and I thought them all wonderful as well as difficult. But it was Diana Adams who excited not only my ambition but my adoration. Every chance encounter in a hallway, on the street, or through a window was duly recorded in my diary.

While she by no means took me under her wing as a protégée, Diana did show a certain quiet interest in my progress. I am grateful now for this definite and yet somewhat distant approach; it discouraged dependency, a quality many teachers and coaches encourage for obvious reasons. Perhaps Diana felt some responsibility for me, and in one way or another she seemed to like me. At the end of my first month at the School I mentioned in my diary, "Diana gave me a rubber ball. . . . She is so nice to me. . . ." Well, I thought it was nice, but its implications might not have been. But just as I interpreted her "Good Luck" as bursting with encouragement and personal interest, I determined that the rubber ball meant the same thing. It therefore would never have occurred to me not to use it. I became the only one standing at the barre in class, every class no matter who taught, clutching a small rubber ball in the palm of the hand that was not holding on to the barre.

Balanchine had apparently suggested to some dancers in the company that they hold a ball to train their hands correctly. He didn't want just a long, smooth, curved hand, he wanted there to be a real hollow in the center of the palm. But the ball wasn't any fun to use.

There was also no disguising it; it was red—a stigmata. Nevertheless, I could not *not* hold the ball; I had been advised to by a person I respected. I made the unconscious choice not to have it traumatize me but to have it teach me—and it did.

Shortly after this I had cause for worry: Balanchine chose eight girls for the company, two as members and six as apprentices. The fact that they were all older than I and from "D" class—I was in "C" class—wasn't much consolation. Although I knew that first-year scholarship girls couldn't be chosen, I could not bear thinking that I might not be as advanced as these other girls, even though I could see clearly that I wasn't. They intimidated me, but I wouldn't admit it, even to myself. I bravely wrote in my diary that day, "I had a very good class, even if I wasn't chosen."

Precisely two weeks later my tone had reason to change.

DECEMBER 9

DEAR DIANA — You'll never guess what happened! I was chosen for a part in *The Nutcracker*. I will be an angel with seven other girls. We don't do anything but stand, but I'm thrilled all the same. . . .

DECEMBER 15

DEAR DIANA — This evening at 5:30 P.M. was our first rehearsal for angels. It wasn't on stage, though. I thought the rehearsal would be just us eight, but everyone was there. The first person I saw was Diana Adams. Then Mr. B and then Jacques d'Amboise. I push in the throne. I'm enjoying this so much.

DECEMBER 16

DEAR DIANA — At 5:00 P.M. we had a rehearsal on stage. I pushed in the throne and then two girls brought on the table which Lucy and I then hooked on. Mr. B came up and took my hand. He asked me my name and gave me some directions to do in regards to my "huge" part. Tonight at 8:30 P.M. was the first performance. Diana and Jacques did it. They were perfect. I'm just in another world now.

Today the angels in *The Nutcracker* are performed by the tiniest girls in the School, but in 1960 they were the biggest, thus my part. Before pushing on the throne, we sailed onstage in our angel gowns with halo hats and pretended to play little gold musical instruments. It was during the assembling of the throne for Marie and the prince to sit on that Mr. B had stopped the whole rehearsal and come over to me. He held my hand and asked, "What's your name, dear?"

"Suzanne Ficker."

"Well, dear, when they bring on the table, you have to hook it to the throne. See this little hole, well, that's where you hook it."

I felt as if I were ten years old and would have swooned had I not had such an important task to execute. I guessed that out of all the angels he must have chosen me and thought, "She looks responsible, let her hook it in." I developed an enormous detailed drama in my mind about our exchange and the reasons for it. After that I could never relax until I had hooked the throne.

We stood onstage for the remainder of the act watching all the various divertissements. I learned everything, including the Sugar Plum's pas de deux and the Dewdrop's dance and secretly planned and hoped that if anyone in the whole second act was injured I could save the day and dance their part, any part.

After this modest stage debut with Balanchine's company and what appeared to me to be special notice by the man himself (needless to say, one could not begin to count how many girls' hands Balanchine had held while asking them their name over the years, and I've little doubt each felt as special as I did), I entered into a period of time where I seemed to grow extrasensory receptors to his every step, nod, word, and glance. I had, in short, been smitten with the fear, awe, respect, and love that is probably an integral component of all the girls who have ever danced under this man's inscrutable gaze. It required no proof, other than his simple quiet presence in a room, to believe, with calm certainty, that he could make or break a career. I kept a count in my diary of any and all Balanchine sightings. What my jottings did not convey was the sheer internal excitement of being near him in any fashion.

> Mme. Doubrovska taught class. Mr. Balanchine came in. I did okay. Lucy said he was watching me. . . . I had a good class. Mr. B came in. Mme. Doubrovska made me and a few other girls do a combination all by ourselves. We were scared. . . . I went to class. Guess who came in? Yes. Mr. B

When he wasn't watching me in class, I found occasion to watch him, but it wasn't in class, and I wasn't alone—it was with a whole brood of like-minded young girls.

DECEMBER 30

DEAR DIANA — . . . After *Nutcracker* I went to Mme. Doubrovska's apartment with other girls in my class. We had tea and talked. As we were leaving, we looked out the window and saw

Mr. B in his apartment. . . . I'll never forget it. [Balanchine lived with his wife in the same building as Mme. Doubrovska.]

Mme. Doubrovska probably spied on him daily. Then in her mid-sixties and still a dancer to reckon with, she had known Balanchine all her life, and she had no less interest or respect for him than those of us not yet twenty. She was the dancer on whom Balanchine had created the then-notorious and technically revolutionary role of the Siren in his 1929 *Prodigal Son*. Critics often referred to her as the first prototypical "Balanchine dancer" because of her long elegant legs, voluptuously arched feet, and graceful extensions. But in 1929 her height, five feet eight inches, was considered a hindrance to her career; she often towered over everyone, including her partners.

Balanchine, on the other hand, found the sheer visibility of tall dancers delightful and spent his whole life championing them. I confessed to my diary, after only two classes with her, that "Doubrovska is my favorite teacher. I feel more at home with her." I cannot help but think that we tall dancers had a certain affinity with each other. We were the great tall minority, and although Balanchine did much to change this over the next few decades, in 1960 we were still relatively rare creatures. Diana, of course, was also a tall co-conspirator, something I had been happily aware of ever since her visit to Cincinnati.

Ten days after I saw Balanchine at home there was another incident. *Dance Magazine* was planning an article on the first fifteen young dancers at the School of American Ballet to be sponsored by the Ford Foundation program. A photographer came to Mme. Doubrovska's class and ran around the room snapping us in action. Hopefully and immodestly I wrote, "She snapped at me mostly." After class both Balanchine and Diana arrived to pose with us for a group shot. It was a somewhat arduous process because the photographer kept saying, "One more, just one more . . ." as we all gritted our teeth and tried to look appropriate—grateful, young, and talented.

But no event with Balanchine could ever be less than momentous. Suddenly, while the photographer changed film, he looked straight at me and said, as if to himself, "A few years, maybe less." My heart started beating so fast I was afraid he would hear it. Well, it could have meant just about anything, but I quickly set to work deciding what and became convinced it meant that he might take me into the company in "a few years, maybe less." I prayed it would be "maybe less."

I was flying so high on this comment and all its implications that I began not only to work harder than ever in class but to practice

signing my autograph in my diary—Suzanne Eden Vonne Ellohnov.
I planned to have need of it soon. But there was always new cause
for dismay about where Balanchine's attention was directed.

FEBRUARY 14

DEAR DIANA — This morning's C class wasn't very good. Mme.
Doubrovska told me that I wasn't working very well. After class,
I apologized. She said that maybe I was tired. During pointe
class she said that I shouldn't come to her class tomorrow. I'm
all upset.

I was crushed. I thought I was working well, trying to deserve my
scholarship, and then this, from my favorite teacher. I went home in
tears. No one was home, so I stewed alone. Finally I picked up the
phone in a frenzy and called the School. Mrs. Gleboff answered, and
I said, "This is Suzanne Ficker. I want to speak to Mme. Doubrovska!"
There was a long silence and then, "Mme. Doubrovska! No one
speaks to Mme. Doubrovska!" I explained that Mme. Doubrovska
had told me not to come to class, and I wanted to know what I had
done wrong. She said she would ask her, and I hung on the phone
for what seemed an interminable time until she returned. "Mme.
Doubrovska just thinks you've been working too hard and that you
should go out and have a soda and go to a movie. You're much too
serious."

I was not consoled, especially when I learned the next day, while
I was supposed to be at the movies, that Mr. Balanchine watched all
of class. It was the longest he had ever watched, and I could surmise
only that Mme. Doubrovska knew he was coming and didn't want
me there because I was a disgrace to her class. Too humiliated to
confess my failure, I wrote in my diary, "Oh, well, I'll have to make
it up." I didn't realize the chance would come the very next day when
Mr. B walked into the studio, not to watch but to teach.

FEBRUARY 16

DEAR DIANA — Mr. Balanchine taught C class today. It took us
a half hour to hear and perform the principles of a plié. Boy
what a thrill! I had a good class, but nothing came of it. [Although
shortly after this my scholarship was renewed for the following
year.]

I was in earnest that it was thrilling to have one-third of the entire
class devoted to learning the "principles of a plié." (A plié is a simple
bending of the knees in a turned-out position and is one of classical

ballet's most basic movements. It is the first one a child learns and often the last one to be done correctly.) It did not bother me that my thighs were aching and that we had forfeited a lot of valuable time in which to show him what we *could* do (we couldn't plié, according to him, and so we went no further). It was a foreshadowing of the thousands upon thousands of pliés to come in his classes.

Although the New York City Ballet was still only twelve years old at this time and its performing seasons were shorter than they would be in later years, Balanchine was an enormously busy man, and he almost never taught at the School. He was in charge of an empire— a company of fifty dancers, a constant struggle for the money that meant survival (the seven-million-dollar grant from the Ford Foundation was still three years away), a repertoire of forty ballets to rehearse and cast. He had also over the past twelve months restaged or choreographed nine new works, including the brief but dynamic *Tschaikovsky Pas de Deux*, the not-so-brief and dynamic *Donizetti Variations*, the celestial *Monumentum Pro Gesualdo*, and the heartbreaking epic *Liebeslieder Walzer*.

Despite his hectic schedule, Balanchine was organized enough to be able to do as he pleased, so he came and taught this class. Mme. Doubrovska knew that he was going to and wanted me to rest for it. I think she felt protective of me, her past looking her in the face, although I was never teacher's pet. That role was reserved for the bolder, more talkative girls. Mimi Paul, also a scholarship girl who was eventually to become a ballerina in the company, was in my class, and she gave off a daunting air of continental sophistication; she spoke French to Mme. Doubrovska, which I thought both enviable and rude.

I did have a couple of friends at SAB, to have a soda with after class or walk home with, but they were never confidantes. I was a little younger than many of the girls, I was shy, and I had my mother and sister. Also, we didn't have money for a social life. My emotional ties were still in Cincinnati, although distance eventually changed that.

When the company began its season at the New York City Center, the School sometimes gave us tickets, but when they didn't it was the fashion to try to sneak in; it cost $4.95 to buy a ticket. On my one and only attempt at this stretching of the rules, an usher came up and asked if I went to SAB. I said yes, but before she could say another word I had run down the stairs and out of the theater. My guilt got the better of me, and there was always my scholarship to consider.

Although I was slowly seeing the repertoire of the New York City Ballet and learning who all the dancers were, I remained in love with all ballet and would alternate with Bev waiting in line for hours at

the Metropolitan Opera House for standing room to see Margot Fonteyn in *Giselle* or the Bolshoi in *Swan Lake*. My allegiance to Balanchine
himself was total, but not to the exclusion of the classics and all the
dancers I had read about in the Cincinnati library. It is just as well
that I saw all these companies that year, because once I joined the
New York City Ballet I had little time or interest to see other companies. By then I knew I was already in the best company.

There was one dancer from my Cincinnati days who became, along
with Balanchine and Diana, a constant focus for me. I had, after all,
danced with Jacques d'Amboise as an armchair for years; he could
only compare favorably in person—and he did. I developed a full-
scale crush on New York City Ballet's tall, dark, handsome, married
leading man. I noted, as with Diana, every encounter—none was too
insignificant—in my diary. When Jacques took my adagio class, contact was finally made.

> This afternoon in adagio my partner was Jacques d'Amboise. I
> shared him with another girl. I had a very good class. I know
> he likes me personally. . . . Jacques taught adagio class. On the
> first combination, he asked me to demonstrate. Was I thrilled!
> He also did one other step with me. . . . Adagio was taught by
> Mr. Magallanes. Jacques didn't take. Darn it.

Between toe shoes, pliés, and crushes there was academic school to
consider. I struggled through my various subjects, some done entirely
by correspondence, and passed, barely. Mother was concerned that
all her girls finish school; she knew all too well the prospects of
survival for a girl without a high school education. But I knew I was
not heading for an academic career and would on occasion skip school
to have lunch at Schrafft's after morning class because I was ravenous,
or go downtown to buy a new pair of toe shoes.

Toward the end of the school year I developed a painful right hip.
It was a typical overworked, overstretched young dancer's ache, but
I went to the doctor for X rays. "There is nothing in the bone, so I
can breathe again," I reported in my diary after receiving the results.
To my horror I was told to take a few days off. It is only in retrospect
that this injury is startling. It was the same hip that twenty-five years
later would have something "in the bone" that would end my career.

A few days after I was back in class, there was another big blow.

JUNE 15
DEAR DIANA — I had an okay class this morning. This afternoon
Mr. Balanchine watched pointe class. I did very well, I think,

under the circumstances. Susan Kenniff and Rosemary [Dun-leavy] got into the company. I'm so happy for them, but I want to get in too. Work, work.

Shortly after this I left for Cincinnati for the summer. It was not quite the end of the year, but I had received permission from the School to leave early in order to dance with the Cincinnati Summer Opera as a guest artist. For the past few summers Donna and I had partic-ipated as dancers in various operas that were presented by the Cin-cinnati Opera under the supervision of Nelle Fisher. (These performances were presented at the pavilion on the Cincinnati Zoo grounds—often to the accompaniment of trumpeting elephants and roaring lions.) When we first auditioned for this job, I was underage (being only twelve), and neither of us played the castanets which the newspaper ad said was a requirement. I lied about my age, and Donna and I bought castanets and at the audition stood surreptitiously along-side a girl who was clacking and rolling hers loud enough for the three of us. There were other requirements that I felt right at home with: wearing huge amounts of body and eye makeup and veiled bikini outfits with a jewel in my navel, carrying John the Baptist's head on a platter, and hootchy-kootchying around in what I thought was an alluring manner. All my friends and family used to laugh at me and make the usual jokes about not being able to see me standing behind my spear because I was tall, straight, thin, and shapeless. But this summer no one laughed; I was the famous home-town-girl-makes-good-in-New-York, and in *Manon* I was featured in a Mozart-style pas de deux, with a powder-puff-blue wig, toe shoes, ballet steps, and publicity photos.

I spent the rest of the summer seeing Donna and various old friends. On August 20 I planned to return to New York on the three o'clock train. It was a Sunday, so at eleven o'clock my father came over and took us bowling. It was the only time I saw him that summer.

When I arrived back in the city, Mother, as usual, had changed apartments. Our lease was up at the Ansonia, and with the prospect of Donna, my grandmother, and my great-aunt coming to stay for a while, we needed a bigger place. We now were installed on East 84th Street in a basement apartment where we still never saw the light of day but could finally unpack our boxes.

Mother sold Bev's baby-grand piano and bought an upright because the baby grand couldn't fit in any of the three rooms. The tiny narrow bedroom held the trundle bed and nothing else. Donna was coming to study modern dance at the Juilliard School, and for many months there were six of us, all women, three generations, living on East 84th Street. But when I arrived from Cincinnati, no one had returned from various summer visits. I was alone. New York City Ballet was in season, and I went to a few performances, ate dinner at the YWCA, and played solitaire, waiting for ballet classes to begin. With no one around to protest, I went on my first diet.

I don't think I really needed to, but being at SAB had shown me that part of dedication meant always being on a diet, or at least saying that one was. I hadn't taken class for two weeks, and I wanted to feel disciplined. For four days I ate nothing all day and for dinner had beef bouillon, a hard-boiled egg, and a tomato. I lost a lot of weight—and a lot of strength. I realized that nothing gained, or lost in this case, overnight or by drastic means, could last, and on the fifth day I went out with a friend, who took me to dinner at the Waldorf, and had a huge steak and a baked potato with sour cream.

The family arrived home, SAB began, and I was back in the old routine. But within a month, my routine was shattered; my dream came true.

OCTOBER 23, 1961

DEAR DIANA — This morning Mr. B came to watch class. When it was over, Barbara Horgan, the secretary, asked Teena [McConnell] and me if we would like to be in Mr. B's ballet company. Oh, I so happy.

CHAPTER THREE

Initiation

᪥

I mmediately after my opening night debut in the corps de ballet in two works, Balanchine's *Stars and Stripes* and Todd Bolender's *Creation of the World*, Janet Reed, the ballet mistress for *Stars*, came backstage to inform me that if I couldn't "learn to do piqué

turns better" my days in the company were numbered. I was horrified. I thought that I turned well, and that if I didn't she should have
told me sooner so I could have practiced more.

I no longer had to worry about losing my scholarship—I had to
worry about losing my job, a job I was increasingly dependent on for
spiritual nourishment, as my family was for financial nourishment. I
earned $80 a week during rehearsal time and $110 during the performing season, so I had now superseded my mother as the big
breadwinner. The addition of my salary to the family coffers was
much needed. Life in New York had proved to be even more expensive than Mother had anticipated.

I didn't lose my job, but I did lose my name. Mother had already
changed her name to Holly, an anglicized form of her maiden name.
Convoluted Russian names were not fashionable in the New York
City Ballet roster, and by now I had decided I wanted an American
name. I picked up the phone book one day and ran my finger through
the F's—I thought I'd keep the F—Suzanne Freed, Suzanne Fairfax,
Suzanne Fields, Suzanne Ford . . . I marched into the office the next
day and asked Barbara Horgan, Mr. Balanchine's personal assistant,
"How does someone change her name?" "Well, who do you want
to be?" she said. "I want to be Suzanne Farrell." I thought it sounded
elegant.

My new working schedule required other changes. I was just beginning eleventh grade in school, but having less time than ever to
study, I switched from PCS to Rhodes on Fifth Avenue and 52nd
Street. It was closer to City Center, where we performed, and classes
began earlier in the morning, at eight, so that I could actually attend
three before the ten-thirty company class. I took the subway, changing
twice, from East 84th Street to school. I had received a partial scholarship and paid the rest of the tuition from my salary; Mother remained adamant that I finish high school, even though it seemed
increasingly likely that I might succeed in the ballet world. As the
months went by and I spent more and more time onstage, my academic schooling became a constant source of friction between Mother
and me; I simply could not keep up with my classes when I performed
until eleven o'clock each night and had rehearsals all day. But the
conflict had only just begun; being under contract to the New York
City Ballet did not mean, to Mother, that I was really going to make
it.

Like all new girls in the company, I was learning many parts within
one week—a horn in *Fanfare*, a swan in *Swan Lake*, a monster in
Firebird, a sassy saloon girl in *Western Symphony*, a white snowflake
and a pink flower in *The Nutcracker*, and a "tall girl" wearing one of

those beautiful white tutus in *Symphony in C*, which I had so admired in Bloomington. Though the circumstances were different (and considerably more professional), I was, in certain respects, continuing my favorite childhood pastime: being someone else, someone more specific, more amusing, more mature, more important, more beautiful, and more worldly than just plain sixteen-year-old Suzi Ficker. But as I instinctively knew, I loved the stage not because it provided an escape from myself or my humdrum life but because when the curtain went up I could be whoever I wanted to be, and that was true freedom—to be myself.

As time went on I came to understand something about Balanchine that was contrary to the frequent analysis of him as a man who required and requested "mechanical" dancers without "personality" and "soul." (He was not opposed to real soul, only its common substitute: ego.) Never has a man encouraged dancers so much to be themselves—soul or no soul, personality or no personality—and never has a man appreciated the diverse, individual results more than he. As a dancer, I have been visible testimony of this for over twenty-five years, and I am as proud of this as of anything in my life.

That first season Balanchine was choreographing Mendelssohn's *A Midsummer Night's Dream*, an enormous, full-evening production of Shakespeare's tale of lovers in a world turned upside down by fairy dust. I was cast as one of four tall fairies in Titania's retinue; Diana Adams was Titania. One day while we were rehearsing in the big, drab sixth-floor studio at City Center, Diana came up to me and said, "Mr. B wants you to watch Titania." I swallowed calmly and nodded.

This was so monumental a suggestion that I didn't dare even to fantasize how wonderful it would be actually to dance the Queen of the Fairies. Diana didn't have an understudy. When Balanchine cast a favored ballerina in a role, he saw only her doing those steps and refused to have other girls behind her also learning the part. This caused enormous consternation in the administrative offices, where the concern was for the stability of programing and casting, but the New York City Ballet was Balanchine's kingdom, and his way inevitably won out. His policy was to cause me a great deal of trouble, however, within a few years, as in ballet after ballet he refused to give me an understudy, while the administrators fretted. But for the dancer whom Balanchine had chosen as his one and only for that specific image or movement, this was both an enormous responsibility and a profoundly affecting show of trust, appreciation, and, on occasion, love. As I was to learn, there was no underestimating the effect on a dancer of having George Balanchine's good faith.

Ironically, by the time the première of *Midsummer* rolled around in

January, Diana was indeed indisposed with a pregnancy (later she miscarried), and Melissa Hayden danced her role. Meanwhile, I did precisely as I was told. I had been told to "watch," not to "learn," and so I watched . . . and watched . . . and watched, and so I did learn. But I think I learned it differently than if I had been told to learn it. Instead of learning only the steps, I learned the ballet, its whole conjured world; there is a difference, and I have never forgotten that.

This observation of such a coveted role was so exciting to me that I told no one. I didn't dare, partly out of natural reticence and partly out of instinct; this could cause trouble with my peers. This was the first and only occasion where Balanchine showed a professional interest in me that wasn't public knowledge in the company, and I had a little time alone to absorb the possibilities. Meanwhile there were many other ballets to wrestle with.

After the New York winter season, I went on my first company tour to upstate New York. Two performances were memorable, both because of mishaps. In Albany I was thrown on with only two hours notice in the "Russian Dance" of *Serenade* (the same music to which I had choreographed *The Kingdom of Diana* several years earlier). Though I was not officially an understudy, I loved the idea that I was finally able to save the day with my performance. I was one of four corps girls who echo the steps of the soloist and thought afterward that I had done quite well under the circumstances, until Diana came up and took the wind out of my sails. "Yes, you did all the right steps, but you did the principal girl's counts." For a while there had been two principals and three corps girls, but I had been oblivious, dancing my heart out to the music.

At one point on the tour the company split into several concert groups in order to dance in various smaller theaters and schools. I was with the *Allegro Brillante* group headed by Melissa Hayden and Nicholas Magallanes. We were in Batavia on the tiny, well-waxed stage of a high school auditorium. When the curtain is raised on *Allegro Brillante*, there are four couples already moving with fast runs and jumps in a tight circle. Before the curtain was all the way up— crash! I was down, flat on my rump. The audience of high school students broke into loud laughter, and my initial physical pain dissolved into humiliation. I wanted to leave the stage in shame, but I didn't. I heaved myself onto my feet to the sound of whistling eleventh-graders (kids my own age) and finished the ballet. I have never particularly minded falling onstage since. Nothing could ever be as cruel as that first time, and even then I realized that I only *felt* destroyed. I wasn't. Both of these unpleasant situations taught me something, and learning something, however small, became my new rule. Balanchine never minded mistakes, even stupid ones, but he did mind repeated ones, and I planned not to make any.

Back in New York I was selected to learn one of the three tall Fates in a revival of Ravel's *La Valse*. This haunting ballet about a decadent society had been created for Balanchine's beautiful wife Tanaquil Le Clercq five years before she contracted the polio that ended her career in 1956. Patricia McBride, a very young principal dancer, was to dance her role, and Miss Le Clercq was teaching her the part. It was an important and emotional event for everyone, and for me my first demi-solo part. We wore gorgeous long black-and-red tulle halter gowns and high ponytails held by black ribbons and rhinestones. Now I looked dangerously attractive, and to add to the illusion I curled my long, scrawny ponytail into tight ringlets. Bev and Mother came to the première, and Bev exclaimed as the curtain was raised and a spotlight revealed the three Fates, "Oh, there's Suzi. Look, she has her hair curled." On my second entrance Bev turned again to Mother, "Look, there's Suzi, but . . ." My hair was straight as an arrow. To my great chagrin, it simply would not hold a curl but, unlike dancing on the wrong music, I had no control over it.

After the performance we were all so thrilled by my debut that we stayed up the entire night, and Mother went out about 4:00 A.M. to get *The New York Times*. Sure enough there was my name, my new name, in print, listed along with my fellow Fates. It was my first review in a New York newspaper; I had arrived, and Cincinnati seemed far away. I took out a ruler, carefully underlined my name, cut out the article, and pasted it in my scrapbook.

In July of 1962 the company set out for a six-week West Coast tour. I had never been west of Ohio, and California presented me with a hot, slow, sleepy climate that I found very inappropriate for dancing. Nevertheless, after a performance of *Swan Lake* in San Francisco, danced by Melissa Hayden and Jacques, I came offstage after my final passionate swan-waving exit and burst into sobs. Everyone was terrified. Finally Jacques approached me, and I confessed to him, "It's just so beautiful." I really felt that I was a swan onstage and Tschaikovsky's music had entered my veins and possessed me. Later, when I had composed myself, I wondered if part of me might be Russian. I have had many occasions to wonder this since.

On August 9, three days before the end of the tour in Ravinia, Illinois, I was informed of my first solo part. I was sitting on the side of the outdoor stage, sewing ribbons on my toe shoes, watching a rehearsal of *Serenade*, and waiting for my rehearsal of *Western Symphony*. Suddenly the rehearsal stopped, and the ballet mistress went up to Balanchine and began whispering and gesticulating in a worried manner. He listened in calm silence as all eyes grew wide and ears grew long. At the end, he turned and pointed a finger at me. "Oh, let her do it. She doesn't have anything else to do." And so I was cast to dance one of the three principal girls in *Serenade*. It was a Thursday, and the performance was Sunday, the last performance of the whole tour. I had three days and one chance.

Jillana, who was supposed to dance, was injured, so I was to learn the Dark Angel role, the messenger of Fate, in the ballet that had been echoing through my own life for some time now. *Serenade* was the first ballet Balanchine choreographed on American dancers, on American soil. It is one of his most famous and is considered one of the New York City Ballet's signature works. With its shadowy lighting, girls in long, pale blue tulle skirts, and implications of great emotion and passion, it exemplifies Balanchine's reaction to Tschaikovsky . . . and to plot. There is no story, yet there are many stories, many moods, many emotions, many loves. But they are abstract, the dancers aren't human, their movements represent forces, energies, and these energies are disturbed, whirling like forces of nature and then subsiding before rising again. Throughout there is an ominous, foreboding quality, represented most specifically by the Dark Angel, in the form of a woman—Balanchine always saw fate in a feminine form. She leads the man blindly to his destiny, only to lead him away again.

I didn't, however, consider any of this on August 9; I thought only about learning my entrances, my exits, and the steps in between. That is how I learned what *Serenade* is about, that is how I learned what every ballet is about. Balanchine was a simple man to whom intellectualizing meant little; physical and aural experience was the route to comprehension. He never procrastinated or delayed or avoided understanding by talking.

When scheduled rehearsals were finished that day, the ballet mistress taught me the part, and Diana, who was to dance the waltz girl in the ballet, was there to try singlehandedly to describe the complex formations and interactions I would encounter in a ballet of twenty-six swirling bodies. I would not have a rehearsal of the whole ballet with the company because of other scheduling, so trial and error was the name of the game. My only protection was knowing my own choreography. I spent the next two days humming and memorizing morning, noon, and night, on the bus, in class, in my hotel room, in the pool, and in bed. I even went into the dark, empty ballroom at the hotel to rehearse the ballet in my street clothes. I learned my part backward as well as forward and I quizzed myself by picking a moment in the music and asking what I was doing at that same moment. I think this was the beginning of my being able to hear just a couple of notes of music and know where I was, physically, inside those notes. I've never again prepared for a role so desperately or in such a vacuum.

Sunday arrived, and as it was the last day of the tour, Mrs. Fagin, a local patron of the company, gave a party in the afternoon at her estate. Despite my nervousness, or perhaps because of it, my diary devotes most of its entry to the wonders of this mansion and the food that was offered.

> . . . They have a horse, an orchid house, and a charming log cabin which can house a small family. It's equipped with kitchen, bath and beds. First we had apples and peaches from their garden. Then we had the meal. Chicken, hamburgers, corn on the cob, salad, potato chips and drinks. For dessert there was cherry pie, or angel food, or blueberry pie with ice cream. Everyone had seconds on everything. I ate so much that I had to lie down in the cabin. . . .

It doesn't sound much like a girl who would have a big debut in a few hours! I did note, however, after taking a taxi to the theater extra early:

> . . . I was so nervous that I could hardly put my make-up on. *Serenade* went very well in all fairness to myself. I was so relieved when it was over though. At the end of my first entrance Diana said, "Very good, Suzanne." Nicky [Magallanes] said that I really did an excellent job. Once I got out there, it was really heaven. Even more so with Diana dancing with me. . . .

There is a section in the ballet where Diana has her back to the audience, facing me, and she mouthed, "Nice job." I was flying and proceeded to throw in a triple pirouette, and then someone else commented, "That was nice, but was it really necessary?" I thought so, it being an expression of my feelings. All this triumph, and the most important set of eyes wasn't there to see it. Mr. B had flown back to New York to prepare for the company's upcoming European/Russian tour. But I've little doubt that he had his spies reporting back to him. Nevertheless, within a few weeks I was worried that I had already lost his interest.

> I went to class at City Center at 10:30. It wasn't very crowded, which made it a lot nicer. Mr. Balanchine taught an exceptionally

good class. I had a pretty good class and worked very hard, but still couldn't do much. I'm terribly depressed because Mr. Balanchine doesn't pay much attention to me anymore. He's beginning to spend a lot of time on Marnee [Morris].

I didn't have much time for brooding, since we were departing for Europe that evening. We were to be gone three months, and Mother had arranged to accompany me. Never having been abroad before, we both acquired our first passports. Everything was a first for me, including flying in an airplane.

Kay Mazzo's mother and Marnee Morris's mother also came along on the trip as chaperones for those of us under eighteen who were supposed to do some academic studying between performances and sightseeing. They weren't too successful. I roomed with my mother, and in most cities after arriving at our hotel Mother would go out scouting to find a cheaper one. My salary and per diem were, for these months, our only income, so we watched our pennies very closely.

Besides my battle with an ever-elusive diet, the next several months were most notable for what happened not onstage but off. The day after we arrived in Hamburg, Jacques and Victoria Simon, a dancer with the company, were hit by a trolley car and hospitalized with bruises, cuts, and scrapes. Vicky lost a few front teeth, and Jacques cracked several ribs and had a slight concussion. Mother immediately offered her nursing services, and so while the rest of the company was asked not to visit the invalids, Mother and I went off to the hospital with supplies.

> I brought Jacques flowers and Vicky some magazines. . . . I like Jacques so much, and he's been very nice to me. I wish I wasn't quite so shy, then we'd be able to speak more easily and be able to have more fun together. . . .

Jacques delighted in exaggerating his aches and pains to elicit my sympathy. He always called me "Suzaahn," which I thought strange but affectionate. I considered his attention the noble kindness of my legendary favorite male dancer, worried enormously about his health and prayed for a speedy recovery.

The company opened on September 1 to a curiously mixed response:

> The audience enjoyed *Raymonda* very much and they went wild for *Western*, but something awful happened in *Liebeslieder*. Ham-

burg is a very cultural city and takes pride in its marvelous opera company. Well, the singers in *Liebeslieder** were just awful and Mr. Balanchine found this out too late unfortunately. During the middle of the first part of the ballet, the audience started clapping and shouting, "Stop the singing," only in German. I was watching in the wings and was horrified and felt very sorry for Mr. B and the dancers. The papers played it up real big with headlines of scandal in the opera house. As a result, the ballet isn't being done until we get new singers. . . . After it was over, Mom and I got a delicious cheesecake. . . . I'm really very upset about *Liebeslieder* though. Now maybe I won't do it. [I had been told to watch Diana's part in the ballet along with Gloria Govrin, who had already danced the part.] The tour is not getting off to a very good start.

The next day things were looking up:

Mr. B called me over and introduced me to a man and started discussing the costumes [for *La Valse*, which was substituted for *Liebeslieder*]. It's just a little thing, but the fact that Mr. B chose me meant a lot.

Within two days we were in Berlin and I was receiving attention from a different man. Kent Stowell, who now directs the Pacific Northwest Ballet with his wife, Francia Russell, was then a promising young dancer in the company and was my partner when I was learning *Liebeslieder Walzer*. He was friends with Conrad Ludlow, one of the company's principal dancers and its most coveted partner, and Mother and I often found ourselves eating a meal with them or playing cards. But Kent kept making passes at me to my great consternation. And then, after a sobering day of sightseeing behind the Berlin Wall, he gave me my first kiss.

The deed was done, but the earth didn't move. Neither Kent's feelings nor my own made much of an impression; I had other things on my mind. By the end of the tour we had resolved our roles and become good friends; I was seventeen at the time, and aside from some vague knowledge about "consequences," my education and interest in sex were almost nonexistent. The consequences I did know about were divorce; after all, for several generations no man in my family had managed to last, and most were bitterly resented. We never, ever, openly discussed at home the intimacies between men

---

Liebeslieder Walzer is a ballet danced to piano accompanied by four singers.

and women, but I knew from observation that they were painful and usually unsuccessful.

My next significant debut came about in as haphazard a manner as my *Serenade* debut and revealed, in no uncertain terms, the first signs of the competition that was to become a permanent part of my life. We had moved on to Zurich after Berlin, and while rehearsing *Apollo* onstage at the Opera House, Balanchine was again the recipient of a whispered message from a ballet mistress. In the rehearsal Diana was Terpsichore; Jillana was Calliope; young, long-legged Patricia Neary was Polyhymnia; and Conrad Ludlow was Apollo, substituting for the still injured Jacques. We were, in 1962, still performing the full version of Balanchine's 1928 Stravinsky work with the birth scene and the final ascent to Mount Parnassus, and I was one of two hand-maidens in the birth scene. Balanchine walked over to Diana and continued whispering and then that fateful finger rose and pointed to me . . . and to Pat Neary.

"Stand next to each other," he said, and we did. I knew that I was shorter than Pat and started to worry. "Diana, stand next to them," was the next order. We three stood facing him, but two of us had no idea whether looking tall or short was wiser at that moment. Both Diana and Pat were taller than I, so I struggled to look taller. "Stand still," Mr. B said with quiet amusement, and then with finality, "Nope, she's definitely shorter, just not tall enough." That was one problem I had never expected to have.

Later that afternoon John Taras, a ballet master with the company, told me that Mr. Balanchine wanted me to learn the second solo girl in *Concerto Barocco*. I was thrilled but couldn't help thinking that I would never figure out how this company worked. The real story was that *Concerto Barocco*, Balanchine's crystalline visualization of Bach's *Double Violin Concerto*, was being revived with Diana as the first soloist and Pat Neary as the second. Diana, however, was having knee trouble and could not do the première, which was to be in Cologne in one week. Allegra Kent was flying over to dance her part, and Pat was considered too tall to dance with her, so the role fell to me. I was, in fact, also a good bit taller than Allegra—but shorter than Pat. What the *Apollo* lineup was all about still mystifies me, unless it was to show Pat that she was indeed taller than I. In a ballet company being the right height at the right time can make all the difference in the world. It has also, on occasion, been used as a simple explanation of inexplicable casting by a man who cast ballets precisely the way he wanted, for his own reasons, all the time.

Concerto Barocco is a relatively small work with only eight corps de ballet girls and three soloists, two female and one male. Lasting eigh-

teen minutes with no scenery and white leotards and skirts for costumes, it is a simple ballet, but one of profoundly spiritual origins
and intentions. Dancing it, one's physical movements and one's soul
seem to share in the purity. That is why everyone wants to dance
Concerto Barocco; it is eighteen minutes of salvation.

Pat was upset. I had considered us friends, and on occasion we
had roomed together. She had a wonderful sense of humor, but now
she was crying, and it seemed to be my fault. I went up to Mr. B and
said, "Pat's crying; maybe it's not right." He was curiously impassive,
saying simply, "Well, that's not very nice of her." I was to learn
then—and later when it backfired on myself—that Balanchine did
not take kindly to outside pressure about his casting. This was his
kingdom; he took care of all his subjects and was angry if they proved
ungrateful.

Poor Pat was told to teach me the role she was to have danced,
and she did, through her tears. It was one of the most uncomfortable
rehearsals of my life. I was compelled to learn fast, very fast; I knew
this was my only chance. I learned the ballet but lost a friend.

Diana also helped me; she had danced the other solo girl, and the
two do a lot of syncopated dancing together. "I'm on one [the count
of one] and you're on two . . . I'm on three and you're on
four . . . I'm odd, you're even. . . ," she explained. I learned both
parts.

Allegra arrived from the States, and on September 23 we danced
Concerto Barocco. Before the performance, for good luck, Diana gave
me a little gold mouse pin with a rhinestone eye and painted whiskers.
I named him Barocq and from that night on pinned him inside my
bra for all important ballets. His long wiggly tail was scratchy, and
he was probably a visible bump where I should have had a cleavage,
but I didn't care; Diana had given him to me.

The performance went by without mishap, and I received many
compliments, all duly recorded, only once again Mr. B wasn't there.
He had skipped Cologne and then Frankfurt and would rejoin us in
Vienna before leaving for Russia. I began to wonder if he would ever
see firsthand the results of his last-minute casting. Eddie Bigelow,
Balanchine's good friend and one of the company's managers, told
me years later that he was constantly reporting back to Mr. B on my
progress and performances. Though I took it as little consolation at
the time, Balanchine also knew how a dancer danced and would dance
under pressure; he didn't need to see it.

Diana, Balanchine's other trusted informant, came backstage after
the performance with a comment that I have never forgotten. It was
about one of the small, subtle things that make a ballerina a ballerina.

At several points in the second movement of the ballet I stood in a simple pose, facing Allegra, after a great deal of exhausting dancing, my back to the audience. Diana said that however tired or out of breath I might be, I should disguise my breathing and not let the audience see my ribs moving in and out or my shoulders heaving up and down. The stage is not the place to remind the audience that one is human; illusion is what they are paying for. I remembered, I practiced, and I have not breathed visibly onstage since. There is really no need to huff and puff when dancing. One simply lets the musical beat become one's own heartbeat, and the heavy breathing, which is a kind of resistance to the music, stops. To many, stamina in dancing often means the ability to withstand the length, speed, and complexity in a variation. To me, it is a palpable quality in the music that I absorb and then follow.

Shortly after my *Concerto Barocco* debut, I started to notice some clicking noises followed by pain and swelling in my left knee. It was the beginning of a chronic problem, but I remained silent on the subject, afraid that if I said anything I wouldn't be allowed to dance. Every evening after performance I soaked my knee in ice and prayed that it would hold me up the next day. In a moment of confidence I confessed my weakness to Jacques, who promised to keep my secret.

Despite my knee Mother and I managed to do a considerable amount of sightseeing in each city. Mother was an avid and organized tourist who made sure that we visited every zoo in every city. When I was rehearsing and unable to go with her, she took plenty of photographs to show me later what I had missed.

Our time in Vienna was spent at the embassy getting Mother a visa for Russia and buying books and canned foods to take with us, even though we had sent over trunks in advance. We were warned that the food might be neither plentiful nor palatable, and we were going behind the Iron Curtain for almost two months. This was Balanchine's first visit to his native land in thirty-eight years; he had emigrated just before Stalin consolidated his power. In those four decades he had become the single most influential force in classical dance in the West, and now he was returning, with an American passport and his American family, the New York City Ballet.

It was an important and emotional occasion all around, and the terms were set when Balanchine stepped onto Russian soil in Moscow to the greeting, "Welcome to the home of Classical ballet!" "No, America is now the home of Classical ballet, Russia is the home of Romantic ballet," was his now-famous retort, and throughout the following weeks, despite a generally favorable and at times wildly enthusiastic reaction to the company, he refused to be treated as the prodigal son come home. He remembered too much of the physical and spiritual deprivation and artistic conservatism during the Revolution and in the years that followed, and he retained a passionate hatred of communism to the end of his life.

I was far too preoccupied at this time packing cans of tuna fish, icing my knee, and rehearsing my various ballets to absorb the historic significance of our trip, politically or artistically. I just wanted to dance well for my boss.

During our three weeks in Moscow, we shuttled around town dancing at two different theaters, the Bolshoi Theater and the Palace of Congresses, which, with a seating capacity of six thousand, had the most enormous stage I had ever seen. Because Mother was staying in Russia for only a week, I shared a room with Gloria Govrin for the Russian leg of the tour. Gloria was a young, very talented dancer who was learning many solo parts. She eventually became a soloist with the company, and with her great height, voluptuous body, and sly sense of humor was one of Balanchine's beloved exceptions to what a "ballerina" was expected to be visually.

The first shock was our hotel room. After walking down a long, dark corridor and picking up the key from a threatening-looking babushka, we entered our room: two narrow, camplike beds, a little dresser, and a version of a bathroom. On the dresser was a radio whose volume we could regulate but not turn off. One morning I said to Gloria, "I nearly froze last night," and when we returned from rehearsal later there was an extra blanket on my bed. One whole floor of the hotel was off-limits, and we deduced that it was full of little cubicles with men and women monitoring our every word. Despite the novelty of Russia, I soon began my countdown: "Only forty-nine more days before we get back to New York."

As the tour proceeded, I began to learn things about the company from Gloria. It was my first real taste of gossip, and my Puritan values were tested. But, however innocently, I myself was the object of two married men's flirtations. One night Jacques, now recuperated from his accident, sitting behind me at a performance of the Russian opera, reached forward and kissed me on the cheek. I thought as little of it as possible, said nothing, and prayed that nobody saw it. Several days later I recorded:

> I sat with Jacques on the bus coming back [from performance]. We had fun talking. He said some nice things and said that his project on this tour was to take care of me and to see that I eat well.

Looking back, I realize Jacques, who loves to tease, must have been having a field day because of my gaucheness and lack of sophistication. I, on the other hand, was happy to have his attention but a little alarmed about the reference to food, since I was, at least in theory, on a diet. Mr. B also showed concern over my stomach.

He always traveled and roomed with his company, flying economy class, eating economy food, riding buses, not limousines, sleeping and eating in company hotels. I often saw him giving a taxi to a dancer before himself, saying that it was more important for them to get to the theater than for him. He was a true democrat—where ballets and casting were not concerned.

Sitting in the huge impersonal communal dining hall of our hotel, Mr. B was assigned to the table next to mine and came over one evening to ask if the food was all right. The food was not appetizing, with everything disguised in horrible white cornstarch sauces, and members of the company had food fights across the dining room, squirting the butter from what was supposed to be chicken Kiev and throwing rolls from table to table. Eventually Mr. B had had enough and became as angry as I'd ever seen him. He told us we were there as ambassadors from America, and our behavior was outrageous and unacceptable.

Trying to appear contrite, I told him that I liked the omelets well enough. He nodded, marched off to the kitchen, and arranged for them to serve me omelets morning, noon, and night. I must have consumed several hundred eggs by the time the tour was over.

In Moscow, as usual, I was waiting for my rehearsal of *Concerto Barocco*, watching another rehearsal, and sewing my toe shoes:

> . . . Mr. B came along and took me by the arm and led me away. I didn't know what was going on so I asked Mr. B, "What did I do now?" He said, "Nothing, but rehearsal is now instead of later."

My audition with him at the school ran through my mind as he led me down a long, dark, empty corridor. Mother was gone, and "that man" was already taking me away again. I thought any chance moment with him—in the elevator, on the street, passing in a hallway—was a great luxury, although my silent awe kept those moments brief. When he wasn't looking, I would hang my camera out of the bus window, look the other way, and take a picture of him.

Now I followed him into a tiny room, not really big enough to dance in, and there was Hugo Fiorato, one of our conductors, who was to play the lead violin in *Concerto Barocco* the following evening. "I want to go over the tempos with you," Mr. B said. "Just mark the steps and tell me if the tempos are good." I was incredibly flattered. Later, he would always say to me, "Suzi, you have your inner clock, and it's very accurate." He also had an inner clock, an internal metronome. I could physically define a tempo, but he had it all inside his head, and he never made a mistake.

The performance was the following day, but by then I seemed to be doing everything all wrong again:

> I didn't have anything else but *Barocco*. It went pretty well. Afterwards Diana came up to me and said, "Not bad." She also told me to lose a little more weight. I'm really trying. And also to work on my arms. She also gave me some pointers on my make-up. For some reason I'm very upset. Maybe it's just nerves and tension, I don't know. I've been working and trying so hard. I want Diana to be proud of me. I don't want to be in the corps all my life.

Between Jacques watching what I ate, Mr. B feeding me omelets, and Diana's admonition to lose weight, I was starting to panic about the fate of the endless diet. But Diana, who was both a woman and one of Mr. B's favorite ballerinas, was the one I believed. I was not, by the way, fat, but my standards were Diana's. She was always very much concerned about weight, and I did still have a layer of baby fat. My cheeks were round and, by now, my figure was more rounded than it had been. The object of this diet was not, therefore, to conquer obesity; it was to attain the ideal shape for a dancer.

By our last week in Moscow I was feeling desperate, but not because of my weight and not because we were in the middle of the ten days of the Cuban missile crisis. Though the world was focused on the daring exchanges between Kennedy and Khrushchev, and Balanchine was well aware of the gravity of the situation, the company in general kept up such an appearance of outer calm that most of us remained, as usual, more concerned about our careers than our lives. I was preoccupied with my left knee:

> I don't know what it is in me, but if it doesn't stop I'm going to do something drastic. I stumbled in *La Valse* and fell in *Western*, twice in one night. I just can't stand to look Mr. B in the face anymore. Not that he wants to look at me anyway, I'm so clumsy. . . . Help me.

I refused to acknowledge the real condition of my knee, but within a few days the secret was out. The knee was so swollen by the time we were in Leningrad that I was forced to tell the ballet mistress I couldn't dance. This provided Mr. B and me with a reason to speak.

He asked to see my knee and examined it carefully, asking where it hurt most and reassuring me that it wasn't fatal. He also had a bad knee and always carried with him the necessary equipment. I wrote in my diary:

> He gave me his Ace bandage, which was very wide, and told me how to wrap it. I did so, but it is so big and so long that half my leg was wrapped up. I went to the theater and watched *Serenade* with tears in my eyes.

He also told me that mineral water was good to soak my knee in (considering the sulfurous color and odor of Leningrad water it may well have been), and I spent the next few weeks practically drowning in the stuff. To this day, though, I'm not quite sure he wasn't just teasing me!

There was another treatment to explore at the dreaded Russian clinic. There were people in the waiting room with really severe problems—bleeding, severed limbs, pneumonia, head gashes—but, being American, I was admitted immediately and felt very guilty. The doctor diagnosed my problem as an inflammation of the meniscus cartilage that covers the kneecap and ordered daily hot-wax treatments. It all seemed rather primitive, but I was ready to try anything. They boiled wax and poured it into a rectangular mold until it was the consistency of rubber. It was then placed on my knee and left to cool and harden for fifteen minutes.

My new daily routine consisted of eating, sleeping, writing letters, reading, playing solitaire, and visiting the Russian doctor. I was miserable.

After a week in Leningrad Mr. B flew back to America, while we continued on to Kiev. At the time I knew only that he was gone and that I missed him, but his biographers report that the emotion of being back in Russia, especially Leningrad, where he had grown up and danced, had become too much for him, and he was having nightmares about being locked up and not allowed to leave. So he left temporarily. I did not witness any such problems and did not hear of any through the grapevine, but then he was a very private man. I hoped to be dancing again when he returned on November 17.

Besides attempting some rather frustrating, painful, and pathetic
barres, wishing I could go home, and helping with some paperwork
in the office, I did very little. I could, however, do one thing I couldn't
do when I was dancing: watch. I sat through whole programs, once
with Diana, whose comments I found very informative. Balanchine
returned as scheduled, not a moment too soon, and immediately
rescued both the company and me from the grip of Russian confusion:

> I was sitting alone at the dining table rereading a letter and
> waiting for Gloria when an awful Russian man came over and
> got real close and asked me something. I kept saying "nyet,"
> "nyet," but he wouldn't leave me. Finally Mr. B saw what was
> going on and summoned Nina [the interpreter] to my rescue.
> Mr. B, Betty Cage, John [Taras], Mrs. Molostwoff and Lincoln
> Kirstein invited me to sit with them. Mr. B said that the man
> had good taste and picked the most beautiful girl. Hah! They
> made me drink a glass of vodka Russian-style [one gulp]. It was
> very exciting, but I nearly died from that vodka.

Our next stop was Tbilisi in the Soviet Republic of Georgia. Mr. B
was Georgian, and I now got a taste of the very different Georgian
temperament. The people were quite wild and gay compared to the
citizens of Moscow and Leningrad, and the men were so aggressive
that we couldn't walk alone in the streets. Balanchine's love of women
was considerably more refined, but its origins were apparent. Upon
arrival we were whisked off to a performance by the local ballet
company, which was very amusing. My diary puts it bluntly: "Their
star was a fifty-six-year-old man and he was really very good for
his age."

I had not danced now for almost three weeks and decided it was
high time I did. I told everyone I was ready. But the boss thought
otherwise. Our exchange was prophetic:

> I wanted to dance so badly and I even did the rehearsal, but
> after a talk with Mr. B I'm not dancing for the rest of the tour.
> He said, "Don't do anything." And then he said, "I want you
> more than you want me." (Which is untrue.) He said other
> things which I want to keep to myself, alive in my heart. I like
> him so much and want to dance in his company and his ballets
> so badly, why must I have a bad knee.

I assumed that when he said he wanted me more than I wanted him
he meant as a dancer. He was, after all, married, and I didn't think

he was flirting. I had received my first kiss only weeks earlier and was either too stupid or too afraid to recognize double meanings, one of Balanchine's specialties. I no longer remember the "other things" that he said to me; I do remember the overwhelming feelings he left me with. They were all associated with dancing, or so I thought. Dancing was our common ground. Despite my general misery I must have felt encouraged by our little talk, because I went back to the hotel and practiced my autograph.

A few days later, while I was watching the performance, Mr. B came up to talk again:

> I'd been standing in the wings, but Mr. B said I should sit and save my legs. So he helped me up on the piano and I watched with him. He talked to me. . . . I can never think of anything to say to him, but I'll never forget our little talks. . . .

Soon after, we left by train for our last stop, Baku, on the Caspian Sea, and I was thrilled to be going home soon.

Mr. B and I had one more conversation on Soviet soil. To the evident horror of some nearby mothers, Mr. B came up after closing night and handed me the flowers that had been presented to him onstage. I protested, saying, "But these were given to you," but he insisted, saying, "Well, I give them to you; even though you didn't dance, you deserve them." He asked me how my knee was, and, lying, I said it felt fine and that I should be able to dance *The Nutcracker* when we got back to New York. He said that I shouldn't do anything. "*Nutcracker* is nothing, but the spring season, you will see," and he pointed his finger to me and then upward.

It did not happen that spring but the following winter; still, I cannot help thinking now that above that finger lay *Meditation*, a pas de deux about an impossible love. Perhaps the flowers he gave me were for *Meditation*. I didn't know what was going to happen; he did.

But before this première I had several other important debuts, some planned, some not, which served to pull me out of anonymity and into the spotlight. A few months after our return from Russia everyone was asking, "Who is this girl?" Once it became clear that the great choreographer George Balanchine was showing an interest in a certain female dancer, no scrutiny was too close and no judgment was withheld—on either side of the footlights.

CHAPTER FOUR

Movements

A s Mr. B had ordered, I danced only a parent in the first act of *The Nutcracker* that Christmas, and by February my knee was well enough for more action, which I got immediately. Jacques was holding a small lecture-demonstration for the Friends of City Center, a group that donated money to the ballet, and I was to dance the second solo girl in *Concerto Barocco* with Patricia McBride. The night before, Jacques phoned me to say that Allegra Kent, who was to dance the pas de deux from the second act of *A Midsummer Night's Dream* with him, could not perform. Would I dance it? I said yes without hesitation and then worried about what I had let myself in for.

This exquisite pas de deux, made the year before on Violette Verdy and Conrad Ludlow, is long, languorous, and so sustained as almost to be in slow motion. I didn't know a step of it, so Jacques took it upon himself to teach it to me; he invariably knew the girl's role as well as he did his own. Like Balanchine, he loved to do both parts and had no trouble doing them almost simultaneously.

This was the first of many roles that he would teach me as well as dance with me, and I think there is a certain significance in the fact that, aside from Diana, I very rarely learned roles from other women; it was usually Balanchine or Jacques dancing around the studio pretending to be on pointe. Dancers can be very possessive about the ballets they dance (even though Balanchine insisted, often by cruel example, that no one "owned" a ballet, including one originally made on them), and having the men teach me avoided a lot of competitive tension with other female dancers. I also think I learned to dance differently than I would have if I had had to imitate the movements of other women—I had more freedom, more choices, and less pressure to duplicate. Later on, when I danced more and more ballets that were made on me with no previous interpretation, that freedom increased; unable to see the movement on any other body but Balanchine's, I had to invent my own way of moving—like him, but like a woman on pointe as well.

Mr. B was to direct the "working rehearsal" of the second movement of *Concerto Barocco*, in which Patty had a long extended adagio and I had only one brief entrance. As we gathered onstage to begin, Mr. B suddenly said, "Let's take it from the top"—meaning the first movement. We knew it, but it was not what we had prepared for physically or emotionally—a situation Mr. B loved. The music began, and Patty and I were instantly catapulted into a musical challenge. The rehearsal never even got to the second movement.

The *Midsummer* pas de deux with Jacques went well. I knew it, but I was physically unprepared for all the bourrée promenades on pointe and languid extensions. My feet began to cramp terribly, and by the time we reached the gorgeous slow ending where I extended my left leg sky-high while cradled in Jacques' arms, my foot was numb and I could not point it no matter how hard I tried. The messages from my brain were not reaching my toes, and my foot, high and exposed on center stage, looked like a trembling spoon. Despite this I enjoyed myself thoroughly, and for once Mr. B was actually there to see me dance.

I loved spur-of-the-moment opportunity, and it didn't have to involve a prominent part. Several weeks later I found myself in the wings one night watching *Donizetti Variations*, a fast, lighthearted but technically demanding ballet with a corps of six girls and three boys. Suddenly one of the girls twisted her foot and came hobbling offstage in tears. There was a ten-minute pas de deux before she had to go on again, and I volunteered my services even though I was not an understudy and hadn't rehearsed a single step of the ballet. I had watched it many times, and I loved the music; that was all I needed to plunge in.

They carried the poor girl upstairs to the dressing room, removed her shoe, and gave her an ice bag, while someone else eased her out of her costume and I climbed into it. I whisked my hair up on top of my head, wrapped the little pink silk scarf from her bun around it, shoved on a pair of pink tights and soft toe shoes, and ran downstairs with someone following me fastening the back of my costume. And so with wisps of hair flying, not a drop of makeup, and steps very similar to the correct ones, I danced *Donizetti Variations*. The feeling was not unlike being on the balancing beams and rafters of the skeletal construction sites of my childhood.

Donizetti was a ballet usually reserved for "small girls," so if I had not snatched this opportunity I might never have danced to that lovely music, and when it came to music I had a voracious appetite. I had nothing to lose and everything to gain by attempting to dance *Donizetti*, and I knew that as one of six girls I would not be the focus of all eyes.

I found myself volunteering often in emergency situations after this. I knew it was the best way for me to learn my craft, because nothing in the rehearsal studio can compare to the real moment of quick decision in front of an audience. The only place to learn is "out there," on the edge, when the beginning and end of your career hinges on that one performance, that one moment. It demands a whole different way of thinking, not analytical, critical, or even emotional, but a pure reaction to music and circumstance. I learned this by trial and error, and many performances were far from perfect, technically and otherwise, but I also learned to dance in a way that would mean something to Balanchine.

A couple of nights after the *Donizetti* episode, I was dancing *Concerto Barocco* and had to think fast, but not about dancing this time. Conrad Ludlow was partnering Melissa Hayden in the central pas de deux, and as he supported her in a series of fast pirouettes, her skirt came loose and fell to the ground. This is a very peaceful, spiritual dance, and the spell was broken. Reality fell on the stage, and all attention focused on it; Balanchine's choreography became merely the accompaniment. The dancers continued dancing but their preoccupation with not stepping on the slippery skirt while pretending that it wasn't there was obvious.

I was waiting in the wings for my entrance and decided to pick up the skirt on my first diagonal step. Lunge, step, sous-sous, lunge, step, scoop-up-the-skirt, sous-sous, and I carried it offstage. The audience started to applaud, and I started to cry. I was horrified that I had done the wrong thing; applause was entirely inappropriate at that quiet moment in the ballet. Everybody else had left the skirt in the middle of the stage, why hadn't I? Ever since, whenever I danced a ballet in which I wore a skirt I have tied it with three knots and sewn it in place.

The first ballet made on me was not by Balanchine but by John Taras, and I always teased Mr. B about this in later years. In the spring of 1963 I discovered my name, along with Arthur Mitchell's, on the rehearsal schedule for a "new ballet." It was called *Passage*, later changed to *Arcade*, and it was to a very complex Stravinsky score, *Concerto for Piano and Wind Instruments*.

The ballet didn't have a real story, but it did have an ambiguous, suggestive atmosphere. The first movement was danced by twelve men in bright two-color costumes emblazoned with emblems and crests. It appeared to be set in medieval times, and in the second movement eight women in black, not unlike nuns, accompanied my entrance. I wore a black cape with a large, stiff hood which, when removed, left me exposed, defenseless, and pale. I was the cloistered one, the novice perhaps. I met Mitchell and we proceeded into a pas de deux, shy and tentative at first, then bolder as we reconvened in the third movement for some rather celebratory dancing before I was again led away, and Mitchell was left wondering what had happened.

I was still in the corps de ballet and was overwhelmed to be cast as the lead in a new ballet. I had never been so long on center stage, and I had never been involved in creating a pas de deux. Adagio classes at the School had provided a little technical practice at being handled by a man, but they did not suggest the prolonged physical and emotional contact—and cooperation—that make a pas de deux the most intimate and central part of a classical ballet. And I had never danced with Arthur before, an impressive, elegant black dancer who had become an audience favorite since joining the company in 1956.

Arthur was very kind to me and did not seem to mind dancing with a corps girl who was all elbows. One day in rehearsal I knocked him in the jaw so hard with one arm that we had to cancel the remainder of the rehearsal while he nursed his chin with an ice bag. He was a revered principal dancer, and I was just a kid who had nearly knocked him out, but his sense of humor was indomitable, and the night of the première he sent me a red rose with a note:

Dear Suzanne,
    All the best. I know it will go well. Hit me as much as you want.
                                        Arthur

My career was moving rapidly ahead, but it came to a grinding halt when I found myself with a rehearsal of *Arcade* that conflicted with a rehearsal of another ballet that I understudied. Which should I go to? I was flustered enough to seek Diana's advice. With tolerant good humor, she took a deep breath and said, "Well, dear, you're going to do the one ballet, and you're not going to do the other." Before she even finished speaking, I wished I had never asked.

The day of the première arrived and proved to be rather arduous, not so much because of nerves or tiring last-minute rehearsals, but because Mr. B decided that I didn't look quite right. My costume was a dull beige dress with long sleeves and an underlayer of white petals.

It was a little drab, but I thought that was how I was supposed to look. We finished the final dress and lighting rehearsal on time, but as everyone was parting company with good-luck hugs for the evening, Mr. B, who had been watching the rehearsal, went up to John Taras and said, "You know, the costume's not so nice. Give her something else."

Besides the world première of *Arcade* that night I was dancing one of the ferocious bacchantes in Stravinsky's *Orpheus*, and it was already late in the afternoon. I had planned to go home for a rest or a bath, but instead, at Balanchine's insistence, I walked the ten blocks to the costume shop to have my dress altered. They took off the white petals and put some pearls around the neckline and Mr. B decided that I would wear pearls in my hair. It was the first of many times that he would have my costumes covered in pearls. Later, he gave me real ones—but they did not always signify calm, clear waters.

I felt much prettier in my new costume, but being tucked and pinned at six forty-five when I had an eight o'clock performance was not what I wanted to be doing. I had left my makeup on from dress rehearsal, and when I finally returned to the theater I practically charged straight back onstage for the performance.

Arcade received mixed reviews but nevertheless enjoyed a brief life of several seasons. The press reaction to me was the first of many reviews hailing my "virginal freshness." One critic even went so far as to say, "Young Suzanne Farrell, a member of the corps, danced the faceless role of a bacchante, indistinguishable from nine other bacchantes. A few minutes later in the premiere of John Taras' *Arcade* she was a star." This was definitely a premature assessment of my status, but within two weeks it took on a new resonance, at least if the definition of a "star" is someone who is thrust into the spotlight literally overnight.

There were two other new ballets that season, both by Balanchine. *Bugaku*, a twisty-twiny, Japanese "sukiyaki" (as Mr. B called it) ballet for Allegra Kent and Edward Villella, premièred eight days before *Arcade*, and another Stravinsky work, *Movements for Piano and Orchestra*, was to be unveiled less than two weeks later. Balanchine had cast Diana and Jacques in *Movements* and was working on it while I was rehearsing *Arcade*.

Several days after *Arcade*'s debut, and less than a week before *Movements* was to première, Jacques came up to me and said, "We're going over to Diana's apartment so you can learn her part in *Movements*." I changed into my street clothes, packed my dance bag, and followed him to Diana's house. I had no idea what was going on, but as usual, I acquiesced to suggestions from those I respected and pretended to be calm and intelligent about seemingly ridiculous propositions.

Only years later did the whole story of what had happened become clear to me. Balanchine had championed Stravinsky's music all his life, turning his sometimes lyrical, sometimes wildly modern compositions into accessible visual counterparts. He had even said that were he a composer, his music would be Stravinsky's. I think he felt one of his purposes on this earth was to help people understand and enjoy his fellow Russian's varied and monumental works. *Movements*, though only eight and a half minutes long, was music in the composer's most atonal, complex, neoclassical strain. It made the 1957 *Agon* sound melodic. In short, *Movements* was to be a very important event on many levels, and for this mammoth responsibility Balanchine was relying on Diana as his most Stravinsky-like instrument—leggy, linear, musical, unsentimental, elegant, and, of course, untouchably beautiful. As with *Midsummer*, she had no official understudy, and again as with *Midsummer*, she found herself pregnant two weeks before the première.

It must be explained that these pregnancies were not accidental; the whole company knew that Diana and her husband, stage manager Ronald Bates, wanted a baby more than anything else. Her difficulty with miscarriages was mourned by the whole company, and when she did finally give birth to her daughter, Georgina, we felt that we had all birthed her. The dilemma she faced the week before *Movements* must have been truly agonizing, because her doctor had advised her not to dance, or even to move around much, if she wanted to keep the baby. Choosing between a baby and a Balanchine ballet is something no one should have to do, and perhaps that is why Balanchine was, at least in principle, so strongly against marriage and babies for ballerinas.

When Diana told him that she couldn't do the première, he was apparently deeply shaken. Now he had a dilemma: cancel the première of a much awaited piece of music by his friend Igor Stravinsky (who was to attend the performance) or do the ballet with someone else. But his vision of *Movements* included Diana, and he couldn't see it without her. He was on the point of canceling the ballet when Jacques, who was aware of what was at stake, made a bold suggestion: "Let me teach it to Suzaahn." Jacques already believed in me, and after he had taught me the *Midsummer* pas de deux six weeks earlier, he knew that I could learn quickly. Balanchine rejected the idea, but Jacques persisted, and finally Balanchine skeptically agreed to let Jacques try. It was at this point that Jacques rushed me to Diana's.

We found her stretched out on the couch under a blanket in her tiny living room. There was no use changing into practice clothes, so I wore my street clothes and bare feet. Climbing onto pointe on Diana's slippery parquet floor could only have left me beside her on the couch

with a broken foot, and no *Movements* in sight. Along with the rest
of the world, I had never heard the music, and between Jacques' and
Diana's grunting, clapping, and singing, I didn't manage to learn it.
I did learn the important counts, but most of the ballet was uncount-
able, and I was told to listen for "the big boom," "the second crash,"
"the sixth silent note," or "the sort of pretty music after the messy
music." I thought I was going crazy, but I kept trying to remember
the steps, the angles, the upside-down lifts, and the complicated stage
directions: "Now you run quickly down here, stage right only farther
over than in the last section. . . ." I couldn't do any of it physically,
of course, because Diana's living room was ten feet by twelve and
had a couch and a coffee table in the middle of it.

Despite all this, after about two hours I managed, somehow, to
learn the whole ballet. There were enough steps to fill a four-act *Swan
Lake*, only they seemed to be danced backward and upside down. My
head was swimming in a sea of développés, crouches, lunges, and
strange musical cues, but my body hadn't yet executed one of them.
I went home and tried to write it all down in my math notebook (I
was also studying for a big algebra exam at Rhodes at the time) before
I forgot it, but after filling up twenty or so pages with hieroglyphics
and stick-figure diagrams I gave up the literary approach; I had completed only the first of the five sections in the ballet. Writing down
steps didn't help and never would in a three-dimensional profession.

The next day Jacques and I rehearsed alone, with Gordon Boelzner
playing the piano, and while we sorted out some of the problems
and blank spots, I heard the music for the first time. Diana's and
Jacques's humming proved to have been more correct than I had
thought possible; this was Stravinsky at his most cerebral and stark—
there was nothing familiar to hold on to for security; it was music
unlike any that had ever been danced to before.

I cannot help thinking that the choreography that Jacques and I
showed to Mr. B the following morning was not exactly what he had
taught to Diana—how could it have been under the circumstances?—
but it must have been close enough in spirit and energy because Mr.
B's eyebrows rose and his demeanor changed. Rehearsals with him
were immediately scheduled with the six corps girls. He began al-
tering, fixing and changing things to fit, although he remained as
quiet and calm as usual; the première would go on as scheduled.
Though I had always liked the idea of "saving the day," I could never
have imagined it could mean anything as important, or as revealing,
as dancing *Movements* for Diana Adams on a few days' notice. As I
realize now my presence wasn't just saving the day, it was the center
of the day when all eyes were focused on me, eyes straining to analyze
and to judge.

Two days before the première we had a rehearsal in Studio 2 at the School up on 82nd Street. I was late because I had a two-hour algebra exam that morning and had to take the bus up Broadway to the School afterward. I charged straight into the studio fifteen minutes late, dragging my math books behind me. I thought Mr. B, Jacques, and Gordon would be at the rehearsal, and the idea of keeping them all waiting petrified me. When I barged through the door and found the studio filled with movie cameras, electrical cords, lights, and an entire camera crew, I thought—and hoped—that I was in the wrong studio. I wasn't. At the front of the studio lined up on chairs were John Taras, Robert Irving and Hugo Fiorato (our two conductors), and Lincoln Kirstein, the man who, with Balanchine, had founded the School of American Ballet and the New York City Ballet. Seated on little stools in the center of the lineup were Balanchine and Stravinsky, engaged in quiet conversation. A documentary for West German television was being made about the composer, and the cameras were to record him at the rehearsal of Balanchine's ballet to his new work.

"I'm sorry I'm late," I blurted out, "I had an exam at school. . . ." But before I could offer my excuses, Mr. B turned and with no admonition or comment said simply, "Let's begin." I was stone cold from not having had class that morning, but I didn't have time to consider what an improbable situation I was in; I simply dived straight into the world of *Movements*.

The rehearsal was terrible. I made a lot of mistakes that upset me, even though only a few of us in the studio knew they were mistakes. My body was not as sensitive to the music as it should have been because I had just spent several hours concentrating on what $2a + b = c$ might mean. But, thank heaven, youth has its pliancy, its elasticity, and somehow I managed to scramble through Stravinsky's score.

If I had ever felt inadequate before, it paled beside the way I felt when the rehearsal was over. Balanchine, Stravinsky, Kirstein, Jacques, and the cruel camera eye had witnessed, firsthand, my insufficiencies, and I felt that I had failed them all. I went up to Mr. B afterward and told him what I felt: "I don't think you should let me do this ballet. I'm just not ready for it." It may have been a silly thing to say, but I thought I had to be honest with him—as if he didn't know already. Then a wonderful thing happened. He clasped his hands as if in prayer, made a small bowing gesture, and said simply, "Oh, dear, you let me be the judge." And so I did, forever more.

This brief exchange was a turning point in a silent understanding, and our trust was sealed. I would try my hardest to do what he wanted and dance well, and he would be the only judge, relieving me of having to criticize myself. Dancers inevitably try to do this but more often than not they are not really in a position to see themselves and only smother energy that is best used for dancing. If Mr. B was willing to take a chance on me, the least I could do was go along with him. We were both taking pretty big chances, but if he thought I could do something, I would believe him, often against my own reasoning. I trusted him not to let me be a fool, but rather a tool, an instrument in his hands. In short, I trusted him with my life.

Balanchine introduced me to Stravinsky, and I was awed; I loved his music. I heard only later of an exchange between Balanchine and Stravinsky at this rehearsal: Stravinsky had said, "George, who is this girl?" He knew Balanchine's leading ladies, and clearly I was not one of them. "Igor Fyodorovich, this is Suzanne Farrell," replied Mr. B. "Just been born."

Movements premièred on an all-Stravinsky program that included *Apollo, Orpheus,* and Jerome Robbins' *The Cage.* Mr. B seemed pleased afterward, patting me on the shoulder and saying, "Good, dear." The audience also seemed pleased, and there was an enormous ovation. The reviews were almost universally ecstatic. "It may well go down in history as one of the greatest ballets ever created," wrote Allen Hughes in *The New York Times,* but my personal favorite at the time was by Walter Terry:

> As for Miss Farrell, she is the ideal female figure for the present Balanchine period. In *Movements* ballerina elements—high-lighted personality, gestural idiosyncrasies, projected glamour—are absent. Only the tool of dance image—the body—functions. This is not to say that Miss Farrell is unattractive. To the contrary she is beautiful. But here is the beauty of a body superbly trained so there is not an extra ounce of weight on it and so brilliantly disciplined that, say, a high-swing of the leg is not a trick but rather a command to action. . . .

I was pronounced slim by the all-powerful press, and I was at one with the world—temporarily.

Life was considerably different for me after *Movements:* Balanchine trusted me, I trusted him, and the public, at least for now, thought it was a fine arrangement. It was just as well, therefore, that when there was a costume change for the second performance the press didn't know it was my fault.

The première had been danced, as it is today, in white tights, white leotards, and white toe shoes. Despite the reviews, I felt terribly exposed in so much white. At the time I thought, as most dancers do, incorrectly, that black is more slimming and flattering to the body than white. Acting on this myth, I mustered up the courage to confess to Mr. B that perhaps I would look better in black. He said simply, "Fine." I didn't have to plead, and he didn't ask for an explanation, and so the six girls and I climbed into black leotards for the second performance the following day.

Without doubt Balanchine knew why I wanted to wear black and was sensitive to my modesty, but he knew I would not be modest in my dancing, and since that was what really mattered, he indulged my whim. Once I was onstage in my black leotard, seeing the six girls out of the corner of my eye in *their* black leotards, I knew it was all wrong. We have worn white ever since, but I have always been grateful to Mr. B for allowing me to make a mistake for myself and learn from it. He was, of course, confident enough about his own work to know that *Movements* could withstand a change of leotard color.

But the critics were outraged. It is obviously unpleasant for an artist to be disliked by the press, but their respect and admiration, which Balanchine had finally won after many years, also had a price: now that *Movements* had been pronounced a masterpiece, any alteration, even a change of leotards, was deemed blasphemous. One critic, who championed the ballet, went on at some length to explain his protest:

In its [*Movements*] first performance a week ago last Tuesday, the seven women dancers in it were dressed in white. Their bodies were seen as unbroken units that took on with a bit of imagination the aspect of figures carved in white stone. Because the choreography kept them more or less stationary, it was possible to see *Movements* as a kind of living sculpture. That being the case, this reviewer commented extensively upon the sculptural effect created by the work, assuming that it had been created consciously, that its whiteness had been intended and that it would remain white until it got dirty. When *Movements* was repeated on the following evening, a number of faithful readers rushed out to see the New York City Ballet reenact the white sculptural wonder. They did not see it. Mr. Balanchine, like Shah Jahan, had decided that it might be nice to do the second one in black. Because I was not there to see it, I cannot say whether it was nice or not. I am certain, however, that it looked altogether different than the *Movements* I saw, for the combination of black leotards and white tights breaks the body into two sharply defined components, the torso black and an assortment of limbs white. But the white *Movements* had a colossal success with almost everyone who saw it that first night. Was it fair or polite then to alter it so drastically without warning? There can be little doubt that many members of that second night audience went to see what they had read about in the papers that very day. They paid their money to see what it was the reviewers were excited about, and they were shown something else. What they saw may have been just as good or even better than what they had read about, but that is not the point. They were not given what they had expected and had paid for . . . [Balanchine] was treating his audience in a cavalier manner.

Poor Mr. B took all the blame, now exaggerated to Olympian dimensions. He probably thought all the hoopla merely amusing.

Other girls in the company were, however, becoming increasingly less amused by Balanchine's interest in me. The feeling of alienation from my peers that I had experienced over the past year since the *Concerto Barocco* fiasco in Zurich now reached a new intensity that was not to diminish for many years. On one occasion somebody was stomping around the dressing room with her cigarette, complaining about a certain ballet master's classes. I thought her comments were unjust and said, "Oh, I think it's a good class," and she retorted, "Well, it's easy for you to be happy, you've got everything coming your way." I learned at that moment that keeping my feelings to myself would make life calmer.

The antagonism was not confined to backstage. Some people thought Balanchine's interest in me was too much too soon, and this was brought home to me in a forthright message several days after the première of *Movements*. I now find it humorous, but at the time I was stunned and deeply hurt. As I passed by the security guard at the stage door of City Center, he stopped me and said, "Miss Farrell, you have a letter." My heart skipped a beat; I thought it might be my first fan letter. I opened the plain typed envelope with no return address and unfolded a rather empty sheet of white paper. There, at the top of the page, with my name misspelled, it read:

Dear Miss Farell,
Your *Movement* stinks.

I was so visibly shaken that the guard asked me if everything was all right, and I could hardly take class afterward. I couldn't imagine anyone hating me that much, and it scared me. I showed it to my mother, who was very upset; we thought things like that happened only in the movies, and I wondered if something worse than a letter might be on its way. It wasn't; the note was the end of the episode. It might also have read "P.S. Welcome to the big time!"

There were fortunately more positive reactions to the acclaim for *Movements*. We filmed it for a television broadcast celebrating the first anniversary of Lincoln Center, and Jacqueline Kennedy, America's new First Lady, requested that the ballet be performed at the White House. Balanchine was pleased, but there was a problem: Could we dance the ballet *Movements for Piano and Orchestra* accompanied only by the piano? Mr. B decided we could not, and the invitation was declined.

Two days after *Movements*, I had another big debut, Diana's role in Brahms's *Liebeslieder Walzer*. It was the beginning of my taking over virtually all of Diana's roles during the next few years—*Agon, Episodes, Apollo, Ivesiana, Monumentum Pro Gesualdo*. Diana was to dance only rarely from then on. In 1966 she had her baby and retired altogether. I had learned *Liebeslieder* on the European tour but didn't think I would be dancing such a profoundly adult ballet so soon. The fact that this piece, performed to heartbreakingly beautiful love songs that evoke a powerful atmosphere of physical and emotional love tempered by the grace of social behavior, was completely beyond the scope of my experience didn't seem to bother Mr. B at all. Perhaps he thought it was a good way to introduce me to such things. There were four principal couples, and the other ballerinas were all the originators of their roles—Violette Verdy, Melissa Hayden, Jillana. Among them I must have looked like the answer to "What's wrong with this picture?"

But, as always, the music showed me how to be and my romantic longings were quickly stirred. In the first section we wore long, pale, heavy silk gowns decorated with lace and flowers, gloves, and jewels in our curled hair. In the second section, where we changed into calf-length gauze tutus, our shiny satin, heeled slippers became pointe shoes. The setting was an intimate ballroom furnished with padded chairs, crystal chandeliers, and three sets of double doors.

The doors were flung open for the second half of the ballet, and the dark, starry night sky enveloped the space as the dancing became more intimate, more expansive, and dreamier. But throughout this ballet, despite its opulence and seductiveness, the air is thick with the silent, tragic emotions of love, not in its youthful joy, innocence, or ignorance, but with the shattering, desperate beauty of one who has lived a hundred lives.

Liebeslieder Walzer was Balanchine's 1960 meditation on what was to him the most important thing in life and, though it was cloaked in silk and satin, it was perhaps his most personal statement on the subject to date. Three years later, with *Meditation*, he was to display a different new-old emotion: young, yearning love. It was not as if

Liebeslieder had never happened, but *Meditation* signified a renewal, a change of direction, and the hard-earned conclusion of *Liebeslieder* seemed to come undone.

Just before departing for a two-week tour in July of 1963, the company announced the promotion of ten new solo dancers; I was the youngest among them. This was probably the biggest simultaneous promotion the company had ever made, and it enlarged the previously small roster of soloists to fourteen. Such a massive exodus from the corps de ballet not only emphasizes what a large pool of young talent had emerged in the early 1960s, it shows that my own successes did not happen in a vacuum but alongside those of a lot of wonderful female dancers. Mimi Paul, Carol Sumner, Sara Leland, Patricia Neary, Victoria Simon, Suki Schorer, and myself, along with Patricia McBride, who was already a principal, represented a whole new generation of Balanchine dancers. Without the experience of having danced elsewhere, we did not face the very difficult job of having to relearn what Balanchine's ballets required, as some ballerinas before us had had to do.

I was very happy to be promoted, but my title was not a primary concern; to be dancing every night was. On the other hand, the small salary increase was more than welcome. I was seventeen when the newspapers noted the promotions and *Ingenue* magazine ran a picture of me in their August issue with a caption detailing my young success. It was this photograph that inspired an amusing exchange, a reminder of the world I had left behind. A classmate from Rhodes approached me with shy amazement and said, "Oh, you must be really famous. Your picture was on a page opposite the Beatles!" Confused, I replied, "Who are the Beatles?"

Shortly after this, while dancing in Washington, D.C., at the Carter Barron Amphitheater, a huge, impractical outdoor edifice that looked and functioned as if it had been abandoned unfinished, I received a beautiful bouquet of flowers at the stage door. It was my first performance of *Movements* outside New York, and I was touched that someone seemed to know how important this ballet was. The accompanying card, however, was a mystery, and after that first anonymous letter about "my *Movement*" I was perturbed to read, "Love, Igor," in a scrawled, disguised hand. I was frightened that this might be an eccentric man who planned to give me trouble: Mr. B had told us stories of the "old days" when an admirer sent flowers to his preferred ballerina, expecting then to wine and dine her and take her home for the night. I showed the note to Eddie Bigelow, and the mystery was solved. The flowers were a gift from Tanaquil Le Clercq, and the note was humorous. The "Igor" was supposed to be Stravinsky. My trepidation turned to ecstasy, because even though I had never seen her dance, I admired her enormously and would have liked to be her friend.

While we were on tour, she and Diana had occasionally invited me to their hotel rooms for an evening of cards; we all loved to play—and I don't remember who won. I think they both knew all too well how lonely and isolating it can be to have been singled out in a ballet company, and they were very kind to me.

My next big public event came on opening night of the fall New York season. The excitement of the night was not, however, my debut as the adagio girl in *Concerto Barocco,* but the performance of Tschaikovsky's *Allegro Brillante,* which heralded the return of another of Balanchine's wives to the company. I had never seen Maria Tallchief dance, but her international reputation had preceded her, and I was as curious as the audience to see this great ballerina. Her marriage to Balanchine had been annulled in 1952, and he had married Tanny a few months later. Maria had remarried also, had a child (the dissolution of her six-year marriage to Balanchine was officially explained by the fact that she wanted a child and Balanchine did not), and returned to dance and tour all over the world with various companies, often with Erik Bruhn as her partner. She was rejoining the company where she had created many great roles, after a hiatus of several years.

She was, at the time, the most famous dancer associated with the New York City Ballet, and the house was sold out. The air crackled with expectation and adoration. I could not help also being curious about her on another level; she was, after all, only the second of Balanchine's five famous wives I was to meet.

The program order was *Donizetti Variations, Allegro Brillante, Concerto Barocco,* and *Symphony in C.* Maria danced *Allegro* with André Prokovsky, a recent foreign import, and she caused a sensation from her first entrance to her last.

I danced *Barocco* next, partnered by Jacques, with Pat Neary dancing the second solo girl. This took a little extra concentration because the second girl was the role I knew first, and I had constantly to restrain myself from moving on her counts, which were now no longer mine. I had an almost neurological reaction to the music, and dancing to the adagio girl's notes threatened, at least musically, to unhinge me. The ballet, however, proceeded without any problems. Except that the audience gave me my first serious ovation. Instead of enjoying it, I was surprised and embarrassed; instead of feeling privileged I felt isolated, off balance. Perhaps sensing this, Diana, who had been watching, came backstage afterward and did not say that it was good or bad, only, "Don't you think you should lose a little weight?"

The next day the critics singled me out all over again. Allen Hughes wrote in *The New York Times*, "It was in *Concerto Barocco* that the greatest solo delight of the evening was to be found, and Suzanne Farrell provided it . . . a gentle lyricism less frequently encountered in NYCB." But the only opinion that really mattered to me was Mr. B's, and as he, too, was pleased, I danced on, trying to ignore the side effects of success.

Three days later I performed Titania in *A Midsummer Night's Dream* for the first time. Balanchine always put considerable emphasis on having a tall Queen of the Fairies alongside a shorter Oberon, who was danced by Edward Villella. I had never worked with Eddie before, but our tempestuous onstage scenes when fighting over the little page, as well as our final reconciliation, went smoothly enough. Titania's real dancing, however, is not performed with Oberon but with two other partners.

In the first-act pas de deux I was to dance, also for the first time, with Conrad Ludlow as Titania's cavalier. Conrad was a perfect partner—he gave a ballerina the ultimate gift, her freedom. Dancing with Conrad, which I was to do many times over the next years, was quite simply heaven; he seemed to be able to absorb every possible misstep or snag and leave his partner looking calm and impervious. But later, Titania dances with a very different partner, under very different circumstances, and with this pas de deux I had trouble.

After some irresponsible tampering by Puck, Oberon's right-hand man in fairyland, a weaver named Bottom is turned into a donkey, and after a little further magical confusion, Titania awakens and falls in love with him. There follows a pas de deux between the two. Titania is overcome with amorous feelings, and Bottom, though oblivious to the depth of her sentiments, allows himself to be showered with her love. A superb donkey head, worn with tremendous dignity by Richard Rapp as Bottom, had been designed by David Hays, and it was to this sweet, slightly comical visage that I was supposed to react with great affection and romantic longing. It is one of Balanchine's most charming, most humorous, and ultimately most touching dances; it is the central dance in the ballet and the clue to Bottom's dream, a dream that carried so much meaning to Balanchine and which he could quote at length from Shakespeare's play:

The eye of man hath not heard, the ear of man hath not seen, man's hand is not able to taste, his tongue to conceive, nor his heart to report, what my dream was.

I had not read the play in 1963, but I figured that Mr. B would show me all I needed to know. And he showed me, and showed me . . . and showed me. And I couldn't get it right. The lightness, the sweetness, and the playful affection that I needed to interact with Bottom in a convincing manner seemed to be beyond my experience. Mr. B, patient beyond all reason, danced Titania with Richard Rapp in rehearsal while I watched, trying to learn and imitate. He was so wonderful, scratching Bottom under the chin, crowning one long donkey ear with a garland, showing Bottom how to partner his precious cargo, and bourréeing across the studio, pulling Bottom behind.

Eventually, exasperated that I seemed unable to cuddle or even communicate with my beloved Bottom, he said to me, "Don't you have an animal at home that you play with or talk to?" I opened my eyes wide, on the verge of tears, and said, "No, Mr. Bal-an-chine." "Oh, that's too bad, you should have one," he replied, and I nodded in agreement.

We were still living in crowded quarters on East 84th Street, and the addition of one extra mouth, animal or otherwise, did not seem appropriate. Nevertheless my boss had given me an idea, which I took as a suggestion, so on my way home I stopped into the local delicatessen, which had a cat, and asked if there might be any extras around. As fate would have it, the in-store cat had just had kittens, and I offered to buy one. "You can't buy one, but you can have one," the man said and led me into the back room where three kittens were skidding around on the floor. I chose the only brown and white one, but as he was already spoken for, I held up the two black and white ones that were left. Since they both looked the same to me, I settled on one.

She was white with black patches on her bottom and a black mask across her eyes like Zorro. I took her home, named her Bottom, of course, and talked her little head off. She quickly became the friend I had never had before, and there was nothing I didn't tell her for the next twenty years. She was the only one who ever knew everything about my life, my feelings and my dilemmas, but she told no one; she was my very best friend.

I immediately told Mr. B about Bottom (also called Girl), and she became a constant topic of conversation between us. He was a great cat lover, always telling us in class how much we could learn from kitties about speed, grace, line, mystery, and not putting our heels down. He was probably impressed that I had taken his passing statement about my lack of a pet so seriously, but the results were visible, and I danced Titania with a new understanding.

Within a few weeks Mr. B told me about the pas de deux to Tschaikovsky that would be made on Jacques and me, within two months

I received his letter from Hamburg, and life was never to be the same again. Perhaps Mr. B knew I might need a cat to talk to, and Bottom arrived, all ears, just in time.

When Mr. B finally met her, their relationship was testy, to say the least—she didn't really approve of anyone but me, especially not men—and he would often say with stubborn seriousness, "If there's one thing I'm going to do, it's conquer this cat!"

Despite her ungracious behavior, Bottom was invited the following year to be photographed for Tanaquil Le Clercq's charming book *Mourka: The Autobiography of a Cat.* Mourka was Mr. B's and Tanny's own high-flying feline. Bottom was cast as the young love interest of Mourka (they met on the dance floor), the world's "first astrocat," who discovered he "could do more for the nation through my elevation." But, alas, their romance was bittersweet and short-lived as a result of Bottom's youth and desire to go out dancing every night. She didn't want to become "Mrs. Mourka."

After many years Mr. B was finally able to make peace with Girl, but not before several scratching wars, one of which resulted in a terrible gash on his cheek that he explained to everyone in class the following morning as a razor cut.

CHAPTER FIVE

Crash Course

A s a partner, Jacques d'Amboise was physically the right height for me—even when I grew five inches standing in pointe shoes he was still taller—and *Meditation* was the ballet in which Balanchine first paired us. (*Movements* was Jacques' casting with Balanchine's approval.) It was the beginning of a long, successful partnership. But during the first *Meditation* rehearsals after Balanchine returned from Hamburg in the fall of 1963, there was another less expected and less conventional partnering match-up that was to affect the casting, choreography, and probably the content of many future ballets.

Although Mr. B was almost sixty years old, he was as young in body and spirit as a man half his age, and he considered it necessary to demonstrate not only every step of choreography for each dancer, male and female, but to do all the partnering of the woman as well. His skills in this department, unwitnessed by the public, were unparalleled, and the fact that on pointe I towered over him by several inches seemed actually to make things easier—he fit underneath me where I needed the support. I discovered what he no doubt knew: we complemented each other visually, and he would often comment on our physical compatibility with sly ambiguity—"Look how well we fit together."

We did not, of course, present the standard picture of a ballerina and her cavalier, but Balanchine had had a lifelong love of women taller than himself. He liked the clear visual metaphor that it presented of the woman, feminine yet in command, and he had invented an entirely new way of presenting a female dancer to her audience. During rehearsals for *Meditation* and for the next twenty years of his life he never tired of showing male dancers how to hold and handle a woman, and he never failed to delight in the fact that he could always partner with greater ease, grace, and strength than even the tallest and strongest men. It became obvious that he liked to demonstrate this more often than necessary; the poor young man would stand to one side with a slightly strained expression of admiration while Mr. B and I danced the most complex movements with smooth success. And so *Meditation* was not only the beginning of what could be called an artistic partnership but also a very real physical one that took place in the studio day after day.

"What! No flowers!" were the first words out of Jacques' mouth when the curtain was lowered after the première of *Meditation*. He and Mr. B went on to say how wonderfully it had gone, but Jacques's comment stuck in my mind. He made it sound as if I should have had some, so I asked him, "Who would send me flowers?" "Well, your mother," he said and simultaneously burst a romantic bubble— I had thought only admirers who loved your dancing sent flowers, not that they could (or should) come from one's mother.

Only eight months before *Meditation*, the New York audience and critics had witnessed *Movements* with the same two leads, and though they liked the Tschaikovsky pas de deux, some shock waves (which Balanchine no doubt thoroughly enjoyed) were generated by the radical differences between the two works—one the height of cool abstraction and the other in the words of one critic "probably Balanchine's first excursion into open sentimentality." Once again Balanchine had proven himself unpredictable and impossible to categorize. One month later he proceeded to cap the distinction by producing *Tarantella*, a charming, tambourine-shaking, technical tour de force for Edward Villella and Patricia McBride, to the witty, bright tunes of Louis Moreau Gottschalk. Nothing could have been more different from *Meditation*.

My off-white chiffon dress in *Meditation* was never altered, but Jacques' costume was changed directly after the premiere. He had worn a kind of eighteenth-century velvet vest with full puffy sleeves and black tights—very much the haunted poet look. Balanchine was dissatisfied, and for the next performance Jacques wore trousers and a very simple gray store-bought jersey shirt; he looked ready for a game at the country club. Although the dance was clearly Balanchine at his most Byronic, he wanted the action to take place in the present moment and not in the easily identified Romantic ballet world of sylphs and forlorn young men. *Meditation* was a contemporary story.

Another break with tradition was my loose hair instead of the usual tight ballerina bun. It was the beginning of a career of loose hair, and I loved it, feeling at the time that it gave me a distraction to hide behind, a veil for my insecurities, or anything else that needed to be concealed. I subsequently discovered that when my hair was down I danced in a wholly different way, a loose-hair kind of way—less inhibited, more dramatic, more flamboyant. There were only one or two "hair-down" ballets, as they came to be called, in the repertoire at the time, but there were many to come. Long, free-flowing hair signified something very feminine, very vulnerable, and very intimate to Balanchine.

Within one week of *Meditation*'s première my hair was back on my head, slicked back in a little topknot dripping with diamond teardrops. It was my first attempt at the sparkling, spinning, and high-flying Dewdrop in *The Nutcracker* and it went well . . . as far as it went. I was a big jumper in those days and while landing from a grand jeté split leap I felt something pull underneath my left foot, the horse-kicked foot. I hobbled through the finale of the ballet just before it had time to swell and found myself the next morning at the doctor's office. It was not serious, just a sprain, but it needed time to heal, and the doctor prescribed huge, thick, lace-up, flat-heeled, black orthopedic shoes until it did. I was horrified. Here I was, all of eighteen years old, just beginning to appreciate the results of adolescent changes and the delights of dressing up, and I had to wear old women's shoes! Humiliated, I stayed home as much as possible, praying desperately for my ligaments to mend.

Before my injury Jacques had been choreographing a new ballet on me to one of Shostakovich's quartets, and the moment I felt well enough to resume rehearsals I did, although it was rather too soon. The ballet involved four dancers—hence the title, *Quatuor*. Robert Maiorano, a dark, handsome boy, played a dark, handsome boy; Jacques played an older, dark, handsome man; and Roland Vasquez played my dark, handsome father, all of whom were vying for my attention. The music, appropriately, was tormented, and thoroughly confused—now this was high drama! But the drama in my left metatarsal proved to be more real, and Mimi Paul danced the première.

By January 20 of the new year, though my foot was still weak, I danced my first Terpsichore to Jacques' Apollo. I simply refused to wait any longer for a completely healed foot to emerge from my big black shoes, so I donned a tight pair of pink toe shoes and felt better immediately. My performance was probably a little more cautious than it might have been. With one foot bound in adhesive tape I felt like a cat with boots on, and I had a distracting urge to shake off the constricting accessory. Since then, except in absolute emergencies, I have avoided putting anything inside a toe shoe that was not a part of my foot; I could control my feet but I could not control Dr. Scholl's inventions.

I had learned the role of Terpsichore but, as usual, was not scheduled to perform it that evening. Melissa Hayden was to have danced the role; instead she replaced Maria Tallchief in *Scotch Symphony*, so I replaced her in *Apollo*. It was my first time onstage in over a month, and Jacques was supportive, both emotionally and physically.

It was becoming a more and more frequent occurrence that I was thrown on in a new part, and Jacques was there to catch me. His conviction and security gave me enormous comfort as I started to dance new ballets as fast as I could learn them. Our energies, in fact, were amazingly well-matched, and our mutual abandon resulted in a kind of natural eruption on stage. We encouraged each other and there were no apparent limitations to our daring. I would never have had a career to write about had I not found—and relished—such freedom on the stage, and while it was Balanchine who offered it, it was Jacques who literally traveled with me when the curtain was up—and down. While Mr. B was undeniably taking an unusually serious interest in my dancing, we were by no means speaking on a daily basis, whereas Jacques and I were and would often get together after morning class or after a rehearsal and experiment with a complicated turn, promenade, or lift, trying always to do it bigger, faster, smoother, and higher.

Jacques, who already enjoyed considerable fame and reputation, was never satisfied performing what he knew he could do, and I, with a small but growing reputation, felt the need to improve and learn, not preserve or reproduce what had worked before. I might easily have fallen into the trap of early success and spent my time perfecting my most noted qualities, but judging from the reviews, they all concerned my virginity, and I didn't see what that had to do with anything. Besides, I already knew there was more at stake than public acceptance. I sensed that I was involved in a world at New York City Ballet that was not dictated by the public's whim. On the other hand, Balanchine's whims were taken with the utmost seriousness, and he had a distinct dislike for dancers with self-imposed images of themselves.

Balanchine didn't like the packages, deals, or high-strung temperaments that arrived with celebrities, as was made clear around this time by the rapid entrances and exits of Erik Bruhn on our stage. The great Danish classicist came and left the company twice in the course of several years for a total of about three months performing time, and by his own admission it was the worst experience of his life. One could be sure that if Balanchine was presented with a finely tuned finished image, however beautiful, he would try to expand it, nurture it, and extend it. Obviously Bruhn and Balanchine had different ideas about dancing, and this example, along with numerous others over the years, undoubtedly strengthened Balanchine's now-famous resolve to have no "stars" in his company. The fact that within a year I was presented to the public in what could easily be regarded as a star's schedule of performances might seem incongruous, except for one important detail—I was *his* star, and my greatest wish was to serve him.

Two events of immeasurable importance to the New York City Ballet took place during the first few months of 1964. The Ford Foundation, which had given me the scholarship at SAB in 1960, issued the single largest grant to ballet in American history, and the vast majority of it, over seven million dollars, was given to Balanchine's two institutions, the School of American Ballet and the New York City Ballet.

This meant both security and a future, the two rarest commodities in the American dance world, not only because of the money, which was always in short supply, but also because of the prestige. Never before had such a powerful and wealthy financial establishment put so much faith in the work and judgment of one man, and an "artistic" one at that. One of the grant's many stipulations was that Balanchine legitimize himself by accepting a salary, something he had always refused to do before. Characteristically, he used his $10,000-a-year stipend to pay the salary of Barbara Horgan, a longtime company employee who then became his personal assistant.

To many, especially in the modern dance world, the Ford Foundation's concentration on Balanchine seemed an undemocratic gesture, but it turned out to be a very wise one. During the next twenty years the success of Balanchine's work made the United States, and specifically New York, the center of the dance world, and everyone, including modern dancers, profited from this.

Balanchine now needed only one more thing to fulfill his grand plans—a frame for his ballets whose depth, width, and height would match and contain his visions—and in April of 1964 he got it. An impressive group of accomplices—Lincoln Kirstein, Nelson Rockefeller, Philip Johnson, Morton Baum, Betty Cage, and others—had conspired to build Balanchine a theater at the new New York arts complex called Lincoln Center, and on April 20, after years of controversy, planning, and building, the New York State Theater was unveiled at a gala opening in which I danced *Agon*, a recent addition to my repertoire, with Arthur Mitchell. This small but epic Stravinsky ballet had been made seven years earlier on Diana and Arthur, and so, as with Jacques, Arthur's experience and unfailing good humor did a great deal to get me through this very special evening; I simply let him manipulate me in the pas de deux, an effective approach for this athletic ballet.

Four days later, at the official opening of our new home, the company presented a redesigned and expanded production of *A Midsummer Night's Dream* in which I danced Titania. The New York State Theater was a large-scale family affair, and it was the first time Balanchine had ever been consulted about stage size. The result was a stage bigger than we had ever performed on regularly, constructed of crisscrossing wooden panels covered with gray battleship linoleum that was to set a precedent for dance stages all over the world. The little bit of bounce to the floor spared our legs, feet, and backs some of the enormous physical resistance of gravity's pull. There is no way of knowing how many careers were prolonged because of this construction. The welfare of his dancers' bodies was of paramount importance to Balanchine, and there were to be occasions when he refused a tour because it would entail dancing on stages that would put us in peril.

The sheer dimensions of our new stage put us in peril, however, for different reasons. We were not used to jumping that far, running that far, or being carried that far, and the whole company suddenly seemed to be out of breath. We danced all the same ballets, but now we had to cover twice as much space in the same musical time and a certain amount of retraining was in order. I feel sure that this is one of the main reasons that Mr. B began teaching company class on a much more regular basis than he had previously. Suddenly he found himself with the convenience and freedom to extend and expand, and, like a scientist in a laboratory, he experimented in every direction, technical and otherwise.·

Despite all the encouraging attention I was receiving from Mr. B, I did not always feel that I knew what he wanted or what he meant by some of his seemingly extreme demands. I believed in him and wanted to please him, but I could not understand why, if he cast me in his ballets every night, there was so much wrong with me in class the next morning. Although I was convinced he was a genius, it also occurred to me that he might be just a little eccentric . . . until he challenged me to pirouette his way in class one day and changed my life.

It was shortly after moving into the State Theater, and we were in eleven o'clock morning class in the huge, windowless main hall on the fifth floor. Like every other ballet dancer on earth, I had been taught to turn from a fourth position with one leg directly in front of the other, both knees bent in plié ready to push off into as many pirouettes as possible. I was what is called a "natural turner," having no fear of spinning around on one leg as fast as I could, and the results more often than not were smooth multiple pirouettes. Turning was not one of my problem areas, but Mr. B made it a problem, or so I thought. He asked me to start my pirouette, and I settled into a nice, comfortable fourth position.

Thinking I was ahead of the game, I straightened my back leg, knowing that he liked it that way, although it still felt foreign and unorthodox. I thought I was giving him what he wanted, but he didn't think so at all.

"Why don't you try a big fourth?" he said. I shuffled my legs a little wider and looked at him for approval. "Bigger." Again I shuffled a few more inches. "Bigger." Now I was feeling really uncomfortable with my legs so far apart that the notion of pushing off for a turn was becoming a fantasy. "More," was the next suggestion, and though I silently tried to accommodate him, he knew what the rest of the dancers were thinking—no self-respecting ballerina would ever take such a wide stance before a turn.

"More." By now my legs were so far apart that I risked losing my grip and slipping to the floor in a split. If this was a Balanchine experiment, I wished he had used another guinea pig. Now that I felt thoroughly ridiculous—which was not helped by nervous twitters from the other girls, all hoping they weren't next on the turning block—he smiled in triumph and said with enormous satisfaction, *"Now* turn." Never in my life had I turned from such a deep lunge, and my instincts told me to shuffle back to where I had begun, but I looked at Mr. B and thought better of it. He seemed so happy and excited, and I did after all want to please him. Half defiantly (I was sure that I would fall on my face) and half curiously I turned . . . and turned . . . and turned.

While these pirouettes were perhaps not the cleanest or most precise I had ever done, they were the most glorious in ways I had not felt before; it was a feeling I had never known and have never forgotten. Mr. B watched with his head held high, and when I finished, he was the only one in the whole room who was not astonished that I was still upright. "You see!" he said with a little smile and held his finger up in the air like a magician who has just pulled a rabbit out of a hat. He was not a bit smug about my success—our success. The dynamic of our interaction had changed; instead of being teacher and student, now, at least on some levels, we were accomplices.

The turn that had begun with such painstaking resistance and hard labor resulted in such a wonderful sensation that I decided then and there that this man knew exactly what he was doing—even when he asked for what seemed physically impossible. "Impossible" went out of my vocabulary; things were merely "different." If he wanted wider, he would get wider; if he wanted smaller, he would get smaller; and if he wanted me to stand on my head I would ask only whether I should be facing front or back. That pirouette was really the beginning of our spiritual understanding; indeed, it was not about pirouettes at all, it was about believing in someone even when you might doubt.

Now that I had turned this way once, I could never again turn the old way. It was that simple. I never went backward into a stingy fourth position again. It was, I suppose, a turn of faith, but that was not frightening to me. Not to turn, not to believe, to refuse Balanchine's wisdom—that would have been frightening.

I discovered another interesting fact about a large fourth position. While the conventional fourth telegraphs to your audience "pirouette time," as if there were a billboard on your chest, a Balanchine fourth keeps them guessing, and the power of surprise in dancing cannot be underestimated. From a wide fourth one could not only turn but also step into arabesque, swivel into a chassé, bourrée to one's partner, or just stay there and smile. It meant freedom and flexibility which to some might be the hell of indecision, but to me was heaven.

Despite my overall technical proficiency I did sometimes worry that I didn't really excel in one specific area of dancing. While I could turn, jump, extend my legs, and point my feet, there was always someone who could turn faster, jump farther, lift her legs higher, and point more beautifully. I was a kind of good jack-of-all-trades, which could be very dull indeed except for the one thing I did have, probably the thing Diana had seen in Cincinnati: I could move, and if I could incorporate what Balanchine wanted with my movement, it might blossom into something—it could be anything. I think that was interesting to Balanchine. With no image to uphold and no glory in any single area of technique, I never had the debilitating worry that I might lose my strongest point. I had no strongest point, and the result was freedom and flexibility.

Five days after opening our first season at Lincoln Center, I danced one of two female solo parts in a new Balanchine ballet, and that flexibility was put to good use, at least physically. *Clarinade* was set to jazz music composed by Morton Gould for Benny Goodman, who played the clarinet for the first performances. The ballet was a lighthearted excursion into Balanchine's easygoing, hip-swaying American soul, and if it had occurred to me that Mr. B saw me only as the girl in *Meditation*, this ballet changed all that. There were four movements: "Warm Up" with Gloria Govrin, Arthur Mitchell, and five couples; "Contrapuntal Blues," a pas de deux for Anthony Blum and myself; "Rag," a solo for Gloria with four girls; and finally "Rideout," the finale.

I wore a turquoise leotard with a turquoise polka-dotted black skirt; Gloria was in shocking pink; we both had ponytails. The men were in pants and cut-out T-shirts. My dance with Tony Blum was very long and acrobatic, based on a thirties craze, the marathon dance. Mr. B had discovered that I never got tired, and I became his marathon dancer, executing everything from a "mopping" step, where I hung over Tony's shoulders while he swooshed me around the stage, to a form of moonwalking twenty years before Michael Jackson put it on the map.

There was one other movement Mr. B devised that made me feel decidedly uncomfortable. I had to sit on Tony's thigh, facing him, while he moved his leg underneath me and I swayed my legs around; it seemed to go on forever. This embarrassed me, especially when Mr. B was watching. In hindsight I can see that although *Clarinade* itself was not a particularly profound ballet and was short-lived, its real importance was as a stepping-stone for a kind of jazzy movement that Balanchine would perfect several years later in "Rubies," the second section of *Jewels*.

Our inaugural season at Lincoln Center was only three weeks long, and it was followed by a two-month layoff during which I went on my first concert tour as a guest artist from the New York City Ballet. Jacques never took a vacation and was always organizing extra work for himself and other dancers when the company was not in season. It was a chance not only to dance in different theaters for a different audience but to make extra money; in those days even dancers of Jacques' fame made very little money, and he had a wife and four children to support. There was to be an arts festival in Munich at the end of May, with stars from the Bolshoi Ballet among other international celebrities, and Jacques asked me if I would like to go along with Patty McBride, Eddie Villella, and André Prokovsky and be his partner in *Scotch Symphony* (in the Munich Ballet's production), "Five Pieces" from *Episodes*, and the pas de deux from *Stars and Stripes*.

This was a very exciting prospect. I felt it was a great honor to be included with these principal dancers. Besides, I had never danced any of the roles before, and it would be wonderful exposure and experience without the pressure of Mr. B and the all-knowing New York audience watching. But Mother and I were worried about appearances of a different sort. I would be traveling alone with Jacques, and we thought some people might get the wrong idea. We agonized for some days over the decision and finally did what we had always done—we asked Diana.

Mother telephoned, and Diana, always wise and practical, said, "People will think whatever they want to think anyway, so go and enjoy yourself and let them think whatever they like." So off I went to Europe unchaperoned.

After the festival, Jacques and I continued on to Bayreuth for a performance of *Stars and Stripes*, and it proved especially amusing to hear John Philip Sousa's patriotic marches resound in a theater so imbued with the weight of Wagner's dramas. The following day Jacques suggested we go swimming, and as we sat in the sun at the public pool I felt a hand on my back. "You know, Suzaahn," said Jacques, "you don't have to let me do this." I replied with corny composure, "I know. Don't worry, I'm the Rock of Gibraltar." Away went the hand, and that was the end of the flirtation; Jacques was very much a gentleman.

I was flattered that my childhood idol liked me, but curiously enough this brief episode put an end to my crush; once it was no longer only in my imagination, the romance was gone. I remained grateful to Jacques, however, not only for talking to me and dancing with me but even for flirting with me, because it made me feel pretty, and I was beginning to notice a curious trend. As Balanchine's interest in me increased, it seemed as if I were wearing a "Do Not Touch" sign. It became a joke among the men in the company that if anyone bruised me in partnering—and I bruise very easily—his job would be in peril; but it was a joke nobody laughed at.

At this time my interest in the opposite sex was still dormant. I was busy dancing, and I was still trying to finish high school. I would come home from dancing a lead in a new Balanchine ballet and have to study for a history exam and then get up six hours later to go to biology class, but it was clear where my preference lay. My teachers at Rhodes understood the situation, but they respected their work as much as I did mine. After I had delivered a rather pathetic essay one day on Archibald MacLeish, my English teacher reprimanded me, "I know it's very nice to be a ballerina, but wouldn't it be nice to have excellence in literature also?" It would have been, I suppose, but it was simply not possible.

One night, tired after performance, I broke down and said flatly to Mother, "I just can't finish school." She relented. By this time she was seeing my name and picture in the papers, and perhaps she finally thought that maybe I really wouldn't need a high school diploma. I never got one, but I was also receiving a very different though no less important education in the world of Balanchine.

By now I had danced quite a few of the major female roles in the Balanchine repertoire—*Serenade, Concerto Barocco, Agon, Apollo*—but I had not yet been in a tutu and tiara, the crowning symbols of a real ballerina, one with poise, confidence, glamour, and unshakable authority. It was three days before my nineteenth birthday, and Mr. B had cast me in one of the most revealing, vulnerable, and ecstatic parts he had ever choreographed for a woman, the second movement of Georges Bizet's *Symphony in C*, written when the composer was only seventeen years old. This was the ballet that had made me want to join the New York City Ballet back in Indiana five years earlier. But it had never crossed my mind that I might be wearing the tiara of the adagio ballerina within a few years.

Tying one's hair back from the face was revealing; tying it back with flowers was revealing but soft and pretty; tying it back and putting on a glittering crown was a revelation; it required blue blood. And then there was the short, tight, fluffy white tutu, enhancing everything and hiding nothing; it feels more naked than a leotard. And so with the lights dimmed and the music trembling, the ever-solicitous Conrad Ludlow led me out of the back right wing of the huge outdoor Greek Theater in Los Angeles, and I bourréed toward the center of the stage and the soft spotlight, looking as regal as I could. The performance went well—even the famously nerve-racking balance on pointe with one leg held high to the side went well.

Balanchine had originally choreographed *Symphony in C* in Paris two years after I was born, and it had been presented at the first performance of the New York City Ballet. It has since been danced by over forty companies around the world; like *Serenade*, it remains one of the cornerstones of the Balanchine repertoire. Mr. B was a man of the moment, however, and despite the ballet's world renown and seeming perfection, a few months after my first performance, he changed a step in rehearsal one day. It was a small detail, but it has since become perhaps the most famous single moment in the ballet.

I was in profile in a deep penché split on pointe in the center of the stage, holding both of Conrad's hands for support. It had always seemed that there was just a little too much music for the movement down and up however slowly it was done. "Can you touch your head to your knee?" Mr. B asked, and everyone onstage looked astonished; it was a weird, unorthodox, acrobatic thing to ask for in the middle of a very classical adagio. I bent down, put my forehead on my knee and mumbled—I was completely upside down—"Like this?" "Yes, like that." He gazed at the effect for a moment—it looked wickedly impressive and very beautiful. Ever since, ballerinas all over the world have been splitting their bodies in two directions. At the time I told Mr. B I felt like one of those pendulum birds on the edge of a vase in a flower shop that dips its beak down into the water while its tail shoots straight up. He looked at me a little curiously and said that was an interesting assessment.

More accurately, what Balanchine had suggested was simply the ultimate extension of a conventional classical movement. The arc traced by the legs mirrored the music; this was perfectly complemented and completed by the arc of the head and neck to the knee. It is a specific example of how, and why, Balanchine extended the vocabulary of his craft overall, with tradition and through tradition, but never in spite of it. He was visually uninhibited and chose to give movements their full musical value and depth, and, as with this penché, it often called for a step of a rich and passionate nature that had not been dared before.

On one occasion this feat of flexibility caused me considerable embarrassment when a rhinestone on my tiara caught on my tights at my knee, and as I tried to rise again, I watched a long pink snag from my tights begin to unravel in front of my nose. Without a hand available to disengage the thread, I was presented with two choices—either being stuck on center stage upside down for the rest of the movement, or ignoring the problem and continuing to dance with my tights coming completely unraveled around my head. Relishing neither prospect, I bent my head back down to my knee, praying for divine intervention, and got it. The thread broke and I rose up triumphantly to meet Conrad's puzzled gaze—"What on earth were you doing down there?" There I was, attached to my own knee at a profoundly beautiful and much awaited moment in the ballet; it was a real struggle not to laugh, but I was still wearing my crown and controlled myself until we were offstage.

Some time later Mr. B again used me to change another arabesque in another well-established ballet and that change has become, like the Bizet penché, a mystery of physical execution. During one of the most climactic moments of the pas de deux between the Sugar Plum Fairy and her cavalier in *The Nutcracker* he declared, uncharacteristically, that he wanted to try what could only be called a visual trick. He arranged for a small, thin metal slide, pulled by wires, to be cranked invisibly across the stage and, instead of doing the usual choreography, I was to step onto the slide on pointe, in arabesque, holding my partner's hand while two stagehands, in opposite wings, pulled the wire and me across the stage. The effect was magical, and to this day audiences are thrilled and baffled by the seemingly impossible feat. Mr. B was equally thrilled with his optical illusion, and I was thrilled to be his guinea pig.

Mr. B thought I had a good head for crowns and, shortly after *Symphony in C*, he offered me another one. A revival of *Ballet Imperial* (now called *Tschaikovsky Piano Concerto No. 2*), a big Balanchine ballet originally made in 1941 for Ballet Caravan, a predecessor of the New York City Ballet, was scheduled to be danced for the first time by the company in October of 1964. Our move into the State Theater enabled Balanchine to do what he had always wanted to do—big productions of ballets that would have looked cramped on the stage at City Center. *Ballet Imperial* had been designed by Balanchine as a grand tribute to the splendor of Imperial Russia, a celebration of his Russian heart and heritage and his spiritual fathers, Petipa and Tschaikovsky. I had never seen the ballet. The new production was to be a full, lush display with elaborate new scenery outlining old St. Petersburg and gorgeous formal blue-and-gold satin-and-velvet tutus and tiaras designed by Mme. Barbara Karinska. A Russian émigré like Balanchine, she was the company's official costume designer and had dressed numerous Balanchine ballets and Hollywood movies in her opulent creations. In a land dominated by Balanchine's stark black-and-white leotard ballets *Imperial* was a major costuming event. It was also a dance event of prodigious proportions.

The ballerina role had been designed on Marie-Jeanne, a compact dancer of great physical prowess, and for her role Mr. B called several of us to learn it or rather struggle with it. It was being restaged by Frederic Franklin, who had danced it in the Ballet Russe, and it required many hours of arduous rehearsal; it was the most technically difficult ballet I had ever learned as well as the longest. The ballerina makes her first entrance to a cadenza solo full of turns stopping on a dime and flashy jumps at breakneck speed; followed by a very long, soulful pas de deux; and then a finale full of fouettés, fast intricate footwork, and big saut de Basque jumps. Although I was overwhelmed at the prospect, I was cast for the première, partly out of default when other dancers were injured or reluctant and partly because Mr. B wanted to see me out there. The critics up until now had been kind and fairly indulgent about my new prominence in so many ballets, but after dancing *Imperial* I was reprimanded in *The New York Times* for "not being sufficiently authoritative." They thought it required an established ballerina.

Mr. B didn't care what the papers said. He told me I was wonderful and cast me again and again, no doubt exacerbating the already growing suspicion within the company as well as the press that he was blinded by an infatuation. But Mr. B, infatuated or not, was never blind; he was, beyond all else, even beyond his own feelings, professional. I believe he had a bigger design, a further-reaching vision, than merely having a perfect performance of *Ballet Imperial* on a given night. He obviously had already chosen to commit himself to me, and he had plans, serious plans, for what he might do with me. But he had already lived a hundred different lives in the ballets he had choreographed before I was even born, and for us to continue forward together I had to pass through his past. And his past, even his loves and personal passions, were in his ballets. All those movements, all those pirouettes, all that music, all those stories and styles, all that romance, all that beauty and joy and heartbreak, all of that was who he was. I am convinced that he wanted me to catch up to him, and I had to do it quickly so that we could meet in the same place in 1964.

During the fourteen months following *Meditation* I danced fifteen new ballets, including *La Valse, La Sonnambula,* and the Sugar Plum Fairy in *The Nutcracker,* and though officially I was still only a solo dancer, every one of them was a principal part. I skipped through the natural hierarchy of progression because I think Balanchine felt there wasn't time. A dancer's life is short, and if he had nursed me through years of experience we probably could never have met up in the place where we could work together. He needed whatever it was that he saw in me, and I needed him to tell me what it was and what could be done with it. I think this is why Mr. B felt the urgency to throw me out onstage night after night and watch me flap my wings, hover, and try to remain airborne—which I did, some times better than other times. But I never gave up. I always gave everything I had.

I was so busy at this time rehearsing, performing, and absorbing new roles that I never had the perspective to realize what was happening on a deeper level; in dancing Balanchine's life onstage, I was becoming part of it offstage. There were some signs. Ten minutes before the curtain was to rise on the first performance of *Ballet Imperial* I was standing at the barre backstage warming up, when Eddie Bigelow called me over to the doorway leading to the dressing rooms. He handed me a little square leather box with a fleur-de-lis emblazoned on it in gold. I said, "What's this?" He just answered, "Open it." Inside, wrapped in crepe paper, was a very thin silver chain with a little teardrop pearl in its center. I was deeply touched and thanked Eddie for being so thoughtful and giving me such a special good-luck gift. He held his hands up in protest, saying, "It's not from me." Then who? Eddie looked a little uncomfortable and said, "Well, I'm not supposed to say, I was just told to give it to you." The stage manager was calling "Onstage for *Imperial*," and so, with other things to think about, I couldn't pursue the mystery until later.

This was the first present I received from Mr. B. I was flabbergasted. Until now we had only worked together and made small talk about our cats in the elevator. I wore the necklace every day, not onstage but for class and rehearsals, and it has since become imbued with my perfume, my skin, and my heart.

A couple of weeks later Mr. B gave an interview to *Time* magazine, and he said about me: "She is an alabaster princess, you couldn't design a better figure." I charged over to the dictionary to look up alabaster. Our conversations started to become a little more personal, and he began to make comments on the paleness of my skin and how I reflected the light. Until now, like most young girls, I had thought that a tanned skin was the height of attractiveness, and this was the first time anyone had complimented me on my whiteness.

Monumentum Pro Gesualdo was Stravinsky's and Balanchine's eight-minute hymn to commemorate the four-hundredth anniversary of the birth of the composer Gesualdo. Made on Diana Adams and Conrad Ludlow in 1960, it was danced with six couples in white practice clothes. It had not been performed during Diana's absence from the stage, and now Balanchine wanted me to learn it and perform it in tandem with *Movements*.

These two ballets had not been performed together before, but they have been ever since, with only a brief lowering of the curtain between, in which the ballerina takes off her skirt and changes partners. Danced together they were a revelation in stylistic contrast—*Monumentum* so classical and pure, *Movements* so modern and stark. In dancing both I discovered the joy of appearing in a certain style and then in a completely different one moments later. These dances are short but chock-full of physical and spiritual wonder, and during them every bone, muscle, and vein feels that it is being explored.

Diana came to rehearsals to help put *Monumentum* together, and after one rather confusing session she sent me a note that clarified not only certain musical questions but captured the essence of the ballet itself. The letter had a cat-paw print on it from one of her pets.

Dear Suzanne—

I couldn't find the right word today, *not* lyrical, and not really romantic. I think it is "gentle." That is the difference with *Movements*. Mr. B says it should be like a *lamb*. I'm not sure what he means, but I think he told me once "madrigals" are for shepherds. If this doesn't make sense to you, forget it, enjoy it and good luck as always.

Love,
Diana

Don't let me ruin you. It should also be *on the note*. Tell Mr. B you are correct about third movement, lifting the knee after the back bend, on *three*, not two. Sorry. Also the flex, everybody at once, as we talked about—O.K.?

Diana was quite a lady. She offered me not only her wisdom and encouragement but freedom to dance differently from her; it is a rare gesture, especially in a great ballerina. This was an invaluable note suggesting certain elusive qualities in the ballet but not insisting on them. Like Mr. B she seemed to trust my judgment, and for the première she sent me a beautiful old Russian medal of the Virgin Mary. The card with it read, "This is a medal the boss gave me, and I give it to you now, to bless all that you dance and give you good fortune—With love, Diana." This was our last collaboration, and it was as if she were completing her role as my guardian angel and passing on her mantle of authority. I was moved to tears.

Although it was clear to everyone by the beginning of 1965 that Balanchine's interest in me was very real, no one but he knew just how far he was willing to go to promote me, to proclaim his belief, or to declare his love. He had displayed interest in more talented dancers than one could count. But the next ballet that he made on me changed all that, and everyone, including my mother and me, realized that the basic dynamic of our relationship changed; he was no longer leading me—he saw me leading him. I was called his muse, a category not listed in the program, and when *Don Quixote* premièred the whole world had an image of his muse in action.

Part

II

CHAPTER SIX

The Don and Dulcinea

I had never read Cervantes' tale of *Don Quixote*, so when Mr. B told me sometime in the early part of 1965 that he was going to make a big three-act ballet about a man who is searching for his ideal and that she was going to be me, I was enormously flattered and rushed out to buy a copy of the book to find out who she was. I read and read . . . in the bath, on the bus, at dinner, at breaks between rehearsals, and after four hundred pages Dulcinea still hadn't made her entrance, although she was described frequently enough in rather daunting detail by Don Quixote. He calls her "My Lady," and proclaims that ". . . a knight-errant without love was like a tree without leaves or fruit, or a body without a soul." He continues:

> . . . her name is Dulcinea, her country El Toboso, a village of La Mancha, her rank must be at least that of a princess, since she is my queen and lady, and her beauty superhuman, since all the impossible and fanciful attributes of beauty which the poets apply to their ladies are verified in her; for her hairs are gold, her forehead Elysian fields, her eyebrows rainbows, her eyes suns, her cheeks roses, her lips coral, her teeth pearls, her neck alabaster, her bosom marble, her hands ivory, her fairness

snow, and what modesty conceals from sight such, I think and imagine, as rational reflection can only extol, not compare.

I knew now how I was supposed to look—but I still had no real idea who I was or what I'd be doing. Frustrated, I paged through the rest of the book quickly, and by the time Dulcinea appeared she had been transformed into the ugly prisoner of wicked enchantment and I didn't know what was going on anymore. I realized that Dulcinea resided more in the mind of Don Quixote than anywhere else, and since my talents were physical and visible, I wondered how I might appear without appearing. I worried that the whole expedition into sixteenth-century Spain was beyond my literary capabilities. When I told Mr. B that I was trying to read the book and confessed that I found it rather overwhelming, philosophically and otherwise, he nodded kindly and said, "Don't worry, dear, you don't need to read it." I should have known that he would tell me everything I needed to know; it would be in the ballet.

Balanchine's longtime Russian friend Nicolas Nabokov was to compose the music for *Don Quixote*. When we were introduced for the first time, he took a long, hard look at me and said, "You know, George has always wanted to do this ballet, for twenty-five years he has wanted to do this ballet, but he always said, 'I never found my Dulcinea.' " Mr. B told me the same story a few days later.

In his usual way, Mr. B did not choose to explain Dulcinea to me verbally, but he began involving me in the larger process of putting together what was to be the company's longest, most complicated, and most expensive production to date. With three acts, seven scene changes, a forty-foot giant wielding a sword, a thirty-foot rotating windmill, a miniature puppet theater, firecrackers, a corps of pigs, and a cast of thousands, including a horse, a donkey, and children, *Don Quixote* was Balanchine again defying his "neoclassic," "emotionless" self by presenting a story that was epic not only physically but philosophically. His version was to have no relationship whatsoever to the nineteenth-century Petipa ballet, a comic tale of a witless old dreamer and a pair of witty young lovers. The love story in Balanchine's *Don Quixote* was the one Cervantes described between the aging Don and his beloved, Dulcinea.

Rather than detailing the story or explaining my character, Mr. B showed me the world I would inhabit. I saw the miniature sets designed by the Spanish painter Esteban Francés, the costumes at Karinska's, and I heard the Nabokov music. It was environment, not literature, that gave me the boundaries that were my freedom to be Dulcinea.

Don Quixote was a rite of passage for me on many levels—on dancing "off-balance," on being a ballerina, and on being Balanchine's ballerina—and I think it is interesting to note just how unorthodox my dance education was because I danced in George Balanchine's company. While most ballet dancers in the world were performing the nineteenth-century classics—*Swan Lake, Giselle, The Sleeping Beauty*—I was dancing the twentieth-century classics—*Apollo, Symphony in C, Liebeslieder Walzer*. Because I worked for Balanchine I was never asked to fit into the mold of the world's idea of a classical dancer with her grand demeanor, polite arabesque, and rounded elbows. Instead of perfecting a precedent, I was encouraged—as were all of Balanchine's dancers—to set one, if I dared. We started breaking the rules at the very first rehearsal.

The company ended a tour of the southwestern United States on March 15, 1965, and the New York season, in which *Don Quixote* was scheduled to première, was to begin just over a month later. There were a few weeks vacation following the tour, but as usual I did not go on vacation, having neither the interest nor the money. Instead of sitting on a beach in the Caribbean, I went to the New York State Theater. Because the company was not in season, it was very quiet and dark, and I had to turn on the lights in the small fifth-floor rehearsal studio. It was a little creepy being alone in such a huge theater. But suddenly, while I had my leg on the barre stretching, the heavy double doors squeaked open, and I peeked up to see Mr. B's face peer around the corner. He had seen the light under the door and was about to turn it off (he didn't believe in wasting energy, even if it was Con Edison's), but when he saw me he said, "Oh, I thought I might find you here. Do you want to work?"

We began putting together my third-act variation the following day, and as far as I know this was the first actual choreography he did on the ballet. The third-act Dream Scene was the dancing climax of the whole ballet, and I think beginning there gave him the roots and the atmosphere for the rest; knowing where it would end told him where it might begin, and where it had to go. As with *Meditation*, Gordon Boelzner played the music for us, and so began a pattern that was to recur many times: the three of us in a studio experimenting, dancing, laughing.

Gordon had joined the company as a pianist a few years before I had, and Balanchine trusted him musically. There was a wonderful give-and-take rapport between us with Mr. B dancing away in the middle of the room saying, "Well, maybe try this . . . yes, but more . . . more. . . ." while I tried to show him what he had just done and Gordon interjected, "Well, now, wait a minute, Mr. B, you don't have a repeat there. You just put it in, but it's not written here."

And we'd all have a good chuckle and relocate ourselves within the score. Gordon prevented musical disasters—and musical comedies.

This variation was long, the longest I had ever danced, and Mr. B probably wanted to see if I could sustain its demands, which were both technical and dramatic. He had observed by now that I neither perspired nor got out of breath, but in this dance he pushed me over the limits of what I had done previously. The beginning was difficult, full of a repeated rhythm that I had to absorb into my body without the aid of any conventional ballet steps. "I want pulsing, pulsing," Mr. B said, and it was for me to lunge, fall, withdraw, reach out, yearn, stretch, spin, and tighten with the music. In the course of these rehearsals we first developed what came to be called my "off-balance" movement. It was to be much commented upon and seen as one of my trademarks.

Classical dancers are trained to be "placed" with square shoulders over square hips over symmetrically turned-out legs, the body extending in various directions around a stable vertical axis that is always in a perpendicular relation to the stage. It would appear to be physically wise to maintain this symmetry at all times for the purpose of staying upright, but when I did a high kick or fast inside turn I would put so much energy into it that my recovery was not always perfectly "on-balance." I was unafraid of falling—which was crucial for this kind of attack—and as I scrambled to regain my "center," Balanchine became intrigued watching my various recovery techniques.

He found square, proper, academic dancing "boring as hell," and one day as I fell out of a turn into a backbend lunge he said, "Can you do that again, can you fall more . . . lean more . . . bend more?" I said, "Let me try," and he countered, "Is it impossible?" He always took into account the fact that he had never been on pointe himself and that he might be asking for something actually "impossible." (In reality he knew more about the physics of being on pointe than most dancers who have been up there all their lives.) By now I knew nothing was impossible, at least physically, and replied, "No, it's not. Let me work on it." If I couldn't repeat the movement immediately, we would leave those places sketchy until the next day or the next rehearsal when I could. He never worried about etching steps in stone like some choreographers, because he was secure in his craft and knew that his medium, space, could not be carved or molded by an idea but only by the dynamics of the moment.

Mr. B wanted me to be "off-balance," and it was surely one of the most unorthodox requests any well-trained ballet master could make. In *Don Quixote* we broke one rule after the other and climbed through the walls of balletic convention to discover a whole new place to inhabit. It was not the conventional space defined by dancers of up and down, left and right; it was a tilted, revolving circle. The air there was delightfully unpolluted, and best of all, there were no laws until we made them.

This new kind of movement might sound haphazard, improvised, or arbitrary, rather like so-called modern dance, but it was none of them, which is what amazed everyone. I did not feel imperiled but exhilarated, and, more surprising, I never felt out of control. I knew where I was at all times, even when I was somewhere I had never been before, the crucial reason being that one can be effectively off-balance only when one knows exactly where on-balance is. I could be happy in either.

The expected distortions of off-center motion didn't occur because of a number of factors—the most important, speed, Balanchine's great innovation. One had the impression of a dancer moving smoothly through familiar classical positions or of classical phrases unfolding in a slightly unorthodox relation to gravity. We also had the benefit of carrying tradition with us. I was on pointe (a very useful medium for traveling onto new planes). I was turned-out (and therefore when I "turned-in" it was a choice and as such became an effective and dramatic quality instead of the usual human stance). My knees were straight, my head held high, my hair in a bun, and my body in a beautiful chiffon costume—it looked classical because it was classical and yet it was totally different. This was, needless to say, all very exciting for Mr. B and myself, and he must have felt like the chef who first discovered that viscous egg whites could be transformed into a thick, light froth.

It proved essential to the laboratory atmosphere of experimentation that I had still not developed an image of myself, nor had I allowed myself to import the ridiculous but pervasive notion that I must be perfect, classically or otherwise. Balanchine always said, "Perfect is boring," and I believed him. Had I not, had I thought my dignity— as well as my posture—was in constant jeopardy because of what this man asked, I would never have been Dulcinea, and the next twenty years of my life would have been perfectly boring. Making balletic goulash with Balanchine was a great deal more satisfying and fulfilling than the lonely splendor of perfection.

There was one other notable technical emphasis in the "Dream Scene" variation, and it was in direct contrast to my off-balance forays. It was a very vertical upright motion and became one of the motifs, along with the music, of Dulcinea's presence. Bourrées, the small, light, fast, traveling movements of the toes on pointe with straight legs, are one of ballet's most basic, most beautiful, and most difficult steps to master. Bourrées were of extreme importance to Balanchine; they appear in virtually all his ballets, denoting a dramatic, feminine, and transporting moment; and mine were terrible. They had all the usual problems of wooden legs, feet that didn't point at all times, and knees that separated several inches between each step, ruining the gorgeous effect of a filigree blur. Being the psychologist that every good teacher must be, Balanchine knew that the only way to make his dancers practice a certain movement enough was to put it in a ballet where the public would be watching, so Dulcinea became a "bourrée" girl, and I have had reason to thank her many times.

We finished the variation after a few rehearsals, and as the company was still on vacation I got into the habit of going to the theater alone at night and, without music, rehearsing by myself. I could hear the music in my mind and would hum to myself—always dancing in tempo—and go through the variation three times from beginning to end without stopping. This was eventually exhausting, but it was also very revealing. By not pausing, stopping, or fussing over any specific step or moment in the dance (every dancer's favorite rehearsal technique), I discovered the overall rhythms, dramas, highs and lows, stops and starts, climaxes and quiet moments in it, which were, after all, what it was about. To Balanchine, dancing was never the execution of a specific step but musical movement with a beginning, many middles, and an end. I realized that, with numerous climactic moments, I had to calibrate each one, give each its full value without it being like the one before or the one after, and all of them were dictated by the music I heard in my head. There were many mood changes, from highly emotional and yearning to aggressive and abandoned, from wild and exotic to quiet and vulnerable. Everything I'd always wanted to be and to feel I had in five minutes of dancing. It was a tremendous event in my life, and Mr. B gave it to me.

In my solitary evening rehearsals for *Don Quixote,* I developed a love of working alone, even without musical accompaniment, that was to last the rest of my life. Even with an audience, dancing has always been a very private affair to me, and in rehearsals I found privacy essential. Then I could falter, slip, laugh, talk to myself, or do something fabulous, without the pressure—or thrill—of a witness. With the barriers down, I could explore options, which is what I think rehearsals should be about. For the same reason I have never believed in overrehearsing a part (which I rarely had the chance to do anyway); it can be a setup for disaster when the elements of the moment don't conform to what is expected, and it can easily kill any spontaneity on stage.

As with *Meditation*, I had no understudy for *Don Quixote*. This caused a great deal more consternation in the management offices than before; instead of a pas de deux, *Don Quixote* was a three-act ballet scheduled for fourteen consecutive performances at the end of the spring season after five weeks of regular repertoire. What if I became sick or injured? The public had bought tickets to this enormous, expensive production, and the company stood to lose a lot of money and good will. There was good reason for raised eyebrows, but Balanchine was not a man of reason on this occasion because he was involved in what was to him a much more profound event— believing in me was no small part of it—and he was in a position in his life where he could insist on exactly what he wanted. He had proved that his judgment and his talent were the best around. There was one more factor in this seemingly unequal equation that made it all quite logical: he knew (though maybe others did not) that nothing short of death would keep me from getting out on stage and dancing my best night after night for two weeks at the end of the season; belief can make a person very strong physically as well as spiritually. The understanding between us, silent as it remained, was now operating on many levels—musical/technical, off-balance/on-balance, on pointe/off pointe—and now it became onstage/offstage. It began at the Tip Toe Inn on 74th Street and Broadway and wound up two months later at the Dunkin' Donuts across the street.

After full company rehearsals began for *Don Quixote*, I would go to all of them even when I was not involved because I wanted to know where I'd be living as Dulcinea. It was a natural progression of events that, after these long days where Mr. B and I were so involved in our work, we started going out to dinner together. Actually it was not so much going out to dinner, it was simply that neither of us had eaten. It was often midnight before we left the theater, tired and hungry but excited about *Don Quixote*. Mr. B was living at the time with Tanny at the Apthorp on Broadway and 79th Street, and as I was now living with my mother and sister on 76th Street just off Broadway, we would walk uptown together. He would ask, "Have you eaten anything today?" knowing full well that I hadn't had time, and I would answer in kind, "No, have you?"

By that time of night many restaurants were closed, but the Tip Toe Inn, an inexpensive Jewish restaurant-bakery and bar, was open late, and we would stop in and sit in a booth under the bright neon lights and eat. I usually had a cheese omelet, a habit left over from my Russian days, while Mr. B ordered some rather foreign-looking ethnic dish. Often Eddie Bigelow came with us, and we were like three nomads walking anonymously up Broadway at night, dressed in nothing in particular, looking like no one in particular, but inside pulsing with the day's events. It felt like anything but a date with Balanchine, and yet we were becoming close, telling each other stories, talking about what I would wear in various sections of the ballet, substantiating each other's work.

Mr. B and Eddie would invariably have a beer and vodka and encouraged me to join them, but I had not yet learned how to drink and usually stuck to iced coffee. People no doubt saw us sitting there together, but I didn't think there was anything to see, anything romantic, that is, and having Eddie along was the assurance—or insurance. The conversation was always animated and light, never touching on the feelings that were stirred by *Don Quixote* or each other. Mr. B knew that I was a shy, religious girl, and I knew that he was married and that I was not the first girl he had taken to dinner. Besides, he was far too intelligent to do anything to make me uncomfortable. No doubt he already knew that things were getting convoluted and having a social threesome with Eddie kept appearances innocent.

I realized only in retrospect that Eddie was in fact acting as my bodyguard. When Mr. B couldn't be with me, Eddie was always around to take me to dinner and escort me home; I never had occasion to socialize with anyone else, especially a prospective suitor. Eddie and I became the best of friends and have remained so, and when things heated up with Mr. B, he became my confidant—but he was also Mr. B's. He carried Balanchine's heart on one sleeve and mine on the other.

After dinner when Balanchine and Eddie walked me home, Eddie would stay in the lobby while George—at his insistence I started to call him by his first name though I rarely felt comfortable with the unfamiliar familiarity and never called him George during working hours—took me up in the elevator to the eighth floor. "I'll deposit you," he would say with a grin, but he meant it, and I think he wanted the door locked after he left. If my mother was home (she still worked mostly at night), they said hello and made small talk, and he would always try unsuccessfully to cuddle Girl before leaving. Our comings and goings were all very proper, and later, even when they crossed the line, the atmosphere of propriety remained, which served, in retrospect, thoroughly to confuse the issues.

As Dulcinea I was to appear in several different guises, one of which was the Virgin Mary. I could not help feeling this was presumptuous, but because she was in Mr. B's hands, I knew she would receive appropriate presentation. There was something else about the portrayal that made me feel very strange indeed. At the end of the Prologue, in the first act of the ballet, I was to be wheeled out on a little cart in a simple dress, a veil around my head, holding my hands in the Virgin's pose of palms together facing inward to her heart. In rehearsal we didn't have the cart, so Mr. B put a chair in the middle of the studio, and I stood on top of it. Richard Rapp, who had been such a wonderful Bottom when I danced Titania, was to be Don Quixote, an acting role, not a dancing one, and, of course, Balanchine did the part to teach him what to do. There I was balancing on the chair one day in my black leotard and black tights, trying to look spiritual, when suddenly Mr. B, as the Don, fell to his knees before me, his sword in his hand, his head bowed.

It was a gesture of adoration and supplication to the Virgin, but it felt strangely real. I was to open my hands and bend over and lightly touch his shoulders with my fingers, then resume my original pose. That was the end of the scene. Mr. B didn't look as if he were pretending, and I was overwhelmed to be in the position of standing over him and blessing him—the man I'd seen in *Dance Magazine*, the man I had written about in my diary, the man who taught me class, the man who was the embodiment of American ballet. Suddenly it was as if I were in charge, as if I were saying, "Yes, go on. I believe in you." Every time we rehearsed, the same thing happened, and it was staggering. But it was not romantic, not yet.

The world première of *Don Quixote* was at a gala benefit on May 27, and when Mr. B told me that he was going to perform the role of the Don perhaps I shouldn't have been surprised, but I was. Balanchine was now sixty-one and had not performed onstage since he had done Herr Drosselmeyer in a televised production of *The Nutcracker* seven years earlier. The role of Don Quixote, while not calling for tights or pointed feet, did require a great deal of bruising, acrobatic behavior, because the Don was rarely at rest, as was appropriate for a man of chivalry living in a cynical world. He was endlessly fighting the windmills of his imagination and tripping, falling, kneeling, and crawling, being dragged or pushed or blown up when he was not wielding his sword to defend the honor of Dulcinea.

But it was not the physical strain of the role that unnerved me about Mr. B's decision—I knew he was as agile and energetic as any young man—or even the fact that beyond the usual demonstrations in the studio we had not rehearsed together. It was the decision itself, to portray Don Quixote and dance with me in public, that I found so moving. But he considered the ballet a public statement, as he was later to explain in an article in *Life* magazine with a quote that has become as famous as the philosophy it describes.

Woman is the goddess, the poetess, the muse. That is why I
have a company of beautiful girl dancers. I believe that the same
is true of life, that everything a man does he does for his ideal
woman. You live only one life and you believe in something
and I believe in a little thing like that.

It didn't seem to me such a "little thing," especially when it looked
as if I had been chosen to be that ideal; it was a very serious situation.
I didn't, however, feel pressure, I felt profound commitment.

Despite my confidence in Mr. B, when the final dress rehearsal
came on the afternoon of the gala and Mr. B still hadn't practiced
with me directly because he was overseeing the whole production,
I did worry a little about some of the physical logistics between us
in performance. (Even Diana sent a note that evening wishing me
good luck "with your new partner.") I had to lead him not only
spiritually in the world of Don Quixote but, literally, through the
ballet; the spontaneity and vulnerability in evidence that night were
all too real.

A half hour before the curtain was to rise, he appeared backstage
in full regalia—swooped-up mustache, goatee beard, black eyebrows,
and the billowing white shirt and knee-length pants that he wore in
the Prologue. He looked wildly theatrical and seemed very much
pleased with the effect. But he was also very emotional, and when
you consider that he had been planning this event for so many years
and that now I was a part of his plan, it is not surprising that I danced
that whole evening with tears in my eyes. I saw only him, nothing
else. We danced entirely for each other, and in a curious way all the
emotion was a relief, a release of everything that had been building
up between us without any direct expression. The ballet became a
kind of public courtship, a declaration, where dance, mime, and ceremony mingled with our real lives and emotions so deeply that our
onstage and offstage selves became interwoven.

My first entrance in the ballet was after the opening scene in Don
Quixote's study, a place filled with giant books containing the lives
and wisdom and dreams of men that came to life as the Don performed
his first act of chivalry against tiny armored men (played by children)
to save a beautiful blond girl. He was a man with a quest in a world
that had abandoned quests.

The stage filled with smoke, and the scenery parted to reveal a
long, steep staircase to one side of the stage. I entered, dressed in a
simple blouse and skirt, carrying a basin of water. My feet were bare,
and I had no dance steps, I only walked. I was a servant girl. I crossed
the stage and opened the curtain beside the staircase, and as it parted

a bright light warmed the room. I went over to the chair where the exhausted Don Quixote was sitting and knelt by him, placing the pan of water between his feet. In the first performance Mr. B suddenly realized that his feet were too far apart and shuffled them closer together for me. Even then, he was very helpful. Taking the single pin from my hair, I let it fall and, bending over, I washed and dried his feet with my loose hair—a reference to Mary Magdalene washing Christ's feet.

After easing his feet into big buckled boots (lined with a dusting of baby powder so his bare feet would not stick), he rose and began to walk forward, standing straighter, encouraged by my presence. I ran to him. He had forgotten his sword, and no knight traveled without his sword. Mr. B never told me what to feel, but inside I was saying, "Don't believe what other people say. Don't care. Just go your way. We'll go on together." Here the music built to a great crescendo. During this scene I often heard a snicker from the audience. The simplicity and unmistakable religious symbolism made many people uncomfortable, but Balanchine was not a man embarrassed by his faith, or others' fear of it. Unlike many things in the ballet, this passage was never changed.

After he was standing, appropriately garbed, my job was over. I picked up the basin and walked to the stairs. Don Quixote turned toward his servant one last time and saluted me with his sword— "My Lady"—and it was here, as I climbed the long staircase into the light, that Dulcinea's theme was exultantly heard.

More than any other single element in the ballet, it was this passionate yet simple music that gave me the final clue to being Dulcinea. I cannot explain it; it was in the music—soft, gentle, mournful, and sweet, taken from an old Russian folk theme. When planning the ballet with Nabokov, Mr. B had said to him, "Don't you remember this?" and sat down at the piano and played a melody—or what he remembered of it—from his youth. It was music that had been haunting him all his life. Nabokov orchestrated it, and it became my theme.

Once I reached the top of the stairs, the scene was over, and I scurried as fast as I could down the stairs backstage, put on the Virgin's crown and veil and climbed onto the rickety little wooden cart that was her altar. "Go, go," I cued the stagehands. I was wheeled out in my Virgin pose, and Mr. B knelt before me. Over time, the cart, which took up too much wing space, was altered, and the Virgin appeared on a pedestal in rays of light with an unmistakable halo. I preferred the simplicity of the cart, but it was impractical, so the grander vision prevailed.

After a stagehand lifted me off my perch, I ran to a little makeshift dressing room on the side of the stage for a quick costume change into white tights, a pale silver powder-puff tutu, and white peasant blouse. After being bare in the Prologue, my feet had inevitably swelled, and I had to squeeze them into my white toe shoes and convince them quickly to dance on pointe, a whole different mind-set from flat-footed motion. I twisted my hair into a bun, secured it with a few flowers, grabbed my long thin crook and ran to the wing to be dragged onstage by my accusers. No longer the Virgin, I was Marcela, a shepherdess, blamed by the townspeople for the death of a young poet who "died of love for Marcela." I was flung before the jury and, resisting, fell to the ground. Mr. B kept telling me in rehearsal, "Oh, you don't have to fall so hard," but I loved to fall, really fall, not like a graceful ballerina but as I imagined a shepherdess unjustly accused. While the townspeople were shaking their fists at me and threatening me with stones, Don Quixote and Sancho Panza— played with unerring faithfulness by Deni Lamont—rode into town, the Don on his old nag, now converted to the great steed Rosinante, and Sancho Panza on Dapple Gray, his trusty ass. These four-legged characters never missed a performance or the chance temporarily to steal the scene by relieving themselves in the middle of the stage.

Waving his sword, Don Quixote scattered the townspeople and came over to me, helped me up, bowed to me, and walked me to the center of the stage where I danced a beautiful variation. It was filled with a delicate motif of walking on pointe, knees lifted high, forward, backward, and in circles around my staff, very simple and very touching. In the midst of all this sweetness, the music builds to a great climax, and Mr. B suggested that I do three fast consecutive step-up double turns in arabesque. It was a precarious, tricky sequence with no time or place to cover a mishap; if the first turn was off, it was difficult to continue. I thought it was wonderfully dangerous. It became a moment everyone on stage waited for: "Will she make it?" At the end of the dance I went over to the Don, who had been watching from one side, and before bourréeing off, my crook over one shoulder, I put a kiss on my fingers and passed it to his lips. This gesture of affection was specifically choreographed by Balanchine, a most unusual request by a man who avoided the obvious and the sentimental in his work; he knew the power of a kiss, and therefore rarely used it.

Several seasons after the première, Mr. B added another dance for me earlier in the first act. I was a gypsy woman called Zoraida and wore a long black wig and a burgundy-and-gold brocade and velvet costume with burgundy-heeled slippers. I was a fortune-teller in the town square, and at one point I begged for alms, and only the Don gave me something. I thought it was great fun to be so flamboyant and colorful in a dance full of seductive backbends and big kicks, but Balanchine decided it added nothing to the ballet, and after a short life, it was removed.

At the end of the first act the Don and Sancho Panza were invited to a ball at the royal court where the second act took place. There was an ominous, funereal atmosphere here with the women clad in sumptuous black-and-gold dresses with enormous hoop skirts and white ruffled necks, and the men in black-and-gold brocaded vests. After a sarabande for the couples there was entertainment for the Don, five very different dances.

Following these festivities the court people put on *commedia dell'arte* masks with huge Cyrano de Bergerac noses and began to dance with Don Quixote, pushing him, taunting him, bumping into him, and twirling him. They brought out a little wooden donkey, placed the Don and Sancho Panza on it, and lit a firecracker underneath. It blew up, and the riders fell to the floor, bewildered and bruised. The symbolism of Christ's entrance into Jerusalem was unmistakable. Then a throne was wheeled on, and in another piece of Christian symbolism they placed a red cape around the Don's shoulders and a crooked gold crown on his head and pushed him onto the throne. The stage filled with smoke.

As he sat, beaten and alone, the stage was quiet, then the soft soothing trumpet of Dulcinea's theme sounded as I came onstage in a shaft of light. This was my only entrance in the second act, and I was a vision, the Don's vision, but more real to him than anything that he had just endured. I bourréed onstage through a portal on a diagonal, the dark stage lit only by my light. Mr. B called it "Suzi's light," and the request for it was heard often between Mr. B and the stage manager.

I wore a long beige chiffon costume with an Empire waist and a headpiece of flowers and gold ribbon with a pearl at the center of my forehead. This headpiece, one of the most beautiful I ever wore, was designed by Mme. Karinska and Mr. B during a costume fitting. I had on my dress, and Mr. B looked at me and said to Mme. Karinska, "Maybe something on her head, maybe some flowers?" She leaned over a vase filled with small silk flowers, scooped up the entire bunch, held it to the back of my head and said, "Maybe with a little gold around it." Mr. B threw up his hands in satisfaction and said, "Yes, perfect!"

For the première of *Don Quixote* Mme. Karinska gave me a beautiful old medal of Joan of Arc from her large collection. She probably thought I would need a lot of spiritual strength; she sensed from the way Balanchine fussed over my costumes how he felt about me.

In the ballet, I went over to the Don and took off his red cloak and crooked crown, helped him to his feet, comforted him, encouraged him, and led him back to his course. This vision of Dulcinea was his salvation. Danced entirely in soft spotlights, our pas de deux was filled with heartbreaking tenderness. He crawled on his knees after me as I fed him, symbolically, out of the palm of my hand. I held him, I cradled him, and I consoled him.

The first night this was all too real, as Mr. B was not entirely sure of where to go when. I had to keep my wits about me as he adjusted the choreography while we went along—he was to have his arms up, and I was to bring them down to his side, but he left them down, so I brought them up. His sword got caught in my skirt briefly, and his attentiveness to unraveling it became a new gesture of solicitous sweetness. A few moments later he murmured to me, "What's next?" and, with him before me, we faced forward, and I reached over his shoulder and pointed the direction. The choreography could not have fit the moment better, as I literally guided him to downstage right. There was, of course, nothing visible in that corner; it was where his dreams were born.

The press often referred to this gesture as highly symbolic of Balanchine's overall meaning, which it was, but Balanchine was also preoccupied with fingers and the ability to point, or not point, for another, more obvious, reason, which I discovered when I reached up to hold his left index finger for support during a turn, and it wasn't there. In a gardening accident a few months earlier he had lost the first joint of that finger, and as we had never rehearsed that turn together, I was unprepared to do it unaided. It was a rather ludicrous moment in the midst of so much attentiveness, and I will never forget how strange it felt. Despite these various unchoreographed moments, or more probably because of them, I think this pas de deux, our only real one together, revealed feelings that hadn't been planned, and it was quite a revelation to have it happen onstage in front of an audience.

The ballet continued. The court people awakened, oblivious of my presence; they were the cynics without vision or faith, and as the Don turned to follow me, his resolve renewed, a courtesan's hand blocked the way and covered his face with shaving cream. Blinded and looking foolish, he continued to follow me, arms held high with dignity, and the curtain fell. His vulnerability was tangible, and my eyes filled with tears again.

During the intermission that followed the second act, I went to George's dressing room where Michael Arshansky, another Russian émigré who doubled as makeup and wig man, was adjusting his beard before the final act. I just wanted to tell him how much I loved *Don*

Quixote and loved dancing Dulcinea. I didn't manage to say much of anything, but he understood. Welcoming a chance for comic relief, he clowned around the room gleefully with the shaving cream still all over his face.

The last act opened with a short scene in front of a curtain where the Don was captured in a huge net like an animal and left lying on the side of the stage. The curtain rose on a courtyard in front of the iron gate of a palace; it was another of Don Quixote's visions. This section contained the most actual dancing in the ballet, aside from the second-act divertissements, with a corps of sixteen girls in beige chiffon, two solo girls in pale blue, two cavaliers, and me in pale pink chiffon with Conrad Ludlow as my partner, the Knight of the Silver Moon. After an introductory dance with all the girls, I proceeded into my pas de deux with Conrad, which was followed by the first girl's variation, the second's, the first cavalier's, and then mine, the one we had first worked on the previous April. These variations were very different from anything Balanchine had made before, very syncopated with the beat of the music and full of turned-in movements. But unlike the atonal turn-in of his Stravinsky ballets, these were turned-in lyrically, and the effect was riveting and powerful.

During all this dancing Don Quixote was supposedly lying to one side of the stage in the shadows, but on the first night, when I went toward him in my variation, I saw that the net was empty. Mr. B had crawled offstage and was now standing watching in the first wing—he had two jobs that night and didn't want to miss a thing. After my variation he crawled back under the net. My solo ended dramatically; I whirled around and fell to one knee in profile, my face in my hands. It was very appropriate for all the pent-up emotion, foreboding, and technical fireworks that had preceded it. There was enormous applause that first night. I did not want to remove myself from the world of the ballet, so I just stayed on my knee, face hidden. It seemed like an eternity. The conductor, Robert Irving, waited until it was quiet again before beginning the coda. This final whirlwind was no less wild than my variation, and again I ended on my knee, face in my hands, but now the dream was over, and danger lurked nearby.

Merlin flew onstage in a swirling black cape, and tried to capture me. I ran offstage and entered again with a fast spinning, jumping, off-balance diagonal that apparently had my mother and Bev as well as Diana on the edges of their seats in terror that I'd be face down at any moment. The scenery broke apart, and Don Quixote emerged for his final fencing battles against a windmill and the forty-foot armored giant. He was pummeled, dropped from the windmill, and beaten to the ground again before being stampeded by a herd of pigs.

At last he crawled into a cage in which he was carried home, back to the study where his trials had begun and where he was now prepared for death. He was dressed in a white nightshirt and laid in his bed, as a long funeral procession passed before him. There were penitents in chains, monks in black cloaks and hoods carrying crosses, priests swinging incense; it was the endless black stream of purgatory, and everyone was swaying to and fro. The audience became decidedly restless over the implications of this scene—"Where do I place in this lineup?"—but Balanchine, thank heaven, never changed it or short-ened it. Meanwhile I had changed back into my servant girl's clothes and again came onstage as the Virgin at the apotheosis of the funeral march. I stretched my arms toward Don Quixote, and as he in turn reached for me, he rose, literally, on an elevator platform beneath the bed. His white gown grew with him until he was fifteen feet tall and then suddenly, poof, he collapsed back to earth, back to his bed and his humble surroundings.

I entered again as the servant girl in bare feet, and this time I closed the curtains, darkening the stage. I picked up two splintered pieces of wood, and the music stopped. In total silence I walked across the stage holding the two sticks in the form of a cross. Music would have been an intrusion; it was the absence of everything that was impor-tant. The silence was eerie and unnerving, but Mr. B had always told me to walk slowly—"Don't feel uncomfortable, don't rush it, take all the time." He wanted it to be uncomfortable, he wanted everyone to be waiting, to feel the loneliness that life can have. I placed the cross on the dying Don's chest and, sighing, fell onto him. This was the cue for the orchestra to resume playing.

The Don reached out one last time to his few loyal friends and died. I cried and held on to his lifeless body before sliding off the bed and ending once again on my knees, hands covering my face in grief. But on the first night, as I tried to move my hand off his chest, I felt another hand move. Although he was supposed to be dead, Mr. B had lifted his hand and held it strongly over mine. It was both funny and improper for him to have moved, but I savored the comfort. I needed it, and I doubt that many people in the audience saw it. I was emotionally overcome. It was the end of the ballet, but what had happened between us was the beginning of something else.

After the final curtain fell that first night, the applause flooded in and with it the reality of where we were; it was time to bow. Mr. B had sent me a huge bouquet of red roses, which I received onstage, and we bowed together, over and over. The ballet seemed to be well received, especially by a gala audience that traditionally sits on its hands, but no small portion of the applause was for Balanchine's performance. His appearances onstage were rare, and here he had embodied a role that he so clearly was living, not just acting, that this night had already been marked down in the history books.

On one bow he pushed me forward to the center of the stage. I looked about for him, but he was gone. Like a magician, he had vanished; he was offering me to the audience, and I was bewildered to have lost him—I realized I had just found him. Success for me from then on existed only together—mine was his, and his was mine. Neither existed without the other. When the reviews of *Don Quixote* rolled in full of suggested improvements for the ballet, but with praise for me, I was hurt and angry, and it became a kind of crusade for me to prove them wrong; but I could do this only by dancing.

There was a big champagne party on the promenade of the theater immediately after the performance, and I had bought my first evening gown for the occasion. It was white with an Empire waist and silver beading, and around my neck I wore the pearl George had given me. I also wore a pair of long white gloves given to me as a good-luck present by Lucia Davidova, a very elegant Russian friend of Balanchine's. The accompanying note read, "With admiration and love, for good luck, from Lucia. P.S. These are washable." And so with my washable gloves and my hair in a skinny ponytail I finally felt sophisticated, though when I look back now I must have seemed more like a girl at her high school prom. But in its way, this was a coming-out party for me.

Mr. B waited outside my dressing room looking very dapper in his tuxedo and bow tie, and there was a twinkle of excitement in his eyes. Taking his arm, I walked with him through the side door of the stage and up the stairs to the theater's promenade and the party. We both felt wonderful, and we felt wonderful together. I don't think either of us really wanted to be swallowed up in a big social event at that moment, but it was a necessary courtesy to the patrons that Balanchine be there, and when we arrived, there was an enormous fuss made over us, and it was all very merry. With champagne glasses in hand, we toasted everything—the ballet, Nabokov, the theater, the patrons, and each other. The band played, and we danced together, and over Mr. B's shoulder I saw my mother and Bev watching us from the balcony. I waved, but tonight was a night I wanted to be with George, and we kept on dancing.

After an hour or so, with social duties fulfilled, we left the party, and George again waited while I packed up my dance bag and changed back into my more comfortable street clothes. We sneaked out the side door of the theater into the dark night. It was well past midnight by now, and we walked slowly up Broadway together, arm in arm. We wanted to be alone to feel what we were feeling, to talk about the ballet, to compliment each other, to be quiet together, to be happy together. It was, after all, a stolen moment when we should have been at the party, or I should have been in bed, or he should have been home with his wife—but we didn't think about any of that. We stopped at the twenty-four-hour Dunkin' Donuts on 74th Street and sat on stools under the glaring lights and had coffee and cream doughnuts. George was still in his tuxedo. Nothing was off-balance now.

CHAPTER SEVEN

European Dining

T he reception of *Don Quixote* was curious. Although Balanchine had requested not to be reviewed—critical opinion of his performance was somewhat irrelevant—the temptation to comment on the master's portrayal of Cervantes' hero was too great, and he received raves. Reservations, however, about the ballet as a whole were strong and would remain so for the next thirteen years of its difficult and fragmented life.

The man who had said that dance was about itself and needed no story had produced a long, allegorical tale about life, death, and love that was full of costumes, characterization, and episodic action sequences, and now he was "spanked," as he called it, by those whom he had persuaded to like steps for their own sake. They insisted on categorizing him when, in fact, he was inventing another category. In *Don Quixote* every step, gesture, and musical theme was rife with philosophical and religious symbolism. Ultimately the blame came to rest on Nabokov's music; it was condemned as unsubtle (one reviewer referred to it as "movie music") and generally inadequate for the profound themes of faith and redemption.

This was certainly not the first time Balanchine was given negative notices; he had been receiving them all his life, though by 1965 his legend was growing, and they were harder to come by. But he had learned from experience and was ambivalent at best and amused at worst about the critics and their pronouncements. Contrary to belief, he did read reviews on occasion, but only to keep himself apprised of current opinion. He had a kind of confidence in his work that was at once awesome and humble. I remember sitting with him after class one day, having coffee in the theater canteen below the stage. He had brought the paper, and I read to him from it: " 'George Balanchine, one of the three greatest choreographers in the world today . . .' " and he said to me dryly, "Well, Suzi, who are the other two?" Sometimes he would not recognize anyone else, but then again, sometimes he would not even recognize himself.

Although he was indifferent to the critics, Balanchine felt an enormous responsibility to the public, many of whom found *Don Quixote* hard to accept. He knew he was asking for trouble by having an idealist as the hero of the ballet rather than the more familiar buffoon. But Balanchine was, above all else, a deeply religious, even mystical man. He was a teacher, not just of ballet steps—they were merely his medium—but of how to behave, of how to serve something bigger than one's self. And in *Don Quixote* his blatant belief shocked his audience.

My personal success in the ballet, as well as Balanchine's, was somewhat undermined by the critical response. On the one hand, none of it mattered because he had said what he wanted to say, and that was good, but he did not consider his craft solely a means of self-expression; he felt a responsibility. If the public found what he said unclear or not effective, he considered his mission unfinished. I think this is one reason *Don Quixote* became famous as the most tinkered-with ballet in the repertoire. Not a season went by that Balanchine didn't add, subtract, or change something in it, always trying for a better way to seduce the audience into enjoying and accepting it.

Despite everything, the ballet generated enormous interest, not only because it had the familiar classical form of a full-evening extravaganza, but because it was proclaimed to be autobiographical. Balanchine's decision to play the role of the Don himself appeared to confirm this. The notion that the enigmatic ballet master was spreading his own life and personal beliefs across the stage at the New York State Theater was intriguing. When I read about this interpretation, it increased the confusion I was already feeling. If it was true that life and art were becoming mixed up, I wondered whether it was Don Quixote and Dulcinea out there on stage, or George and I. Not surprisingly, I was more comfortable being Dulcinea. She had her role delineated and choreographed; she had a beginning, middle, and end. I was just a teenager. But I did know one thing, and I knew it well—how to dance, how to be Dulcinea.

It did not matter whether George loved me or loved Dulcinea. My work, his work, our work, the company's work were the only things worth taking seriously. Besides, if George loved my dancing, that was good enough for me; when you believe as I did, you are not yourself anymore; you are your work.

Another aspect of the *Don Quixote*-as-autobiography theory bothered me more. The papers frequently referred to the significance of the age difference between the Don and Dulcinea, implying that this was the love of an old man for a young girl. I didn't like those implications. The facts were undeniable: Balanchine was sixty-one and I was nineteen, but I never felt he was old. When we were dancing, we were in the same time frame, a musical-emotional time frame, with the same understanding, and our ages were completely irrelevant. I was making him younger and he was making me older, and we met in the middle; our internal metronomes were perfectly calibrated with each other.

Balanchine was also accused of making the Don too emotional, too full of self-pity. The image of him crawling on his knees to Dulcinea was repeatedly referred to as one of the most revealing moments in the ballet. Being a part of that image, part of that emotion, I am unable to judge this with objectivity, and for that I am grateful.

The night of the *Don Quixote* gala was the culmination of many emotions that had been building up between us, and in a way the performance was a relief, an explosion, a kind of spiritual consummation. One is never quite as vulnerable as on that first night when, wanting to be understood, never before having danced a particular ballet before an audience, one feels that moment is the only moment in one's life. Until then I had not really been aware of the personal feelings between George and me. I had never before been so imprinted with someone else's feelings. On many levels *Don Quixote* brought us together—I have often thought that was the ballet's real purpose—and from then on things became clear, and they were clearly complicated.

There were fourteen consecutive performances of *Don Quixote* during the next ten days, with matinees and evenings on Wednesday, Saturday, Sunday, and Monday. Contrary to the administration's fears, I not only never missed a performance then or for the next four years, I thrived on the responsibility. I became stronger, healthier, more confident and more daring in my dancing. I also became thinner, which was fine with me, but Eddie Bigelow made it his business to make sure I was fed and rested whenever possible. After the matinees he would get me a grilled cheese sandwich and iced coffee from the coffee shop across the street and bring them to my dressing room. There were only a few hours between performances, so rather than go out or return home, I preferred to stay in my makeup, eat, work a crossword puzzle, or take a nap on the dressing-room floor. One afternoon just as I was about to eat my sandwich, there was a knock on the door, and it was George saying, "Do you want to go up to my office and rest?"

I protested that I was fine where I was, but he insisted, saying, "It's cold in here, and it's much nicer up in my office. There's a big wonderful chair and . . ." Dressed in my theater robe, woolly leg-warmers, and the grubby old pair of toe shoes that I used as slippers, and clutching my grilled cheese, I shuffled up to the fourth floor. It was indeed a great deal nicer up there. At that time Balanchine still had a sizable office (as the years went by it decreased measurably as the administrative faculty grew), and it had a lovely homey atmosphere. There was a rug on the floor, a piano piled high with musical scores, drawings of stage designs on the walls, lots of interesting old books, in English as well as Russian, and an alcove where he had a hot plate to boil water for coffee. I climbed into the big plush armchair, and we started talking about *Don Quixote*, about the performance, about other ballets.

"Go ahead and eat," he said, and I unwrapped my sandwich and began to chew. I was a little uncomfortable being there with him alone, although technically there wasn't anything improper about the situation. I became increasingly dismayed when he went down on his knees beside me, holding on to the arm of the chair, and before I knew it I had uttered the classic line "Shouldn't you be home with your wife?"

I didn't really want to know. I would have liked to avoid the whole subject, but that was a naive fantasy; I was beginning to love the man.

So the first time I had amorous feelings toward a man, I was instantly thrust into a triangle, a very public triangle. From then on, in the midst of so much excitement and success onstage, I felt, offstage, a slowly gnawing guilt, although I could not see what I might be doing wrong. The last role I could ever imagine for myself was as a marriage wrecker. Even if I was madly in love I would never, ever, have asked George, or any other man, to leave his wife for me. As it turned out, all the trouble happened anyway, of its own inevitable accord.

But it didn't happen quite yet—and in the meantime there was a great deal of fun to be had in a much more visible environment. George had originally planned to perform *Don Quixote* only once, but he had such a good time with it that over the next few years he did one or two each season. Sometimes I would ask him to dance it with me, and he was happy to oblige. His appearances were never posted on the casting list; they would be announced over the loudspeaker as the lights in the theater dimmed: "In this evening's performance of *Don Quixote*, the role of Don Quixote will be danced by George Balanchine." It was an amazing thing to hear, and the audience would applaud its good fortune.

Because of Balanchine's own physical involvement and the extravagance of the production, *Don Quixote* enjoyed a long and successful life in the publicity department (possibly more successful than onstage). Everyone wanted to capture Balanchine in action, and the press office was flooded with requests for photo sessions. The office politely tried to consolidate requests, knowing Balanchine's dislike of being photographed—also he was a very busy man—until they discovered that he was positively eager to pose. He thought nothing of wrestling himself into his elaborate makeup, beard, and armor and standing for hours with me while the cameras clicked away. To everyone's great surprise, as soon as a roll of film was finished and the photographers were being encouraged to leave, George would hold up his hand and say to me, "How about another costume? Suzi, go and change into your other costume," and the cameras would be reloaded. It was a period of great energy and enthusiasm, and the result was photographs of George and me as the Don and Dulcinea all over town.

This publicity culminated in a long article in the August issue of *Life* magazine's international edition with George and me on the cover. The article became a much quoted source of Balanchine philosophy and wit, and of me he said, "Suzanne has a phenomenal presence. Her soul is in her eyes." It was a beautiful thing to say, and it made me think that he could read my soul. He knew me before I knew myself; this also gave him an edge over me.

George had become my most avid publicist, and the first thing he did after *Don Quixote* was promote me to principal dancer, the only promotion at that time. Two weeks after the New York season ended in June, the company was embarking on an eleven-week tour of Europe and the Middle East. It was to be my second tour overseas, but things had changed a great deal during the past three years. No longer a corps de ballet member with a bad knee, I was now Balanchine's newest ballerina, and he made no secret of the fact that he wanted to present me as such. On the other hand, I was still only nineteen, and, as in 1962, my mother came along as the company's nurse, and Beverly, who had never been to Europe, came along for the fun of it.

I had never been to Paris, but George had told me all about its architectural beauty and gastronomic delights, and I was thrilled to be going to a place he loved so much. We were there for only a week but that was plenty of time for the City of Lights to exert its magic and provide the perfect frame for romance. Upon arriving from the airport at the Hotel Le Havre, the company hotel I had signed up for in New York, I found my expectations of old world Paris more than well met. I was neither fussy nor spoiled when it came to living arrangements (at home I still shared a bedroom with Bev), but my sense of privacy was shattered when I realized that the toilet was down the hall and resembled a rusty old iron grate, and the sink and the bidet were in the middle of the bedroom I was sharing with Mother and Bev. Some people called it quaint, but it was too quaint for me, and when George asked me later at the theater how I liked my hotel, I confessed that it was a little rougher than I had anticipated.

"Oh? Well, I think there is an extra room at my hotel. Maybe you could move in there," he immediately suggested. After rehearsal, Mother, Bev, George, and I walked over to the Hotel St. Anne, and to my great surprise and pleasure were shown a lovely big, bright room with a private bathroom and a huge bathtub. I considered it providential that there happened to be a vacancy in George's hotel! I didn't become suspicious until later when I saw that George's room resembled a closet with a bed that folded up into the wall. He had given us his own room, but he would never admit it. It was a Don Quixote–like gesture of gallantry; it was also very convenient for us to be in such close proximity.

If I'd known what he had done, I would never have accepted the room, which he knew, and when at the end of our stay I found the bill had already been paid, I learned my lesson. For the rest of the tour I never complained to him about our accommodations. When we changed hotels in other cities, which we frequently did to find something cheaper, I didn't tell him about it.

My first performance as a principal dancer with the company was opening night at the Paris Opéra when I danced *Agon* with Arthur Mitchell. All of Paris had turned out in its finery, and the theater was magnificent, ornate beyond description, with hundreds of chandeliers lighting the gilded decorations. Backstage was Byzantine, with endless long, dark, mazelike corridors, and it proved all too easy to get lost and never find the stage; echoing cries for directions emanated from bewildered dancers trapped in foreign hallways.

There had been a great deal of publicity about the company's first visit to Paris in nine years, and much had been written about me and my quick rise to stardom. I did not want to disappoint Paris, and I was so proud to be representing Mr. B that when my entrance in *Agon* arrived I felt I had a lot to prove: that I was worthy of Mr. B's high praise, that I was not just an infatuation, that I could really dance. I ended up showing a great deal of energy, but it was not the kind I had intended; the first glimpse Paris had of Balanchine's much touted ballerina was of her lying flat in the middle of the stage.

The opening step of the *Agon* pas de deux is an unpartnered diagonal sequence of high kicks, low drags, and spinning turns on half pointe, and I went for it as if I were shot out of a cannon. I was still adjusting to the extremely steep rake of the stage, and as I kicked my right leg up to my nose, my left leg went out from under me, and I was down with a resounding crash. I saw Arthur spin on by me doing the steps I should have been doing. Five seconds into the dance, and any image I had wished to create of speed, elegance, or technical brilliance was erased from memory.

I had wanted to impress, and I had. My heart sank, but I was up in a flash, continuing where I had left off. The fall was probably a good thing in several ways: it showed that I wasn't about to play it safe even on such a high-pressure occasion, and I realized immediately that I could not possibly better such a splendid slip, so any nerves I had disappeared. Falling in front of thousands of people shocked me, but it never scared me, and there is an important, visible difference between the two. Once recovered, I felt bolder than ever. The worst had already happened, and now there was a new challenge: they knew I was human, so now I could go on and try to convince them that I was not entirely human by dancing beautifully.

The audience didn't seem to hold the mishap against me, and in the following night's performance of *Liebeslieder Walzer* I had a lovely but embarrassing moment after my "whispering" duet in the first section of the ballet, when the applause would not stop and the quiet melancholy of the ballet was interrupted for several minutes. It was quite inappropriate at that moment, and although Mr. B had a well-known dislike for applause both in the middle of a ballet or for a star dancer, on this occasion he was thrilled; he wanted everyone to like me as much as he did, and he never lost an opportunity to thrust me in front of the audience, even for an unscheduled appearance.

A week or so before closing night in Paris Mr. B suggested Jacques and I dance *Meditation* in the last performance. I thought it was a bad idea. "George, it's just too sentimental, and they won't like it," I told him. "When they think of a pas de deux they expect the 'Black Swan' and 'Le Corsaire,' flashy, technical things." I don't know why I questioned his judgment. Mr. B insisted, and to my great surprise, it was a sensational success. The French adored Russian romanticism; so much for trying to second-guess the boss.

Since *Don Quixote*, George and I had no longer needed the chaperoning of Eddie Bigelow, and every night in Paris we had dinner together alone. Mother and Bev followed their own schedule of sight-seeing all day, attending the performance at night, and then going off by themselves or back to the hotel. They remained conspicuously silent on the subject of my late-night suppers with George, but I figured that they knew whom I was with; I was in good hands. Mother trusted us, and she never asked any questions about my late evenings, which seemed natural enough at the time but rather unfortunate in retrospect. It was the beginning of four years when a lot of important things about George and me went unsaid by all participating parties including ourselves. This is partially explained by the importance of "the moment"—at any given moment we were having too much fun to discuss anything as far away as consequences or the future. Paris was the ideal setting for our courtship.

Although we had only a little time after performances and during the day between rehearsals, George made it his business to introduce me to the delights of French culture, which for him began with the restaurants. We both felt a newfound freedom in being together, which we had never felt in New York, and he was uncharacteristically enthusiastic about taking me to the most extravagant dining spots, where we were inevitably seen by the Paris smart set as well as the press. We went to Maxim's, Fouquet's, and Brasserie Lorraine. I wore my best dresses, and he ordered champagne and introduced me to red wine and pâté de foie gras. We also discovered a quiet little bistro where they had a wonderful dessert, La Mystère, which we would share. It was vanilla ice cream covered in chocolate, and inside was a crunchy surprise—the "mystère."

It was an idyllic week with lots of dancing, very little sleep, and walks along the Seine arm in arm. I felt like *Gigi* come to life. To underscore the notion, a prominent patron invited us to a party at his Paris mansion, where we were serenaded by violins beside the fountain and toasted everything we could think of with champagne. Maurice Chevalier attended, and when I asked him for his autograph, he very kindly obliged me with a signed photograph to add to my collection.

Despite the Continental education I was receiving, I was still a child in many ways, with my hair in its perpetual ponytail and my movie camera by my side. George was most tolerant about being filmed for my home movies, mugging and making silly faces on top of the Eiffel

Tower for me one afternoon. We felt and looked like typical giggling American tourists, and neither of us cared about what an onlooker might have thought.

George made a special point of showing me two of the city's most treasured art works, both of which enchanted me. First he took me to the Musée de Cluny on the Left Bank to see *The Lady and the Unicorn* tapestries. As we walked by the six huge hangings in the vaulted room he explained to me that five of them represented the senses. The last and most poignant has the beautiful but mysterious title *À Mon Seul Désir* (To My Only Desire) and depicts the young maiden embracing a coffer of jewels, a gift from a lover perhaps. Her white unicorn is seated patiently beside her with the most touching expression of innocent adoration upon its sweet face. George told me the legend that a unicorn can be captured only by a virgin; it will come and lay its head in her lap. He loved the title *À Mon Seul Désir* and said he wanted to make a ballet for me about the story of the unicorn. He bought me a book on the tapestries, and whenever I look at it, I still feel a curious emotional pang.

The other thing he wanted to show me was the Botticelli exhibition visiting the Louvre, and as we stood before *The Birth of Venus* George told me with great seriousness that I looked like her. Although she was ravishingly beautiful, she did not have a lot of clothes on, and I blushed at the compliment and its implication. "It's very pretty," I murmured.

Our next stop on the tour was La Scala opera house in Milan, which not only had a more steeply raked stage than the Paris Opéra but seemed to be built vertically all around; you couldn't get anywhere without climbing endless flights of stairs. When we weren't working George took me to the elegant arcades, and we stopped at every window to admire the bags and shoes. He insisted on buying me several handbags—not big, roomy dance bags for toe shoes and leotards, but the elegant little purses nothing fits into that every lady should own. He would admire a pair of shoes, and within minutes we were inside the shop and the shoes were on my feet. He thought my feet were most important and took a special pleasure in buying me shoes. My favorite were woven white leather sandals with high heels covered in metal like tap shoes. Late at night, after performance, after a meal, when walking along the cobblestone streets, we would be silent except for the rhythmic clicking of my shoes. Every now and then George would say, "I just love to hear you clip-clopping along," and we would count out the musical rhythm.

Much as I appreciated these gifts, I felt uncomfortable about George's generosity, but when I protested he would always say that the company didn't pay me enough anyway. It gave him obvious pleasure to shop with me and watch me model shoes, but I became hesitant about mentioning something I liked because I knew that I would immediately have it. Several months later, back in New York, he designed a little black Persian lamb jacket with a black fox collar for me at the fur shop of an old Russian friend. But when I managed to pay for it myself, he proceeded to buy me a white mink jacket trimmed with ermine as well. He was a very insistent man, even where his generosity was concerned.

Day by day George and I were becoming closer and closer. Being in Europe gave us the chance to be alone together in a way that could never have happened in New York. Living in hotels and being together every evening made it all too easy to forget the reality of our home lives and their responsibilities. Had this tour not taken place when it did, in the immediate aftermath of *Don Quixote*, the course of our relationship might have been very different. Perhaps things would have come to a head sooner, or later, with more frustration, but Europe provided us with powerful evocations of how it could be, of how it might be. It was never to be that simple, but we did go back several times during the next few years, sometimes to dance, sometimes to rest, to be able to feel that way again.

Despite all the excitement of being with George, eating with him, shopping with him, dancing for him, unanswered questions remained in my mind. I knew that when I was dancing we were on the same level, that we spoke a language of music, movement, and emotion that was the same; but when it came to life offstage, I often wondered why he wanted to be with me. I was still an unsophisticated girl from the Midwest with little conversation aside from ballet, while he was a man of enormous culture and education.

Our next city in Italy was Spoleto, but after Milan George returned to New York for two weeks. He didn't tell me why he had to go, and I didn't ask. I presumed it was for some business or other, but I missed him terribly. While we were in Spoleto, I had a free day, and Bev and I took the train to Rome to visit the home of our religion. We walked around St. Peter's Basilica and saw Michelangelo's *Pietà*, and I discovered that even in the Vatican Italian men consider pinching women their divine right.

As I had in Milan's cathedral, I did a lot of praying, and for the first time I questioned my faith. I didn't feel much control over what was happening between George and me. There were unspoken problems. George was married, and in Rome, standing on the founding rock of Catholicism, I had reason to worry, although I felt that I was being honest in my actions; I knew that our work was honest. I could not answer for George, I just had to trust him. I decided to put it in the hands of God. I asked Him to push me in the right direction, trusting where I went to be His will. During the ensuing years, when the situation became a great deal more pressured than it was in 1965, I found myself spending even more time in church. By then there was really no one else I could talk to who didn't have a vested interest in my actions.

In Europe, however, there was little time for such ponderous worries before we were off to Venice to dance at the exquisite little Teatro La Fenice. George was especially sorry not to be in Venice with me, and before leaving he gave me full tourist instructions. He made me promise to take a gondola ride down the Grand Canal—and it had to be at night—and to go to the Piazza San Marco for an Italian ice cream—"They have such wonderful ice cream!" So after the performance one night Mother, Bev, and I bargained with the gondolier and climbed into his smooth black gondola for a long ride around the canals, but I was feeling more than a little sorry for myself that George was not with me, and I let a few lonely tears fall into the canal.

We then sailed down the Adriatic to our next stop, Dubrovnik, where George was to rejoin us. We were in morning class the first day on the outdoor stage in the heat of the midday sun when he appeared. John Taras was teaching class, and as soon as Mr. B showed up people ran over to hug him and say hello. I stayed at the barre, knowing that the best way for George to see me was when I was dancing.

Finally a dancer came up to me and expressed what was obviously current company opinion. "Why don't you go and say hi to him? You know you're the only one he wants to see." Although the company had probably been buzzing about George and me, this was the first time anyone had dared to mention it to me. I was startled and took the advice as an order. I went over to George to say hello. After this episode I became increasingly aware that we were being watched and probably second-guessed by the company. This was unpleasant but unavoidable, and within a few months, when the press got into the spying-and-predicting act, it was to seem rather benign; at least the company was family.

Our appearances in Yugoslavia were part of the Dubrovnik Festival, and our stage was a temporary platform erected in the center of the local citadel. Our dressing rooms were converted prison cells in the catacombs of the castle, with only a long, winding stone staircase leading up to the stage. It became blocked at frequent intervals by an overload of girls in bushy tutus. But the naturally theatrical setting of the fortress more than compensated for the lack of modern stage conveniences. Because it had been built on the city's highest precipice, we danced with the Adriatic on one side and the audience on the other and very little in between.

I was to dance *Scotch Symphony* with André Prokovsky the first night, and I was especially excited knowing that George would be there to see it. The performance ended up being a great deal more dramatic than intended because as soon as the lights dimmed and the music began, a great howling gale of wind roared across the stage from the sea and did not cease all evening. Unlike the breeze from the fans that are sometimes placed in the wings for certain ballets, the wind was out of control and seriously threatened to alter the choreography; I danced the entire ballet with my calf-length tutu around my neck, and my center of gravity was never where I expected it to be. It was a real battle with the elements, but I persisted, and the ballet was completed without mishap. George thought it was a wonderful effect; I think he loved seeing me overcome less-than-ideal circumstances because it brought out not only the trouper in me but some unplanned off-balance movements as well.

After the performance we went out for a reunion dinner at the elegant Hotel Argentine where he was staying (Mother, Bev, and I were staying with a family in a pensione-style arrangement), and I had yet another new theatrical experience. After an elaborate meal ending with some very potent Turkish coffee, a curtain parted to reveal a small stage, and a belly dancer emerged in her glittering but scanty finery. I was embarrassed; George, of course, was not. This was a rather tame exhibition, to say the least, but I had never been to a nightclub before. It wasn't that the dancer didn't have much on— a sequined bikini and a large rhinestone in her navel—it was that there was so much of her to begin with.

While she proceeded with her jiggling, undulating maneuvers, I watched with a kind of awed fascination. Although I cannot pinpoint what, I probably learned from this woman something of interest about performing that I might not have learned elsewhere. It has been my experience to absorb more about dancing, performing, and various effective gestures, facial as well as physical, from people who are not professional ballet dancers than from those who are.

Traveling six days later to Athens, we succeeded in trading one ancient outdoor theater for another more famous, the Herodes Atticus Theater at the foot of the Acropolis. It was spectacular, with acoustics better than Carnegie Hall's and a platform stage open on all sides to the amphitheater; our wing space was the stone tunnels of the theater's original structure. Appropriately, we danced *Apollo,* and it was a humbling experience to dance this ballet and suddenly find oneself upside down in a backbend staring up at the beautiful symmetry of the stonework of Apollo's countrymen.

Our restaurant haunt in Athens was a little outdoor bistro called the Dionysus on the precipice of an extremely steep hill, and our favorite dessert was, predictably, the mysterious Coupe Dionysus, which we ate while holding our knees securely on the table legs to prevent the whole thing from falling down the hill. We thought it was all very romantic.

On the ninth of August we flew to Israel for an appearance at the Israel Festival which consisted of a single performance in Jerusalem and seven in Tel Aviv. The company was booked into a somewhat primitive motel that resembled a kibbutz with a single large dining room and a menu of unusual Israeli food that prompted a re-creation of the food fights of our Russian-tour days. Some of the company chose to move out to the nearby Hilton for more American-style service and prices, but we stayed, and so did George.

There were two more brief stops before we ended our tour with two weeks in London. In Salzburg, George, ever vigilant on the culinary trail, discovered a little fish restaurant called the Forelle where we went regularly, and in Amsterdam he asked Patty McBride and me to chaperone him at a press conference. Neither of us said much; George was fond of bringing along "a little beauty" to confuse the situation. The power of the visual was, after all, what he had based his work on, and he was not opposed to using its influence even at a press conference.

I was especially excited to be dancing at the famous Covent Garden opera house in London, the scene of my childhood memories of Moira Shearer and Michael Somes. I was surprised to find how small it was to have had so much history and sentiment attached to it until I discovered that its special charm lay in the intimate atmosphere between audience and stage. The company's critical reception, however, was often less than intimate, and it was my first taste of the ongoing feud between the conservative British press and all-American Balanchine. This was the New York City Ballet's third visit to Britain, and on each occasion Balanchine managed to offend British ballet tradition.

The complaints were various: dances without costumes or stories that produced ballets without heart and soul and girls who thought nothing of kicking their legs well above what was considered decent. The latter reminded some critics of the Rockettes, an allusion Balanchine no doubt agreed with; the difference was, he liked the Rockettes. The British complained about our unruly arms stabbing out in all directions (the company's arbitrary "arms" were admittedly one of our hallmarks, even back home), and one headline complained that there was "Nothing New" on a program consisting of *Prodigal Son, Allegro Brillante, Monumentum/Movements,* and *La Valse.* This brought out the crusader in me, but George deflated the situation with his now-famous retort—"You can't speak too loud or too much in England. If you are awake it's already vulgar." The British concern with propriety was directly opposed to Balanchine's notion of what was interesting—he was bored by "polite" dancing.

Our gastronomic forays in London were somewhat limited, but George did introduce me to the British pub where he delighted in pints of draft beer which, in one of his few agreements with English custom, he liked at room temperature. I often think that over all those years of knowing each other we had only two major disagreements, from which neither of us wavered: he always wanted the company to be bigger and bigger, and he liked warm beer.

We returned to New York on September 12, and within ten days our fall season opened with fifteen performances of *Don Quixote,* followed by several more weeks of repertoire in which I debuted in two more ballets, *Swan Lake* and *Raymonda.* By now I was dancing at least once every night, often twice, and had leading roles in twenty-eight ballets, one-third of the entire repertoire. For the audience, I had become unavoidable. This was the hardest year of nonstop dancing I had ever had, but throughout I remained healthy and uninjured, and I think no small part of my endurance came from my new relationship with George. I was in love with him, and the energy love inspires can be neither measured nor underestimated. We were feeding off each other, and the power was astounding. I felt omnipotent; I could dance anything, anywhere, all day long, day after day, week after week.

In October, toward the end of the New York season, George left for Cologne to oversee productions of his work, and while he was gone we wrote to each other almost daily. His letters were invariably undated and scribbled on hotel stationery.

My Dearest Dul, [Dulcinea]
This is just to tell you that there is no news since I wrote you last. My days are the same routine; morning in the theater, pouring water into the sieve. This afternoon I talked to about twenty reporters, some of them trying to spank me for being mechanical and soulless monster. Thank God, soon I'll be nearer to you!

Love you, miss you,
Pest you-George

The derivation of "Pest" came about because on one occasion he asked if he was bothering me about something, and I teased him by saying that he was a pest. On the bottom of the letter the "mechanical" and "soulless" man had drawn a little black bug.

Balanchine had a great passion for English words; he loved puns and double meanings, and he was a master of the ambiguous phrase. This often resulted in tears for one dancer and grins for another, such was his subtle way as a teacher. Less subtle but always amusing were the handwritten notes that accompanied the enormous bouquets of flowers he sent me for performances. These bouquets were so numerous and so huge that every night the sinks in my dressing room were filled, and I walked home looking as if I had just raided a florist shop.

One of Balanchine's favorite word games was to describe his dancers as various animals, depending on their physical and mental attributes. Within the vast menagerie there were two general favorites, the thoroughbred horse, with its perfect breeding, grace, and speed, and the cat, with its flexibility, independence, and unflappable demeanor. In an interview with the columnist Earl Wilson, he said in response to a question:

> How can you praise her? She has speed, alertness, understanding. Her muscles are flexible. She responds beautifully. It is like the cat family. There are lions and tigers, pumas and leopards, and they are all different. Why? It is the body's chemistry. Suzanne is a cheetah, the fastest. Others are lions, slow and lumbering. Yes, Suzanne is a cheetah. . . .

He finished by saying, "As long as I'm alive, as long as I can work, I will always have new dances for Suzanne." Twenty years later this statement turned out to be true, but at the time, though I was still only twenty, I was wise enough to know that a dancer's career was short and that Balanchine's obsession with any given career could be shorter still. Because he was going to live "forever"—as he often told us, and I believed him as I believed everything else he said—it stood to reason that he would outlast my career and could certainly outlast his current interest in me as an instrument of his profession.

Every dancer in whom he had taken an interest had walked a tightrope, lifted up there by the greatest choreographer in the world. But this kept everyone literally on her toes; it certainly kept me on mine. To be eternally interesting to Balanchine, to surprise him, was my greatest wish, and I think I developed a certain kind of desperation in my dancing because of this. Fortunately the desperation was never negative, or self-destructive, but it was, I think, probably always apparent in my performances. It not only made them better, it gave them a momentary liveliness that was different from anyone else's. Dancing was the most important and stable thing in my life, it was the best that I was capable of being. To offer less rather than more was not a possibility for me; it was death.

I never took Balanchine's interest in me for granted, even though he showered me with numerous assurances that his interest would not wane. If my dancing had ever suffered, if I had ever thought that I could get by with less onstage because of George's feelings for me, our offstage relationship would never have worked.

One of the more amusing reality checks I developed for myself at this time was a private system for judging my dancing progress. I would hang the current season's brochure on the refrigerator at home, and after each performance I would mark the appropriate ballet with a grade—"VG" for very good, "G" for good, "X" or "E" for excellent, "N" or "No" for no good. If I had done something extraordinary, like an unexpected balance, I would draw a long line next to the ballet, and if I had whipped off an unusual number of turns, I'd mark down how many. This was really just an upgraded version of what I had done in my diary when I was a student. I was merely keeping tabs on myself. Needless to say, my assessments rarely coincided with the critics'; but, unlike theirs, no one saw mine.

A few months later I received an unusual phone call from Betty Cage, the company's manager. She said, "Mr. B wants to give you *Meditation*, and I am sending over the papers." Until then I had never thought about ballets as being transferable objects of value, financial or otherwise. But shortly afterward I received a very official-looking document that gave me proprietorship of the ballet. It meant that I would receive royalties every time it was danced. But *Meditation* had no financial worth to me; it was simply one of the most valuable things in my life. In some ways it had been the beginning of my life, and it was one of the tenderest and most beautiful gestures I ever received. In giving me this ballet, George was giving me the best of himself.

There was another, more frightening aspect of being the object of so much attention. Much as I adored George, I was also overwhelmed and perplexed by our convoluted lives. As I was to find out, having Balanchine's undivided attention had its unpleasant side. He was a man used to having his own way, and he could be as possessive as any man in the throes of a romance. But being George Balanchine, he also had persuasive powers that easily outmatched my own less experienced resources.

CHAPTER EIGHT

Pearls

᠍᠍ᚎᛁᚏᚎ

W hile George was still in Europe, in October 1965, I was waiting for a bus one day and bought a copy of *Newsweek*. Inside I read that Maria Tallchief had "withdrawn" from the company in mid-season, offering her now-legendary explanation: "I don't mind being listed alphabetically, but I do mind being treated alphabetically." The article also stated that Patricia Wilde had announced that she would be departing at the end of the season. It was the first I had heard of the scandal, and apparently the resignations had taken Balanchine unaware as well. The article went on to report various ballerinas' comments on their director's less-than-democratic casting policy, calling them "casualties of Balanchine's emphasis on youth." (Clive Barnes, who had recently been named dance critic of *The New York Times*, continued the categorization a few weeks later in an article that referred to Balanchine's focus on "the young, brave and heartless.") *Newsweek* summed up the various signs of trouble as indicative of an overall "simmering discontent within the New York City Ballet."

At this point I was sitting on the bus, and my spine began to tingle. Undoubtedly certain facts and opinions were true, but I had never seen them stated in such a bald-faced manner. So far my name had not appeared, but I knew with certainty that I was at least one good cause, if not *the* cause, of the "simmering discontent." Naturally I felt defensive—Balanchine had determined my position within the company, and the fact that he chose to like me at this time was my good fortune. I certainly wasn't suddenly going to dance badly or care any less about George or my work because of outside pressure. But the pressure was there.

By the time I finished reading the article, I had arrived at the theater, and already there was something else to worry about—I *was* mentioned by name. All dancers complain with good reason and without good reason—it is part of the daily routine; but another idea had been suggested in the article that I didn't like one bit, and I was to hear it, and read it, constantly for the next four years. "For Pygmalion Balanchine," the article declared, "Farrell is not only the alpha but the omega of his young ballerinas. The exquisite Farrell is the latest in a forty-year series of Galateas that include Danilova, Geva, Zorina, Tallchief and Tanaquil Le Clercq."

It was one thing to be in competition with one's competition, it was quite another to be at the end of a long list of George's glamorous, talented wives. The obvious implication that romantic involvement with one's boss was inevitable left me feeling outnumbered and out of control. I hated being on a list, anyone's list.

Similarly, I disliked the frequent comments about my youth, how good I was for my age; I wanted to be seen and judged on my dancing alone. In the same way, I didn't see why I should be relegated to the role of most recent delegate in a phantom "series," however illustrious its members. I tried to take solace in one of Balanchine's most confident remarks—"I disagree with everybody and I don't want to argue"—but it was not so easy. The gossip and public opinion were beyond my influence; more and more the only place where I had control, where I could "argue," where my actions made any real sense was on stage.

Things on the home front were also unsettled. My mother was not my confidante, but we had had several significant exchanges. We were probably both equally confused about the right and the wrong, the good and the bad, of the situation, but when Mother started hearing things outside our front door, the whole affair took on a more serious tone. We had always cared very much about what other people thought of us, so when our neighbor offered her opinion, Mother was upset. "Balanchine is very interested in your daughter," the neighbor said. "He's in love with her." Mother, feigning ignorance for the sake of propriety, said, "Do you really think so?" The woman looked at her severely. "You'd better be careful. He'll treat her like all the other ones. She won't last long. He likes them for a while, he's in love with them for a while, and then he moves on to someone else." This was indeed often said of him.

That evening Mother sat me down and said with great seriousness, "Suzi, the man's in love with you." I, of course, was uncomfortable admitting such a thing to my mother and defended our relationship by connecting it to our work—that was our mutual passion. "Mother, we're just very good friends," I said, "and we love to work together, and we've become close, but he isn't really in love with me." I also said one thing that I felt more strongly than anything else; it meant survival to me. "I'm different from the others, I'm different," I cried. I had to be.

"Well, you're playing with fire," Mother said. "The man is not infallible. He has been married; he *is* married. He has a pattern." This I could not deny; but I could change the pattern.

"Maybe you should meet someone your own age," Mother suggested. But at that point I was not interested in knowing a man just for the sake of having a boyfriend. I was happy with George, and I was happy with my work, and I didn't see how they could be separated now without turning the clock back. Nevertheless, this was the first time we had openly discussed the issue; nothing had been mentioned in Europe. Mother had planted the seeds of discontent by suggesting other options, and she was a very forceful woman, the undisputed general in our family. Until George came along, she had been the only adult influence in my life and I had good reason to trust her instincts: we had come to New York penniless and alone and we had far more than survived.

I had thrived, for the most part, of course, because of George Balanchine's influence, artistic as well as personal; he was without doubt the most important man in my life. He was also the only man in my life and the first for whom I had ever felt trust, affection, and gratitude. I never, however, regarded him as a father figure. Quite the opposite—it was for him that I felt the first stirrings of adult love, and it was because of this that I was so confused about his feelings. I could not forget that he had another life, a married life, a life he never spoke about, never explained, a life I didn't dare ask about—he had at least two separate lives, and I had only one, the one with him. I had graduated from my first kiss to being the "other" woman, and if I let myself think about it long enough, my mother's suggestion about "someone my own age" rang in my ears.

It was wildly ironic that by the time I met Roger, Mother's fears about George had been set aside and she had become his most vocal advocate; it meant that Roger and I were engaged in an uphill battle against the two people I loved and respected most, Mother and George. As I was to discover, they had between them an emotional artillery force primed for action if necessary.

During the fall season after the European tour, several anonymous notes had been left for me at the stage door. They were all short, respectful, and complimentary about my dancing. Eventually a poem arrived comparing my images in various roles—as Dulcinea, as the Sleepwalker in *La Sonnambula*, as the Swan Queen in *Swan Lake*, and as Titania in *A Midsummer Night's Dream*—and I realized the author was scrutinizing me very closely indeed. He signed himself "The Poet," and several weeks later I received a small package with an accompanying note saying that it was very presumptuous of "The Poet" to assume that I liked his poem, or even liked poetry at all and perhaps perfume would be a more appropriate offering. Inside was a bottle of Réplique perfume, which I genuinely liked. George also liked it, but I did not tell him where it came from.

Just as I was becoming intrigued about who this person was, I started noticing a young man in the audience every time I danced. He sat rather conspicuously in the first row to the left of the conductor, practically on top of the stage. When I received yet another note saying how much he liked the way I bit my lip in *Irish Fantasy*, I was convinced that the figure in the front row with opera glasses was "The Poet." Only someone sitting that close could have seen such a thing. It made me realize that even when I thought I was being inconspicuous on the side of the stage during Jacques' variation, I wasn't. After that I never forgot that onstage everything counts, everything shows, there are no rest moments even during rest moments.

At night, as I emerged from the stage door, I began to notice a tall, slim, dark figure lurking in the shadows and knew this must be my admirer. It took several months before Roger summoned up the courage to emerge and introduce himself. "You were always with someone," he explained to me later. And indeed I was always accompanied by either George or Eddie. I had been touched by his poem, his perfume, and his patience, so when he timidly asked me to have coffee with him, I said perhaps some afternoon.

Roger was only a couple of months older than I and lived at home with his parents, who were both lawyers. But, unlike me, he seemed to have considerable freedom to come and go as he pleased. He was Jewish but said he was an "unconscious" Christian—he had been very moved by *Don Quixote*—although I didn't care one bit what his religion was. On our first real date he took me uptown to the Cloisters on my day off and bought me a beautiful book with reproductions of medieval art. On another occasion he proudly produced tickets to the hot new Broadway show *Man of La Mancha*. This musical version of *Don Quixote* had received far more acclaim than Balanchine's version, and I was determined, out of loyalty, to dislike it. Despite this, I enjoyed it thoroughly and cried voluminously. What was so startling, so refreshing and unique to me about being with Roger was the lack of pressure. We were just two kids having fun, enjoying each other's company. I had rarely felt so carefree, but things quickly got out of hand.

Mother, not surprisingly, developed an instant dislike of Roger.

Though he was extremely intelligent and well educated, she complained about his beard—she thought he was a hippie—and his background, but basically she objected to him on principle; if he had been anyone other than George Balanchine, I am convinced that she wouldn't have liked him either. By now George had charmed Mother—he had had a lot of practice charming mothers—and they had become confidants, at least where I was concerned. It must be remembered that my mother had almost a genetic suspicion of men in general, but now she was convinced of George's trustworthiness, and she never changed her mind about him again. What mother would not have been charmed—he was generous and endearing, always appearing laden with gifts and flowers; he was sophisticated and gentlemanly, often inviting Mother to sit with him to watch me dance; he was courteous, stable, unhysterical, and protective. On one occasion when he came to our apartment he told her, "You've not only given me a ballerina, you've given me a family." In short, to Mother, Balanchine represented the one thing she had always lived—and survived—without: male security, financial and emotional. He was also the greatest choreographer in the world, he was obviously in love with her daughter, and for the moment this seemed perfect to her. Bev was also very fond of George; they played the piano together when he visited. Although she tried to remain neutral in all this domestic upheaval, in the end she, too, agreed with Mother. Roger didn't stand a chance, and neither did I. With Balanchine and Mother united, defeat was certain and I was completely overwhelmed.

One day, following a violent argument with Mother about Roger, I fled the apartment to meet him, and in my desperate state asked if we could drive out to Manhasset, Long Island, where the Marist teachers Brother Paul and Brother Damian lived. Jacques had introduced me to them after several performances, and I thought they might be able to give me some impartial advice. I felt caged, and I needed to talk to someone outside the situation, someone who could tell me that I wasn't going crazy, that I wasn't wrong to want some freedom to develop on my own. Because Mother and George were the people I loved most, I could not simply disregard their wishes. I felt like a high-stakes commodity; my choices and actions existed to make everyone else's life smoother, but I was beginning to wonder where, if anywhere, my own feelings fit in. I was torn apart trying to make everyone happy. I hadn't yet learned that this was an impossible dream.

We arrived very late at night at the school where Brother Paul and Brother Damian taught and lived. Not only did they tell me that I wasn't crazy—they knew what a difficult and unusual situation I was in—they gave me some very wise advice, which I did not take. Since I obviously couldn't resolve the dilemma with my mother, they suggested I move out, get my own apartment and put a little space between us. Unfortunately I didn't have the time or stamina for so much emotional disarray while I was dancing every night.

Getting my own apartment might have solved many problems, but even though I could have afforded it, I couldn't do it. If I had moved out, I would inevitably have relocated virtually next door because I had to be near the theater, and it seemed ridiculous to pay two rents instead of one. I also did not want to face the reality of breaking up the family; the three of us had not been apart since arriving in New York. I decided to try a stoic approach instead. Silly me. Within a week Mother and I were fighting again, and again I left the apartment in the middle of the night with nowhere to go. After calming myself down a little, I walked several blocks downtown and found myself at the door of Betty Cage's brownstone. I rang the buzzer.

Betty, the New York City Ballet's wise, self-effacing manager, had saved the company from disaster so many times I thought perhaps she could help me. I explained my problems, and she listened sympathetically. We both had the advantage of knowing that, although a lot of my difficulties were typical mother/daughter struggles, the situation was considerably more delicate and complicated because it involved the feelings of George Balanchine, and the repercussions could be cataclysmic. Betty, like Brother Paul, suggested that I get my own apartment, but after I explained my unwillingness to do that, she came up with another solution that she had used successfully for the past twenty years with the company. She judiciously wrote out a contract to be reviewed and signed by Mother and me. It contained provisions like, "Suzanne will be allowed X number of phone calls each day and can go out X number of times each week." I took this pathetic piece of paper home to Mother, and we both signed it and agreed to follow the rules. But the contract was rendered null and void when Roger gave me a pearl ring.

If Mother had felt threatened by Roger before, it was nothing compared to what she felt when she saw me wearing this token of attachment. It was a lovely ring with two pearls—one black and one white—surrounded by little diamonds. It had been in Roger's family and signified, to us, our engagement, although I had never announced this fact to anyone—I may have been naive, but I wasn't stupid. I wore it on the ring finger of my left hand, the only place I wore any ring, but I did not flash it around or wear it in the theater. I suppose I accepted the ring partially to escape from the guilt I felt in regard to George's marriage. This was my first encounter with a "real life" romantic dilemma and my awkwardness was apparent. Any professional grace I had mastered didn't help me in this world of confused personal feelings. It was as if I had developed a three-dimensional intuition onstage that far exceeded my emotional maturity offstage.

Although Roger and I had tried to keep our relationship private, there was very little about me or my whereabouts that George wasn't aware of. He was very intuitive, and there had been occasions when he had asked me to walk home or have dinner after performance and I replied, "I'm sorry, I'm not free tonight." At times, I even said I had plans when I didn't, just to feel that I could have some space of my own. I was beginning to resent having to account for myself at all times, especially since, when I was an inconvenience to him, he left me without any explanation.

Roger was tolerant about our situation. He respected Balanchine enormously, but he was also worried about me. I wasn't able to sleep for nights in a row, and all the worrying was wearing me down. Life seemed impossible, and I was prepared to marry Roger to resolve some things. This is not to suggest that I was not also in love with him, but in my state I scarcely knew. I realized that marrying Roger would create numerous other problems, but at least we'd no longer all be at the present impasse.

In the end it was not my decision; it was George's. One day shortly before we were to leave on tour, George saw the ring on my finger and exploded. "I don't like it. Take it off," he demanded. He never mentioned Roger by name or even by implication; he didn't need to. We both knew what he was talking about. I was frightened to see him so angry. It had never happened before, and I took off the ring. I never put it on again. I gave it back to Roger. George had won the war, and I was left with fractured emotions—great anger that he was interfering in what I thought should be my right of decision, and great love for him too in whatever way I was then capable of defining the term.

Despite the turbulence of our emotions at the time, I knew that we were meant to be together in our work—I still didn't know if that meant privately as well or not—and that our work and our mutual respect, admiration, and understanding were more important than anything else, including my yearnings for some kind of phantom freedom. Someone had to be eliminated, and poor Roger was the most expendable of the principal players. I realized that I couldn't have everything at the same time—but that didn't mean I would never have it.

Roger defended his position, but he knew from the beginning that our romance was far from the usual kind and involved a great many important feelings besides our own. A lot of people have given up careers for love (if I had persisted in marrying Roger I knew mine would be in serious jeopardy), and I know there are times when it is the only thing to do. But it was not something I could do, not then anyway. I needed to dance, I had to dance, I loved to dance, and Roger knew it. This did not mean that during the following months he didn't call to inquire how I was and see if I had changed my mind, but I never did. I had learned one rather unpleasant lesson that I didn't soon forget.

Because Roger had come and gone so quickly and yet so significantly in my life, I used to wonder occasionally over the years what had happened to him. Almost twenty years later I received a letter from him telling me he had married and moved to California.

About a week after I had returned Roger's ring, the company traveled to Philadelphia for several performances. One morning there was a knock on the door of my hotel room. It was George. He handed me a little wrapped box and told me to open it. I thought perhaps it was a peace offering, and I was quite amenable to calling a truce. It was, but it did anything but pacify me. Inside a leather jewelry case was an enormous pearl ring surrounded by diamonds. It was strangely similar to the one Roger had given me—only a great deal bigger. I said, "I cannot accept this," and handed it back to him.

Furious, he grabbed the ring and threw it across the room. Frightened, I got down on my knees to scramble under the bed for it. I stood up, put it on my finger, and said, "All right, I'll wear it. Thank you. I have to go to the theater now. See you later." And I grabbed my dance bag and left. I was incensed at being so manipulated. But I also understood. I saw that he was hurt and confused, and I cared deeply about his pain. I had behaved in a way that was contrary to what he expected and wanted; I was different. I kept this ring, wore it, and came to love it. I still wear it with pride and humility.

It was never quite clear whether or not the ring was intended to symbolize our present or future union in marriage. It was never spoken of as such, and obviously it could not be an official engagement ring. George was married, but I think, at least to him, it signified an exclusive attachment. More directly, to me, it signified love in all its gaucheness, desperation, and beauty, and I loved those qualities in him. His decades of experience with women had not made him either cynical or too wise, only, it seemed to me, more vulnerable. The ring was given out of love, and I accepted it out of love. In a way we were protecting each other, tripping over our hearts in the process.

This somewhat absurd situation was not, of course, prompted only by jealousy. The fact that George Balanchine was who he was did not make him any less human in affairs of the heart, but there was another undeniable and perhaps more significant reason for the extremity of the situation. We were both so deeply involved in our work together that he would have considered my dating someone else or marrying someone else a catastrophic threat to that relationship. I had the advantage of already knowing that I would never desert him spiritually and never be closer to anyone else.

His history of marrying his leading dancer of the moment indicates that for him there was no rational separation between work and personal intimacy—his life was his work and his work was his life. An offstage relationship was perhaps a way of temporarily securing what was as necessary to him as air—and just as intangible. He often explained why he liked to marry his ballerinas—"If you marry a dancer you always know where she is—in the studio working." Similarly, Maria Tallchief has expressed a bittersweet explanation of her marriage to Balanchine: "When we married it was as if I were the material he wanted to use." In giving me this pearl ring perhaps he was hoping to attach us symbolically when it wasn't possible in any other way.

I did experience one terrifying emotional repercussion from this episode a few months later, when everything had ostensibly been patched up and put together. While rooming with a friend on tour, I woke up screaming, sweating, and thrashing about. Never before had I wakened in such acute physical pain from a dream. The image itself was vivid and wrenching: George and Mother were pulling on one of my arms, and Roger and what was probably myself were pulling on the other. I felt myself being dismembered. My roommate, another dancer in the company, was frightened, but she knew enough about Roger and George not to be too surprised; if George's feelings about me had ever been restrained, they were no longer.

Nightmares aside, I had good reason to wonder just what George had been thinking during all these dramatic events. Surely he realized that I was desperate—so desperate that I would break off with him and fall in love with someone else. Surely it occurred to him that his marital status—which I had no reason to think was going to change—

made my now extremely public romantic involvement with him very uncomfortable for me. But we never talked about any of this.

Despite all the offstage stalemates, when it came to work, Balanchine and I were never less than professional, and I realized just how much solace, sanity, and discipline a craft can provide. Three weeks after I scrambled under the bed after the ring, I was in the première of *Variations*, a truly experimental Balanchine/Stravinsky work, in which there was also a great deal of physical turmoil, only this time it was highly choreographed and I was in control.

Dancing was our common ground, and every time we worked, there was the same sense of discovery, of mutual excitement and respect between us. It was as if our spirits agreed even when our hearts did not. Even on occasions of great personal tension between us, it was not uncommon for there to be a knock on my dressing-room door after the performance. There would be George, saying how well it all had gone or how he liked the way I had done a certain step that night; and I, filled with the thrill of dancing for him, would say what a wonderful ballet it was, what a wonderful step he had devised, and we would for the moment be as close as we had ever been. Emotional friction suddenly disappeared beside what was really important to both of us, and that never changed. No matter how many painful situations might arise to separate us, it was always dancing that united us, as it had from the beginning.

Our heightened personal emotions did not drain our creative or physical energies but actually seemed to consolidate them. All our gripes and troubles were left outside the studio door. Work was the saving grace, the one therapeutic outlet. The calm single-minded focus was psychologically healing, but it wasn't merely a survival tactic; it was why survival was necessary, it was the chicken *and* the egg. If anything, I felt more committed to be an energetic, daring, good dancer when things between George and me were rough. Dancing was the bottom line—the line that would support or hang me.

It seemed that the more complicated my life became, the more time I spent in the theater, and the more I danced, the more I needed to dance. But I also needed to dance when I was happy. It was as if in between all my happiness and sadness I learned how to dance, really to dance. Joy and tribulation contributed to both my capacity for moving in space and for being moved by music. I think this was true for Balanchine as well. However he may have felt about events of the past, he was as ready for work as I was. Dance was our tactical maneuver. He made parts in his next four ballets on me—and altogether in five of the six ballets he made over the course of the next year. The last of them was "Diamonds."

CHAPTER NINE

Diamonds

⮡⟐⟐⤆

S travinsky dedicated *Variations,* which he composed in 1965, to the memory of Aldous Huxley, and indeed, the piece synthesized a brave new world into five explosive minutes of seemingly undanceable music. There were no recognizable themes, no melody, and no sentiment. Balanchine was eager to make its visual counterpart, but because the music was so complex and suggested so many different possibilities to him, he decided to use an unprecedented format. He choreographed three entirely separate dances, which were to be performed consecutively, to the same music. The effect if filmed might have shown the three dances performed simultaneously on a horizontally split screen.

Despite the unorthodox approach, Balanchine was not inspired by the chance to present a choreographic tour de force, although *Variations* was indeed one. His purpose, as always, was to teach, to educate the ear and the eye to the wonders of Stravinsky's composition. On this occasion he chose to mimic the music by presenting what amounted to a virtual assault on the senses, destroying all assumptions and preconceptions and substituting in their place a magnificent three-dimensional array of dry, plastic movements soldered together by sheer wit—musical, physical, and even intellectual.

The format was simple enough. The first part was danced by a corps of twelve girls in navy-blue leotards and skirts performing large symmetrical designs that reminded some viewers of a Busby Berkeley dance routine. Part two was danced by six men in simple gray-and-white practice clothes performing in unison but with far greater complexity than the girls had. Like a giant double helix, they were always connected as they wound themselves up into an impossible situation, wrestled themselves into another, and then unwound onto each other's shoulders in a pyramid formation. It was genetic engineering according to Balanchine.

Part three was a solo for me wearing a long-sleeved white leotard and skirt, with my hair in a ponytail. Never before had a ponytail bounced in so many directions in such a large space in such a small amount of time. If physics was the subject, my solo was the atom bomb. Unlike the dancers in the previous sections, I was unrestrained by having any relationship to anyone else; my existence related only to the music and the space, and the possibilities—and dilemmas— were infinite.

The dynamics of the contrasting repetitions retained an energetic logic: when the music was most unfamiliar on the first hearing, the visual counterpart was the simplest; the second time around, the music was less shocking, but the physical formations were somewhat more complex; and the third time around the music felt like an old friend, but onstage I was popping around, looking as disjointed as the music had first sounded. On each occasion, the equation remained balanced. Balanchine was a master mathematician as well as a physicist.

Part survival and all play, my choreography, by design, was so fast and so apparently reckless that it looked spontaneous. I was flying around the stage doing everything under the sun except conventional ballet steps. I was off-balance, as I had been in my Dulcinea variation, but the music was atonal, and the movement was correspondingly sharp, unpredictable, and unemotional. Yet, however startling and "modern" the ballet appeared, it remained entirely classical—like the music. Once again Balanchine had shown just how deep and broad a launching pad tradition can provide for those who know it and respect it enough to use its real, unlimited power.

Putting *Variations* together required great musical sensitivity, not so much to "understand" or "interpret" but to hear crucial moments in the score. Some parts of the music were more specific than others and took on certain sounds or rhythms that could be identified, and these became anchors and signposts for me to be finished with one movement and get myself to the back corner for the next. Between these friendly blips, squeaks, and scratches were sections of music that we called "messes." And there were a lot of "messes" where the orchestra sounded as if it had been anesthetized. During these sections Mr. B would say to me, "Just swim around for a while," and so I'd "swim around" until a high note signaled that it was time to come up for air on the other side of the stage.

I slunk like an inchworm, jumped in circles, kicked on diagonals, and finally, a few worlds later, took a huge arabesque reaching to the heavens, dived to the floor, and caught myself in an acrobatic walkover before striking a classical ballet pose and running offstage. I felt like a musical note dancing around in a Disney cartoon. *Variations* was the most extreme I had ever been, as far from Dulcinea as anyone could imagine, but it felt equally divine.

The ballet was hailed as a masterpiece, and because it had involved such fun, such unpredictability, and such exhilarating concentration it really felt as if we had robbed the bank and everyone was applauding our getaway. As before, the password was trust, but *Variations* pressed the meaning even further. If ever a ballerina had cause to worry that she might look foolishly out of control onstage, my solo in *Variations* could have been introduced in court as evidence. I had no idea how I looked while dancing this ballet, but I did know how I felt and I had to trust that feeling.

There is no mirror onstage, and even if there were it would be an inadequate gauge. As Balanchine once explained, "The mirror is not you. The mirror is you yourself looking at yourself," and they are two very different things. I knew Balanchine would not put me in front of thousands of people if I didn't look good; he had no reason, ever, to make any dancer look bad. After all, when we were dancing his ballets, we *were* him—and he was us. Physical fear is limiting, but psychological fear is debilitating. The reward in overcoming both is a great one; having danced *Variations* with both success and pleasure meant I could dance anything—and anything is a fantastic prospect. I felt Protean.

When Balanchine said of me in an interview several weeks after the première, "Without her there would be no *Variations*," I think that more than anything else he was referring to my "musicality," a quality that had been attributed to me many times already and from now on became the single most frequent characterization of my abilities. At the time, although I felt complimented, I didn't really know why. When one reviewer described me in *Variations* as possessing "all the innocent musicality of a thrush," I was baffled in a way that I never was when they said I was thin.

Mr. B never mentioned my musicality to me, although he obviously liked the way I synchronized my movements to music. He also could see how much music affected me, physically and emotionally. I always felt a special rhythmic rapport with the conductor, especially Robert Irving, a superbly sensitive maestro, who was the company's musical director for over thirty years and Balanchine's musical alter ego in the pit. Certain specific musical forms—a waltz, a polonaise, a mazurka, a polka—are eminently countable and rhythmically danceable; they virtually tell you how to move. But other music, like much of Stravinsky, doesn't tell you what to do; but it did tell Balanchine.

In *Variations*, I never knew precisely where I was in the music, but

I knew approximately, which was more than enough. Ever since I had learned *Movements* in Diana's living room to Stravinskian silence, I had felt in tune with his music, even when there was no tune in the score. He made sense in my body, not because I had figured him out—that was an intellectual fantasy exercise for others to enjoy—but because I listened and, energized, let my body ride the waves. If I had had to stop and think, I wouldn't have danced a step.

It was at this time that I had my last encounter with the composer himself. Stravinsky was visiting the theater one afternoon, and Mr. B suggested I dance *Variations* for him, an impromptu private performance. While Mr. B stood quietly to one side, Stravinsky perched on a little stool in the center of the stage near the footlights, cane in hand, chin leaning forward—he looked so small to be such a musical giant—and I charged through *Variations*. Afterward, while I was in my dressing room, George knocked on the door to say "Igor" was leaving and I murmured, "I so love his music." George said conspiratorially, "Tell him, tell him," so I chased down the hall after the disappearing little figure, shouting, "Mr. Stravinsky, Mr. Stravinsky." He stopped and turned and I said meekly, "I just want to thank you. I so love dancing to your music." He hugged me and said, "Oh yes, dear. I can tell."

It is perhaps only a personal truth, but I believe that a dancer who tries to analyze the music, to interpret every note physically, to accentuate the obvious climaxes, will bypass what music is really about. It is a definition of time, and that can only be spontaneous. Moving with music is not an intellectual feat; it is an emotional, physical, sensual response to a given moment of time. Tempo, the speed with which a score is played, is not a stable element of musical production and therefore can never be relied on in performance. To me, being able to adjust to the tempo on each separate occasion is essential to one's sanity as a dancer, because no two conductors are alike. Expecting one tempo guarantees you won't get it.

I have danced fast *Symphony in C*'s and slow ones and hundreds in between; no two have ever been alike, and that is what is exciting about tempo. It is open to interpretation by the conductor (within certain confines), and it is the dancer's job to respond appropriately. One of Balanchine's most important innovations in dance was to declare—and insist—that music be the first priority to a dancer.

This law was truly revolutionary in a craft where so often the tempo is established by the dancers while the conductor merely tries to follow their needs and adjustments. In Balanchine's world the dancers were in service to him, but everyone, including him, was in service to the music. Even today this priority more than any other single element separates the New York City Ballet from other companies.

Three weeks after *Variations* premièred, the company unveiled another major Balanchine ballet. *Brahms-Schoenberg Quartet* was as melodious and romantic as the Stravinsky was not. Arnold Schoenberg's 1937 orchestration of Johannes Brahms' *First Piano Quartet* expanded the aural scope of this beautiful music, and the enlargement served Balanchine's purpose perfectly when he decided to choreograph a ballet to it. A huge production involving fifty-five dancers in four separate movements, *Brahms* is a forty-minute dance extravaganza performed before various draped Viennese backdrops by girls in long, luscious tutus designed by Karinska.

That Balanchine had been choreographing to both Brahms and Stravinsky in alternating rehearsals during this time was testimony to not only his enormous energy and range of musical knowledge but his physical discipline. Each season at least two new ballets were announced, and more often than not they were both by Balanchine.

The first section of *Brahms*, the Allegro, was led by Melissa Hayden, André Prokovsky, and Gloria Govrin; the Intermezzo was a gorgeous pas de deux for Patricia McBride and Conrad Ludlow; the Andante was led by Allegra Kent and Eddie Villella, and the last section, "Rondo alla Zingarese," by Jacques and myself. Dressed in full gypsy regalia of black and pink, streaming with colorful ribbons, I found the Rondo a harking back to my days as a super in *Carmen* with the Summer Opera in Cincinnati, and I flung myself with gusto into the hip-thrusting jauntiness, spinning turns, and silent repartee with Jacques.

As with *Variations*, there was a great deal of amusement in rehearsals as Balanchine demonstrated repeatedly for the corps of men just how to move with the energy and abandon of Hungarian gypsies. I will never forget this sixty-two-year-old man dressed in baggy gray pants, a cowboy shirt unbuttoned at the neck, and soft rubber shoes stomping around the studio with such youthful conviction, rhythmic energy, and polish that he easily outclassed everyone else in the room.

With this energetic example to emulate, Jacques and I turned the fourth movement of *Brahms* into a wild display of flamboyant yet elegant fun that always brought the house down—and often threatened to take us with it. Knowing that I could handle impromptu situations gave Jacques the freedom to do a great deal of throwing, flinging, and last-minute catching that gave the piece an effective atmosphere of danger. In one section of the movement after several big, leg-kicking lifts, I finished with some pirouettes, and Jacques needed to give me a little push to reverse my momentum so I could exit before his variation. Push came to shove on one occasion when the teasing and tantalizing ended up with me down on the apron of the stage with one arm falling over the footlights into the orchestra pit. It was an extremely close call. Taking advantage of the extra drama, I jumped up, gave Jacques a "woman-scorned" look, and slunk off. Mr. B, who had been watching in the audience, ran backstage. He was furious, and I had to "cover" for Jacques, saying that it was our mutual abandon that had conspired to throw me into the orchestra pit.

Playing it safe might have prevented a possible physical disaster, but it would have been a moral disaster if either of us had held back in our performance. Curious as it may sound, the fact that I ended up on the floor more often with Jacques than with any other partner was, to me, a sign of our success. Jacques' generosity as a dancer was something I learned a great deal from and rarely saw matched by anyone else. It was as if together we had a kind of silent conspiracy. As free as we were disciplined, we knew the two were not opposites but dependants. We were terrific sparring partners—everything depending on the moment.

Dancing with Jacques always involved maximum energy, but not always at such a flamboyant level. We developed the habit of doing warm-ups together backstage. Sometimes they were to warm up before a performance and sometimes they were for no reason other than to work. Often the area was dimly lit while the performance was going on and in the shadows we would hold on to the cold metal barre and count out endless pliés and tendus to the accompaniment of whatever music was being played or to our own silent counts. No one watched, no one expected anything, no one required applause.

A solitary barre also provided a chance to exercise one's discipline: while there was an angel on one shoulder offering the challenge, there was always the devil on the other shoulder saying, "Nobody's looking at you, so why not save it. Take it easy, do it tomorrow, do a little less." I played a kind of game with myself and acted "as if" someone were watching—my own conscience most likely—just as I walked down the street "as if" someone were watching. It is a most useful game for keeping spirits high while tricking the ever-present devil.

Brahms-Schoenberg Quartet garnered the usual bag of mixed reviews. When I was in a ballet, I was in no position to judge the judges, but as with *Don Quixote*, I was angry at the lukewarm reception and told George one day, "You know if I don't do anything else in my life, I'm going to prove to these people that this is a wonderful ballet." Surprised at my anger, he replied calmly, "Oh, dear, that's very sweet of you, but don't you worry about it. You can't be a one-woman army, and you can't change the world in a day. We are on another cloud." Despite the wise words, *Brahms* remained a real focal point in my life, another beautiful ballet added to my Balanchine crusade. I was determined to dance it so well that it would receive its due.

Although Balanchine always did all the casting for his ballets, he began around this time to ask me which ballets I would like to dance during a season. I marked the upcoming season's brochure, but because I loved all the roles I performed, and I performed so many I ended up circling everything. I decided that the exercise was one of courtesy more than anything else, so I learned to send the ball back to his court, asking him what ballets he would like to see me in.

I began to receive various offers to perform in Broadway shows and movies outside the company's jurisdiction, and I always took them to Mr. B, asking him what I should do. He would peruse the offers and then always say, "How much will they pay you? If it's a million dollars . . . well . . ." and his eyebrows would rise as he grinned. Of course, it was never a million dollars, and although he never said, "Don't do it," he did say, "Oh, dear, you don't need it." I didn't mind the fact that he always advised me against outside projects— my work with him was undeniably the most important thing—but I did sometimes think of the time he had spent in Hollywood in his youth, and I would have liked the same experience. But he was many years past that point in his life and had no interest in nostalgic experiments. He had learned what he had to learn and moved on; I caught him at a later stage.

Although I might have enjoyed making a movie, I didn't feel deprived that I hadn't. There was, however, one movie that Balanchine wanted me to be in, and it didn't pay anything close to a million dollars. Arrangements had been cobbled together to film a full-length color version of *A Midsummer Night's Dream,* and I was cast as Titania. This project, unlike most dance films, was intended not merely as a record of Balanchine's choreography; there were plans afoot for theatrical distribution by a major film company.

We shot the entire two-hour ballet in a studio warehouse on West 54th Street in ten days during a break between seasons in June of 1966. Because time and money were at a premium, we did virtually every scene in one take after an initial blocking rehearsal. This left some of us feeling pretty insecure about the results, but Balanchine seemed calm enough even after seeing the daily rushes, so we proceeded on schedule. Breaking an unwritten New York City Ballet rule, Balanchine asked me to wear the pearl necklace he had given me; this was, after all, the movies, and the law of no personal jewelry was not in effect.

After many thwarted plans the film finally opened at the Little

Carnegie Cinema over a year later. The reviews were good, but it
enjoyed only a brief run. A ballet film of Shakespeare's comedy was
not a high priority with the moviegoing public, which was flocking
to see Dustin Hoffman's performance in *The Graduate*.

During the first week of July 1966 the company traveled up the Hud-
son to Saratoga Springs, New York, to open our inaugural season at
the Saratoga Performing Arts Center in an enormous outdoor auditorium built on a beautiful grassy incline in the midst of Saratoga
State Park, surrounded by public golf courses, a swimming pool, old
mineral baths, and a wonderful little town already famous for its water
and its racetrack.

Company morale was high as we chose roommates and proceeded
to set up house together in little boxlike apartments at an unfinished
complex called the Ash Grove Farms. Those who could drive rented
cars to commute from theater to grocery store to home to swimming
pool, but those of us who couldn't drive were at the mercy of the
occasional bus or a lift from a friend. I asked Eddie Bigelow to teach
me to drive and began a summer of dancing and driving lessons, a
curious combination of transportation methods that has since become
almost a rite of passage for young company members.

We opened the three-week season with *Midsummer*, still fresh from
being filmed but now radically altered when danced with the real
moon and stars in the distance, the trickle of nearby running water,
real fireflies, dragonflies, and moths mixing themselves up with the
children in the ballet who were impersonating them, and the cool
night breezes. It was as if Balanchine had always intended this ballet
for this theater; the magic was palpable.

Because Balanchine was staying with Tanny in a small cottage out
at the farm owned by Richard Leach, who had been the founding
force behind the whole Saratoga Performing Arts complex, I saw less
of him than usual, although there was the occasional dinner *à quatre*
with Eddie and my roommate, Gail Crisa.

Gail was my age, but in every other way we were opposites. We
became good friends and usually roomed together on tour. Although
I never confided all my troubles to Gail, she knew enough about my
relationships with Roger and Mr. B to keep quiet, and I relied on her
discretion.

One week after opening in Saratoga, Balanchine, Arthur Mitchell,
and I were back in New York City for a single performance of two
new Balanchine ballets. A Stravinsky Festival was to be held at the
new Philharmonic Hall directly across the plaza from the State Theater
at Lincoln Center, and Balanchine had been asked by Lukas Foss, the

Festival's director, to choreograph some balletic diversions for the evening. Balanchine was limited by the fact that his designs would have to fit in front of the orchestra on the small apron of the wooden concert stage, but he was a man who could work miracles while accommodating less-than-ideal circumstances.

It was to be the first evening at the new concert hall devoted entirely to Stravinsky's compositions, and to commemorate the occasion Balanchine chose two pieces of music that he was not only familiar with but had choreographed several times before. *Ragtime,* a jaunty, jazzy romp for Arthur and myself, had enjoyed a previous life six years earlier in a dance made for Diana Adams and Bill Carter. The second work on the program was a viola solo entitled *Élégie-Elegy.* This represented the ballet's third reincarnation. It was to have a fourth fifteen years later in 1982 as one of the very last ballets Balanchine made.

In the 1966 version he pared the earlier versions down to a solo for me, retaining the notion of dancing in one place under a spotlight. This proved a useful idea given the Philharmonic's limited space. The dance itself was completely untechnical in nature, full of caressing, sad, yearning arm movements and evocative poses, a kind of universal, all-embracing image of mourning. (The 1982 version was even smaller in scale, with me kneeling on the floor in very personal gestures denoting what to me had become a very personal grief—for Balanchine, for myself, and for us both.) My costume in 1966 was a reproduction of my *Meditation* dress, only black. Although the color was appropriate to the subject, I found it strange to be dressed in black by Balanchine. It was the first of only two occasions when he thought of me in black. With very few but significant exceptions he dressed me in white for twenty years—he would always explain that white costumes complemented my pale complexion.

Mother attended the Philharmonic Stravinsky evening, and while she was talking with Mr. B after the performance he told her that he wanted me to dance *Élégie* at his funeral. He never mentioned it to me, but in telling my mother he knew I would hear of it, which I did, with great trepidation. I didn't like to think about his death; he seemed more alive to me than anyone else, but I consoled myself by deciding as I had before that he would probably outlive my performing career.

Two weeks later, back in Saratoga, I was out of mourning and in a white bikini, not at the local pool (I would never have worn anything so revealing in real life) but onstage.

Bugaku, designed in 1963 for Allegra Kent and Eddie Villella, was undoubtedly one of Balanchine's most provocative ballets, in which he had made elaborate and intricate experiments using Allegra's exceptionally loose and languid limbs. It was my first experience with such an overt display of sheer stretch, and in hindsight I see that it was the first time Balanchine cast me in what was clearly a sexy role.

I danced this ceremonial Japanese-style ballet with Eddie Villella, and the fact that he was much shorter than I, especially when I was on pointe, served Balanchine's purpose. *Bugaku* was designed very specifically around the formidable tension between a muscular, virile, and earthy male presence and a soft, delicate, but extremely flexible female one.

The center of the ballet is a long, intimate, and stunning pas de deux in which the male dancer molds and shapes his partner into physical positions of the most extreme nature. Predictably, the ballet was hailed by the critics as a ritualized wedding ceremony and consummation. But, whatever his purpose at the time, Mr. B repeatedly explained to me that *Bugaku* was *not* intended to be a wedding celebration.

But after telling me what it was not, he did not tell me what it was. The music, especially commissioned from Toshiro Mayuzumi by the company, had slow rumbling drums and percussive pulses, but the overriding sensation was of instruments being extended past their intended abilities. As I tried to match these straining climaxes physically, the question became, how stretchy can you get? The answer was as stretchy as you could . . . or dared. In other words, the apparent sexual tension in the ballet was not something conjured in the performer's mind, it was in the music.

Bugaku was the first ballet in which I was called "sexy." This caused literally howls of laughter at home, where I was still called Bean on occasion. I consider sex in ballets a very delicate subject. It was also one of Balanchine's primary touchstones—the profundity of physical connections was, after all, the subject of his craft, and he was a specialist—and part of his genius was undoubtedly his ability to treat something so personal, so intimate, and so universal with such raw and yet spiritual implication.

If a step or movement is played only for its sexual suggestiveness, it immediately becomes something other than itself, and the result is a limitation. If, on the other hand, the step or movement is given its full musical and physical value without the trappings of a specific intention, sexual or otherwise, its power can be limitless—it will suggest to some, it will comfort others, and while it may provoke one person, it may be a beautiful image to another. I have never believed in foreshortening any movement's options by imposing one's own experience on it. If there is eroticism in the music and the movement, it will speak for itself; if the dancer chooses to emphasize this aspect, it is the beginning of vulgarity.

.   .   .

Directly after Saratoga the company embarked on a two-and-a-half-week tour to Washington, D.C., followed by our annual visit to the Ravinia Festival outside of Chicago, where I had danced my first Dark Angel in *Serenade*. Mr. B did not come on the tour but left for Europe on business and to get some rest. Since Roger had vanished, we had drifted back to comfort and closeness, and now we wrote to each other frequently.

My twenty-first birthday came while George was away, and it seemed to take on great significance for him. He repeatedly reminded me of it:

> Dear Suzi,
>   Just received your letter. I am so pleased that you like yourself in the picture. [The company had been invited to a private screening of the edited *Midsummer* film.] This encourages me to praise you as a dancer again. After all, you have agreed with me that you are not so bad. You also should say that I am not prejudiced. You probably did not receive my telegram wishing you happy birthday. I did not know the address and wired to North Shore Hotel, Chicago. Stupid!!! [We were staying in Evanston just outside of Chicago, but I got the telegram anyway.] Here in Paris, I went to church where you used to go, near St. Anne Hotel, and as I entered on the left side there was a little chapel of St. Suzanne—how strange! I've placed two candles wishing for your two knees be well. Please rest well after your hard work. Let your knees and feet be quiet for awhile. Let your brain work—read *War and Peace*. God bless you.
>   Love, George
> P.S. Do you have room for two more? [He had sent a clipping of two little kittens.]

My knees were not especially bad at this time, but ever since the Russian tour Mr. B had known that they were potentially my weakest joints—most dancers' bodies have a vulnerable spot, if not two—and he was always concerned for them.

Knees aside, I was becoming increasingly stronger as a dancer, more in control, more familiar with my own abilities and more aware of how to use stage space. Brute strength for a female ballet dancer is virtually useless; technical knowledge, femininity, facility, and experience are her real strengths. Because I danced so often in so many ballets, I sometimes teased Mr. B that I was his truck driver, and this comment inspired a humorous poem, sent from Paris, dedicated to me "in recognition of your service to me as a truck driver." The verse

was rather risqué, and it was signed "Lord George B." I thought
perhaps it was to commemorate my coming of age, and I was flattered,
but I hid the letter and blushed when I thought of it.

Whatever George may have been thinking or wishing privately
because I had turned twenty-one, his deepest feelings, as always,
emerged in his work, and the next ballet he used me for was anything
but a sexual invitation. "Diamonds" was a foray into his Imperial
Russian heritage in all its austere, crystalline beauty, and there he
put a crown on my head and gave me a consort—but not a king.
Balanchine often explained that in the world he guarded that was the
way life should be between men and women.

Sometime in the early months of 1967 he told me about his plans
to make a full-evening ballet based on precious gems—no story, only
an evocation of the gems. Just as Balanchine loved to feed his dancers
champagne and caviar and clothe them in fine perfume and French
silk, now he wanted to cover us with precious stones. *Jewels* was a
landmark ballet for many reasons. Its popularity with the public made
it worth its weight in gold at the box office; it gave many dancers
roles that made them glitter as never before; and it contained choreography of dizzying variance, wicked wit, and shattering poi-
gnancy. It became famous as the first full-length plotless ballet.

Originally Balanchine had chosen four gems upon which to set the
ballet—Emeralds, Sapphires, Rubies, and Diamonds—but a Sapphire
section was dropped because the ballet would have been too long,
and perhaps he couldn't decide on any "blue" music. For the first
section, "Emeralds," he had chosen the quiet, moving strains of Ga-
briel Fauré; for "Rubies," Stravinsky's bright, bouncy *Capriccio*, and
for "Diamonds," Tschaikovsky's majestic and passionate *Symphony
No. 3.*

Mr. B asked if I would like to be a Ruby or a Diamond, but, like
his questions about what ballets I would prefer to dance and, later,
whom I would prefer to dance with, I think this was a gesture of
courtesy, not a real question. He had already decided that I would
be a Diamond—clear, cool, hard, and lasting, but also a mysterious
prism that reflects the entire spectrum. "Diamonds" was the last
section of *Jewels* and the only tutu ballet Balanchine ever made on
me. It was unusual that he was making one at all at this time; more
and more his medium required either the starkness of practice clothes
or the soft femininity of long chiffon dresses. But "Diamonds," like
Ballet Imperial and *Theme and Variations* (both made in the 1940s),
represents Tschaikovsky in his grandest manner and requires the
classicism of a crisp tutu and a glittering tiara. Again, like the two
other aristocratic Russian ballets, "Diamonds" brought out Balan-

chine's own grand manner, derived from Petipa and the czarist court, where propriety, hierarchy, and impeccable manners ruled the occasion with ceremonious conviction. "Diamonds" represents Balanchine's last excursion into the world of large-scale tutu formality; perhaps it was his final word on the subject, or perhaps he had already used all the music he thought appropriate to it.

Although *Jewels* is without story, it is not without motifs, and I have always felt that the thread that connects the three gems is woven by walking. Each of the three sections makes a statement about a very specific style of walking—"Rubies" tips the scale at one end with a turned-in, cocky kind of strut, a Stravinskian strut; "Emeralds" has a low, delicate walk marked by a slow, underwater weightiness, a very French allure; while "Diamonds" tips the scale at the opposite end with a proud, high, exposed kind of prance, like a Russian thoroughbred.

"Diamonds" opened with a beautiful waltz for twelve girls, followed by a long pas de deux for Jacques and me, a scherzo, and finally a polonaise with sixteen couples. Despite Balanchine's limitless imagination on the matter of getting from one place to another, when we began working on the pas de deux he couldn't decide how Jacques and I would enter. "You know, I really don't know how I'm going to start this, so we won't waste time on it," he announced. Memories of *Meditation* and trouble with entrances to Tschaikovsky filled my mind. As before, Mr. B said, "Let's skip it and pretend you're already in." Being "in" meant being on center stage for the beginning of the pas de deux. Jacques immediately dropped to one knee, and, grasping his hand, I extended a leg high to the side. The slow diagonal entrance that became such a harbinger of what was to follow was not fixed until the whole pas de deux was already set. Once again, Balanchine worked backward with great foresight.

As in *Meditation* and *Don Quixote*, I begin this diagonal, my first entrance in the ballet, from the stage right back wing, and I was beginning to feel that this lonely, faraway wing had my name engraved on it somewhere. Jacques entered from the opposite front corner, and to the very quiet sound of a single French horn we approached each other with the simplest of walks, laced with courtly intricacies. It was very difficult to make an entrance with great ceremony and yet no steps, no technical fireworks with which to catch the audience's attention. One somehow had to produce an atmosphere full of almost eerie foreshadowing that would make them sit on the edge of their seats even though very little was happening physically.

This entrance was a great lesson to me in dancing without dancing, in being interesting without steps, in being alone with a single sound instead of the aural comfort of a full orchestra. Presence would have to be everything. Contrary to what I had expected, the lonely horn did not encourage me to retreat or emphasize the loneliness onstage. It made me want to fill the void, but I was given nothing with which to fill it—except an overwhelming feeling of vulnerability. That is probably what Balanchine had in mind.

Perhaps it was because the diagonal was tacked on at the last minute that it had a real sense of mystery about it; I felt like an oracle, prophesying what was to come and whence it came. At one point I did a certain step and finished with a leg and an arm in a position that prompted Mr. B to say, "Wonderful, you look like an arrow shooting through the air." This was a comment, not a command or even a request, but the image stuck in my mind, and the "arrow" started working its way, unforced and unchoreographed, into the pas de deux. At another moment I was upstage left in sous-sous on pointe, about to run toward Jacques across the stage, and knowing what a beautiful headpiece I would be wearing, I thought, "I'll model my headpiece," and held one hand gently to the back of my head with the other arm extended as if I had just shot an arrow from my invisible bow.

Had Balanchine objected to these details, he would have said so. He said nothing, and that was enough of a nod for me. Mr. B set the parameters of the movement, sometimes with great detail and sometimes without any detail, and within those limits he allowed for enormous freedom not only of movement but of spirit. I think sometimes he was grateful not to have to spend precious time deciding which arm should be up when it was not something that really mattered. Moving with conviction, shape, and energy were his concerns.

In gorgeous contrast to the various images of support, presentation, separation, and reconciliation between Jacques and me was a turning sequence of great visual and musical beauty. Technically the steps consisted of two inside pirouettes stepping directly into two outside pirouettes on the other foot, ending in supported attitude front and then switching immediately to attitude back with my face and one arm raised upward. After a building tremolo, the music reaches a climax and ends almost in silence with a haunting echo following in its wake. Sometimes I finished my turns on the music and let the echo follow me, sometimes I became the echo, sometimes I was both. In other words, "musicality" to me was not defined by hitting the turns and finishing on any specific climactic notes, but in shaping the physical sequence into the musical one in any number of legitimate or even illegitimate ways. But there was always one connecting factor:

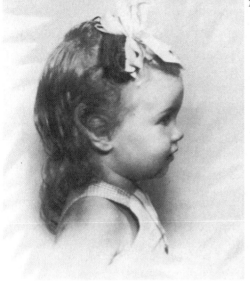

At two

As Clara in The Nutcracker *with the Ballet Russe, 1955*

My mother, Donna, with me on her lap, my father, Robert, with Beverly, and Donna (Sug) standing

4

"Oh, dear, you let me be the judge." ▶

My first tutu—I'm twelve years old, with John Lankston in Cincinnati

Mme. Doubrovska teaching the first Ford Foundation Group at the School of American Ballet ▼

6

7

After the première of Meditation, *1963, with Jacques
d'Amboise, the only time he
ever wore this costume*

5

The Don and Dulcinea

Left to right: Sir Frederick ▲
Ashton, me, George, Margot
Fonteyn, Rudolph Nureyev at a
party, 1965

With George in Rome

Christmas decorations:
George holding Top, me
with Bottom, and Bev

14

15

▲ *Choreographing*
Slaughter on Tenth
Avenue, *with Arthur*
Mitchell

At the Saratoga Race
Track with Oklahoma
Trail and unknown
rider—a publicity sho
for Jewels

Watching a rehearsal

A Midsummer Night's Dream: *Oberon, Edward Villella, receiving instructions from Mr. B; Conrad Ludlow behind me*

Paul and me at our wedding reception

Cooking in Brussels with Top, Middle, and Bottom

With Maurice Béjart at Brussels' customs

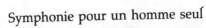

21

As "The Young Girl in Rose" in
Nijinsky—Clown of God

With Jorge Donn in Bhakti

22

23

24

25

26

Island living . . . and dancing

Cinderella and friends, 1981

27

Meditation *with Adam Lüders, 1981*

"Diamonds" with Peter Martins

Mozartiana

Revisiting Van Cleef and Arpels, Paris

In Memory of . . . *with Joe Duell and Adam*

With Adam in **Davids-bündlertänze**—*the only moment in the ballet that he and I meet*

Going to dinner with Larisa
Lezhniná, Alexander Kurkov,
Elliott Erwitt, Toni Bentley, and
Yuri Zhukov

34

After Scotch Symphony *with Elena
Pankova*

35

36

Leningrad, 1989

Vienna Waltzes *with Adam*

With Lincoln Kirstein, November 26, 1989

37

38

in dancing one is in the energy business, and music is the senior
partner. Sound is not music's sole attribute, it has an energy of its
own, and sometimes that energy requires more time. I think it is this
interaction and respect for the music that binds a dancer inside it,
forming a true musical movement.

The "Diamonds" pas de deux is one of the most beautiful Balanchine ever made, supremely classical in style, epic in scope, ritualized
in manner, and yet in the midst of its unmistakable grandeur there
lurks immense sweetness and vulnerability. Tschaikovsky was certainly Balanchine's accomplice in evoking this indescribable atmosphere of quietly controlled passion, but it was Balanchine who
devised the form. In some ways the entire dance could be viewed as
the buildup to one of the simplest yet most breathtaking final moments in a dance between a man and a woman.

Throughout the previous ten minutes there had been a glorious
blend of victory and surrender between Jacques and me, of leading
and following, initiating and receiving. It is a dance full of the paradoxical tensions between a man and a woman, but its beauty lies,
not in rivalry but in submission; "Diamonds" is about the majesty of
service and the glory of humility. And so Balanchine had Jacques
drop to one knee beside me in the final pose and, with head bowed,
kiss my hand.

That Balanchine spent his life building pedestals for his ballerinas
to stand on is no secret, and although some might protest the position
as one of inequality, no one who has been there has ever complained.
It is the most humbling and beautiful place I have ever been. Balanchine was a feminist long before it was the fashion: he devoted his
life to celebrating female independence. Some years later, Arlene
Croce, the esteemed dance critic and author, described this quality
most eloquently:

> If George Balanchine were a novelist or a playwright or a movie
> director instead of a choreographer, his studies of women would
> be among the most influential artistic achievements of our
> time. . . . Of course the autonomy of the ballerina is an illusion,
> but Farrell's is the extremest form of this illusion we have yet
> seen, and it makes "Diamonds" a riveting spectacle about the
> freest woman alive.

That illusion of "the freest woman alive" was a vision of possibility
Balanchine gave to all of us—not only those who saw his ballets, but
those who danced them as well.

Paradoxically, this independence could incorporate and transcend the support and strength of a man; a partner enabled movements not possible alone, and this is why, to Balanchine, a male dancer's nobility was not to be found in bravura pyrotechnics but in the self-effacement of supporting a woman on pointe. Male dancers have a long and illustrious history of egotistical preoccupation, and it was one of Balanchine's most difficult jobs to find and teach men to dance with a woman not in spite of her but for their mutual glory.

This is a sophisticated concept of service, and I feel that dancers like Jacques who dared, while all the world was applauding the charisma of a Russian defector, to trust Balanchine with not only their careers but their egos were true pioneers. Moral leaps reach even further forward, in time and space, than physical ones.

The scherzo, which immediately follows the pas de deux in "Diamonds," has a number of very fast entrances by four demi-soloist girls and boys and the two principals. It was here that Jacques had several short but action-packed solo dances full of big jumps and turns, and I developed the habit of watching his consecutive à la seconde turns from the back wing and betting on him; offstage betting (OSB) was not illegal. "If he pulls in and does a good pirouette finish," I would say to myself, "I'll have a good performance." I believed in betting on my partners; they were risking as much as I was, although this particular gamble didn't come until the ballet was almost over. These games I played with myself weren't superstition, they were sources of renewed energy.

There is very little in the way of excitement and glamour that can equal Balanchine and Tschaikovsky in a polonaise, and "Diamonds" proved no exception. With the girls in long white gloves and the addition of sixteen boys, the stage was filled with the blinding glitter of not only scenery and costumes laden with rhinestones but the sheer exaltation of thirty-four bodies moving with the precision of a Russian court presentation. In the midst of all these interweaving bodies I took center stage in a simple arabesque penché and Jacques promenaded me around in two slow circles. It was as if we were the central stone in a mammoth setting, and this moment epitomized one of Balanchine's choreographic jewels. It was his wisdom about energy contrasts that shaped the moment: while all the other dancers were generating enormous power with their movements, Jacques and I were quietly understating the moment and the music, almost oblivious to the whirling dancers around us. Mr. B had been focusing in class on our hands, he wanted to see each individual finger separated from its neighbor, and I took this opportunity, while in the penché with one arm extended before me, to model my little finger for him. Perhaps no one else noticed, but that didn't matter; it was a tiny detail that I knew he, standing in the front wing, would see. "This is for George,"

I would say to myself, relishing this silent covenant between us.

Immediately following, as the music built slowly, Jacques and I backed up and joined everyone else on stage for the grand tableau before the final pose. It was here that I said to myself, in time to the music, "Thank you, Mr. Tschaikovsky."

Jewels enjoyed immediate success. Mr. B was friendly with M. Arpels of Van Cleef & Arpels, and, in a mutually profitable publicity heist, I went with George to the Fifth Avenue jewelry store one day in full makeup with my gloriously studded "Diamonds" tutu in a plastic bag. The store was closed and the glass cases were opened. While cameras clicked away, George and M. Arpels threw priceless jewelry at me. They even took the crowns of Empress Josephine and the Czarina out of the vault and put them on my head. We were like children locked in a candy store. It was enormously amusing as each master eyed his work—George would say, "Look at her, look how wonderful she looks," while M. Arpels agreed, "Yes, look at that setting of diamonds and sapphires, what a magnificent setting."

In "Diamonds" Balanchine had placed me, in a great public ceremony, on a pedestal where I felt humbled and also physically removed, even from him. The ballet was not intended to separate us privately, but, as with *Don Quixote*, it left me feeling idealistic, not realistic.

CHAPTER TEN

Traveling Steps

J ewels had its world première on April 13, 1967, and two days later I danced another role for the first time, the "Sanguinic" section of Hindemith's *The Four Temperaments*. It was a ballet that, for one reason or another, I was to dance very rarely, perhaps only twenty times in my whole career. The last time was twelve years later when Mr. B awakened in the hospital after heart surgery and called the ballet mistress, saying that he had had a dream and I must dance "Sanguinic" again. I did, although Mr. B was not there to see it; but he obviously already had.

Four days after the first performance of *Jewels*, the New York State Theater was host to another première, not of a new ballet but of a new medium for ballet. A huge white screen was spread across the stage, and as the lights were lowered, the movie version of *A Midsummer Night's Dream* had its first public screening.

George seemed very pleased with the whole project, and while I was happy that he was happy, what I saw on the screen bothered me. It did not look the way I felt when I was dancing, and I realized that dance on film is at best an entertaining record of a ballet's logistics, at worst a serious misrepresentation, physically and otherwise.

Wearing my first offstage Karinska evening dress—a long, close-fitting, strapless black gown with a blue silk lining and the requisite bust pads—I attended the gala première escorted by George. Other friendships were not really possible for me, given the high ratio of jealousy in my situation not only from George but from other female dancers. I realized that the isolation was my choice: I had chosen to be a dancer, and being interesting to Balanchine was a full-time occupation. At the time I had neither complaints nor resentments; I accepted it as simply the way my life was. In retrospect, I realize that the fact that I had no outside points of reference meant that I made various important decisions in a social vacuum.

George was not only my date in a romantic sense but also almost my only friend. He was not, I hasten to add, a confidant—only God and Girl knew all my thoughts—but he was a pal, and, curiously, we shared a mutual interest in playing games with only one player. We both began the day in our respective apartments with a cup of coffee and several games of solitaire, and we both liked to solve a crossword puzzle between rehearsals at the theater. These pastimes gave the comforting illusion that problems were solvable . . . at least some problems. On occasion, before a performance, I would raise the stakes and become unusually competitive by playing six different games of solitaire in a prescribed order; if four were successful it meant I would have a good performance. I doubt that George indulged in such "if" games, but perhaps he did.

I spent more hours with George than with any other person. We had class, rehearsals, coffee breaks, costume fittings, conversations, performances, and dinners together. We did everything but sleep together. Sometime during the spring of 1967 George moved into a rented studio apartment near Lincoln Center, and we began to have breakfast together. Stopping by the Tip Toe Inn on the way down from 76th Street early in the morning, I'd pick up a cheese Danish for George and go over to his apartment for coffee before walking with him across the plaza to the theater.

His studio was bright and cheerful, with a nice view, but the furniture consisted of only the basic necessities; it was certainly not set up for my benefit. Typically, I found out only after the fact that George had moved. And typically, there was still never any discussion between us of the whole situation.

Now that he lived alone, George had more time to be with me. He would often take me to dinner at some of New York's most fashionable restaurants, like Le Cirque, the Oak Room at the Plaza, and the Russian Tea Room, where it was guaranteed that we would be seen and end up in a gossip column. I think he was proud of me, and I was proud of him, and we were proud to be together.

Other people, however, were decidedly distraught. I overheard complaints by other dancers: "When Suzanne's finished dancing, Mr. B waits outside her dressing room and then they go out to dinner while the rest of us go on with the performance." I cannot deny that this happened on occasion, but more often than not I was in the last ballet, so frequently we were the last people to leave the theater. When I wasn't, I tried to remedy the situation by taking a long time getting out of my costume and makeup and dressing. I would tell George that when I was ready I'd meet him in the first wing.

Eventually I confronted him. "George, don't you think we should stay for the rest of the performance?" He had also heard the complaint, and he was not a man who liked having his actions questioned. "You know, dear," he replied, "I give them a company, I give them ballets, I give them rehearsals, I give them class if they want to come. I already give them everything." Aside from the fact that I wasn't about to challenge him, what he said made a certain amount of sense to me. At least I needed it to for my peace of mind.

When we were together I would tease him on a related subject. "If I weren't a dancer," I said, "you wouldn't look at me twice." "And if I weren't a choreographer," he agreed, "you wouldn't look at me twice," and we would both laugh and take a good long look at each other.

In late August of 1967 I danced for the first time with an unexpected partner. Following the company's annual visit to Ravinia, a small group of us traveled with Balanchine to Europe to perform for six days at the Edinburgh Festival in Scotland. It was the first time I ever saw or danced with Peter Martins, who was to become the most important partner of my later career. At the time I did not consider a future alliance, especially since Peter was then a member of the Royal Danish Ballet and was not Balanchine-trained. Balanchine, with his usual foresight, thought otherwise.

Because the festival provided a wonderful opportunity for prestigious European exposure, Mr. B agreed to forego his usual democratic dogma about touring—if anyone tours, everyone tours—and only about twenty-five dancers traveled. Nevertheless, the programs were ambitious: *Agon, Bugaku, Tarantella, Donizetti Variations,* the second movement of *Brahms-Schoenberg Quartet, Meditation, Movements, Concerto Barocco,* and *Apollo*—a composite Balanchine festival.

When, at the last minute, Jacques was injured, the schedule was immediately altered: I danced *Meditation* with Conrad Ludlow, and *Movements* was replaced by *Ragtime* and my solo from *Variations.* I danced at least three of the five ballets every night, and *Apollo* was scheduled for each performance. Balanchine was determined not to cancel it despite Jacques' absence. John Taras, who often scouted for Balanchine, flew to Denmark to take a look at the Royal Danish Ballet's youngest Apollo, and after a series of long-distance phone calls Balanchine agreed to import the twenty-year-old dancer for one of his most subtle and poetic male roles. Peter had never even met Balanchine. There was risk on all sides, but Mr. B remained calm throughout the entire experiment.

Until this time I had danced Terpsichore only to Jacques' Apollo, but as long as Mr. B was there to oversee everything the prospect of seeing an unfamiliar face and body opposite me did not cause me great consternation. I simply had one extra problem to be aware of along with the small raked stage and the marathon programs—there would be a big blond at the end of my finger instead of Jacques. But the dynamic was altered as I immediately became the ballet's knowledgeable veteran, a job that had always belonged to Jacques. We had only one day to rehearse before the first performance, and it was devoted mostly to compromising, musically and technically, between Peter's and Balanchine's slightly different renditions of the ballet. As the week proceeded we had more rehearsals where Mr. B began to take Peter's performance apart and then reassemble it.

No major mishap occurred during the first performance, which under the circumstances was probably remarkable. Mr. B was pleased, and that was the extent of my emotion at the time about my new partner, except that I was grateful to him for making it possible to do *Apollo* and for putting himself on the high wire without a net by dancing for Balanchine.

Peter and I communicated primarily through movement, with little verbal discussion. Technically and rhythmically we had some very different notions about Stravinsky's music. There were also physical adjustments to be made: his arms were longer than Jacques', so I had to change my reach accordingly, and the way I fit into the crook of his hips, his shoulder blades, and torso was different, but a good fit nevertheless. We had a mutual preoccupation with becoming physically compatible, not a bad way to learn about a partner. I did not think, "Here is the partner of my dreams." He was more like a new part of the wall I had to scale to reach Mount Olympus. I didn't even think about how handsome he was. And he was very handsome.

Mr. B, on the other hand, was probably much more aware of the interesting visual impact that Peter and I made together (as part of the picture, neither Peter nor I was able to be objective) and, while he said nothing at the time, he proceeded to ask Peter to be a guest artist with the company in New York the following winter. Over the course of the next few months we danced together in *The Nutcracker*, *Liebeslieder Walzer*, and "Diamonds."

With Jacques becoming increasingly vulnerable to injury, Balanchine, as an expert and practical company director, saw the potential in Peter—as a dancer and as a partner for me. Our physical attributes complemented each other long before our temperaments did—his heroic head, broad shoulders, and huge hands were encompassing, creating a very secure and romantic dancing environment for me as well as the audience, and I responded with a somewhat bolder and more daring approach to movement.

Following the week in Scotland, the company had a layoff period, and while most of the dancers returned to the States, George and I flew to Paris. George justified this by explaining that the visit would be at least in part work-related—and he certainly did spend many afternoons meeting with various European contacts—and that my presence would be helpful in doing publicity for the *Midsummer Night's Dream* movie.

Ultimately, of course, it was to be a nostalgic return to the city where he had first courted me openly. I was now twenty-two, and perhaps George thought Paris might encourage the personal side of our romance. It did—we had a wonderful time eating, walking, lighting candles in churches—but we had separate rooms, and though we spent all day and all evening together, I had my café au lait in my room alone each morning. If George would have liked it otherwise, he only occasionally pressured me. Between his marriage, his paying for my trip (which I could not have afforded), and the "work-related" justification, my conscience would have been unable to cope

if we had had a physical affair. Perhaps I was still as backward as
ever, but I was not about to risk everything—my career, my relationship with George, our work, and my sanity—on an impulsive
Parisian escapade.

This time in Paris proved to be the calm before the storm because,
within a few months, it became clear that even though George was
patient with me, everyone else was becoming increasingly impatient.
A private private life was a fantasy, I suppose, in a world where so
many people depended on Balanchine not only for their work but for
their emotional sustenance. Nevertheless, I think that at times we
both hoped, like ordinary people struggling through a personal life,
that it might be possible. It wasn't.

Immediately after the Edinburgh season, Pat Neary abruptly left
the company. She made no secret of the fact that I was the cause of
her departure, declaring that Balanchine's favoritism to me left no
room for any other dancer to progress.

By late October the company was back rehearsing in New York
before going to Chicago for a week of performances. Opening night
was a gala benefit of *A Midsummer Night's Dream* in which I danced
Titania, and the performance was followed by a champagne party
which, as was now customary, I attended with George. As usual, we
clinked glasses, made toasts, mingled with patrons, and had our
photos taken doing so. Two days later the *Chicago Sun-Times* ran a
photo of George and me with the caption: "Miss Farrell, who dances
the role of Titania in the New York City Ballet's *A Midsummer Night's
Dream*, is engaged to Mr. Balanchine." The accompanying article elab-
orated on what was truly news to me:

> George Balanchine, choreographer of the New York City Ballet,
> and ballerina Suzanne Farrell confirmed it at the champagne
> party at the Pick-Congress that followed the opening at the Au-
> ditorium Theater: They'll wed shortly. Miss Farrell will thus
> become the sixth Mrs. Balanchine. And George is maintaining
> his strict policy of marrying only ballerinas. All five wives, in-
> cluding Chicago's Maria Tallchief Paschen, were dancers.

There was that list again with me at the end of it. It was as if I were
simply the next fateful incident in the cosmic pattern of George Balanchine's many lives. I was hurt, and I was furious. George was still
married; he wasn't even free.

Later that morning when I went to the theater, no one, not George,
not Gail, not other dancers, not the stagehands, not the administrative
staff, said a word about the article. At the time I was too angry to

bring it up with George. When he made no attempt to deny the rumor, I felt even more cornered. It occurred to me that he had regarded the pearl ring he had given me as an engagement ring, although I never did. It was as if everyone knew something about me I didn't know. I was even afraid to show the article to Mother; she would have thoroughly approved of it.

Shortly after this I decided again to try to put a little distance between George and myself. Things between us were becoming more convoluted and more difficult, with no resolution in sight. I told George one night at dinner that I thought it would be best if we didn't have dinner together anymore and limited our relationship to the studio, where the turmoil was absent. He was very upset, although he probably took some solace in the knowledge that this was not prompted by the presence of another man in my life. There wasn't anyone, and he knew it. But I was trying to grow up, and maybe that was more dangerous.

Mr. B started losing weight, and the management became worried about him—he was sixty-three and in generally good health, but with so many lives depending on him and so many people who cared about him, he was closely watched. A member of the staff approached me and said, "Mr. B's so thin, we're worried about him. Do you know what's wrong?" and I confessed that we had not been going out together (they knew this already) and then, to my astonishment, it was suggested to me, in no uncertain terms, that I see him again, take him to dinner, and make him happy.

The company had been all too aware of the ups and downs of George's relationship with me, and if his mood was affected, everyone felt affected. This was made most apparent to me one day when one of the company's more prominent male dancers suggested a solution to the current tension. "Why don't you just sleep with him? It doesn't have to mean anything. Is it such a big deal?" I was deeply shocked. I had never thought of sex in that way; my life would certainly have been simpler if I could have.

At this point, the whole situation may start to seem slightly surreal. For me, at the age of twenty-two, it certainly was. My engagement to Balanchine was announced in the papers. He never denied it to the press—either because he felt it was understood in some way between us, or because he didn't choose to dignify the rumor. I didn't deny it to the press either—because it would never have occurred to me to speak to the world at large except through Balanchine or the company.

I expected to be taken care of, but I resented the form that care sometimes took. I loved Balanchine, and I wanted him to love me in the same way—at least not to *not* love me. I was flattered by his attentions, personal and professional, yet I wasn't prepared to face the consequences of where those attentions might lead. I'm not convinced, even to this day, that he was, either.

And we never talked about any of it. Maybe we both knew there was no rational, painless solution to the dilemma—that any talk might upset the delicate balance which allowed the ideal of our collaboration on stage to continue.

I did, however, comply with the suggestion about having dinner with George again, but not without feeling that this outside interference was unfair. By Christmastime George had gained a few pounds and was over at our apartment decorating the tree (he thought that Bottom should replace the star at the top), exchanging gifts, and having a jam session at the piano with Bev. I was happy to have the tension of the last few weeks relaxed, although everyone else seemed a little happier than I was about this purely cosmetic solution.

Several weeks before the new year, George and I were having dinner after performance at La Comédie, our favorite neighborhood French restaurant near Lincoln Center. The maître d', who knew us well and was grateful for our late-night business, invited us to spend New Year's Eve at his restaurant. They were planning a celebration with hats, noisemakers, champagne, and piano music. To my great surprise George thought it was a wonderful idea and booked a table for two.

It was to be our first New Year's Eve together, but I was startled at George's enthusiasm, knowing that because of certain memories he found this time of year painful and was apt to become maudlin. I had little enthusiasm for the excitement about New Year's myself and was always glad to dance in *The Nutcracker* performance that evening and then go home to bed.

New Year's always reminded me of the first time I was allowed to stay up as a child. I was ten years old, and Mother, perhaps because she knew it was the last time my father would be there for the holidays, gave in to my pleadings to stay awake for the magic moment. It was traditional for all the neighborhood families to gather in their front yards wearing funny hats and at midnight to set off fireworks, blow bugles, horns, and the colorful paper noisemakers that roll out like snakes. Not having the money to buy these special instruments, we used our old aluminum pots and pans, and I will never forget smashing my two lids together while looking over at my mother hitting a metal spoon against the burned bottom of a crooked saucepan. I was crying, and never again did I want New Year's to mean anything. Nevertheless, George and I dressed up and went to La Comédie, and at midnight the lights went out, and, wearing masks, we went through the motions of celebration. At least we had real paper noisemakers.

Within a few weeks there was genuine excitement when we premièred a very experimental new ballet. The company had danced the previous July in Montreal at Expo '67, and Balanchine, touring the various exhibitions, first heard the "music" of the Greek mathematical composer Iannis Xenakis. It was played in conjunction with a light show that structurally mimicked the sounds, and I think that idea intrigued Mr. B. Xenakis' *Mestastaseis & Pithoprakta* consisted of sixty-one different sounds each made by a different orchestra member. Balanchine's ballet *Mestastaseis* had twenty-eight dancers dressed in white, forming a huge mass that altered its form through appropriate motions with the accompanying sounds.

Pithoprakta had Arthur Mitchell and me with a corps of twelve dressed in black. With my hair loose and parted on one side, and wearing a white-and-gold fringed bikini, I danced a pas de deux with Arthur, who was bare-chested and wore sparkling long trousers. The motif of the dance was that we barely ever actually touched; but, as was often the case, this had come about by accident. Before the première we had filmed our dance as a record of the choreography, but because Arthur was unable to be there I danced the pas de deux alone. Mr. B thought this looked interesting, and when Arthur returned he told him only to pretend to partner me; thus our interactions took on an alienated tone. The première on January 18 was greeted with both cheers and boos, but despite rave reviews the ballet lasted only a few seasons, largely because the music was so difficult for the orchestra to play.

Ten days later I was in another of Balanchine's experimental works, only this one was forty years old and was considered one of his enduring masterpieces. *Prodigal Son* tells the story of the fall and redemption of the biblical character, and its recent revival had provided Edward Villella with one of the greatest roles of his career. I asked Mr. B if I might dance the Siren who lures the Prodigal Son into the depths of greedy sensuality, a part originally designed for my beloved teacher Mme. Doubrovska. I was curious to explore a darker, more earthy role. Because at one point the Siren has to walk on her knees, Mr. B was concerned that the role might be a physical strain on me, but my knees were fine; I danced the ballet without injury.

Before performance one evening I was warming up with my leg on the barre in arabesque when George walked by. He asked how I was feeling, and I said, "Fine, but my back feels stiff and I can't seem to get a decent arabesque. . . ." Then I realized that the Siren doesn't have any arabesques, which is unusual considering that this is one of ballet's most commonly used positions. Looking at me with a straight face, Mr. B said, "Yes, she just wasn't an arabesque kind of lady." Indeed, none of her movements is directed behind her; all are in front of her or underneath her where she is in diabolical control.

Eddie was amazing in the title role, and his intensity onstage was tremendously energizing, as it was in *Bugaku* and *A Midsummer Night's Dream*. These were the only other ballets I ever danced with him— all ballets where our height discrepancy was ideal for Balanchine's dramatic purpose—and as a result we never became close friends offstage the way I did with Jacques. Eddie also puzzled me because he didn't attend Balanchine's classes. I was so loyal to Mr. B on every level that it was difficult for me to understand why everyone would not want to be taught by the best teacher around. Complaints that his classes were damaging to the body baffled me. I still cannot help suspecting that the "damage" referred more to the ego than the body because, unlike most teachers, he had neither the time nor the interest to pamper that sensitive but anatomically elusive organ.

In April 1968 I again shared Mr. B's past when he decided to revive the dance section from the Broadway musical *On Your Toes*, which he had choreographed in 1936 with his first wife, Tamara Geva, as the Strip Tease girl and Ray Bolger as the Hoofer. At the time the show made history for several reasons: it produced the first full-scale ballet within a musical that actually advanced the plot, and, at Balanchine's insistence, it introduced a new credit in the Broadway play-bill: "Choreographer." Three years after its première the show was filmed with Vera Zorina, Balanchine's third wife, and Eddie Albert in the main roles.

I adored the Richard Rodgers music and knew that in this production I would have the chance to look as worldly and seductive as I dared. The plot, about backstage jealousy and murder, was serious tongue-in-cheek humor, a quality I had not had occasion to test publicly since my appearance as a four-leaf clover back in Cincinnati. As the Strip Tease girl, I would also be required to die onstage, another enticing professional opportunity.

Balanchine was in very high spirits while he was re-creating *Slaughter*—he invited Richard Rodgers and Ray Bolger to the theater for their suggestions, and he requested permission to use the original red barroom set, a wonderful pop-expressionist décor rife with *trompe l'oeil* humor. Arthur was cast in the Ray Bolger role, and another of Mr. B's many guises was revealed, the Broadway hoofer. While Arthur was to sport tap shoes, I was to dance in high heels for the first time onstage. Heels immediately alter one's equilibrium and stride, and this gave me an immediate feel for the ballet's style—unclassical, sexy humor.

My first entrance in the ballet was on a miniature runway on a stage within the stage. Dressed in black fish-net stockings, pink high heels, and a tight, short, fringed pink costume (later in the ballet, when things heat up between the Hoofer and myself, I changed into a black version of this costume), I had to entertain the audience of men by rolling my hips, kicking my legs, shimmying in circles, and finally removing a garter and flinging it to a lucky bystander. Embarrassed to perform this full out in rehearsal in front of George, Arthur, and my peers, I had no such trouble when the curtain went up in front of thousands of people. It was a powerful demonstration of my uninhibited performing nerve, which was in direct contrast to my real-life inhibitions. I was simply more at home onstage than off; it was where I was most alive, most happy, most in control, and, I suppose, most removed from dilemmas I couldn't handle.

The critics did not greet *Slaughter* with high praise. Those in the know thought that the man who had made *Agon, Monumentum/Movements,* and *Jewels* should not be devoting his valuable time to lightweight Broadway material. But Balanchine had time for everything, including pure fun. "I am a circus man," he once said of himself, and he never underestimated the value of sheer entertainment—or an audience's hunger for it. Disregarding critical advice, the public flocked to the theater, and *Slaughter* became a box-office sensation.

After a gala preview on April 30, the ballet had its official première two days later on a program that finished with another new Balanchine ballet whose somber, celestial beauty should have quieted all fears that the choreographer's interest had returned to Broadway. Performed only once, *Requiem Canticles* was a tribute to Martin Luther King, Jr., who had been assassinated in Memphis a month earlier. Set to Stravinsky's 1966 composition for contralto, bass, and chorus, it was more ceremonial procession than dance, with a large corps of dancers in bare feet and long white robes carrying candelabras. Wearing a simple white dress, I walked among them, searching but not finding, and in the final image, Arthur Mitchell as Dr. King, dressed in purple robes, rose above us, ascending with the choral voices. The evening ended in silence.

These were to be the last two dances in which I would work with Balanchine for some time. Our offstage relationship found a resolution of sorts during the year, but before the final emotional battle—we never had an artistic one—we traveled one last time to Europe together for work and play.

At the end of June, before the Saratoga season, the company had a two-week layoff, and George and I flew to Paris for a few days before taking the train to Brussels, where a benefit screening of the *Midsummer* movie had, at long last, been arranged. It was the only European showing of the film and my first visit to the Belgian capital. After the screening there was a party at which George and I each spoke a few words, and we were introduced to the man who had made Brussels one of the centers of the European dance movement, Maurice Béjart. With his trademark beard and black turtleneck he cut quite a dramatic figure. Our conversation, however, remained minimal in a mixture of French and English. This was probably the first time Béjart had seen me dance, and I had no notion then of how important it would prove to be.

With a few days left before we had to return to New York, George and I flew to Rome where we stayed at the Hotel Raphael. We spent our time between restaurants sightseeing at the Vatican, where for the first time I saw Adam and God touching fingers on the ceiling of the Sistine Chapel. It was a gesture that I had danced with gratitude many times in *Apollo*. On a less artistic excursion we hired a horse and carriage to take us around St. Peter's Square and had our photo taken by an Italian ice cream vendor.

Back in New York later that fall, George, always a patriotic American, encouraged me to vote in the presidential election and, in a rare liberal gesture, insisted I vote for Hubert Humphrey. Within a few months I made another important choice, but, significantly, I made this one alone. It had political repercussions of its own within the New York City Ballet and provoked the biggest scandal of my life.

Part

III

CHAPTER ELEVEN

Collision Course

Late one Monday night in November 1968, Paul Mejia told me that he was in love with me. We were standing by the open door of my apartment after he had brought me home from dinner. I thought to myself, "Oh my God," but I only murmured, "Thank you for dinner," and quickly shut the door. Fortunately, Mother was at work. I undressed and went to bed. I had rehearsals and a performance the next day, but I lay in the dark unable to sleep.

Would I tell Paul that I loved him too, or would I try to preserve peace and tell him that I didn't? It was a terrible decision to have to make, and I didn't make it that night. If it was going to be a repeat of the Roger fiasco—and I had every reason to believe that the pressure would be even worse—I had to decide if it would be worth the battle; if it would be fair to everyone or anyone; if I could survive. But I did know one thing: if I told Paul that I love him, I would be willing to face the consequences, all of them. As it turned out, there was one that I could not imagine.

This was the latest dilemma in my life, but the events leading up to it had not happened overnight. Paul was a young dancer in the company, and we had been casual friends for several years. Before my debut in *Bugaku* I had, to my great surprise, received a bouquet of roses that was not from George. The accompanying note wished me good luck and, after comparing me to a pearl, was signed "With great admiration, Paul R. Mejia." While it was typical enough for dancers to give flowers or a little gift to another dancer for a debut, it was unusual for me to receive such a token of good luck because of my isolated position in the company.

Several months later Paul surprised me again by asking if I would take adagio class with him at the School of American Ballet. Although I was by now a principal dancer with a large repertoire of ballets, or perhaps because of it, I was anything but complacent about my abilities and often went to the School to take extra adagio classes. If Jacques was available he would sometimes come to partner me; company members were requested to bring a partner so as not to deplete the already small pool of male dancers at the School.

Most men considered me too much trouble because of Balanchine's ever-watchful eye, so I was startled by Paul's bold invitation. After class we walked down Broadway to Howard Johnson's, had coffee ice cream sodas, and talked about Mr. B. Paul was a nice, quiet boy with good table manners.

So began a friendship, a rarity for me. Paul was two years younger than I and had been born in Peru of an American mother, who had trained at the School of American Ballet, and a Peruvian father. At the age of eleven he moved with his mother and sister to New York, where he was accepted at the School, which he attended for seven years before entering the company. As a young boy he had played the little prince in *The Nutcracker*, and his musicality impressed Balanchine, who subsequently paid for Paul to have piano lessons. Later, when Paul expressed an interest in choreography, he attended a workshop Balanchine gave on the subject.

Over the next few years Paul and I remained friendly, but no more. Our age difference and the fact that I was somewhat taller than he did not suggest any romantic possibilities to me; those were all involved with a man forty-one years older than myself. Nevertheless, there was a certain sympathy between us, and it centered around our mutual love and respect for Balanchine. My life and thoughts were so focused on dancing for Balanchine and doing what he wanted that I think I would have been quite incapable of becoming close to anyone who did not have the same deep admiration. It wasn't snobbish, it was just a fact of my life, and all Paul and I ever talked about was Mr. B and ballet.

Usually dressed in a bright red sweater and black tights, Paul became one of the small but constant group of company members who took Balanchine's class religiously every morning. A sort of camaraderie developed among us when Mr. B suggested a movement or a tempo that looked or sounded impossible. We would try and fail, try and fall, or try and succeed, it didn't really matter which; it was the approach and the willingness that Balanchine was interested in and that ultimately tied us all together. Any company hierarchy was completely negated as we were all reduced to amazement at what he got us to do.

During Paul's first few years in the company, Balanchine had displayed a certain interest in him, as he did with many young dancers, using him as a stand-in for Eddie Villella when choreographing "Rubies" and casting him in several solo roles, including one of the four men in *Agon* and the principal boy in the third movement of *Symphony in C*. At the beginning of 1967, when Mr. B added my Zoraida gypsy solo to the first act of *Don Quixote* he also added a juggler's dance for Paul.

Before things became complicated, Paul and I actually performed together on several impromptu occasions. During the filming of the *Midsummer* movie Paul had acted as Eddie's stand-in for Oberon, so when Eddie was injured on tour in Toronto a few months later, Paul danced the role for two performances. Melissa Hayden was dancing Titania in the matinee, and I watched from the audience with George. After the first act George turned to me and said, "Well, it was okay," and then went backstage and told Paul, "It was fine, but your feet are lousy, but there is nothing you can do about them. But do it again tonight and when we get back to New York we'll work on it." This was a typical enough Balanchine-as-ballet-master pronouncement, and it was not necessarily negative, but Paul was deflated.

Propelled by emotion, Paul danced the evening performance, with me as Titania, and I was aware of an unusual intensity during our altercation in the first act. When I repeatedly refused to let him have my little page, he not only shook his fist in appropriate rage, but I heard him mutter, "Death! Death!" It was the first time we had danced together onstage, and while I was impressed by his dramatic involvement, I was nearly reduced to giggles by his unprecedented vocalizing.

About a year after this episode I danced with him again. *Brahms-Schoenberg Quartet* was scheduled to be performed on the second night of the company's New York winter season, but Jacques was injured and the role had been taught to John Prinz, a talented young dancer in the company. During the afternoon rehearsal with Mr. B, John danced so full out—after all this was a big chance for him—and with so much eagerness that when he landed from a big jump he fell on his elbow and broke it. It was about three-thirty in the afternoon, the performance was at eight, and once again I was without a partner for *Brahms*. Reluctant to cancel the whole ballet, George asked if I had any suggestions, and I replied, "The only person I would feel confident with would be Paul."

By this time Paul and I had taken many adagio classes together, and I trusted him as a partner; I knew that even if he was unsure of the choreography he wouldn't drop me, and at this late stage the basics were all-important. George said fine, and rehearsals were immediately scheduled to teach Paul the role.

The three of us went into a small studio, and George and I started throwing steps and counts in Paul's direction. He caught most of them. After he had learned the essential partnering with me, Mr. B insisted that I leave to rest for the performance, and he finished teaching the ballet to Paul himself. Because time was at such a premium, his first entrance was cut. I came out alone and did a certain amount of improvising to fill up the stage. Later that season Paul was taught the ballet more thoroughly, and we danced it once more, but it was the last time Balanchine ever paired us.

At Christmas in 1967 George and I were invited to Paul's mother's apartment for a "Russian" Christmas celebration. She had produced a big buffet of Russian specialties, and with the encouragement of numerous vodka toasts everyone was very merry. Paul, who still lived with his mother, had just bought a piano, and he and George played for the guests. After the festivities, George and I left together, as we had arrived, and Paul, as he told me later, received some wise words from his grandmother. He had confessed to her that he was in love with me—he was then all of twenty years old and had already survived crushes on two other ballerinas, Patty McBride and Kay Mazzo—and she said, "You'd better watch out, she's Balanchine's girl." Because he was either very naive or just plain stubborn, Paul refused to believe this and replied, "Oh no, they're just friends. They just work together."

Meanwhile, he and I continued our adagio class when possible, and once a month, on a Monday, the company's free day, he would take me on a real date. Dressed in a three-piece, pinstriped suit he would pick me up, and we would go to a fancy restaurant where he'd spend his whole paycheck. It was on such an occasion that I first saw *Gone With the Wind*, followed by dinner at the Rainbow Room. Paul did not tell me then that he was in love with me, and I didn't guess it—another romantic problem was the last thing I was looking for. But I did enjoy his company. He never pressured me and never asked me about my relationship with George, which I didn't want to talk about. It was refreshing.

Although I loved meeting George's Russian friends and learned a lot from them, they were, like him, a great deal older than I and often talked in Russian about things that had happened before I was born. With them I tended to feel inadequate or simply decorative; as an instrument, I met Mr. B on his own level, but socially and emotionally I was insecure, except with a few people—Gail, Roger, Paul—my own age. I read *War and Peace* between rehearsals, but not even Tolstoy could compensate for experiences I had not had time to live through.

Curious as it may sound, at twenty-two I was trying, without much success, to eliminate romance from my life, and Paul didn't confuse me the way George did. Ironically, our infrequent dates took on a romantic atmosphere not so much because of any passionate feelings between us but because I felt I was always being watched, so going out with someone besides George, especially a young man, was immediately an occasion for secrecy, a real cloak-and-dagger situation.

The secrecy spread—Paul and I would meet for breakfast before class at the Éclair, a bakery on West 72nd Street. Mother would still be at her night job in the morning so she didn't see me slip out, and, as time went on, Paul would pick up croissants and come over for breakfast before she got home. By the fall of 1968 the situation was becoming ridiculous; the more Paul and I tried to hide our friendship, the closer we became—a bitter irony.

One morning after breakfast we boarded the 104 bus down Broadway to the theater, and who should be sitting on it but George. Innocent as we were, we probably looked, and certainly felt, guilty. There were some uncomfortable greetings, just as there were a few weeks later when Paul and I met at the church I attended on West 71st Street one Sunday morning and there was George standing in the aisle.

I don't know exactly when I realized that I *was* in love with Paul. I was so haunted by possible confrontations that my emotions were reined in. I felt guilty about every moment or thought or feeling I shared with Paul—or anyone else. Nevertheless, I decided to tell Paul that I loved him.

Mother made no secret of the fact that she thought my interest in Paul was practically illegal. Eventually she became so irrational on the subject that I moved out. I found a small one-bedroom apartment on West 56th Street and moved in with what I could carry. The situation had gone way beyond a mother/daughter clash. She defended her behavior by saying, "Suzi, you'll never understand, you're not a mother." I think she saw my life and career disappearing.

George, on the other hand, was not hysterical; but when he realized that Paul and I were serious he did something he had never done in all the previous years of our relationship. He asked me to marry him.

And he said he wanted us to have a child. "Imagine what a wonderful, intelligent, beautiful child we would have." This sounded very strange coming from him. Children had never entered my mind, and it was no secret that Balanchine thought ballerinas shouldn't have them. There was still, however, no mention of divorce. As before, certain names remained unspoken between us, and now Paul's was added to the list. George was desperate, but it was simply too late. Perhaps it had always been too late.

Because of work, we inevitably saw a great deal of each other, and I was as committed to him, my dancing, and the company as ever. My relationship with Paul did not diminish what remained, always, the most important thing in my life: my work. As before in times of crisis, dancing was my emotional and spiritual anchor. But while George knew my allegiance to him was more than just professional, it was not enough for him. It broke my heart not to be able to give him everything he wanted, but I couldn't. I couldn't and survive at the same time. This was something I could not explain; I just felt it.

Our unique relationship had proved itself so often to both of us, and it might not have withstood consummation. The physical side of love is of paramount importance to many people, but to us it wasn't. Our interaction was physical, but its expression was dance. We both had histories suggesting that marriage might not be the answer— George had had numerous marriages, and my family had barely survived the one that produced me. I didn't want to go home with George and be married. Even if it had been bliss, I think we would have lost something on another level. The thought frightened me.

All the same, I did consider the prospect. It would have given George what he thought he wanted. But I could not see what it would have given our work that we didn't already have. I knew that I didn't need to sleep with him to be cast in his ballets. He didn't need to sleep with me to reveal my potential as a dancer. He had tried many times before to unify his artistic and emotional passions of the moment, but the history of his many marriages suggested only insecurity to me. Balanchine needed to choreograph to live, just as I needed to dance to live. Neither of us needed to be married to live.

Mother kept saying to me, "It wouldn't be so bad to be Mrs. George Balanchine," and I would say, "No, it wouldn't," but there was something more. "You can't always have what you want," she'd say. I knew that in defying his wishes I was risking everything to preserve what we had, our ongoing ability to work together. I knew that I could love him best onstage where I was at my best. Offstage we were both confused, sometimes stupid, emotional human beings, but onstage we were bigger and better than ourselves.

Because I couldn't give George everything he wanted, I became committed to making it up to him in some other way. I think this commitment lodged itself in my subconscious and made me a better dancer. It became quite simple—every time I danced, it was life or death to me.

During the fall of 1968 I was so torn and confused about the situation that I did not sleep for weeks. I could still dance, but I did not feel I could make an intelligent decision. Eventually, just as I had done about Roger almost three years before, I went to see Brother Paul to hear an objective opinion. I told him that I thought I was in love with Paul, but so many people were horrified by it that maybe I had lost my senses. He said that I shouldn't doubt myself and that if I was in love with Paul, that was wonderful.

When George realized that I could not be verbally convinced of his point of view, he tried a different approach. He became distant— which brought Paul and me closer. Paul seemed like the only person involved who cared about my feelings and emotional wretchedness. The winter season was to end in February, and we decided to get married during the break that followed. Having committed ourselves to each other, we saw no reason not to go ahead with the inevitable. A long engagement would have only prolonged the war, and the tactics being used were tearing me apart. I wanted peace and thought that once I married, George would have to let me go.

Four days after Christmas my sister Beverly was married, and I, of course, was in the wedding party. Although I was happy for Bev, the occasion was difficult for me: Mother wouldn't talk to me at the reception, and I could not help wondering why both my sisters had married the men of their choice without Mother's interference, yet it didn't seem possible for me to do the same. Later that evening I danced the Sugar Plum Fairy in *The Nutcracker* and felt grateful for the peace and freedom I had onstage. By now, they didn't exist anywhere else in my life.

I didn't know how or when to tell George that I was going to be married. I had gone to Betty Cage with my Roger problems, so I went to her again, and while she couldn't tell me a good way to say it, she did tell me not to tell George while we were rehearsing *Don Quixote;* it was too emotional a time for him. In the end I didn't have to tell George anything; Mother did it for me. She had called up Betty, begging her to do something, to intervene, to stop this marriage. Betty refused to interfere, saying that if Paul and I wanted to marry we should be allowed to. Mother then called George and told him that not only was I getting married to Paul Mejia, but Betty was encouraging us! But George never mentioned this to me. It was a nightmare.

Meanwhile, working on another front, Mother confessed her dilemma to Kate Kahn's mother back in Cincinnati, and Mrs. Kahn suggested that I might talk to a certain Father Richard McCormick, a Jesuit priest and theologian, who was an acquaintance of her family's. One day I received a phone call from him; he introduced himself and said that he was passing through New York and would I like to meet. While I was reluctant to discuss my problems with a virtual stranger, he was persistent, and eventually I agreed to have lunch with him. He was very kind, and before I knew it I had poured out my heart to him.

After hearing the whole convoluted story he asked, "What would you like to do?" I replied, "I would like to marry Paul." "Well, then I think you should," he said, and offered to perform the ceremony. Mother probably felt betrayed; Father McCormick was supposed to have talked some sense into me, instead he became one of my few allies.

We decided to be married on February 21, the first Saturday of the layoff following the ballet season. We didn't put an announcement in the newspaper—we knew better than to advertise the event. All the arrangements were shrouded in guilt and secrecy, but the word got around, and one day I received a summons from Mme. Karinska. I went over to her costume shop, and she asked me what I would be wearing for my wedding. I hadn't given it much thought and said I'd probably just buy something. "You can't do that," she cried indignantly and insisted that she make me a wedding dress. One of the few people to give this important moment in my life its due attention, she said, "You must look as beautiful as possible when you get married." Ever since giving me the Joan of Arc medal several years earlier she had sensed the problems in my future, and now she showed sympathy for a decision very few were sympathetic about. She designed a lovely, simple, short white lace dress and a beautiful headpiece; she knew my head well.

On February 16, before the end of the season, George had flown to Europe to stage an opera for the Hamburg State Theater, so he was not in the country when Paul and I were married. Because there was such conflict, and it seemed that few were happy that we were getting married, we had a very small ceremony in the little chapel of the Church of St. Paul the Apostle, two blocks from the theater. Gail was my maid of honor, and Ricky Weiss, a friend of Paul's in the company, was best man. Even Ricky asked Paul just before the ceremony, "Are you sure you want to do this? You might be giving up your career."

Mother attended the ceremony and cried audibly throughout. Paul's mother gave a reception afterward, but my mother did not come. No one from my family came. Many of my teachers from the School attended as well as a few company members and staff, and I was grateful for their show of support. I think a lot of them believed that this marriage, however painful it might be at the time to Balanchine, would also act as a bucket of cold water that could cool the highly emotional situation between us.

We left the reception in a taxi and spent our wedding night in the International Hotel at Kennedy Airport. The following morning we flew to Hawaii for our honeymoon. When we changed planes in San Francisco, Paul pulled my jacket down from the airplane rack and rice fell out all over the floor. I joined our fellow passengers in looking around for the newlyweds; the guilt about marrying did not soon leave me. At the airport check-in in New York I had remarked humorously to Paul that our baggage had been tagged with my initials, "SF," and only when we reached Hawaii without our luggage did we realize what had happened: our bags had stayed in San Francisco. Despite this shaky beginning, we had a lovely time swimming, lounging on the beach with tropical drinks, and adjusting to the unbelievable fact that we were finally alone together, and five thousand miles from New York no one seemed to disapprove of our union.

We had traveled on an inexpensive package deal, and during one sightseeing bus trip to a volcano, the tour guide asked jovially, "Anybody here just married?" Since we were the only couple under sixty, everyone looked at us, but we were reluctant to admit the fact. It was a bittersweet beginning.

As soon as we returned from our honeymoon I learned from a newspaper article that George had obtained a Mexican divorce on February 5, seventeen days before Paul and I were married. Within a few weeks, when George returned from Europe, I realized that my marriage had solved nothing.

One afternoon in early April during the rehearsal period preceding the spring season, the phone rang and Paul answered it. It was one of the company's staff members with a very strange request—that Paul please not come to the theater. In effect, he was fired, but he would continue on the payroll. He was to be paid for staying away from Balanchine. Astonished, angry, and terribly hurt, Paul would not agree not to talk to the press, and the following day another call came withdrawing the whole request.

The first sign that Mr. B was not going to tolerate Paul had come during a rehearsal for Paul's juggler dance in the first act of *Don Quixote* sometime in January. No voices were raised, and no names were mentioned—the whole company was watching, and you could have cut the air with a knife—but Mr. B found Paul's interpretation inadequate. "Can't you beg, don't you know how to beg?" he asked him repeatedly, as Paul stooped lower and lower and begged harder and harder.

I knew my career might change when I married Paul, but I honestly didn't believe it would. I believed that as long as I danced as beautifully as I could for George, in time he would forgive me and come to understand. He eventually did, in his way, but I don't think that he ever forgave Paul. It is ironic that our loyalty to Mr. B first brought Paul and me together and then, in turn, separated us from him.

As the rehearsal weeks proceeded, there was no noticeable change in my scheduling, but Paul had decidedly fewer rehearsals. George returned from Europe on April 10. He had stayed abroad several weeks longer than planned, apparently because he was devastated by my marriage. Eddie Bigelow, Barbara Horgan, and Lincoln Kirstein had all flown to Germany, not only to see the première of the Glinka opera he had directed, but to console him and try to reason with him. I know this only from other people's reports. I never heard it from him directly, but it was said that he even threatened not to return to America. At the time I only knew that when he did return he was distant and would not speak to me. If we happened to meet in a hallway, he would turn and walk the other way.

There was one other change. I was called to teach "Diamonds," a role for which I had never had an understudy, to Kay Mazzo, a young soloist in the company. While understudies and second casts were normal situations in company life, they were not for me. At George's insistence, I had never had understudies for roles that he had choreographed on me, and while it was, of course, his prerogative to change that policy, it indicated a definite change in his attitude toward me. Perhaps he wanted to remind me that the exclusivity he had given me could be taken away at any time.

Nevertheless, once the season began I was cast, as before, in the roles I always did, which gave me some measure of hope that time might heal the wounds. On one occasion, after a performance of *Swan Lake*, there was a knock on my dressing-room door, and it was George. While this was something that had happened hundreds of times in the past, it had not happened since my marriage, and I was tremendously happy to see him. He wouldn't come into the room, so we stood in the doorway and he said, "I just wanted to tell you how wonderful you were tonight." "You see, George, nothing has changed," I said to him hopefully. His face remained impassive. He said nothing and left.

As the distance between us seemed to grow with time, I became increasingly upset. Frankly, I missed him. I loved him no less and no differently because I had married Paul. Obviously I could separate things that he couldn't. In this we differed, but the real world had never been our world.

In despair one day I went to his office and offered to leave the company if things were too difficult between us. He said, "No, that's not necessary, dear. But perhaps Paul should leave." My nightmare of being torn asunder was coming true. The ever-increasing tension between the three of us came to a head on May 8, 1969, the most surreal day of my life.

It was a Thursday, and the annual Spring Gala Benefit was scheduled for that evening at nine o'clock. The program was to consist of two previews—John Clifford's ballet *Prelude, Fugue and Riffs* and Jerome Robbins' *Dances at a Gathering*—and *Symphony in C. Dances* was the first Robbins première by the company in thirteen years, and the hour-long ballet to Chopin piano music was to become one of his most acclaimed. Eddie Villella had been cast in the third movement of *Symphony in C*, but because he was one of the eight principal dancers in the Robbins première, he asked not to dance *Symphony in C*.

The third movement was a role that Paul had danced on numerous occasions over the past two years, including the previous Saturday, and he presumed, not unreasonably, that he would replace Villella. But it was Deni Lamont, who had not danced the role for some time, who was cast. Paul interpreted this, probably correctly, as a direct slap in the face. Being both very young and very Latin in temperament, he was simultaneously furious and miserable.

He came to me and said quite simply, "I can't take this anymore. I have to leave." Feeling that my world was quite literally falling apart around me, I did something rash and unconsidered. I could not get to see George, so I sent a message via the staff, from Paul and me, saying that if Paul didn't dance the third movement of *Symphony in C* that night, we would both resign from the company.

This was an entirely uncalculated gesture of sheer desperation on my part. It had the form of an ultimatum, but, incredible as it seems, I had never intended it to be one. In trying, however awkwardly, to reconcile my life with Paul and my life with George, I had succeeded only in achieving ever greater separation from the latter. I felt that I could not survive another day under these circumstances, and my message was intended to convey this.

Both Betty Cage and Eddie Bigelow phoned, begging me to withdraw the message. They knew Balanchine well enough to know his reaction to an ultimatum, but I did not see as clearly as they and insisted they give George the message. Subconsciously, I probably wanted and needed an outright confrontation; something had to change in a big way.

Paul and I went to the theater and looked at the casting. His name was not there, but mine remained for the second movement of *Symphony in C*, and in a blind daze I went to my dressing room to prepare. It was still several hours until performance. Even now dancing remained the only place where I felt any security. After I had put on my makeup and sewed my toe shoes, there was a knock at my door. It was Mme. Pourmel, the petite Russian wardrobe lady who so devotedly guarded our precious costumes. My white tutu was already hanging on the rack in my dressing room, but Mme. Pourmel tiptoed over and silently took it off the hanger and clutched it in her arms. I looked at her, and she started crying. "Suzanne, you're not dancing tonight," she sobbed. It was then I knew that I was no longer a member of the New York City Ballet.

Stunned beyond tears, I went to find Paul, who had been sitting in his dressing room. We stared at each other in disbelief. At nine o'clock, we walked numbly through the side door backstage into the auditorium and sat in the audience to watch the performance. It was absurd, but we didn't know where else to go. *Symphony in C* had been canceled, and after numerous last-minute program changes— which were apparently attempts to salvage the situation with Paul and me—*Stars and Stripes* replaced it. Nothing I saw on the stage that night seemed real, not because it was all so beautiful, but because *I* did not feel real. I was living someone else's life, not my own.

At about one o'clock the next morning after the performance and party festivities were over and the theater was empty, I went back to my dressing room and packed up my things—my black fishnet *Slaughter* tights and high heels, my half-sewn toe shoes, my lucky toe shoes, my *Apollo* curls, my makeup and eyelashes, my rhinestone earrings, and all the little cards from George wedged in the corner of my makeup mirror that had arrived with such huge bouquets of roses. The last thing I put in my theater case was the medal of the Blessed Virgin that George had given Diana and she had passed on, so trustingly, to me. My whole life was in that small black suitcase. I was a dancer without a job, and I felt as homeless as any bag lady.

The ephemeral nature of dancing took on a new meaning for me that night. One day I was one of George Balanchine's ballerinas; the next, my name was erased from the company's roster. I was twenty-three, and I had good reason to think my career had ended. Two days later "Diamonds" was performed for the first time by another dancer, but I was not there to see it.

CHAPTER TWELVE

Exile

❧

G| eorge and I didn't see each other face to face that night, and
we didn't say goodbye. It was not a mature mutual decision
at a time of extreme anxiety; it was a momentary explosion. I did not
leave the New York City Ballet solely because I was supporting my
husband. His professional dissatisfaction was a timely catalyst for an
inevitable break between George and me. Although this separation
could have been accomplished in a more graceful manner, I am convinced that at this time it was necessary.

Looking back, I regard the severance as a stroke of fate, just as our
initial union had been. Our whole relationship was in danger of being
destroyed. Too much had passed between us, and the air needed
clearing. If I had not left, married or unmarried, the situation would
only have worsened, although it is frightening to imagine how.

At the time, reality hit with a resounding thud when instead of
waking up from a bad dream the morning after the gala, I woke to
newspaper articles that made it evident that our resignation was irreversible. There were not only detailed reports about the fateful
phone calls of May 8 and who was to "succeed" me onstage at the
State Theater but even predictions about my future prospects: they
were dim.

I was now a Balanchine dancer without Balanchine, and there was
real curiosity about my ability to survive professionally. Was I too
much the product of one man's style, vision, and physical training
to be able to function in the outside dance world where the nineteenth-
century full-evening classic ballets—ballets I had never danced—were
the criteria of ability and artistry? It felt very lonely being a Balanchine
spokesman without a forum. The resource that I'd always relied on
when all else failed was no longer available to me on a daily basis.

One thing, however, was clear to me from the start: no matter what
happened, or did not happen, I was going to remain faithful to what

Balanchine had taught me. The fact that our personal lives had clashed did not mean I no longer believed in him, his work, or his philosophy. My problems with George were personal, not artistic, and I did not suddenly think in anger, "Well, he's not really as good as I thought he was," or "I don't miss dancing his ballets," because he *was* as good, and I *did* miss them. But he had also taught me the value of the moment, and the fact that my "now" no longer involved him didn't lessen my loyalty. I had committed myself to him once, and my allegiance did not change because my good fortune had. My exile would be the greatest test of just how much I had learned from Balanchine—not only about dancing but about life.

I had to continue taking class. It was the only thing I could think of to do each day, but I did not want to take classes from any other teacher. His was the only way I would consider dancing. All I needed was an empty studio, and knowing that the State Theater was always open, Paul and I went over late one night, long after performance was finished, to do a barre.

The security guard at the stage entrance stood up and said, "You can't come in here." He was a nice man who had known me ever since the theater opened in 1964, but he had obviously received strict orders from higher powers. I had not realized just how angry Balanchine was at me, and months later the same thing happened again when the company was not even in town but in Saratoga. I was with Lee Roy Reams, an old friend from Cincinnati who was appearing in a production of *Oklahoma!* at the State Theater, when we were stopped by the guard. "But she's with me," Lee Roy replied. "I know exactly who she is, and she's not allowed in this theater," the guard countered. Lee Roy was furious, but by now I was resigned to the situation. Not even having an empty space in which to work by myself made me feel true loneliness for the first time. Finally, Paul and I started renting little studios around town, which was not only expensive when we had no income but embarrassing.

Having no contact with the company, much less George, I had no idea what he was thinking, but when he finally broke his public silence, this is what he said to the press:

> Could anyone really think I would change a whole program just to keep someone from dancing? Paul was being used according to his ability. Fortunately, or unfortunately, I must make the artistic decisions. . . . I'm disappointed in Suzanne. . . . After this, it would not be good for the company if they returned. . . . She is an exceptional dancer, and we will miss her. . . . Many other companies would be delighted to have her.

Never was he more wrong. I received no job offers, and it was not because the dance world didn't know I was available. Fear, I think, was the reason. Most major companies all over the world had at least a few Balanchine ballets in their repertoire and hoped for more, and they didn't want to risk hiring me and possibly alienating George Balanchine. That may have been unfair to George—they undoubtedly didn't ask him about it—but we were hot goods, and no one wanted to touch us.

Several weeks after our departure the phone did ring one day in our quiet little apartment, and it was Eugene Gamiel who was in charge of the West End Symphony. The orchestra had a single performance scheduled for June 9 at Brandeis High School, and he asked if Paul and I would like to dance something. We immediately said yes and then had the problem of not being able to perform anything we knew. If George wasn't allowing us in the theater, he certainly was not going to let us dance any of his ballets, so Paul choreographed a pas de deux for us to Mahler's *Symphony No. 1,* and we threw ourselves into rehearsals with all the enthusiasm our deprivation had engendered.

Since I did not own any costumes, I made one out of a nightgown I had, and for a headpiece I took the gauze off my wedding veil and wore the Karinska design on my head. She was uncredited on the program, but I didn't think she would mind. I grasped desperately at any connection to my so-distant yet so-recent past. Nostalgia and sentiment were my daily companions. The performance went well, and a number of significant people in the dance world attended, curious to see what had happened to me since my exile. Paul and I began to feel like the side show in the circus. Mother, however, did not attend, and the silence between us deepened.

Meanwhile, Paul started choreographing another dance for us to Delibes, the *Sylvia Pas de Deux,* and we premièred it, in the same costumes, at Brother Paul's high school auditorium in Manhasset for an audience of children. These haphazard gigs were unpaid, but it was a way for us to keep dancing, and we were grateful.

In July we went to Cincinnati to perform *Sylvia* again at the Summer Opera where I had danced as a child. Over the years I had become something of a celebrity back home; they had given me the key to the city in 1965, and the university awarded George an honorary doctorate in 1967. I was touched that they invited us despite the fact that I was not to be accompanied by Balanchine or the New York City Ballet.

Later that month Paul and I bought two cheap excursion tickets on a charter flight to Europe. We needed to get away from New York,

where we were becoming more and more paranoid about our neb-
ulous situation. Meeting anyone we knew was increasingly difficult;
there was nothing to say. After almost missing the plane, which
departed from what looked like the cargo area, we arrived, after a
bumpy flight, in Brussels, where we both promptly became violently
nauseated after having some soup. We had to wait eight hours for a
train to Paris. Finally, in despair, I said to Paul, "Whatever happens
in our life I never want to come back to Brussels again," and he
promised me we wouldn't.

After a little relaxation in Paris, we traveled to Vienna and Milan
where we took class with the Vienna State Opera Ballet and La Scala
Ballet. By now we realized that we had no future in the American
dance world and thought that in Europe we might be able to design
a new life without the shadow of the past hovering over us. Everyone
was very polite, but no one offered a contract.

Back in New York we hired an agent to try to get us work, and on
my twenty-fourth birthday we danced *Sylvia* with the Huntington
Ballet on Long Island. We were becoming a one-pas-de-deux act, and
in our real desperation not to disappear entirely from the public eye,
we started branching out and doing things besides dancing. People
were eager for interviews, but they wanted to discuss only the one
thing I didn't want to discuss: my break with Balanchine. I had never
before had to deal with the world without Balanchine's advice and
protection, and it was a rude but sobering awakening.

For the first and only time in my life I said yes to everything
our agent offered, which included modeling some wild Vidal Sas-
soon hairdos in *After Dark* magazine for which we received publicity photos as payment. We danced *Sylvia* on the Dick Cavett show,
but the camera decapitated me for most of the dance; and we went
on "To Tell the Truth," where the audience had to guess which of
three men was my husband. One guy was chubby, one was pigeon-
toed, and the third was Paul; we didn't manage to fool anyone.
Kitty Carlisle, who was on the panel, was very kind but had to dis-
qualify herself because she knew the New York City Ballet. Thanks
to her disqualification we received fifty dollars compensation and I
was given some costume jewelry. Our financial situation was not
improving.

One day we received a call from Rudolf Bing at the Metropolitan
Opera and walked across the Lincoln Center Plaza for a meeting in
his office. Very tall, thin, and dignified, he told us that he wanted to
arrange an evening with some ballet at the Met and wondered if we
were interested in performing. Excited by the idea, Paul started to
tell him about a ballet to Prokofiev's *Scythian Suite* that he had been

planning, but Mr. Bing's face darkened upon hearing of it. He wanted to put *Hansel and Gretel* on the program and thought we might do a jig in that. Paul's ballet sounded too elaborate. Wringing his hands, he kept repeating, "But what about my *Hansel and Grate-ell?* This is a most unfortunate situation, most unfortunate. . . ." He obviously wanted my name on his program but didn't want it interfering with Humperdinck's. He was a shrewd businessman; it would undoubtedly have been a publicity coup.

Back in our apartment we began work on two unlikely projects—writing a musical of *The Red Shoes,* whose themes were becoming strangely parallel to my own life, and formulating an exotic Peruvian soft drink from fermented corn husks. After making up a sample batch we drafted a letter to several of the big soft-drink companies offering them distribution rights. We envisioned ourselves rolling in money! It was a humorous attempt prompted by our ever decreasing funds, but at least we got a laugh out of it.

Despite our relatively pathetic lifestyle and plenty of meatless meals, there was one element about these months of artistic atrophy that I welcomed: our isolation gave me a chance to recover from the tension with George and Mother, and the overall sense of relief was immeasurable.

In September 1969, while I was playing with my cats—in addition to Bottom we now had Top and Middle—a telegram arrived from Celia Franca, director of the National Ballet of Canada, inviting me to guest-star with the company on their North American tour. It was the first offer I had received from a major ballet company, and I was understandably thrilled. Paul, acting as my agent, negotiated a very good contract for me, and it was decided that I would dance two performances of Erik Bruhn's *Swan Lake* in Milwaukee. If people had been wondering about my ability to dance the "classics," this would be their chance to find out—and mine.

I went up to Toronto to learn and rehearse the ballet, in which I was partnered by a very nice Yugoslavian dancer named Hazaros Surmejan, and was confronted by the company's restrained English style. Being desperate to dance, to continue learning, and yet knowing that my life had radically changed, I decided to try to fit in stylistically. But it was not possible for me suddenly to shorten my reach, lower my legs, slow down my rhythm, and generally hold back the thrust of movement that was part of my Balanchine training. I felt not only physically suffocated but emotionally confused. To consciously do "less" when all my life I had tried to do "more" for Balanchine seemed decidedly wrong. The ballet masters were understanding and did not insist on trying to alter my way of dancing. I was glad to have attempted the change and to reaffirm that Balanchine's was the only way.

Having resolved this dilemma, I proceeded to enjoy myself. Tschaikovsky was as supportive as ever, and I relished the opportunity to dance both the innocent White Swan and the evil Black Swan. I did, however, have to check myself consciously from dancing the choreography to the same music of Balanchine's *Tschaikovsky Pas de Deux* in Bruhn's Black Swan pas de deux. Mr. B had infiltrated my whole being—my ears, my heart, and my legs.

The performances were a huge and unexpected success, and I was invited back to dance several more times in Toronto at the end of November. I learned *La Bayadère* and their version of *The Nutcracker* in addition to *Swan Lake,* and for the first time since leaving the New York City Ballet I started feeling like a real dancer again. With daily class, rehearsals, and performance I was back in my element, and Paul and I began wondering if we might not move to Canada. There was speculation in the press that I might be offered a more permanent contract, and I let it be known that I was interested. But much as the company enjoyed the publicity my appearances garnered, it is possible they felt that anything more permanent would be politically unwise.

After spending the Christmas season in New York, I was asked back for another performance of *Swan Lake* in April of 1970, and I used the opportunity to try to break the ice with Mother. It was over a year since my wedding, when we stopped speaking, and I thought the time had come. I invited her to the performance in Toronto, and her first view of me was onstage. I was determined to show her that I had not only survived the alienation of the past year but was dancing better than ever. She still collected my reviews, and they had piqued her interest. When we finally saw each other face to face, an hour later, any expected tension was entirely absent; a disaster had occurred.

During the coda of the Black Swan pas de deux I was doing some fast piqué turns in a circle when I heard a loud pop over the sounds of the orchestra. My right leg immediately turned to jelly and I lost all control. Not feeling any pain, I gritted my teeth and sent rapid messages down to my leg. None of them was heeded, and I tried switching the turns onto my left leg. I started praying, unable to believe that this was happening. If only I could improvise my way through the last scene of the ballet . . . I couldn't, and the next thing I remember was being carried offstage and seeing Mother's frantic face as she watched my knee swell up like a balloon.

Mother, Paul, and I took a taxi to the emergency room at the hospital while the performance was finished by another ballerina. Unable even to walk, all I could think was, "Oh my God, I have no New York City Ballet, no Mr. B, and now no leg." It was as if the only thing I had left, my own body, had deserted me.

The doctors were unable to diagnose precisely what had happened to my knee, but they informed me that it was extremely serious and until the swelling subsided, no treatment could be suggested. I wanted to go home to New York, so Paul and I rented a car and drove back. A doctor at Columbia-Presbyterian Hospital drained the fluid and took X rays. The prognosis was not good. I had torn the cartilage, which was now attached only by a thread; an operation was recommended. I went home on crutches to think about the decision, but Mr. B's belief that cartilage can regenerate itself kept echoing through my mind. I decided not to have an operation, to let my knee heal of its own accord. It did, although it was a long, frustrating process.

By the end of May I was off crutches and ready to try my first feeble ballet barre. The School of American Ballet had moved into spacious new headquarters in the Juilliard building at Lincoln Center, and I phoned and asked if I might be permitted to use one of their empty studios. I knew that the School could be off-limits to me, as the theater was, but I felt I had nothing to lose by asking. Mrs. Gleboff was sympathetic and said it would be fine, so early each morning I walked over to the School to work before classes began at ten-thirty.

I came and went to this familiar yet now so foreign place as inconspicuously as possible, but one day, as I was leaving, I ran into the School's director in the hallway. It was the first time George and I had seen each other since my departure over a year before. He nodded politely, and I said a little defensively, "I'm getting over a knee injury, and I was just here doing a barre—they said that was all right. Maybe we can talk sometime?" He nodded again and said, "Fine," and we parted in our different directions.

Paul and I had not been to see the company perform since we left, but during their spring season of 1970 we mustered up our courage and bought tickets to see Mr. B's newest hit ballet, *Who Cares?* I was afraid that I would be overcome with tears when I saw the company and knew I was no longer a part of it, but happily I was able to watch in a state of relatively calm resignation. People in the audience recognized us, but no one spoke. I adored *Who Cares?* and wrote an enthusiastic letter to George—after our brief but civilized hallway encounter I thought there might be a possibility of rekindling contact. But there was no response. Soon after I tried again, and again there was no answer.

I cannot deny that I dreamed about being able to rejoin the company and work with Balanchine again. I also wanted him to know that I was still married and surviving. I had one rule: if he would take me back, I had to be a better dancer than ever. I wanted to deserve to go back.

Living in New York City without a job was growing increasingly difficult, emotionally as well as financially, and Paul and I became more realistic about our future. We decided to look at houses in Saratoga Springs, a town we knew well from our summer seasons with the company. We found a brand-new house that had a backyard, a washer/dryer, a dishwasher, even central vacuuming. We started planning to turn the garage into a dance studio where we could teach local students—our vision of the future became a suburban one—and we applied for a mortgage from the Adirondack Trust Bank. After several months of red tape the phone finally rang one day, and we were told our application had been approved.

Panic immediately set in. Suddenly a life of dancing in an anonymous garage was becoming a reality, and I looked at Paul and said, "I don't want it, I don't want it." It represented never dancing on a stage again, and despite the lack of performing opportunities, I was not ready to face retirement at the age of twenty-four. Paul called the bank and said we had changed our minds.

As one last summer venture we went up to the Adirondack Mountains where I had spent so many summers of my childhood. My grandmother's cottage was located on the mainland of Eagle Bay, and in the center of the lake lay Cedar Islands, the site of a luxury hotel and summer resort during the early part of the century and later, in the 1950s, a boys' camp. It had been deserted for some years, and its "For Sale" sign was bent and rusted. No one seemed to want to buy it, which was not surprising given its state of total disrepair—garbage, bottles, and broken glass washed against its shores, old ceramic toilets and tubs, even a piano, were embedded in the marshes, and there was neither electricity nor running water. The large stone main building was still intact, although every window and door was broken and the roof leaked voluminously, while all the smaller waterfront cabins were in ruins, as were the footbridges connecting the main island to two smaller ones. The place had become a haven for illegal camping parties, and the residue of their festivities and vandalism was everywhere. But to us it looked like paradise.

Paul and I decided to buy Cedar Islands and called the bank to salvage our loan agreement. We saw the place's possibilities, and its secluded, albeit wrecked, atmosphere coincided with our emotional state at the time. It required an incredible amount of work to be even habitable, but work was the one thing we were longing for—in any form. We installed some camping equipment and started clearing the shores of the refuse. I put on my trusty rubber sweatpants, usually used for rehearsal, and waded into the shallow water to collect garbage. We filled hundreds of bags. We washed our clothes, bathed in the lake, and over a bonfire cooked the fish we had caught with string and worms; we were as happy as we had been in recent memory.

Cedar Islands represented a haven, and we viewed its disrepair as a challenge, not a chore. It was to take years of work every summer before it became what we had envisioned the first day we stepped onto its muddy shores, but we were always happy there.

Back in New York several weeks after we had signed our deed of ownership, I received a telegram in the mail from the founder and director of Ballet du XXème Siècle (Ballet of the Twentieth Century), Maurice Béjart, whom I had met briefly in Brussels. His company was going to perform in Montreal, and he invited Paul and me to come see them there and discuss possible employment. I had never seen his company, but from browsing through *Dance Magazine* I knew its reputation of being wildly avant-garde and theatrical with a distinct emphasis on male dancing—it certainly did not sound like a likely prospect for what I might have to offer. Nevertheless, we flew to Canada and picked up tickets left for us at the box office.

They performed a version of Wagner's *Les Vainqueurs (The Conquerors)* and a dance called *Ni Fleurs Ni Couronnes (Neither Flowers nor Crowns)* that was a modernized *Sleeping Beauty*. Viewing the company as a possible place of work, I noticed several things. The music was taped, which infused the performance with a very different, more limited musical threshold than I was used to with Balanchine; and not only did the women have rather simple choreography, they often didn't even dance on pointe. I had also never seen so many handsome, bare-chested men onstage at one time. The company's leading male dancer was Jorge Donn, and while I was impressed by his dramatic attack, I found his thick mane of long blond hair, kohl-lined eyes, and exaggerated movements just a little too flamboyant. He made me blush.

These were all serious considerations, but another aspect of the company caught my attention. There was an intense energy and commitment onstage that I could identify with immediately, and this quality made the stylistic anomalies less significant. These dancers believed in what they were doing, even if what they were doing was not exactly what I had believed in all my dancing life. But I think a passion for something has the effect of overcoming differences and binds like minds together.

Following the performance we had dinner with Béjart and Donn, who were both extremely gentle and kind. Béjart offered me a job. While we were extremely happy to receive such a rare offer, Paul and I worried about how I might fit into this male-oriented company. There had not been any significant female roles in the program we had seen. Paul said, "Well, I didn't really see anything there for Suzanne to dance." Béjart, far from being offended, replied, "I know, but I want to make new dances with her." Needless to say, that excited me. He then said to Paul, "We don't really need any new boys, but if you want to join the company, that's fine, although I can't really offer you a solo contract." The difficulties of the past year had left their mark, and we agreed almost on the spot to move to Brussels and join Béjart's company.

The next day there were some contract discussions, and negotiations threatened to come to a complete standstill when the subject of toe shoes arose—it was a deal-breaker for me. Mrs. Lotsey, the company manager, told me that female dancers were allocated two or three pairs of pointe shoes a month. Spoiled perhaps by Balanchine's generosity, I was used to an unlimited supply of new shoes and often used as many as twelve pairs a week when dancing a heavy schedule. Balanchine's insistence that his dancers have new shoes at their disposal meant that we wore toe shoes morning, noon, and night, for class and rehearsals as well as performances, and the result was the company's unique familiarity with dancing on pointe.

I told her that I could not survive on so few shoes, and she turned red at my arrogance. Job or no job, I could not agree to that. I knew it would compromise my dancing to have to spend so much time on half pointe. I had discovered since my knee injury that the way the skeleton adjusts to being on pointe enables all the weight and strain to bypass the knee joint. She went out of the room to consult with Béjart. She returned several minutes later and, obviously bewildered, added to my contract that I would be provided with as many toe shoes as I needed. I promptly signed on the dotted line.

I had performed a total of nine times over the previous nineteen months, and the notion of full-time work was irresistible. We moved out of our New York apartment, put our few bits of furniture into storage, packed our clothes, placed our three cats in traveling crates, and bought two one-way tickets to Brussels—the city we had sworn never to return to.

Before leaving on November 10, we agreed to one last interview for a dance publication called *Dance News*. I was happy finally to have something to talk about that was real and positive—Béjart and our move to Europe—but the resulting article, once again, focused on the differences between George Balanchine and myself. It was definitely time to get out of town.

CHAPTER THIRTEEN

Through the Looking Glass

W e went to a beautiful Belgian city where we knew no one, couldn't speak the language—neither language, Flemish nor French—and were employed by a man we barely knew. It was, on the other hand, easy to shed the unhappy past, and the idea of living in Europe, where Mr. B had spent many years in his youth, suggested a sophisticated adventure.

The company had found a furnished apartment for us near the theater, which we entered through a movie house. The landlord presented us on the first day with a detailed inventory of every item in the apartment—ashtrays from various hotels, spoons, soap dishes, everything—and warned us that if anything was missing, there would be trouble. The next morning, while I was drinking coffee at the little kitchen table, the handle fell off my mug—the glue had melted—and we decided to move. We found a spacious unfurnished apartment in the center of town that was lit up each night by the flashing red neon of a gigantic Coca-Cola sign. We bought a mattress and put it on the floor, took a door off its hinges and rested it on top of two terra-cotta flowerpots for a table. After investing in a couple of straight-back chairs and nailing a ballet barre to one empty wall, we were settled and camped out, quite happily, for the next year, although the setting did not quite fit my image of European elegance.

On the other hand, the Théâtre Royal de la Monnaie, the company's home base in Brussels, was as old, elegant, and charming as one could wish. Nearby were two studios, one flat and one raked like the stage, in which we rehearsed. I encountered one of the many differences with my Balanchine education on the first day. Class was compulsory. I immediately said to myself, "Well, if I don't like class, I'm not going to take it," but now, as before, I took it every day without fail.

Curiously, considering the company's exaggerated style onstage, class was classical, terribly classical, in the English squared-off Cecchetti style. I wanted to belong and not insult anyone, so I made an effort to give the teacher what he asked for. I did, however, to the administrator's dismay, take every class on pointe while everyone else was in soft ballet shoes. One day the teacher came up to me and said, "You know, you don't have to take class on pointe," and I said, "Yes, I do. I like it up here." I hadn't worked all those years being comfortable on the tips of my toes for nothing, and I was determined not to shorten my extremities.

Because morning classes were a great deal slower in tempo than I was used to, I also determined to do an extra barre each day, a Balanchine barre. Paul joined me and we would give ourselves the kinds of split-second combinations that Mr. B had given. Speed is one of the most difficult qualities to gain, mentally and physically, and one of the quickest to vanish without daily practice. Again, although this type of movement was rarely required in Béjart's ballets, I had worked too hard for it to lose it. As a result, without a speedometer by which to gauge myself, I became even faster.

As I learned more about the company, its divergences from Balanchine's style, beliefs, and emphasis became glaringly apparent. If Balanchine believed "Ballet Is Woman," Béjart believed "Dance Is Man." Their musical tastes were equally different—Béjart's music was electronic, oriental, silent as well as classical, and he was fond of using Wagner, a composer Balanchine considered entirely inappropriate for dance. Balanchine experimented in extending the human body in space, while Béjart, who also used enormous amounts of space, filled it with props, dramatic gestures, voices, elaborate scenery and costumes, and choruses of glamorous, half-naked young men.

Everything seemed to me upside down, inside out, and backward. Yet Béjart's company is probably the only place I could have survived as a Balanchine dancer, which is what I still was. I knew my roots, and they were deeply embedded. Had I gone to a so-called more "classical" company like American Ballet Theatre or the Royal Ballet, I would have had two choices: to change my way of dancing and believing entirely, or to be a side-show display of "Balanchine dancing." It would have been easier never to dance again than to change my belief in Balanchine, but I also didn't want to dance in a vacuum as some kind of anomaly. I had grown up in the New York City Ballet, it was my family, and I needed to feel that emotional bonding. So despite the endless contradictions of Béjart's world with Balanchine's, I could dance there as I believed and still be a company player. And there was one more thing—I could learn something. Balanchine had taught me not only how to dance but how to learn, and that included being able to learn without him.

Béjart was a Frenchman whose name originally had been Bergère, meaning shepherd, and I often thought of him as the keeper of his flock. He had begun his company of about fifty dancers in 1959 when he was thirty-two, and it had become a very controversial force in European dance. While his work was adored by an enormous audience of emotional young people for its grand mystical subjects and theatrical designs, it was simultaneously criticized for the same reasons. A physically striking, energetic, and magnetic man with impeccable manners, Maurice Béjart had a great passion for his work, and that was enough of a common link for me. I liked him. He did not try to remake me, and in return I trusted him and gave him everything I had, just as I had done with Balanchine. I also took a secret satisfaction in knowing that while I was dancing Béjart, I was also showing Balanchine to people; the two were not mutually exclusive.

Although I transferred my present allegiance, I did not forget who was who or what was what artistically. Balanchine was unique choreographically and musically. Béjart's energies were devoted more to the theatrical than the musical. But he was a sincere man who had the same all-consuming zeal for his work that Balanchine did, and the atmosphere in his company was, like that at New York City Ballet, one of consolidated forces working toward a common goal. The work was different, but the approach was the same. It was an atmosphere I thrived in.

I made my debut with the company on December 10, 1970, in a pas de deux entitled *Bach Sonate* that Béjart made for Jorge Donn and myself. It was very classical by Béjart's standards, and he was offering himself, as was I, to extend our mutual resources. I wore a simple pink leotard and skirt, and Donn wore flesh-colored tights. He was Béjart's beloved protégé, an Argentinian discovered at the age of fifteen, and I saw in their situation much of the same relationship that I had had with George. This gave Donn and me an instant sympathy toward each other—we knew what a sublime but precarious position discipleship offered.

Donn was my most frequent partner for the next few years, and given our radically different background and training, we danced well together. He was dedicated, sensitive, and hard-working and had a thrust to his movement that I not only respected enormously but learned a great deal from. Shortly after premièring the Bach pas de deux I danced Béjart's *Romeo and Juliet* to the Berlioz score and found in Donn a most ardent and adoring Romeo—such a partnership was far more than I might have hoped for. I probably absorbed as much from him dramatically as I had from Jacques technically.

Christmas of 1970 was the first holiday Paul and I had spent away from home without family, and for the first time in my life I mailed over a hundred cards to people in New York, including many at the New York City Ballet. I was deeply nostalgic about many people whom I no longer saw every day; it felt as if a flood had washed them all away. Shortly before Christmas, I found a message at the theater from a Mr. Vernon Rader who said he was an American living in Brussels. Apparently we had mutual friends back in Cincinnati. Knowing we were probably alone for the holidays, he invited us to his house for dinner, but being shy, we declined. He persisted, and eventually we accepted. He picked us up and drove us to his house where we were greeted by his wife and fourteen cats. Thus we met the couple who were to make our years in Brussels a great deal easier and brighter.

In late January we embarked with the company on its first American tour. We were to perform for three weeks at the Brooklyn Academy of Music, just across the East River from my former home. Béjart had had an enormous amount of advance publicity that focused on the "avant-garde" aspect of his work; there were even buttons reading, "Béjart is Sexier."

My appearance generated a certain amount of interest; my old audience was curious about my new job, and Béjart wanted Daniel Lommel and me to appear opening night in a revival of *Erotica*, a dance set to the poetry of Tadeusz Baird. This was not my preferred role; it was not very erotic, at least not by Balanchine's subtle standards, just somewhat overt. The scenery consisted of two enormous photographs, one of Daniel and one of me, blown up and hung at the back of the stage—Béjart's film influence at work. He thought it was a wonderful way to reintroduce me to my old hometown. I expressed doubts, but he insisted. I had wanted to be seen in New York for the first time in *Bach Sonate*, because he had choreographed it especially for me.

The critics were appalled by *Erotica* and launched what amounted to a wholesale assault on not only the company but Béjart himself.

They called him crude, insincere, limited, vulgar, and pretentious and dismissed his work as expressionistic pop art. Eventually he wrote a reply in *The New York Times* that read in part, ". . . never before has a rejection of my work on the part of a journalist been interlarded with an abuse which attempts to reduce me to a provincial or worse, a cheap." It was horrible, and day by day we all ached as Maurice grew paler.

The public, on the other hand, either oblivious to advice or piqued by controversy, flocked to Brooklyn. Every performance was sold out, and every night there was a standing ovation. In Europe, Béjart had seduced an audience not made up of strict dance connoisseurs, and the same proved true in New York. He provided extravagant emotional spectacle on a grand scale, and contrary to some opinions, he was not a pretentious man. He was bright, educated, and totally honest about his work. Ultimately, it is always the box office that talks, and we were back in America before the year was over, touring Chicago, San Francisco, Los Angeles, and even New York again.

I was truly incensed at the critical reception Maurice received, especially when my own "special talents" were said to be "wasted" in Béjart's ballets. I felt that only I could pass that judgment; if I didn't feel wasted, I wasn't. Béjart chose to work on another level, a level that I felt taught me something.

Our season in Brooklyn coincided with the New York City Ballet's winter season at Lincoln Center, but I had neither the time nor the inclination to cross the river to see my old company; I was with Béjart now, and I gave him my all. There was, nevertheless, an interesting juxtaposition when *The New York Times* printed on the same page one day a review of Kay Mazzo as Dulcinea in *Don Quixote* and a review of me dancing Béjart's full-evening work *Messe pour le Temps Présent (Mass for the Present Time)*. This was a work about the current state of the world with a scene of people reading newspapers, a disco encounter, and then Donn and me on a platform in white representing pure love in a slow pas de deux. There was no music, just the rhythm of a recited French poem. For the final scene everyone came onstage carrying silent revolving red siren lights. We placed them on the floor and left as the text and music stopped. The audience was left with only a stage of flashing red lights. There were no bows.

This was certainly different from dancing Dulcinea, and it demonstrated Béjart's interest in contemporary political matters, an emphasis that, unlike Balanchine's, became easily dated but never failed to generate strong opinion at the moment. One always knew with Béjart that the audience would either love or hate us, there was no middle ground, and this made it exciting. Immediately after our New

York run, we flew back to Paris, where we were welcomed with almost worshiping enthusiasm.

Back in Brussels I started adding to my repertoire. Paul choreographed a small ballet for a workshop to one of Liszt's rhapsodies, and I learned Béjart's *Fleurs du Mal*, set to Baudelaire's poems, and his *Symphonie pour un homme seul* to Pierre Henri sounds, where at one point I swung across the stage on a rope. Props were no small part of Béjart's visions, and Paul and I had a private joke—"Have chair, will travel"—after we realized just how often he devised choreography around this simple piece of living-room furniture.

From the beginning Maurice had suggested that I watch the repertoire and tell him what I might like to dance. He knew that some things might not appeal to me, and I appreciated his sensitivity. As a result I watched closely, and my initial resistance to certain dances faded. I saw them instead as a new challenge. *Fleurs du Mal* had several leading couples, and while others danced, the rest of us had to remain onstage quietly facing huge, mirrorlike objects. It was a lesson in being resourceful and present without any specific choreography to latch on to for identity. It was also an occasion for discipline when one saw a stray strand of hair in the reflection and could do nothing about it.

Rite of Spring was a tour de force. I objected to the lack of pointe shoes in the female role, but eventually I told Maurice that I would like to try it. With its pagan, pulsating movements, it could not have been more different from the ethereal motion of my New York City Ballet days. Nevertheless, I plunged in and had a wonderful, earthy experience. And it was still Stravinsky's ecstatic music that I so loved.

Boléro was essentially a long solo where I stood on a large orange table surrounded by twenty admiring men. In bare feet, black tights to the hip, a flesh-colored leotard, and ponytail, I had to seduce for over fifteen minutes to Ravel's hypnotic music. The intimidation I had felt during the few minutes of seduction in *Slaughter on Tenth Avenue* paled beside it, but it was a fascinating experience in concentrating while under a formidable hot spotlight. Beginning with one arm, then the other, then a leg, a hip, another leg, an eye, I discovered ways to isolate each in its own mesmerizing capacity before combining them for the final collapse on the table. This company was my home now, and resisting what it had to offer would be resisting my own potential.

Béjart's father had been a professor of Eastern philosophy, and Eastern rituals had a lasting impact on his son. *Bhakti* was a ballet in three parts that celebrated Indian mysticism with elaborate face paint, masks, and a great deal of arm, head, and neck undulating. I danced the third section with Donn. As Shiva and Shakti we had a very stretchy, upside-down, oriental-style pas de deux. I wore a mask of light green pancake outlined in black liner with a red dot on my forehead and long twisted wet tendrils of hair around my face—I was now as far from Balanchine as I had ever been, but I adored the exaggeration that only the theater allows.

To find different interests and nuances in less tightly crafted work than Balanchine's was an experiment in contributing and discovering my own technical resources. I was not beyond adding looks or movements from my former days where they were appropriate; experimentation retained its stronghold in my work.

The new earthiness of my life with Béjart was not restricted to the stage, and one morning when I rolled off our mattress onto the floor I hit my head and said to Paul, "I think we are going to be here for a while, and it's time we had a real home." We found a lovely big apartment, bought some wonderful old antique furniture at Les Petits Riens, the local equivalent of the Salvation Army, acquired several more cats, and installed ourselves quite luxuriously at long last. We started to cook each evening and began feeling the pleasures and security of a comfortable domestic existence.

In the fall of 1971 Béjart embarked on what was the biggest and most successful single project I worked on with him. *Nijinsky, Clown of God*, set to a mixture of Pierre Henri and Tschaikovsky music, was based on the life of Vaslav Nijinsky, perhaps the most famous and possibly the most troubled Russian dancer of all time. Donn starred as the Nijinsky character and I was "The Young Girl in Pink," an abstraction of his wife, Romola. There were readings from his diary threaded through the score, and the ballet became an allegory that included many of his most famous roles—*L'Après-Midi d'un Faune, Petrouchka, Schéhérazade*, and *Le Spectre de la Rose*—all retold with a clown motif, an indication of how Nijinsky's dance roles came to haunt his ravaged mind. I entered on several successive occasions, each time in a shorter and shorter dress, beginning with a gorgeous pink lace gown, brimmed hat, and parasol and ending in a *Bugaku*-like bikini and white tights for the final pas de deux with Donn. After a last dance with his alter-egos, Nijinsky began to decline, and I appeared for the last time as he lay dying. This became one of my favorite Béjart roles.

The ballet was a full-evening spectacle designed for a forum-style theater with a central stage and three ramps projecting into the audience that were used for exits and entrances. It caused an enormous sensation wherever we danced it. In January we took the production to Paris for a two-week run at the 7,000-seat Palais des Sports, an immense arena on the outskirts of Paris that was usually host to ice-skating competitions, boxing matches, and soccer games. The enthusiastic audience that filled the place emphasized what I had been amazed to realize: Béjart, for all the critical controversy about his work, was a great deal more famous throughout Europe at this time than George Balanchine. In fact, Jerome Robbins, thanks to *West Side Story* and his Broadway work, enjoyed a wider reputation than Mr. B. The ovations at the end of a Béjart performance were far more vocal and lengthy than any I had ever known for a Balanchine evening; the screaming matches rivaled those at a rock concert, and tickets sold out as rapidly.

In keeping with the size of the arena, Paris arranged a publicity campaign of prodigious proportions, and our performances became a major media event. I felt I had really seen everything when I saw a gigantic billboard of myself on top of a van traveling up and down the Champs-Élysées. It was Gigi gone Hollywood. We were embraced as visiting celebrities in a way that classical ballet dancers rarely are; it was as if the world had turned completely upside down.

After performance one night, Robert Ricci, son of Nina Ricci and now head of her perfume and couture empire, sent his card backstage and asked to meet me. A small, distinguished, elegant man with graying temples, he reminded me of George; he was even wearing a little red Légion d'Honneur lapel pin just like the one George wore on occasion. He invited Paul and me to his office and asked if I would consider posing for ads for his L'Air du Temps perfume. This was the first perfume Paul had given me; I felt it was Providence calling and agreed immediately, although I didn't know how I could compete with the beautiful crystal doves that graced the top of the bottle.

Several months later we took *Nijinsky* to London where, although the tour was sold out, the reception by the press was vicious. We were called the "Folies Béjart" which "squanders the talents of some very fine dancers . . ." and accused of being "embarrassing," "hollow," "posturing," and "sheer kitsch." Balanchine was not the only dancemaker who offended British taste.

In October of 1972 the company was invited to perform *Nijinsky* for three weeks at the 5,000-seat Felt Forum in New York. I danced every night and heard later that George had attended a performance. We had no personal contact, but I was told that he said I looked very pretty with my pink parasol but that "If I had done the ballet, I'd have made Suzanne Nijinsky." At least he had been interested enough to come, and, naturally, I was curious to know what he really thought, but I never did find out.

Back home in Brussels, Béjart began choreographing a new dance to Pierre Boulez' music entitled *Marteau sans Maître (Hammer Without a Master)*. But by the time of the première, in March 1973, I was in the intensive-care unit of the local hospital with what was to be the strangest illness of my life.

One day after an especially strenuous rehearsal I felt an acute soreness in my right thigh muscle. Because it was winter I reasoned that I had not been sufficiently warmed up and had pulled a muscle or ligament. The following morning there was a distinct lump in my leg, not a typical muscular reaction, and I decided to take it easy in rehearsal. By evening it had grown visibly, and I went to see the Raders' doctor, who was baffled but gave me some anti-inflammatory pills. The next morning the lump was so large and inflamed that I could hardly walk, even dragging my leg behind me, and I had to cancel all my rehearsals. The lump was the size of a fist and throbbed constantly. The doctor came, took one look at my leg, and rushed me to the emergency room. Unable to diagnose the problem, they decided to operate and investigate. The lump was growing by the hour, and the terror of cancer was in the front of my mind.

They loaded me up with sodium Pentothal, and I was transported into bliss as they wheeled me into the operating room. When I came to, I instinctively reached down to feel if my leg was still attached; it was. The lump had turned out to be an abscess of unusual dimensions, and the operating room had to be closed down and sterilized for twenty-four hours after my operation. The wound at the top of my thigh was left open to drain and eventually close up of its own accord, so I was bedridden for over a month. On the other hand, the relief of knowing it was not fatal and did not require amputation was enormous.

The cause of the infection remained a mystery, and for the next five years I continued to develop abscesses on different parts of my body from time to time, although none was ever as large or as serious as the first. Perhaps they were a reaction to the different bacteria indigenous to Europe—I even worried that it might have been the wine! Several months later I developed a painful case of kidney stones, and I became convinced that the pleasures of red wine were taking their revenge.

Once again during a health crisis, Mother came through. It obviously took an emergency to overcome her enduring anger and hurt over my decision to marry, but now she traveled to Belgium at once, and when she arrived in Brussels she and Paul managed to maintain a certain civility. Previously, the only interaction we had had was the occasional letter in which Mother would detail who was dancing my different roles at the New York City Ballet: "So-and-so is doing *Brahms* and so-and-so is doing 'Diamonds.'. . ." Whatever her intent, I hated it. My life was different now, and I refused to be baited into remorse or regret. Mother didn't show any apparent interest in what I was dancing with Béjart; her loyalties remained with Balanchine throughout.

I was, however, glad to see her, and we spent our days in relatively peaceful coexistence, playing cards and talking. I had been ordered to eat red meat because my blood count was so low, and after being a virtual vegetarian for much of my dancing life, I started downing giant steaks every day, a practice I continued, to a lesser extent, for several years.

I recovered in time for a North American tour to Seattle, Phoenix, St. Louis, and Vancouver in the spring, followed by Milan in May, Barcelona, Toronto, Ottawa, and Washington, D.C., in June. Béjart's full touring schedule took us to cities, countries, and continents that I would never otherwise have visited. Although the New York City Ballet toured, it was limited by its size, the expense involved, and the fact that by the 1960s Balanchine was more interested in making new ballets at home than showing old ones abroad. Needless to say, the education in different cultures was illuminating, and the world became a lot bigger place to me than it had seemed even in New York City.

For our visit to Jerusalem in July 1973, Béjart designed a ballet for me to Mozart's variations on *Twinkle, Twinkle, Little Star*. Entitled *Ah, vous dirais-je, Maman*, it was essentially a solo where I was a precocious young student dressed in a short tutu and black neck ribbon, like a Degas dancer, who danced the twelve variations of the tune for my onstage pianist mother. I began the ballet by playing seven notes on the piano (after locating Middle C directly below the first letter of the piano logo), which proved more challenging than dancing the twelve variations.

Every summer we had six weeks off, and Paul and I returned to our island in the Adirondacks. Slowly but methodically, we began rebuilding—a new roof for the house, glass for the boarded windows, a kitchen, new cabins, and even a grass croquet course where before there had been only a swamp. And we bought a snazzy little speedboat.

In the summer of 1973 we drove two hours down to Saratoga to see the New York City Ballet dance for the second time since our departure. In June 1972 Balanchine had astounded the dance world with his most ambitious project to date, the Stravinsky Festival in which the company premièred no fewer than twenty-one new ballets by eight choreographers in the space of one week. Of the nine made by Balanchine, at least three—*Duo Concertant, Violin Concerto*, and

Symphony in Three Movements—were already acknowledged master-pieces. While we had heard something of the festival, we had seen none of the new ballets until now.

We saw *Violin Concerto* and *Symphony in Three Movements*, and while I realized what I had missed, I was happy to know such ballets existed at all, and my belief in Balanchine was reconfirmed. If I was a little sad or nostalgic, it passed. I felt no bitterness; my "now" was in Europe with Maurice, I was happy and I refused to regret the choices I had made.

By August we were back in Brussels preparing a mammoth new production entitled *Golestan (Rose Garden)*. The company had been invited to Iran to perform, and being a man who took advantage of opportunity, Béjart designed a Persian ballet to honor our host, the Shah of Iran. The première was a private showing for the Shah and his wife in Persepolis, a half hour from Shiráz. There, in the middle of the desert, a huge outdoor platform had been erected near the tomb of Xerxes, complete with piped water, electric lighting, and full, though primitive, backstage facilities. It was a model of Persian extravagance. For the audience of the Shah, his family, his bodyguards, and my eleven-year-old nephew, who was visiting us, thick Persian carpets had been strewn across the sand, which was lit by candles. In the center was a velvet divan for the Shah. It was truly a scene out of the *Arabian Nights*, and when the Shah clapped his hands, the performance began.

My part had an intricate pas de deux with Donn and a high-powered variation set to ritual Persian drums. As the lead rose I was dressed in red from head to foot and, among a chorus of girls in green, I was known backstage as the pimento in the olive. *Golestan* was the first, and only, time I actually danced in red shoes. Unlike the ballerina in the movie, I had no trouble getting them off—though the red dye stuck around on my hands for a while.

The large chorus of men wore long white pants and shirts with sleeves that reached to the ground. They were visually effective, but predictably, one by one the men tripped on their sleeves and fell. In rhythm with the beat of wooden instruments came a succession of "boom . . . boom . . . boom," as one after another went down. The bright lights in the middle of the desert attracted some rather enormous insects, and as they hit the lights and fell, dazed, to the stage, their splats and buzzes added to the booms, creating a generally hilarious echo of the musical score. We were, however, unable to vent our amusement; all mouths were held tightly closed to prevent the entrance of shifting desert sands. I believe the Shah thoroughly enjoyed the ballet and was honored to have had a ballet invoking his own cultural tradition.

Following the performance, we were ushered into two silk-and-velvet tents, one red and one blue, each the size of a city block, erected in the desert for food and entertainment. After hors d'oeuvres and champagne in the first tent, we were directed into the second for a sit-down buffet of elaborate and exotic foods, while the Shah and Empress Farah table-hopped, introducing themselves.

In the midst of this unreal splendor and wealth, the medal of the Virgin that Diana had given me and a big Russian cross from George were stolen from my dressing room. I had carried them with me everywhere as a source of strength, placing them like good-luck icons by my makeup mirror in every dressing room in every theater. Now I felt my last ties to Balanchine were gone. I remember saying to myself stoically, "Now I know, I'll never go back to the New York City Ballet." Perhaps my fate needed that last emotional break before it could proceed. And there was one more adventure with Béjart to be enjoyed.

For four weeks in October and November of 1973 the company boarded a small Greek ship for a tour to North Africa with stops at Tunis, Algiers, Casablanca, Tenerife in the Canary Islands, and Dakar. The strange circumstances began when we took a bubble-gum-pink chartered airplane from Brussels to Tunisia, where we boarded the ship that was to be our home for the next few weeks. Aside from the company and crew, the only civilians on board were Béjart's mother and Barbara and Vernon Rader, who enjoyed the run of the boat while we made excursions to shore for performances.

We drew cabin numbers out of a hat, and as we walked along the railing to find our little cubicles I remarked to Paul about the numerous little brown cardboard boxes that lined the hallways. When we awoke the next morning, far from land in a very rough Mediterranean, not one box remained, and the communal breakfast room was filled with some very green dancers. As the morning proceeded, more faces appeared only to say a heroic *"bonjour"* before leaping onto the deck and vomiting overboard; how we were all going to rehearse and dance became increasingly mysterious.

Maurice and Paul alternated teaching class outdoors under the sun on a large deck cleared for the purpose, but every time the ship rolled from one side to another, dancers dressed in everything from bathing suits to shorts and sweatpants went flying from one side of the boat to another, laughing uncontrollably. The lounge inside looked like an old folks' home with people knitting, playing cards and Monopoly, and sipping chicken broth.

Because of the unusually rough seas we were still one day's sail away from Algiers on the morning of the scheduled performance, so we were shuttled to the nearest land in motorboats to board buses that would carry us overland at a more appropriate speed. Upon arrival we found the makeshift stage measured only twenty feet wide, so we had to slice the ballet crosswise to fit on it. The experience of dancing *Romeo and Juliet* with wiggly Olive Oyl legs was unique; every time Donn and I were supposed to embrace, we missed each other's arms, and it felt more like a Chaplin comedy than Shakespeare's tragedy. As the performance ended, we saw our ship pulling into the harbor to pick us up and dock for the night.

While I was promenading on deck one evening with Maurice, he said to me, "Wouldn't it be nice to have a Balanchine ballet?" I mentioned to him that I owned one—*Meditation*—and he said, "Well, how do we get it?" It had not occurred to me before to ask Maurice to dance Balanchine, but now, at his suggestion, I wrote to Barbara Horgan to inquire about the possibility. I received in return the musical orchestration and Jacques, who flew over to teach Donn his role.

It was wonderful to see Jacques again after four and a half years, and we worked together with all the speed and enthusiasm of times gone by. Donn and I performed the ballet in Brussels at the Théâtre Royal de la Monnaie on December 21, 1973. It was a highly emotional night. Donn was more nervous than I had ever seen him; it was the first time he was dancing Balanchine, a man he respected enormously. I wanted Donn to have something as momentous as the occasion, so I gave him a necklace with a small turquoise cross that George had given to me. He didn't want to take it, saying it was too special, but I insisted; I was going for broke this time. The night was uncanny, the choreography felt like my own skin, grafted on after years of absence. We danced the entire pas de deux in tears.

Ten years after its creation, *Meditation,* in all its romantic glory, was once again provocative. The Belgian audience, so accustomed to Béjart's extravagant theater, was stunned by its palpable emotion and simplicity. I was ecstatic to be dancing it again, but I was careful to remember that I was only revisiting an old friend while in a new land—I was not returning. There was another Béjart ballet in production.

We premièred *Il Triomphe* in the Boboli Gardens of Florence on an outdoor stage surrounded by the beauty of Italian horticultural and sculptural art. The ballet, set to Luciano Berio's music, described the stages of Petrarch's life in six themes: Love, Chastity, Death, Fame, Time, and Eternity. I portrayed Laura and was in four of the themes. Each phase was marked by a Roman chariot of Ben-Hur proportions designed in the company's scenic workshop. I entered as Chastity in a chiffon gown covered with pearls with a unicorn by my side— shades of *The Lady and the Unicorn*—only now I did not blush. Death entered and took me, but with Fame I was resurrected before the final tableau, where everyone returned in simple body stockings and white lights and waves raised us to Heaven. I adored the opportunities for high drama—death, resurrection, and even eternal splendor.

Following the Italian season we had our annual summer break, and Paul and I flew back to our island. As we had the year before, we bought tickets for a performance of the New York City Ballet in Saratoga and saw *Symphony in C* and *La Valse*. Although I had danced both these ballets many times, I had rarely seen them and was deeply moved. When we got back to the island, I was very emotional and felt driven to write George to tell him exactly how I felt—it was the shortest letter I had ever written.

Dear George,
    As wonderful as it is to see your ballets, it is even more wonderful to dance them. Is this impossible?
                      Love,
                      Suzi

Part

IV

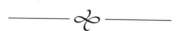

CHAPTER FOURTEEN

Back to the Future

I walked over to West 67th Street and went up in the elevator to the twelfth floor. As I stood facing Balanchine's front door, many thoughts rushed through my mind, but I ignored them all and knocked. I had absolutely no idea what would happen when we saw each other.

Since I had received no response to my previous letters, I had expected none this time. But I had to write. I think I knew somehow the time had come. I sent the note to the theater in Saratoga. Several days later, when we were back on Cedar Islands, Paul came tearing down to the shore where I was swimming, waving his arms. "Barbara Horgan is on the phone."

I ran up to the house dripping water and picked up the receiver. "Mr. Balanchine received your note," Barbara said, "and he wondered if you might be able to meet with him." I told her we would be in the city at the end of August en route to Brussels, and a meeting was arranged.

I did not dare imagine what he might have to say to me, or what I might say to him, or why he had finally answered a letter. It could have been in reference to my dancing *Meditation* in Brussels, or he could have simply been curious to see me.

The door opened, and there stood George. My heart skipped a beat, then a feeling of great comfort came over me. He asked me in, and we hugged each other as we had done so many times before. We were alone, and he uncorked a bottle of his favorite Haut-Brion vintage. I don't recall exactly what we said, but it wasn't much. It was as if we picked up where we had left off. What had happened between us was no longer a problem; it had been absorbed, and we were ready for each other again.

Our primary concern was that I had immediate commitments to Béjart that included a tour to Rome, Paris, and Monte Carlo in the fall. George respected the fact that I wanted to fulfill these obligations. When I left, I had been there barely an hour, and my life had flipped over again. Paul was still unmentioned between us, but I understood that only I would return.

Because of the unlikeliness of a reconciliation with George, Paul and I had not fully discussed the possibility of one, but when he heard what had happened, there was no friction between us. As a dancer, he knew that I belonged with the New York City Ballet and was extremely happy for me. So while it was clear that I was to have a job and he wasn't, we thought that, perhaps in time, Balanchine might relent and take Paul back too.

We flew to Brussels to prepare for our move and tell Maurice that we would be leaving his company. He was very sorry to lose me, but, like Paul, he knew that I was a Balanchine dancer first and last. Curiously, as soon as I found that I would be returning to the New York City Ballet I realized that I had assimilated all I could from my Béjart experience. Much as I loved the company, I was ready to leave; yet not once until this moment had I entertained that notion. Now, suddenly, my muscles and my memories started twitching with different thoughts, channeling themselves for Balanchine.

In Brussels we arranged to have our furniture shipped back to New York, broke our lease, and moved in with the Raders until we left in December. During the summer we had acquired Duchess, a big, friendly German Shepherd whom we took on our final tour with Béjart. In Paris Maurice took us to Maxim's for dinner, and the kind maître d' offered to watch Duchess while we ate. We were duly impressed with this extra service until we found out that not only had the help walked her, they had fed her *boeuf haché* and string beans on a silver platter and charged her meal to our bill!

Our last performance with the company was in Monte Carlo. It was a very emotional occasion with many hugs and tears; I was deeply grateful to Maurice for my four years with him. Just before we left, Donn returned to me George's turquoise cross, which I had given him for *Meditation*. It had served its purpose, and he insisted that it really belonged with me.

Back in Brussels one of our cats had just given birth, so we boarded the plane for New York with nine cats and a large dog. We looked more like a traveling animal act than dancers. With no time to find an apartment of our own, we moved in with Paul's mother, bringing the total in her establishment to five adults and twelve animals. At night the entire apartment turned into one big bed. We lived there for about a month before a duplex in the building became available.

Meanwhile, I unpacked the essentials, including my shawl. (In 1962 I had purchased a flowered black, red, and orange shawl at the airport before leaving Russia, and during my Béjart years I had developed the habit of wearing it, wrapped around my body in any number of ways, for class and rehearsals. It was to become my backstage trademark, good-luck charm, and security blanket; I was rarely without it.) Then I walked over to the New York State Theater. It was all a little unbelievable, and I was nervous. It was five and a half years since I had been in the building, and I knew that many things had changed. I walked down the long, dark corridor to the main hall for class and touched the cold yellow cement wall; it felt like an old friend.

When I pushed open the heavy fire door to the studio I saw what looked like hundreds of dancers. The company had grown since my departure, and there were many very curious, unfamiliar faces. There were some familiar faces, too, all staring at me, wondering what would happen, in the next five minutes and the next five years.

My reappearance posed a possible threat to many dancers, especially those who had been dancing my former roles, but I was equally full of trepidation. There were six other principal women dancers— Kay Mazzo, Karin von Aroldingen, and Sara Leland, who had all been promoted since my departure, and Patricia McBride, Allegra Kent, and Violette Verdy. I was prepared—and expecting—not to be cast as often or favored as exclusively as before.

Jacques, of course, was in class and had saved me a place at one of the portable barres in the center of the studio. We had always stood next to each other. A few people came up and said hello, but basically they were all waiting to see what would happen. Was I better or worse? Fatter or thinner? Weaker or stronger? Faster or slower? And for the many who had never seen me dance, who had only heard stories or seen pictures, I was a kind of notorious legend, and they had the greatest curiosity of all: What was the fuss about? What had Balanchine seen in her? Would he still see it? I wondered too.

At ten past eleven Mr. B, in one of his smart western shirts, came through the back door as he always had, and I could feel all eyes on him and on me, back and forth, back and forth. Unable to stand the tension, I thought to myself, "Well, to hell with everybody," and went over to give him a hug. He hugged me back, and class, to my great relief, began.

I quickly realized that coming back was a great deal harder than I had expected. There were a lot of unanswered questions. Had Balanchine moved on in his work and left me behind with an understanding that had worked for us in the 1960s but would not work for him in the 1970s? The publicity and acclaim that surrounded the 1972 Stravinsky Festival had brought the company new power, prestige, and fame. Balanchine was now recognized as one of the century's towering artistic geniuses. Would I still be useful to him? Would I still interest him?

I immediately started rehearsing many of my old roles and was cast for my first performance in the adagio of *Symphony in C*—the role I was to have danced the night I left the company in 1969. So I literally picked up where I had left off. With the confusion of moving and the tension of returning I came down with the flu and had to postpone the performance by a few days, not an auspicious start. Balanchine cast me with Peter Martins, the young Dane with whom I had danced several times just before leaving. At that time he was still a guest artist. In the interim, he had joined the company and become Balanchine's most eloquent young male dancer.

A little surprised to see him at our first rehearsal—I had never danced this ballet with him before—I said to him jokingly, "Oh, you're still here." There was a certain irony in the fact that he had crossed the Atlantic to come to Balanchine at almost the same time that I had crossed, leaving Balanchine.

In 1967 Peter had not made any enormous impression on me, but now, as he took my hand to lead me on the long diagonal entrance, there was electricity. He seemed like a different person than he had been before, but then I, too, was different. It felt as if we had been partners all our lives; there were no technical problems, no temperamental hitches—here was the partner of my dreams I had never dreamed about. In fact, I had not given any thought to whom I would be dancing with—I just wanted to work with George again. Peter's solicitous partnering smoothed the way for my first trembling entrance before the all-knowing, all-curious New York audience.

Waiting the whole evening for this moment—*Symphony in C* always concluded the program—I pinned the rhinestone crown on my head ten times over, until finally little Mme. Pourmel hooked me into the

white tutu she had so sadly removed from my dressing room six years
before. Peter and I stood in the dark empty back wing while the corps
and demisoloists began the adagio movement.

He said, *"Merde,"* I said, *"Merde,"* and crossed myself twice. I then
pinched myself twice and bourréed out onstage, reluctant and yet
eager. There was no place on earth I would rather have been. The
spotlight was the light at the end of my tunnel. I was twenty-nine
and felt ageless.

Out of the corner of my eye, I saw George in the front right wing,
leaning on his elbow, watching, and I felt a little less lonely. The
performance went by like a dream, and afterward, through the maze
of my thoughts, I heard the waves of applause. Ronnie Bates, the
stage manager, took my arm and told me to go out in front of the
curtain for a solo bow. I protested, knowing this wasn't company
policy—*Symphony in C* had four ballerinas, and the last thing I wanted
to do was ruffle any more feathers in an already tense situation. But
he insisted. "The audience wants it," he said, and I could only presume that he would not have encouraged me without Balanchine's
approval. I went alone, and the audience was very kind, welcoming
me back. Afterward Paul and I went out and celebrated.

A few days later I danced *Concerto Barocco* with Peter and Colleen
Neary, Pat's younger sister—the generations were moving on. Although I had not danced any of these ballets for six years, I remembered the choreography as if it were engraved in my mind and body.
I was quite surprised, therefore, when I had my first rehearsal for
"Diamonds" and realized that in the living room the previous evening
I had performed a ten-minute pas de deux in seven. The next day in
rehearsal with Jacques, I realized my mistake; as soon as I heard the
music and had a real partner to dance with, I remembered the other
three minutes.

On January 26, I danced my first "Diamonds," and in the beginning
of the pas de deux Jacques missed my hand trying for the wonderful
"hands off" effect, and, crash, I was down on my rump. A ballerina
in a tutu down on the floor is particularly unsightly, given the stark
classicism of her image, but despite feeling that this was a most imperfect beginning, I also felt a dizzy comfort—once again Jacques and
I were taking risks, and I felt an odd sensation of gratitude in spite
of my ungainly position.

"Diamonds" had a special meaning for me, and I was extremely
emotional about dancing it again. Unlike *Symphony in C* and *Barocco*,
it had been made on me, and I felt a unique bonding with George in
such ballets. "Diamonds" was the last classic ballet he had done for
me before I left. It was also to Tschaikovsky who always affects me;

I inevitably dance his music with a lump in my throat—and a strength in my body.

Jacques was now forty, and while he was still full of enthusiasm, verve, and passion, his body was not what it had once been, although he was to continue dancing for almost ten more years. The terrible discrepancy between the strength of a dancer's will and his instrument was made clear to me one day when I was walking down the hall with Jacques. "Oh, Suzaahn," he said, "I have always wanted to dance with you again, but now that you've come back to the company, I can't do anything anymore." It broke my heart to see someone know so much and want to give so much and have nature take away his ability. I thought to myself, as a warning, "Dear God, nobody should want to dance that much." But when my time came, I knew exactly how he felt. On the other hand, I believe that wanting it so passionately is what can make dancing truly great.

At the end of that first season in early 1975, I revisited the most poignant ballet of my old repertoire, *Don Quixote*. It was an unexpected experience of stirred memories—wonderful memories but nevertheless memories of something past. Now, instead of George opposite me as the Don, it was the partner of my youth, Jacques; instead of Conrad Ludlow as my support in the Dream Scene, it was a new young man in the company. He was a fine partner, but *Don Quixote* had been that rare Balanchine ballet where the "who" of every role had taken on an extra reverberating meaning. It was now ten years later, and the feelings and pulses and thrusts were different, and I became emotional for different reasons. It was not so much that we were all older in the melancholy sense of time passed, but rather the realization that while *Don Quixote* had performed an unquestionable service in 1965, its purpose had been fulfilled. Perhaps because it was no longer necessary, its fit felt imperfect.

Within three years the ballet was retired permanently from the repertoire. Perhaps George thought it was time to give up fighting windmills; besides, he had other ballets on his mind by then. Ironically, when the last performances were announced in 1978, the ballet received its most enthusiastic and glowing reviews. Anna Kisselgoff, the senior dance critic of *The New York Times*, described Dulcinea's impact: "No words, not even those by Cervantes, could communicate the depth of spiritual solace that her dance images transmitted so sharply and yet without literalness."

Mr. B presided over the final rehearsals for each of the ballets before I performed them again, but he said very little. He watched, as he had done so often ever since my audition at the School. The silence belied the incredible excitement I felt in dancing for him again. I did not forget, ever, that but for his generosity I would not have had the privilege.

I was not the first leading dancer to have left the company under less than friendly circumstances, and I was not the last to want to return. That he allowed me to come back was my good fortune, and I would like to think that, among other reasons, the fact that our differences had been personal and not artistic made the difference. Had they been artistic, we probably never would have worked together again, but I had not left because I wanted to explore the dance world across the street, or because I felt his ballets did not "fulfill my needs."

Now I had the opportunity to proceed where I had left off. But no matter how willing I was, there was the distinct chance that returning might be less than glorious. I had glowing memories, which can be dangerous and formidable competition to the present. Balanchine's ballets did not reside primarily in my mind, however, but in my muscles and body, and each time I danced a role again, they happened of their own accord and their bountiful offerings, not only to the audience but to me, a dancer, increased with every performance—this is perhaps the truest test of a transcendent work.

My pleasures were total, but they were not assured. Like everyone else, I was at the mercy, however benevolent, of Balanchine's whim when it came to casting, but within a week, to my great happiness, I was again dancing virtually every night. I even had the opportunity to dance ballets that I had not performed in the sixties—*Allegro Brillante, Donizetti Variations*. There were, however, some differences—I was not consulted about what I wanted to dance, and now I shared roles, like "Diamonds" and *Don Quixote,* with the ballerinas who had done them in my absence. That was fine with me. But Balanchine's attempt to be "fair" did not really work, and there were a few contretemps with some of my peers. It was inevitable, given the situation, and no one was to blame. Some things hadn't changed: everyone wanted Balanchine's undivided attention and adoration, and everyone coveted dancing each of his ballets. The situation was summed up most succinctly by a soloist with the company, who wryly explained, "Suzanne's coming back is the best thing that's happened to us since she left."

Speculation about the effects of my reappearance on company life was not relegated to backstage. In *The New Yorker,* Arlene Croce surmised that my return could prove to be a "serious crisis" in terms of its possible repercussions on other dancers: "It isn't amusing to speculate, even in private, on what may happen to these girls now that Farrell has returned, or to the less talented ones, or, indeed, to Farrell herself."

On other fronts the public and press had a field day with my return. Had I danced badly there would have been plenty of ammunition— "five years in an alien and diseased repertory" as Croce called my Béjart period—to explain any loss of technique, speed, elegance, or even musicality. The drama was palpable: Had I become a "victim" of Béjart? Had I dried up and lost my enthusiam for Balanchine given our checkered history? Although I felt all eyes on me as never before and was nervous as never before, my solace was still the same—Mr. B's opinion was all I cared about, and his silent presence in the wings each night gave me all the courage I needed and more.

My physical appearance was described literally inch by inch—even the level of my eyelids was commented upon—until I felt as if I had no secrets left. But I also knew that this kind of exposure is an integral part of being a performer. Ultimately, when all the tallies were in, everyone had been very kind indeed, and the general consensus was that I had "improved." I took it all as an affirmation—and tribute— to Balanchine's training. It was said that my arms and hands had a new refinement, that I had mellowed, that there was a new touch of sadness in my movement, that my off-balance was more off-balance, that my dramatic delivery was more dramatic, that I had become more sensitive, that I was thinner. . . .

I still don't know what this all meant, if indeed it was all true. I was never the kind of dancer to compartmentalize my work or my anatomy by focusing on "improving" any specific quality, step, or interpretation. Changes in my dancing—and I've no doubt there were many—were unforced and uncalculated. They were probably as attributable to the way I heard the music on a certain night as to my Béjart experiences. Dancing is a feeling—physical, emotional, and spiritual—and that feeling changes of its own inevitable accord at every moment of your life.

After my reentrance into the company had been accomplished, the next question for everyone, including myself, was what, if anything, new would Balanchine make on me. For the spring season of 1975 a three-week-long Ravel Festival was scheduled, and it provided the answer—a curious one indeed.

The festival had three different programs featuring sixteen world premières, half of them by Balanchine. Although he was now seventy-one and gray, he showed no sign of slowing down creatively or otherwise. Sometime during the frantic rehearsal weeks just prior to the festival Mr. B came over to our new apartment (Paul was not home at the time) and brought a record of Ravel's *Tzigane* to play for me. He explained that this was the music for the ballet he would make with me, a kind of gypsy dance. Periodically he would laugh out loud as he listened to the violin twist the music into an almost corny gypsy hoedown—it was Ravel's version of "Turkey in the Straw"—and while I shared his enthusiasm and adored his good humor, it worried me a little that this dance, whatever it was going to be, would not be particularly "classical," not what either I or the public was expecting from Balanchine in terms of the image of me that he had capitalized on so often before. But I had to trust him and wait for rehearsals to find out. They did not begin until a week before the scheduled première, and in the meantime I had several other new ballets to distract me.

Jerome Robbins, who had joined the company in 1949 as an associate artistic director, had been absent during my tenure in the 1960s and had triumphantly returned the day I departed when his *Dances at a Gathering* had its first performance. During the six years of my absence he had choreographed eleven new ballets, and many of his works were welcomed with an extra measure of appreciation during a time when some of Balanchine's new productions had led many critics to declare that the master's creative juices were drying up. Opening night of the Stravinsky Festival changed this dim prognosis, but meanwhile Robbins had become the company's second most productive and respected choreographer and one of enormous importance to its audience and its repertoire.

Aside from a brief stint during my first year in the company as a horn in *Fanfare,* I had never danced a Robbins ballet, and *Concerto in G* (later called *In G Major*), choreographed for the Ravel Festival, was my first. I had heard, as had everyone in the ballet world, about the various difficulties of working with this supposedly temperamental and demanding choreographer, but my experience did not confirm this reputation.

Jerry often juggled several versions of choreography with an equal number of different casts before deciding which combination suited his purpose best, and *In G Major* was no exception. He designed the ballet's central pas de deux on Sara Leland and Bart Cook, and only later asked Peter and me to learn it and dance the première. This method was unfamiliar to me—Balanchine never changed his casting once he began a ballet unless injury forced him to—and I did not particularly like the audition atmosphere that was sure to encourage insecurity all around. But Jerry was polite, helpful, and accommodating, and he had created a very beautiful, languid pas de deux that I enjoyed dancing. The ballet was an enormous success and became one of the few from the festival that had a future life. So the first new ballet I danced after my return was not by Balanchine.

My second new ballet was by Jacques. *Alborada del Gracioso* was

Ravel *à l'espagnol,* and Jacques made a dance for himself and me with four couples. Since Paul had choreographed a pas de deux for the two of us at Béjart to this same music, it was a bit like changing steps in midstream.

The company was already full force into the festival when Balanchine, Gordon Boelzner, and I finally got together in a small rehearsal studio to begin *Tzigane.* Despite the intense flurry of activity and constant last-minute panics in the theater about ballets whose choreography, costumes, and lighting were finished only hours before their scheduled premières, Mr. B remained the ever-calm center of the storm—he knew he could whip up a little "gypsy number" in less than a week. For me, on the other hand, it was less than ideal. I had waited a long time to work with him again, and I wanted to prolong the experience beyond six days. The music dictated a nine-minute ballet, and Mr. B told me that at one point four couples would join the action, but I didn't know when this might be. We began at the beginning, and he knew exactly how I would make my entrance— I was to mosey slowly onstage from the back left wing, no steps, no pointe work, no pirouettes, just a kind of sultry, draggy schlep. I was miffed. This was the first ballet George would make on me after six years, and my entrance did not appear to herald any great epiphany.

"Well, he's never let you down. He knows what he's doing," I quickly cautioned myself. The music begins with a drawn-out violin solo and then very slowly builds to more rapid rhythms and variations, and so did I. Balanchine's choreographic directions were typically nonchalant and vague: "Oh, maybe walk a little to the left, stop a second, and then walk a little right . . . maybe raise an arm here. . . ."

It sounded like nothing, but before long it started looking like something. He was indicating a mood, an atmosphere, a tone, something that did not depend on which leg or arm did what when. As the music speeded up, the old routine emerged of Gordon playing a phrase or two, Mr. B running around, moving like a seductive gypsy, with me behind him, imitating and memorizing simultaneously. Suddenly he would twist around into some wonderful movement I'd never seen and say to me, "How about that?" and I would say, "It looks great—but what did you do?" I'd deliver up some similar version that didn't correspond to any academic form, and he'd say, "Good," and proceed to the next phrase of music. There were a lot of strangely intricate arm and hand flourishes and many toe-heel-toe, turned-in czardas steps. The flavor of the dance started to emerge.

Finally, he suggested an actual ballet step: "Now, maybe you can do a big arabesque," and, always wanting to give him as much as possible, I did a huge, diving arabesque penché. "We know you can do that," he countered, "what else can you do?" and I flipped out of the penché into a deep backbend, head facing upward. His eyebrows rose as I looked to him for comment, and I knew then the fun had begun—we were experimenting again.

In that first hour-and-a-half rehearsal we completed my whole solo, all five long minutes of it. There were many moments that remained vague, where I felt not altogether sure of my footing, but this didn't bother anyone. Mr. B always saw further than what was precisely delivered; he saw the shape of the ballet, and if its edges remained unfinished, it didn't matter. A ballet's atmosphere evolves, it cannot be carved in stone as long as it remains a musical event.

The following day another rehearsal was scheduled, and Peter Martins showed up for this one. Although I was not privy to the conversation, Peter had apparently cast himself as my partner in *Tzigane*, and George, having no specific objection, allowed it.

During the final moments of my solo, Balanchine had Peter shuffle onstage behind me from a back wing. It was lonely being out there so long in a single spotlight with a single instrument and no conductor—more lonely even than the diagonal entrance in "Diamonds"—and I found Peter's appearance most welcome. The lights brightened, the music broadened into a full orchestra, and the four couples came onstage for the finale of the ballet.

The entire dance was completed in a few days, but I remained uncertain not so much about the actual choreography, what there was of it, as about the flavor of my character. This woman was no Dulcinea and no queen with a crown—but I suspected that she was still a lady of sorts. Several days into rehearsals Lamar Alsop, the violinist, played, and hearing the music with its rightful instrument made things much clearer. Without a conductor Lamar had total control over the tempos, and Balanchine became very animated as he told him that *Tzigane* should be played not with a classical approach but a brash, rather shameless one. "It's like Hungarian restaurant music, a goulash," he kept saying as he snapped his fingers and tapped his foot. I wondered for a moment where I was as I realized that my Béjart training of filling a stage with drama, music, and few actual steps was benefiting this situation more than my fast Balanchine tendus! Balanchine was obviously capitalizing on what I had learned during the past five years.

In the middle of the solo there was a step that made me feel extremely awkward, and the resolution of the problem demonstrates the easy, polite, generous way Balanchine dealt with his dancers' insecurities. After numerous repetitions of the step, I finally wrinkled my nose at Mr. B and hoping for an alteration said, "Is this really right? Do you like this?" To my surprise, he didn't respond to my hint and said that he liked it very much. But he also asked if it was uncomfortable for me and said that if it still felt strange by the time of the première, he would change it. True to his word, five minutes before the curtain was to rise on the first performance he came up to me and asked if I wanted to change the movement. "No," I said. "I think I've figured it out." The movement eventually became so much an integral part of the whole that I no longer remember which one it was.

I could have guessed that I wouldn't be in white for this ballet, but when the costume designer arrived with a solid red drapey outfit I was quite upset. Balanchine, always the gentleman, said nothing, and only later did we go together to Mme. Pourmel for advice. Down in the storage rooms of the theater we found some old costumes originally designed for John Clifford's *Kodaly Dances*. One skirt was made of red, gold, and black shredded ribbons and onto it Mme. Pourmel attached the burgundy-and-beige blousy bodice from my *Don Quixote* Zoraida costume. The combination was perfect, and when I wore it for the dress rehearsal, it gave me the final indication of how I was to move and be. It was as if Zoraida, the failed gypsy of *Don Quixote*, had found her true self ten years later. Perhaps only now was I ready for a flaming red costume.

The première on May 29 was an enormous success, and Mr. B thought the ballet was wonderful. He had a sly grin on his face as the audience cheered him. All critical curiosity about our first collaboration in six years was laid to rest—though Lincoln Kirstein was the only one who managed to capture *Tzigane*'s paradoxical tone in words, with an interesting reflection as to what it might mean.

The music is not exactly a Hungarian cousin to the composer's *Boléro*, but its nightclub overtones cannot be ignored. . . . Farrell did not impersonate a "gypsy"; her body played with theatricalized elements of wildness, caprice, longing, and arrant independence which could be read as intensely secret and personal. Was part of this an echo of her own wandering, of the fact she had at last returned to her tribe's encampment, while proclaiming her own increased identity and independence?

In the opening solo of *Tzigane* there were several moments where Balanchine chose not to choreograph specifically and simply told me to "do something." During the first performance, just before Peter's entrance, I found myself with more music than usual before a final series of fast chaîné turns. Suddenly "something" had a new meaning for me. I held out my palm, fingers splayed, and pointed to its center with the forefinger of my other hand—it was the universal image of a fortune-teller, but I thought of it as a very private gesture: I was pointing to my life line. It seemed appropriate not only to the moment but to my whole reunion with Balanchine.

CHAPTER FIFTEEN

Just Dancing

❦

O ver the course of the next several years the New York City Ballet reached an unprecedented summit of success, financial stability, and artistic grace. There were sold-out European tours where the company was greeted like visiting royalty, Balanchine was honored as never before, the School of American Ballet kept producing beautiful, streamlined dancers of such quality and quantity that the company grew to over a hundred dancers, and, most significant of all, Balanchine's energy and appetite for work continued unabated. In retrospect, these were the glory days, and it seemed as if there were nothing but new triumphs on the horizon.

These years also saw the solidification of my partnership with Peter Martins. The first ballet Balanchine made on Peter and me, *Tzigane*, in which he had a rather abbreviated role, was for some time the only one. This was strange, considering not only how successfully we danced with each other but how closely we became associated, as a couple, with many of Balanchine's greatest ballets; they were all ballets made on other dancers at other times.

Under the aegis of an informal exchange program Peter and I traveled with Balanchine, Violette Verdy, and Jean-Pierre Bonnefoux (both principal dancers imported by Balanchine from France) to Paris in December 1975 to perform and rehearse several ballets with the Paris Opéra Ballet. They were staging their own Ravel celebration, and we danced *Tzigane, In G Major,* and *Sonatine.*

Paris retained its romance and memories for me, but it was now Peter and I who dined with George each night after the performance. I don't think any of us would have had it any other way. I had grown up a lot since my first visit to Paris, and George had obviously reached some kind of peace or understanding about our past difficulties, although it was a subject that would be discussed between us only once.

After our week in Paris, George flew back to New York, while Peter and I went on to Copenhagen for a few performances with Peter's alma mater, the Royal Danish Ballet. We danced *The Nutcracker, Apollo,* and our first *Tschaikovsky Pas de Deux* together, and Peter introduced me to not only his hometown but his family. I was struck by the fact that, in addition to being tall, we both had very short mothers.

We had met up again at a mutually productive time. Unlike Jacques, who was many years my senior in both age and experience, Peter was only a year younger, so our careers and bodies were happily in sync with each other. After joining the company, Peter had for several years rebelled against Balanchine's subtle but unrelenting demands on male dancers and male egos. Unlike some of his predecessors, however, he finally saw the light and revealed a smooth, self-effacing manner and a kind of purity of execution that set the standard for the New York City Ballet's male dancers.

Offstage, our friendship progressed in its own way. After traveling to Denmark on very little sleep, we arrived at the baggage claim area bleary-eyed and exhausted. Peter glanced at me and said, "You look awful." I managed to reply only, "Well, I feel awful," and walked away. After a 9:00 A.M. rehearsal and some rejuvenating sleep, we met for dinner, and I confronted him with his rudeness. "I wanted to see what got you mad," he explained. "Most people would have been furious and gone into a tantrum." "Not much gets me mad," I told him, "so you won't have to try that again." He didn't. And it became increasingly clear to both of us that when we danced together we had a special dynamic. I was the venturesome one onstage, and his assured partnering gave me that freedom.

During the following two years I was in the premières of three major Balanchine works whose differences in style, music, tone, and choreography underscored the almost incredible scope of his musical, cultural, and psychological range. *Chaconne* with its formalities, *Union Jack* with its salute to discipline and order, and *Vienna Waltzes* with

its transcendent romanticism were all presented within eighteen
months of one another. Not only was each radically different from
the others, all three were unlike any previous ballets Balanchine had
made. Each became a unique signature of the company.

On January 22, 1976, Mr. B's seventy-second birthday, *Chaconne*, a
ballet to the evocative dance music from Gluck's opera *Orpheus and
Eurydice*, premièred. It represented Balanchine's third or fourth version of the music, and in this final rendition, the story is entirely
absent except for what lies deep in the movements themselves. Beginning with *Apollo* in 1928, Balanchine had learned the art of elim-
ination. By removing the theatrical distractions of stories, scenery,
costumes, and preconceived interpretations, he revealed the essence
of the music itself. He never wanted to impose an idea—or himself—
on the work of a composer, and it was in this profound respect for
the identity of the music that he was so radically different from other
choreographers. Above all else, he wanted the audience to hear the
music, really hear it, and if his dances enhanced that experience, he
considered his job well done.

In 1963 he had done a version of *Chaconne* for the Hamburg State
Opera Ballet, which means it was choreographed immediately before
Meditation. It was from Hamburg that he had sent me the poem about
the meaning of the *Meditation* pas de deux—the same theme of ill-
fated love runs through *Orpheus and Eurydice*.

Ten years later, *Chaconne* was done at the Paris Opéra Ballet, and
now in 1976 Brigitte Thom, the Paris ballet mistress, came to New
York to teach us the ballet. It was odd to be learning Balanchine's
choreography from anyone but him, and it was immediately obvious
to me that the dances had been made on very different dancers—
there was a position in my part (attitude effacé to the back) that
Balanchine had never choreographed for me in any other ballet. I
didn't think it one of my best, and we developed a silent understanding on the subject. If he suggested it, I would look at him and wrinkle
my nose, and he, always full of alternatives, would usually propose
something else.

The body of the ballet was a courtly set of dances and variations
ending with a magnificent, very long pas de deux and variations for
Peter and myself. It was the most technically difficult dance I had
ever performed. Its classic brilliance in tandem with the brazen wit
of *Tzigane* showed me that I was again deeply enmeshed in the land
of Balanchine's imagination.

But where was the land of *Chaconne*? Just as we finished learning
the choreography from the French ballet mistress, Mr. B decided to
add a whole new section, expanding and deepening the ballet's mys-

tery. An extra rehearsal was scheduled between a matinee and evening performance, and I presumed that Mr. B had a specific purpose—
he never rehearsed just to admire his own work. The accompanist
started playing some completely different music, and during the next
forty minutes Balanchine choreographed what became the opening
pas de deux of *Chaconne*. It also became, curiously, the second and
last dance he ever made on Peter and myself as partners.

The music (also from Gluck's *Orpheus and Eurydice*) was entitled
"The Dance of the Blessed Spirits" and had a sad, yearning, other-
worldly quality. Balanchine added a chorus of nine tall girls dressed
in flesh-colored chiffon, with their hair loose. I was dressed in diaph-
anous white with my hair also loose, and Peter was in a billowy white
shirt.

The pas de deux seemed to unfold in a shadowy place where
gravity had a less definite pull. Our movements were typified by
languid swimming movements as if we were under water—or far
above it. It was Balanchine in a muted tone that became, as he
grew older, increasingly resonant. It was a private world, and yet
at the same time a celestial kingdom; it was Balanchine's idea of
Elysium.

When the lights brightened for the second section and the stage
suddenly filled with dancers in blue, white, and gold costumes, their
hair pulled back, the dancing became public and celebratory. With
such different music, atmosphere, costumes, and lighting, the sharp
distinction between the two sections—one soft and dreamy, the other
formal and classical—was underlined.

Balanchine did nothing without a reason. To him, there was obviously a relationship, if not a progression, between the sensuous
and private and the ritualized and public: for both, ceremony was the
guiding factor. Courtly behavior between a man and woman trans-
lates directly into public etiquette. *Chaconne* exemplifies the importance and beauty of civilized conduct on both levels.

It was immediately greeted as a masterpiece, another rabbit out of
Balanchine's magic hat. Less than four months later another big ballet
carried the display of decorum as far as Balanchine ever took it.

The year 1976, the United States Bicentennial, was filled with celebrations, and Balanchine provided his own unusual addition. *Union
Jack* was devised as a tribute to America by way of its motherland. It
was also a tribute to the company itself, a military metaphor of the
necessity—and beauty—of rank and file. The première on May 13
was in a sense the launch of the last and most glorious stage of the
company's history under Balanchine.

The preparations and plans for the ballet were unusually complex and extensive for a company that performed so often in practice clothes on a bare stage. Hershy Kay was commissioned to orchestrate the three-part score derived from traditional English music; elaborate scenery was designed by Rouben Ter-Arutunian; and military tailors were consulted for accuracy in costuming. Part one consisted of seven regiments, each consisting of nine dancers and a leader, all dressed in similar wool kilts, jackets, sporrans, and berets. I was the leader of the Royal Canadian Air Force regiment of girls, and we danced to orchestrations of Handel's *Water Music*.

Following my regiment, the six previous ones joined onstage for a finale to the resounding grandeur of "Amazing Grace." It was here, as in the opening of the ballet, that Balanchine choreographed seventy human bodies in marching patterns, sequences, and winding steps of such simple intricacy that it astounded his dancers and audiences alike. With no classical technicalities required, the rehearsals in the main hall took on the relaxed atmosphere of a tea party, while Mr. B quietly plotted. First he led one group of men to one side, then a group of women to another, then a third, fourth, fifth, sixth, and seventh and entwined them through each other. There was a great deal of smiling and shrugging of shoulders as we became increasingly bewildered about the whole process, while Mr. B became increasingly pleased with what we thought must be a big, confusing mess.

Finally, when we all understood our specific directions, we put it together, and it worked like the crystals in a kaleidoscope. Only Balanchine was not surprised; he had seen it all in his mathematical, musical mind long before we were able to execute it.

The second part of *Union Jack* was a pas de deux for Jean-Pierre Bonnefoux and Patricia McBride as a Pearly King and Queen in a British music-hall number that included a black umbrella, a whisky flask, a carnation, two little Pearly Princesses, and one donkey and cart.

The final section of the hour-long ballet was a tribute to the Royal Navy with men and women in sailor outfits. My regiment represented the Women's Royal Naval Service. To my great surprise our music was the "Colonel Bogie March," the theme used in the film *Bridge on the River Kwai*, which I had seen as a child on a visiting day with my father. In my strutting and swaggering, with many splits, hip shifts, and other flirtatious movements, all the parades, baton twirling, and pageantry of my youth in Cincinnati found their ultimate expression.

One day I asked Mr. B what my group would be wearing. He said he wasn't sure yet; I suggested a short white-and-blue one-piece culotte outfit I had at home that had always given me a nautical feeling, and he told me to bring it in. Our resulting WREN costumes were a similar style: short white jacket with gold-braid epaulets and gold buttons, short culotte skirt and white naval cap, pink tights, and pointe shoes. It was quite a spiffy costume and never failed to elicit cheers and whistles of approval from the audience.

All sailors were onstage in a marine semaphore for the finale of the ballet, and in regulation stance, legs apart, we spelled out with red and gold flags "God Save the Queen." As cannons boomed to the tune of "Rule Britannia," a stage-wide facsimile of the Union Jack unfurled behind us, and, coming to attention, we raised our right hands in salute while the curtain was lowered—civil servants one and all. The ballet was Balanchine's final statement about the meaning of a company, not just a dance company, but a realm where order and discipline are the celebrated prerequisites to the unison that produces true service.

Union Jack was epic in scope and, happily, became epic at the box office. Company morale had never been higher, and the fact that I was a part of it all meant that I was really back at the New York City Ballet.

During this time I drew on what I called my "Béjart bag of tricks," a collection of theatrical movements, hints, or looks. While *Tzigane* had incorporated many elements from this bag, I found a new one to use in *Union Jack*. Just before leaving Béjart's company, we spent New Year's Eve in Monte Carlo and after the performance went to a cabaret where, among the many sequined, feathered girls, I noticed one in particular. As she meandered down the runway, flinging her boa over her shoulder, she gazed at the floor and looked as bored as all the others. But then, just as she hit the central spotlight, she lifted her turquoise-shadowed eyelids and the light caught her eyes, producing a truly magical, startling effect. "Hmm, Miss Farrell," I said to myself, "remember that." And in the opening walk of my regiment in the first section of *Union Jack*, it found its place. In a square formation we moved from the back of the stage to the center, accompanied by the pounding rhythms of a drum. On the final drum beat, just before turning my back to the audience, I looked up. When this small movement received an unusual amount of comment it showed me, again, just how effective a small detail can be.

The success of *Chaconne* promoted Peter's and my partnership, and in the next few years we did a great many guest performances together when the company was not in season. Mr. B's attitude to these extracurricular gigs was always encouraging; his only concern was that we were well paid. "If they don't give you enough, don't bother," he would say with a grin.

The appearances were usually arranged by Peter and his agent, and we traveled all over the country to perform, sometimes with a local ballet company but more often in some kind of gala occasion with a cobbled together group of international "stars." We usually performed *Tschaikovsky Pas de Deux*, the "Diamonds" pas de deux, the *Agon* pas de deux, or Jerome Robbins' *Afternoon of a Faun*, while the other dancers did pieces from the more traditional repertoire like Petipa's *Don Quixote* and *Le Corsaire*.

Agon, with its stark, neoclassic lines and Stravinsky music, became an instant hit each time it was danced, and I thought this was a real testimony to Balanchine's "popular" appeal with audiences for whom one might have expected the whipping, bravura turns of the old world pas de deux to be the most welcome and accessible items. I also took a silent lesson in seeing how calm one could be before dancing a Balanchine ballet, even a technical one like *Tschaikovsky Pas de Deux*. I watched other dancers straining in their attempt to generate the expected energy for their entrance. With Balanchine, the energy is intrinsic to the choreography and music; one simply has to trust him and allow oneself to absorb and translate it. It is an interaction, not a one-way street.

Afternoon of a Faun was my second foray into Robbins' repertoire, and soon there was to be another. *Other Dances*, a pas de deux to Chopin piano music, was created not for the New York City Ballet, but for Natalia Makarova and Mikhail Baryshnikov. The seventeen-minute dance was enormously popular, and by the fall Jerry had cast Peter and me in its première at the New York City Ballet.

As it turned out, this coincided with our return from London, where we had danced in a gala at Covent Garden in honor of the Queen Mother's birthday. We arrived back in the afternoon to face the prospect of an important première that evening. The resulting performance was an interesting experience in several ways.

Because *Other Dances* had been choreographed on two very small dancers, it became a challenge to have Peter and me, two very tall dancers, execute the same designs in the same amount of time. The fact that we were mentally keyed up by the prospect ahead but physically relaxed from exhaustion proved to be an aid to Robbins' choreography in a way that it never would have to Balanchine's. Although they rely on the dancers' carefree, casual appearance, Robbins' ballets are designed with enormous precision, and endless rehearsals are required to master the laid-back nonchalance that is one of his trademarks. His most frequent verbal suggestion in his re-

hearsals is, "Mark it. Mark it." Every spontaneous reaction is timed
to the letter, whereas Balanchine's far more demanding and intricate
ballets were designed with relatively easy, very flexible movements—
no wonder their ballets worked well beside one another!

The première was an enormous success. In time, I performed several more Robbins ballets—*Dances at a Gathering, The Cage, In the Night,
Goldberg Variations*—and I always enjoyed dancing them, especially
with Peter.

Because of an unprecedented six-week musicians' strike, most of the
1976–77 winter season was lost. Balanchine was now seventy-three,
and it hurt me that the musicians would choose this time in his life
to put him out of work. He had been planning a new ballet, but it
was never completed because of the lost weeks of rehearsal time.
Since he had already told me about his elaborate ideas to stage *Salome*,
based on the Oscar Wilde play, to Alban Berg's *Lulu Suite*, I was at
least able to luxuriate in visions of what I wasn't going to dance.
Mr. B had told me that as Salome I would be dancing alone on a high
pedestal tower with men at my feet . . . but it remained an enticing
dream.

When the season finally resumed in late January, only a few weeks
of repertoire had been salvaged, but a première of sorts was still
presented. Balanchine had admired the choreography of the great
nineteenth-century Danish ballet master August Bournonville all his
life, and now he suggested to Stanley Williams, the distinguished
Danish teacher at the School of American Ballet, that he stage a set
of divertissements and pas de deux from Bournonville's surviving
repertoire. The company now boasted three superb male dancers who
had trained in Denmark—Peter Martins, Adam Lüders, and Helgi
Tomasson—and the ensuing ballet was a tribute to their schooling
and heritage. For a few hectic weeks the company became a mini-
Royal Danish Ballet, which was not so surprising if one considered
just how much of Bournonville's tight, fast footwork, smooth jumps,
and easy grace were also an integral part of Balanchine's contemporary work.

Peter and I were cast in the famous "Flower Festival" pas de deux,
a dance Peter had known and performed all his life. I, on the other
hand, had never danced Bournonville; but I had seen enough of it to
be aware of its potential pitfalls—fairy-tale mannerisms and coy femininity. Not only were these not attributes I coveted, I could not
believe they were Bournonville's original intention. They seemed to
me ideas gathered over the years and passed down with the expected
distortions.

While being choreographically accurate, I decided to approach this ballet with the same energy, musical and physical, with which I danced everything else. I knew I might be criticized for "historical inaccuracy," a term I've never understood in reference to a live art form; and I was right. I was reprimanded: my legs were too high, my movement too broad, my musicality too idiosyncratic. Balanchine, however, adored the whole production and never missed a performance.

In March 1977 Balanchine began work on what was to be perhaps the single most successful ballet in the New York City Ballet's box-office history. Everything about *Vienna Waltzes* suggested romance, luxury, mystery, and sophistication, and it had all of these qualities and more. After its première in June it became the year's most photographed ballet, and performances were consistently sold out. In the Balanchine-as-showman category he scored a hundred. If *Union Jack* was his final statement about company procedure, *Vienna Waltzes* was his last word on the survival of romanticism.

The first three sections, two waltzes and a polka, had music by Johann Strauss the Younger, the fourth section was to *The Merry Widow* waltz of Franz Lehár, and the final movement, to a waltz from Richard Strauss' *Der Rosenkavalier*. An hour long, the ballet was dressed in taffeta, tulle, velvet, and satin, and the yardage of imported French silk was astronomical. *Vienna Waltzes* was Balanchine's tribute to his company and his dancers.

He had told me I would be in the final waltz, but that was all he said, and as rehearsal weeks went by, I caught glimpses of the first four sections of the ballet as he assembled them with his usual speed and good humor. There were incredibly beautiful things going on, and I started to wonder what waltzing angles he could possibly have left for me.

I had noticed another thing: both my usual partners had already been cast in other movements, Jacques in "Tales from the Vienna Woods," and Peter in the "Merry Widow" section. When I was finally called to a rehearsal and realized that I was to have a somewhat absent partner, George explained that he was so tired of running out of men (a perennial problem in the ballet world) that he decided I would do without, or almost. Jean-Pierre Bonnefoux was cast as my imaginary support, who appeared and disappeared with gallant grace and cunning throughout what was essentially a solo for me.

My entrance was from the downstage right wing, George's wing, onto a stage lit by the eerie black chandeliers and magical, mirrored backdrop of Rouben Ter-Arutunian. I walked onstage slowly, luxuriously, in a white satin gown with underruffles, a train, and long satin gloves. At each performance I felt a gentle push from behind as my music began. It was as if George and I went onstage together, and I could feel him following me, not literally but with his eyes.

I began my dance on center stage by acknowledging, curtsying to, and then embracing my partner—only there was no one there. I danced with this figment of my imagination for a while before Jean-Pierre briefly replaced the phantom and then vanished as quietly as he had appeared. Again I was alone with my "other" partner. It is a gorgeous, wistful dance of covered eyes, draped satin, deep back-bends, and twirling ruffles, and it seems to take place on the precipice of a romantic tragedy.

At many moments I knelt down to pick up the long train of my costume, and during a fitting with Mme. Karinska, Mr. B asked her to place a little silver rose just underneath the skirt so that it would show, ever so slightly, at these moments. Later, I decided that my partner was relegated to a phantom existence not because of the lack of men in the company but because I was dancing, once more, with George.

By the time the official première rolled around, one week after the gala preview, Jean-Pierre was injured. During the intervening week he and Patty McBride had been performing the finale of *Scotch Symphony* when suddenly he fell to the floor, obviously in a great deal of pain. He dragged himself offstage, muttering "I've got to get out there, I've got to finish the ballet." I was doing a barre nearby, and seeing just how serious his injury was I literally threw myself on top of him and said, "You can't get out there. You just can't." Patty finished the ballet alone, and it was later discovered that Jean-Pierre had torn his Achilles tendon, one of the most serious of all dance injuries.

I had enjoyed working with him in *Vienna Waltzes;* his European savoir-faire had added a sophisticated dimension to the role. I wondered if I would really have no partner for the première.

As it happened, my beloved Béjart partner, Jorge Donn, was visiting New York. I had done some guest appearances with Béjart in London the previous April, as well as in New York a year earlier (appearances Balanchine thoroughly approved of), and we had kept in touch with each other. Knowing how much Donn had enjoyed doing *Meditation,* I suggested him to Mr. B, and he learned the ballet and danced all the performances that season with great success. Balanchine liked his dedicated approach, and since both Jacques and Jean-Pierre were injured, he invited him to stay for Saratoga, where we also danced *Meditation* and *Bugaku* together. It was a great treat to have my past join my present.

I had been back in the company for two and a half years and was not only frequently cast in roles I had danced in the 1960s but had performed fourteen new ones. As a career goes, mine could not have been brighter. Things were not so promising for Paul. He had championed my return, but his hope that Balanchine might relent and take him back in the company had gone. When we first came back Mr. B had, in fact, encouraged Paul to go to Chicago where Maria Tallchief was establishing a ballet company, but at the time we both thought, probably correctly, that he was simply trying to separate us, so Paul declined.

In the fall semester of 1975 Paul was a resident teacher with Melissa Hayden at Skidmore College in Saratoga. Later, he briefly joined American Ballet Theatre, but the aesthetics were too different from what he knew, and he quit. Subsequently, he took over a small touring company called "Stars of American Ballet," and on occasion Peter and I toured with them.

From time to time, George and I had dinner together, and Paul thought that this was very nice. But if somehow I was getting everything I had once thought I wanted—Paul *and* George—the reality was sometimes less than ideal. Although Paul often came to the theater and was proud to see me dance, there were other times when I went home from some wonderful performance of *Chaconne* or *Concerto Barocco* and refrained from talking about my real feelings. It didn't seem fair.

In the summer of 1977 Paul finally realized that he had to find something more permanent to do. He signed for one more season with "Stars of American Ballet," and a year later he was appointed artistic director of a small company in Guatemala—but it was a thousand miles away.

During the first few weeks of August 1977 the company was involved in presenting several ballets on television. In 1975 the Corporation for Public Broadcasting in conjunction with the WNET series "Great Performances" received funding to film the first "Dance in America" programs. The series, designed to bring various dance performances by different companies and individuals to a nationwide audience, had the potential to reach people who might otherwise never have the opportunity to see what was happening in the American dance world. Because of the problems involved in translating a live dance event into two dimensions, Balanchine had resisted the idea for years before deciding to give it a try. At worst, the results couldn't diminish the works themselves, and at best, the programs might educate and entertain as well as provide a visual record of the real ballet.

We flew down to Nashville, Tennessee, to begin the first of what became an annual filming venture. Of the first five ballets chosen to be recorded I danced in two, *Tzigane* and "Diamonds," both with Peter. (In future programs I would dance *Chaconne, Allegro Brillante,* and *Variations.*) With Mr. B involved both in front of and behind the camera in tandem with the producer and the director—Emile Ardolino and Merrill Brockway—skepticism was kept at bay, and good humor prevailed.

Because of the unyielding demands of time and money, the schedule was very tight, and while I often thought a take had been less than perfect, Balanchine would say it was fine, and I had to trust him. *Tzigane* had been saved for last because it involved the fewest dancers. As midnight approached on the final day of shooting and the threat of triple overtime was imminent, it was decided to film the finale of the ballet with the four couples and Peter first, so that they could be let go. As a result, everyone else flew home the next morning, and I stayed over to film my entrance and first solo. It happened to be my birthday, and Paul had arranged to import a group of musicians to the island, but I missed the party. After one rehearsal for blocking, we did a take at 10:00 A.M., and Mr. B was so pleased with it that we didn't do a second one. This piece of film became the one I like most, probably because the single take captured a certain continuity of energy. There was a piece of torn ribbon that fell from my costume and remained on the stage throughout my solo, friendly testimony to the uncut rendition of that portion of the dance.

Overall, I did not think the final results were a very fair representation of either me or the ballets. Any excitement of the moment was lost in the editing and splicing, and the immediacy of the stage vanished as videotape seemed to spread an even sheen over the nuances of any movement.

I have often felt that if the choice were mine I would keep all filmed footage of my dancing under lock and key. I certainly don't relish the idea of future generations watching a film and thinking that that is how I danced, because it is not. On the other hand, in the imperfect and transitory world of dance, perhaps there is some historical use and some fleeting pleasure to be found in these films. For me, they are merely ghosts of ballets. But as Balanchine was fond of saying, "Nevertheless . . ."

.   .   .

Since my return in 1975, Mr. B had choreographed eighteen new works. Being seventy-four had no apparent effect on his energy level, and in January 1978, he produced two more premières. Both *Ballo della Regina* and *Kammermusik No. 2* were lightning-fast ballets, and between them they contained more steps, turns, complex designs, and witty angles than could be found in a lifetime of work by most other dancemakers. He remained a man brimming with life, but on March 15 he suffered a minor heart attack. This marked a new phase not only in his life but in the company's. He was at home when it happened, and he proceeded to convalesce in the hospital for several weeks and then at home.

I was devastated. Even though the doctors expected him to recover completely, it was a shock to be confronted with his mortality. Until this attack there had been no signs whatsoever of flagging health. He was ever-present, teaching company class, rehearsing new and old ballets, standing in that front right wing each night watching the performance. But all that was about to change.

His illness received very little publicity, and he didn't encourage visitors to his sickbed. A proud and dignified man, he didn't want his dancers, including me, to see him at anything less than his best. I knew the surest way to pray for him was by dancing, so I got out onstage every night and danced for him.

Before his heart attack Mr. B had planned a new ballet for the spring season to music commissioned by Georges Auric. *Tricolore* was to complete a nationalistic triumvirate with *Stars and Stripes* and *Union Jack*. Since he had already decided on the ballet's format, he refused to let his absence halt the production, so he delegated each of its prescribed three movements to a different company choreographer. Peter Martins choreographed the first, Jean-Pierre Bonnefoux the second, and Jerome Robbins the third. The show would go on without him. But it did not survive without him.

The curtain rose on the première on May 18, and by then Mr. B was well again and back in his place in the wings, but it was too late to save the ballet from itself. It was an undisputed disaster, and for the first time we were all faced with the possibility of the company without Balanchine. The next few years were crucial, for while he continued to make new ballets, including two monumental masterpieces, it was now always with the knowledge that each might be his last. This was a knowledge he was more aware of than anyone else. They were wonderful, heartrending, precious years, and they produced *Mozartiana*, the ballet that more than any other changed my life.

CHAPTER SIXTEEN

A Public Prayer

≈ı∾

S ome time after George's heart attack, he and I went to dinner, and to my great discomfort, he began to speak about what had happened between us in 1969. Later I learned it was around this same time that he decided to make his will, an act that he had always been superstitious about. His bad health had jolted him; I think our conversation was part of his final summation.

We went to the Conservatory Restaurant in the Mayflower Hotel near the theater. I had expected the usual pleasant evening of good wine, food, and conversation, but suddenly George started talking about the Bible. I was silent while he recited the Lord's Prayer in Latin and went on to discuss *tentationem*—temptation.

I was not sure where all this was heading until he said, "You know, I was wrong. I was an old man, and you were young. I should not have thought of you that way. You should have had your marriage." Desperately uncomfortable and embarrassed, I kept saying, "No, no, no," but he continued to talk. I felt as if I were listening to a confession I was unworthy to hear.

I don't really believe that George thought he was "wrong," because he wasn't—any more than I was. But I think he had decided to forgive me for what I had to do, and forgive himself for things he couldn't help. In any case, it was the grandest and kindest gesture he could have made to me, particularly since it was so unnecessary—a true *beau geste*, worthy of the knight of La Mancha. I think it brought him, too, a measure of peace.

After dinner George walked me home and said good night at my door. The subject was never mentioned between us again. Several months later, the night before he was to undergo heart surgery, he talked at length to one of his doctors about a past love in his life. "You know, I was not meant to marry her," he said philosophically and pointed upward. "It was God's decision." The doctor was convinced that he was talking about me.

Our conversation that night heightened our sensitivity to and awareness of each other, and some of those feelings are evident in the ballets he made during the next two years, most notably in *Robert Schumann's "Davidsbündlertänze"* and *Mozartiana*. What had not happened between us had enhanced our understanding on another level, not only a dance level, but a spiritual one. If he had thought at one time that he wanted something I couldn't give him, I hoped that now he knew that in truth he did get everything . . . everything I had to give, the best of me.

Shortly after our conversation, George gave me a copy of Mikhail Bulgakov's novel *The Master and Margarita*. In the 1930s it had been banned in the Soviet Union, and it was not until the late 1960s that it was reinstated and at the same time translated into English. It was set in a supernatural world of magic creams, naked witches, flying broomsticks, sorcery, a fifth dimension, talking cats, and clouds that were horses. But at the center was the "thrice romantic" Master, his unfinished novel, and the young married woman, Margarita, whom he loved and who loved him with a "true, eternal, and faithful love." Tragically separated through nightmares often orchestrated by Satan himself, they were finally united and resurrected in death, their "home for eternity," where he would complete his work, and she would guard his sleep.

At about this time, I became mysteriously ill. I cried without provocation, felt desperately unhappy for no apparent reason, and worst of all, I didn't want to dance. I didn't want to do anything. Apathy was entirely foreign to me, and I went in alarm to my doctor who did extensive tests, all of which came out negative. I couldn't understand why I was so depressed at such a wonderful time in my life—I had come back to the company, I was dancing, and Mr. B was making new ballets.

I was sure that the reasons were physical, even though most of the symptoms were psychological. I had always considered depression a weakness, and I refused to think that I had succumbed to it, especially without good reason. Finally, I was put in the hospital for a week for more tests, and the doctors found a potassium-salt imbalance in my system and prescribed medication. I was happy to have some kind of answer, and eventually I pulled out of it. I remember the day I answered the phone and looked at my hand and decided to paint my fingernails; I knew then that I was getting better.

In retrospect, I suppose all this was a deep depression brought on by trying to cope with having both George and Paul in my life. I was constantly juggling the fine line of loving them both, differently and separately. George never asked me about my marriage, but I had little doubt that if anything had happened to it, he would have been the first to know. Mother enhanced the difficulties by remaining, ten years after the fact, unreconciled to my marriage. Neither George nor Mother was compatible with my husband, and it was very hard for me.

Paul and I had eventually come to realize that our marriage would suffer if he did not have fulfilling work, which was why, in September 1978, he accepted the directorship of the Ballet Guatemala. I did not relish the prospect of having him so far away; I was dependent on him for his love and emotional support, but I knew it was not fair of me to protest. He could not find work in New York; so we decided to try this new arrangement. It was the beginning of many years of geographic separation. People have always asked me how my marriage could have survived such long separations. My answer is that the separations—which meant Paul was working—were the reasons it did survive.

The adjustment to living alone was a big one and a difficult one. I was very lonely for some time. Eventually I got used to it, and dancing every night helped enormously. Whenever either of us had free time, we flew to visit the other, and Guatemala provided me with an exotic adventure reminiscent of our Béjart days. Meanwhile, Paul found the dance situation in Central America rather casual. The prevalent attitude, even to dancing, was *"Mañana, mañana."* One day, while I was talking to him on the phone, I suddenly heard screaming, honking horns, explosions and sirens in the background. He explained nonchalantly, "Oh, there's a revolution going on outside my window." Despite the drawbacks, he did manage to restore some kind of professional order to the company, and he choreographed several ballets, including a beautiful rendition of Tschaikovsky's *Romeo and Juliet*. I went to Guatemala for the première and knew that I wanted to dance this ballet. Several years later, at a gala, it became the first ballet of Paul's that I danced in America.

By the end of February of 1979 the New York City Ballet was on tour in Washington, D.C., for two weeks, and I again became mysteriously ill. I was cast for a matinee performance on the last Sunday of the tour, but I awoke that morning feeling so awful that I called the ballet mistress and canceled it. I knew this was last-minute notice, but I also knew I was not fit to go out on a stage. I decided to pack and catch the next plane back to New York, but while I was checking out of the hotel, a terrible feeling came over me. I retrieved my key and ran back to my room.

I was having a miscarriage, but I didn't know it because I didn't know I was pregnant. Like many dancers, I had irregular cycles, and skipping a month or two had never been cause for alarm. It was a horrendous, frightening, and very emotional experience.

After seeing my mother and my doctor in New York, I flew down to Guatemala to convalesce with Paul. Even though the pregnancy had not been planned and it wasn't the right time for us to have children, we were both deeply distressed. I know that some dancers have managed to combine children with a career, but during the years I was dancing I never felt I could do justice to both at the same time. Still, it was a dilemma that the miscarriage brought painfully to mind.

By the middle of March I was back with the company on tour in upstate New York. In Syracuse *Jewels* was scheduled for the evening performance, and I was especially excited because Donna, my eldest sister, who lived there, was to attend. Peter's back went into spasm that afternoon, and with Jacques no longer dancing the role, I was without a partner only hours before curtain time. In desperation it was decided to teach the part, in the little time left, to Sean Lavery.

Sean was a strong, impressive dancer who had joined the company several years earlier, and he was known to be a quick study. Just how quick we were all to find out. Even with the scherzo section cut, there was an enormous amount of complicated partnering to learn for the pas de deux, and Sean absorbed it like a sponge. He was a dancer who could think on his feet, and during the performance we kept in close eye contact for last-minute strategies. The first opportunity came in the pas de deux after we had separated to opposite ends of a diagonal, and I saw Sean snatching a quiet moment to pose. On the edge of taking a plunging penché on pointe, from which he had to rescue me, I only had time to wink at him. Panic replaced poise as Sean charged at breakneck speed to center stage, grabbing me just in time to prevent a full-force nose dive.

It was superb, and I really thought that after that close call we would sail smoothly to the end. We did until Sean tripped on the uneven stage as he was exiting after a series of big jumps. I saw him slip, fall over, execute a complete somersault, stand up, and finish in the correct classical pose. He had unquestionably upstaged me this time.

Peter was out for the remainder of the tour, and Sean was taught the rest of the ballet. With the help of some actual rehearsals, the next few performances were a great deal smoother, although they lacked that extra edge of danger! Dancing "Diamonds" with a younger dancer who was not familiar with it left me in the position of veteran, and I found the change in dynamic affected my performance in a curious way—instead of being the result of a movement, I had to be the cause of it, and the whole ballet took on a new musical resonance.

Although Mr. B appeared to have recovered fully from his heart attack and had returned to the theater, toured to London, and rehearsed ballets, he was still not entirely well. After a great deal of resistance, he was persuaded to undergo triple bypass heart surgery in June of 1979. It was successful, and after convalescing that summer, he was back at work by the fall.

It was within this period of time that Mikhail Baryshnikov joined our company. I admired his prodigious dance abilities and his courage in putting aside his ego and presenting himself in a totally new kind of repertoire. I felt a special affinity with him because I thought we both devoured space with the same passion, and I would have liked to dance with him, but it was impossible because of the great difference in our heights.

It was unfortunate that Balanchine's ill health prevented his working in depth with Baryshnikov, but he did manage to revive two great ballets for him: *Prodigal Son* and *Apollo*. It was in the latter that Mr. B caused something of a public outcry when he eliminated both the opening birth scene and the final ascent to Mount Olympus. Perhaps he thought Misha was too refined a dancer to be convincing as the awkward, gawky young Apollo, or perhaps he just thought it was time to eliminate again, to reeducate again.

I could certainly understand cutting the physical movements if he thought they no longer had the same validity, but I could not see why he cut Stravinsky's score. On one occasion I commented to him, "You don't usually cut music like that." "No, I usually don't," he agreed. There was nothing left to say.

For me the happy result of this revival was that *Apollo* was back in the repertoire, and over the next few years Peter and I danced it many times together with great pleasure.

Although Mr. B's health permitted his daily presence in the theater and he oversaw all productions and casting, he was no longer teaching class on a daily basis, and he had not made a new ballet since 1978. He was still subject to various physical symptoms—dizziness and loss of balance were the most disconcerting—that became increasingly baffling to him and his doctors alike. This was a time in which he revived, revised, and restaged various works choreographed previously and thereby still produced new ballets for the company.

It had become an annual tradition to hold a gala benefit for the School of American Ballet in January, and for such a fund-raising occasion something new, different, or unexpected was usually presented. For the 1980 gala Mr. B suggested we perform Gounod's *Walpurgisnacht Ballet,* an extravaganza he had staged five years earlier for the Paris Opéra Ballet. Brigitte Thom arrived from Paris and, as she had with *Chaconne,* rehearsed the ballet. This time, however, Balanchine had not only me but two other ballerinas, Kyra Nichols and Heather Watts, all learn the leading role. I was having hip trouble and thought that I probably would not dance the single performance.

As the ballet progressed, Mr. B became increasingly involved and excited about what he saw, and by the time of the première on January 24 he had cast Adam Lüders, one of our Danish dancers, and me as the principal couple and revamped, reordered, and rechoreographed much of the ballet. Thrown together with a conglomeration of discarded blue, yellow, pink, and white chiffon costumes from three other ballets, it was one of Balanchine's short, large-scale miracles.

With a cast of twenty-three women and one man, this was definitely the world according to Balanchine, and while Faust's story was absent, the music retained its wonderful, raucous atmosphere, and by the end, with the whole cast onstage, hair and legs loose and flying, the drama was inescapable. One male observer commented, "If that's hell, I want to go there."

For the last tableau, Mr. B had all the girls gather in a diagonal wedge behind Adam and me while I took a flying leap onto his shoulder. After arriving there, I was to, in Mr. B's words, "do something else," so I released one leg into a wide circular motion behind me and placed one arm over my head, palm at a stiff right angle. The effect was of a figurehead on the mast of a ship. Mr. B looked like the cat that ate the canary and said, "Good!" This became the final image.

Walpurgisnacht was greeted with enormous affection, and, to everyone's surprise, what was intended as a *pièce d'occasion* entered the repertoire permanently. Some people found it campy, and while I understood that assessment, I objected to the connotation. It was Mr. B's genius to be able to make a ballet full of extreme gestures tinged with humorous overtones and still be in impeccable taste. The reasons were as simple as the steps: there were no gimmicky tricks and no personality additions in the form of winks, shrugs, or facile communications. The humor was as deeply embedded in the music and choreography as was the wrenching emotion of a profound ballet like *Liebeslieder Walzer.*

During the early spring of 1980 the daily rehearsal sheet announced a "new ballet," and the choreographer was Balanchine. As time went by, four principal couples were called to separate rehearsals: Karin von Aroldingen and Adam Lüders; Heather Watts and Peter Martins; Kay Mazzo and Ib Andersen; Jacques and myself.

The mystery surrounding the ballet grew as time went on. First there was the music by a composer Balanchine had used very rarely before. The ballet, *Robert Schumann's "Davidsbündlertänze,"* was titled after a series of piano pieces composed by Schumann. I was immediately curious as to why I was cast with Jacques. He had all but retired and danced infrequently. During the course of the next few weeks Mr. B designed four very different dances for the two of us, but they hardly constituted traditional pas de deux, for each had an underlying motif where I was the leader, while Jacques, rather than supporting me in the usual manner, was in constant pursuit of my ever-evasive moves. That I seemed to have a character of great independence and elusiveness was not entirely alien to other ballets George had made on me, but here the dynamic between me and my partner was extreme. Our dances seemed to portray a relationship where the passage of time and human aging were of some intrinsic importance to the drama.

This unusual element was underscored by George's failing health, and it was in these rehearsals that I noticed for the first time a real change in not only his physical abilities but also his emotional demeanor. The dances were relatively short, simple, and technically easy, and he assembled and suggested steps with his usual speed, but throughout he remained uncharacteristically pensive, even preoccupied. As we executed some beautiful new movement he did not hold up his finger with glee and say *"Voilà!"* but rather watched quietly, then moved on to the next phrase of music. He was not physically well, and making this ballet was some kind of deep emotional effort for him.

But he had not lost his sense of humor. Jacques and I had been having certain difficulties with the partnering in one section, and I felt it was terrible that any moments of precious rehearsal time had to be spent on our technical inadequacies. Knowing that Mr. B was probably up playing solitaire or ironing his shirts, two of his favorite occupations, I phoned him at eight o'clock one morning and said, "Oh, George, I'm so sorry you have to work so hard to make us look good." He replied calmly, "Don't worry, dear, I have to work hard to make everybody look good."

The next day Jacques and I requested a rehearsal alone to work on one specific dance so that it would be smoother to present to Mr. B at the next official rehearsal. The dance was full of agitation and sudden changes of direction on pointe, and I felt unsure of its atmosphere. To my considerable consternation, just as we began trying to remember what Balanchine had devised the day before, Mr. B walked through the door. Hoping to discourage him, I said, "Oh, George, you weren't called to this rehearsal."

It was abrupt of me, but I didn't want him to waste his energy when we had so little to show him. He ignored me, walked calmly to the front of the studio, and said, "Don't worry, just show me. I want to see if it's what I want." Afterward, I thought it was quite a mess of missed arms and legs, but before I could apologize or offer any excuses, George nodded his head and said, "Yes, it's just what I wanted," and walked out. I shrugged and turned to Jacques and said, "But we didn't do anything." Obviously, Mr. B saw a bigger picture, something far beyond our momentary imperfections, and he liked it.

Of the eighteen dances that comprised the ballet, thirteen were divided among the four couples as duets, three were solos, and two were dances where we all met up together and even, briefly, changed partners. The basic outline of *Davidsbündlertänze*, with its onstage piano and four couples, resembled *Liebeslieder Walzer*, and, as in that ballet, the women began in heeled satin shoes and graduated to pointe shoes. The subject also seemed to be similar: love in different guises, but the Schumann had a very different tone, which escaped me right up to the première. Each couple seemed to represent a different stage or type of love—Heather and Peter were frantic and full of discord, Kay and Ib were young and sweet, Karin and Adam's relationship was the angst of the misunderstood artist and the offered solace, while Jacques and I seemed to depict the older artist in pursuit of a fleeting inspiration—but all these different guises and humors were delineated by the music, not a libretto.

After numerous rehearsals alone with Jacques, I finally formed some idea of the world we inhabited. But when Mr. B called a rehearsal for all four couples and we danced the ballet in sequential order, my bubble world burst. Although there was no actual physical interruption by other couples, it felt distinctly as if they were intervening on my own very particular and personal dream. They seemed to be drawing on our paper instead of their own, and with each new entrance we had to reestablish our emotional territory again. It was not a competitive situation by any means, but there was a definite struggle for existence. All this tension was, moreover, supremely understated, which made its power overwhelming.

I don't know if each couple felt the same strange sense of intrusion about the others, but this obviously created a dynamic that our choreographer had intended. It was as if all the real action happened offstage, while onstage the results, repercussions, and revelations of these loves found some final muted expression. The clues to the ballet's anxious and desperate atmosphere—and there were many—did not seem to cohere, and I felt lost trying to find peace in this confusion.

One afternoon between a matinee and evening performance Mr. B choreographed for me a short, wonderful, quick-footed solo, full of hops, turns, and very staccato movements. At the end, the music hits a final note of certitude, but Mr. B was undecided as to how I should respond. We tried several things—sauté, step, grand jeté into the wing; pas de chat to the knee; chaîné turns into the wing—but none of them satisfied him. Not wanting to leave the ending unfinished, he finally said, "Oh, just relevé and go off." I did the preceding step, which consisted of a few turns, and relevéed as he had suggested. From this position I asked, "Where do you want me to go off?" and pointed to the right wing with my right index finger. "Good," he exclaimed, "that's your ending. They'll all wonder what you're pointing at!" He was right, and just as with the same gesture in *Don Quixote*, the movement took on great significance even though it was devised as a spur-of-the-moment whim. Or was it? Later in the ballet Jacques and I had one final duet, and as we exited Jacques lifted me low under the arms as I opened and extended my legs midair in a wide split. I echoed the length of the gesture with my arm, again pointing ever so slightly as we made our final exit.

By June 12, the day of the gala preview, I knew physically, as did everyone else, exactly what was to happen chronologically, but emotionally the ballet remained inconclusive. Even the costumes were cause for wonder. Here was a ballet with a white costume, but for the first time, I wasn't in it—I was dressed in pale blue, Karin in white, Heather in lavender, and Kay in yellow.

In the early afternoon we had our only dress and lighting rehearsal, and for the first time *Davidsbündlertänze* made some kind of dramatic sense. I could only hope that the feeling would last through the evening. It did, but because each couple had its own entrances and exits, and the scenery by Rouben Ter-Arutunian included long, gauzy draped curtains covering the wings, it was impossible ever to see what any other couple was doing. So my original feeling of existing in a vacuum with Jacques persisted. Unlike any other ballet that I ever danced, I never saw this one as a whole. I feel sure that Mr. B intended this sensation of isolation to add to his overall vision. A few years later, after Karin retired, I danced her role for several performances, and again this element of the ballet was present; I had to control my impulse to move on my former music in order to move on her music. It was as if I were stepping into someone else's life, not my own.

Balanchine told some of the dancers, as well as the press, that the ballet was "about" Schumann and his wife Clara, but this was a biographical idea that he never mentioned to me. No doubt he told each of us as little—and as much—as was necessary to achieve his purpose. Because of the highly emotional nature of the music and dances, *Davidsbündlertänze* received enormous amounts of interpretive reaction.

It was without doubt a very profound, very moving ballet about love, but it had a tragic, tortured edge that made it significantly different from all other Balanchine ballets on the subject (which means most Balanchine ballets). Adam Lüders' final, slow disappearance was not so much the death of a beloved man as a metaphorical farewell to romantic love. In life romance might be the foundation; in afterlife it definitely was not. One year later, in *Mozartiana*, Mr. B explored what was.

If in *Meditation* Balanchine choreographed his life and mine, in his last two masterpieces he choreographed his meditations from the new perspective of his mortality. It was quite an event to behold, to witness, and to dance. In this new light—and it was an illumination— the hugeness of his spiritual faith was dazzling and devastating.

In the fall of 1980 the company embarked on a five-week European tour to Copenhagen, Berlin, and Paris. It was the last tour that Mr. B would make with his company, and the reception in all three cities was appropriately resplendent and grateful. Because of Mr. B's continuing physical symptoms, each day and each performance took on an extra measure of importance to me, so when I developed knee trouble in Berlin I was determined to continue to dance. When Dr. William Hamilton, the company's official doctor, suggested arthroscopic surgery to drain the fluid and repair the cartilage, I decided to go to my other doctor, Mr. B, for a second opinion.

As in Russia eighteen years earlier, he took my leg in hand and examined my aching knee. It was not just because he was my boss or my friend that I trusted Mr. B's judgment about my physical abilities. It was because he had devoted his entire life to shaping, extending, and preserving dancers' bodies, and as a great choreographer and teacher he was an expert on their subtle, intricate workings.

We were in Berlin for only a few days. As part of a larger Stravinsky celebration, we were performing several all-Stravinsky programs in which I was to dance *Apollo* and *Monumentum/Movements*. I knew how important Stravinsky was to Balanchine, and that this chance to present both him and Balanchine in Europe might not happen again. My only concern about my knee was whether I could cause irreparable damage to it by dancing.

George pressed around my knee in several places, asking where it hurt most and how it hurt. Finally, to my great relief, he said, "I think it will be all right if you dance on it." And he was right. But he remained very concerned, and by the time we reached Paris he suggested changing a step in *Apollo* where I swivel around on pointe on a very low bent knee. Now it was my turn to say no. Like so many images and positions in this ballet, the movement had a beauty and sweetness to it that was almost legendary, and I could not envision *Apollo* without it—even if George could.

"George, you can't change that step," I said. "Oh sure, it's just a step," he countered, but I remained adamant: "Well, you can change it, but when we get to that place I'm going to do the original step."

Back in New York I was still reluctant to have surgery. Even if it was only a tiny needle entering the body, I believed it would irreversibly alter the structure of my knee, and I preferred to allow a little time for it to heal of its own accord. The company had a layoff, and with rest the swelling went down. By the time the season opened, I was back onstage without any pain or problems.

By the spring of 1981 Balanchine was working on not one new ballet but four. He had announced a festival to honor the composer who, along with Stravinsky, was the most influential in his life. By this time Balanchine had choreographed thirty-seven ballets to the music of Peter Ilyitch Tschaikovsky, and now he wanted to host an eleven-day celebration of his beloved compatriot that would include no fewer than fifteen premières. Of the new Balanchine ballets there was one that took on a permanent life in the repertoire after the celebration was over. It is one of Balanchine's greatest works, and a ballet that has been surrounded by a mystique rare even for Balanchine.

Mozartiana was haunted from the very beginning—injury plagued its première, leaving all concerned with only a single glimpse at a world Balanchine had dressed in black. Almost fifty years earlier, Mr. B had choreographed what became the first of four very different versions of the music Tschaikovsky wrote to honor Mozart, a composer he greatly admired, although Mozart's clarity, purity, and sublime classicism were quite foreign to Tschaikovsky's own highly emotional temperament. It was obviously music that Balanchine had adored all his life, and now, as he neared the end, he found it necessary to try once more to put it into a visual order.

For this version he changed almost everything—the sequence of the music, the number of dancers, and the choreography. After he had told me that he would use me in this ballet, I acquired a tape to listen to the music. I knew by now that this might be his last ballet. I thought it might help to familiarize myself with the score before we actually began work. To my astonishment, I suddenly heard music that I had known all my life. I had sung Mozart's "Ave Verum" in church as a child, and I thought how wonderful it was to have this music enter my life again at this moment.

That night I had a dream so vivid that I could not distinguish between sleeping and waking. Although we had not begun the ballet and I had no idea of its format or implications, I dreamed about *Mozartiana*. I was in a place composed of tall spires. There was sound, not *Mozartiana*, but a kind of shattering, prophetic, organ-like sound, and I was walking on the vibrating spires upward from one pinnacle to another. It wasn't precarious. My footing was very stable; I was holding on to the air. As I climbed, the light got brighter and brighter, whiter and whiter, until finally I could see, really see. Suddenly the scene changed, and I was walking on the sand by the ocean with Mr. B. It was still very bright, and people came up and looked at me. I responded to their silent, puzzled looks by saying, "Oh, yes . . . that's *Mozartiana*." It was the answer to all questions.

I was not usually susceptible to the influence of dreams, but this particular one was so powerful, and this time with George was so highly fraught with emotion, that the strange spiral vision set a standard for me. Before we even began rehearsals I felt that I had to live up to something.

As on many previous occasions, Mr. B asked me whom I would like to dance with in this ballet. Having been through the ritual before, I gave the obvious answer, "Peter," and he said, "Well, I was thinking of Ib." "Fine," I replied, although I voiced a little concern that Ib was not quite tall enough for me. Already Balanchine had introduced an unusual component.

Ib Andersen was the company's most recent Danish import and a dancer of great passion, speed, and musicality. I had never danced with him. But if I began with any reservations about the prospect, they soon vanished, and Mr. B's intentions became crystal clear. I think he had certain images in mind for this music, and Ib fit those images. I also think it possible that Mr. B saw himself abstractly in Ib's role, and their similar heights allowed for the same partnering that George and I did so well together. In that sense *Mozartiana* was our last dance; there were no understudies.

Rehearsals were fantastic. Mr. B poured out steps and directions and footwork while we scrambled to grasp what he wanted. He began with a long pas de deux for Ib and me, but the entire format was inside out, beginning with numerous alternating variations for each of us and finishing with a duet. Even here the dancing was not at all the usual male/female partnering. Ib and I often danced separately in a kind of dialogue with each other. If most pas de deux indicate a kind of love story, this one did not. We didn't seem to be man and woman, but people with some kind of greater independence and purpose.

The dancing required many stops and starts, and the energy seemed to build backward instead of forward. This, at least initially, felt very awkward indeed. We were clearly treading on new ground, and thrilled as I was to be in the studio working with Mr. B, I was having a hard time mapping the territory that this world described. I felt earthbound, and my dream lingered in my mind.

While reaching for this ballet, I did have an idea about what I would wear, but even here the circumstances were unusual. With entirely new steps, new dancers, and a new occasion, I could not understand why Mr. B remained adamant about dressing it in the original black.

The design for my costume by Rouben Ter-Arutunian was a short, full, round tutu reaching to just above the knee, but something about it was wrong. There were numerous fittings where Rouben and Mr. B fussed and fussed over the skirt, the bodice, the satin, the tulle, the neckline—everything was switched, altered, and changed. Almost daily a new version was produced, but still Mr. B was not pleased. Lace was added one day, only to be replaced by ribbons the next, and on one occasion the bodice was pronounced the "wrong color black." For a man who had a reputation for dressing dancers in practice clothes, George was inordinately concerned about the costume for this ballet.

Finally, the day before the première, we had our first dress rehearsal, and the latest version of my tutu was produced under the recent order: "I want her black, but plain—like nothing, nothing." There was a finality associated to this blackness that was daunting. After the rehearsal I was very upset and teary—the ballet had not gone well, and the costume still felt all wrong.

George came back to my dressing room, took one last look at my costume, and stated, as if he had had a revelation, "You know, I was wrong. I realize . . . nothing is nothing." And he changed it again.

The following day was to be the first night of the Tschaikovsky Festival, and the stagehands were working overtime hanging and arranging the magnificent set designed especially for the festival by Philip Johnson and John Burgee. Consisting of literally thousands of clear plastic tubes of varying lengths, hung as both wings and backdrop, this transparent palace could be altered for each ballet into different designs. For *Mozartiana* the tubes were hung in the arches of an abstract cathedral.

The gala première came and went in a dazed flash. In the middle of the pas de deux with Ib, I heard a tremendous pop in my right foot. Mr. B had devised a wonderful sequence where I stepped up into a double piqué turn holding Ib's finger and ending straight down in a high penché while Ib ran around me and I swiveled directly into a double pirouette. The entire movement was sublime musically and magical physically, like the never-ending water pouring over Niagara Falls. In rehearsal we often began with this sequence, and my right foot had become strained. Now, in performance, something popped.

Reluctant to acknowledge what had happened, I kept dancing. After my exit I said a quick prayer before going onstage again and managed miraculously to finish the ballet. By the time I got back to my dressing room, the swelling had set in, and everyone gathered around to assess the situation. I was scheduled to perform the polonaise of "Diamonds" with Peter at the end of the evening's program.

Because of this last-minute emergency no one, including Balanchine, said anything at all about what had been the première of one of his most amazing ballets. Practicalities prevailed as I determined to dance "Diamonds" despite Dr. Hamilton's advice and jammed my quickly expanding foot into a white toe shoe. I knew if I didn't I would never get it into a toe shoe at all, and I had an hour before "Diamonds" was to begin. I was terribly emotional, not only because I was injured; I was thinking of the repercussions—*Mozartiana* was scheduled for several more performances, and without an understudy I knew if I couldn't dance, the ballet would not happen at all. And I wanted so much to be again in the world I had just inhabited, to explore it further and to dance it for George.

I hobbled through "Diamonds," and the next morning X rays revealed that I had broken a small bone on the side of my foot. I was out for the remainder of the season, and all the prayers and willingness in the world were not going to change that fact. *Mozartiana* was canceled.

The curtain rises on *Mozartiana* in silence and reveals four little girls in black dresses and pink ballet slippers. They form a small semicircle, and in the center I stand, one foot pointed behind, arms rounded to my sides, head bowed. I, too, am in black, but my tutu has underlayers of white tulle. The effect is not of deep, dense black but of one dressed in white with a veil. It is funereal but not morbid, somber but hedged with light.

With the lifting of the curtain, a ghostly breeze fills the stage. The air of the auditorium meets the space of the dance. The quiet sounds of Mozart's "Ave Verum" begin, and I feel the draft touch me. Slowly my head rises, propelling me up onto pointe. I bourrée forward, opening my arms, palms slightly upward. It is a pose from a statue of the Virgin at the Church of the Blessed Sacrament on 71st Street and Broadway that Mr. B knew I attended. Although it is technically not a ballet position, he wanted my arms to open very, very low. It is a humble offering and divine supplication that heralds the beginning of the "Preghiera." I hover about the stage in a series of the simple, quiet gestures of prayer. Vulnerability is the source of my movement. Everything here feels strangely inevitable, prescribed.

Only once before in my memory had Balanchine been so openly spiritual, and in *Don Quixote*, as the Virgin Mary, I was representative. In *Mozartiana* I was less specific, a metaphor for all the beauty in Mozart's music and Balanchine's soul. As the dance ends, I am again surrounded by the four little girls in a classic pose, arms now open and lifted as if framing not so much myself but the power and weight of something higher. The music strains to its finish alone, and I walk offstage in silence.

Mr. B choreographed the "Preghiera" after he had designed the rest of the ballet. He finished at the beginning. During the first rehearsal he asked me to recite the Latin to the "Ave Verum" for him. I had known these words all my life, and they became my guide. I didn't count a note, but just hummed to myself silently, *"Ave, Ave, Verum corpus, Natum ex Maria Virgine; Vere passum, immolatum, In cruce pro homine, Cujus latus perforatum, Vero fluxit sanguine, Esto nobis praegustatum, In mortis examine."* [Hail, true body, Born of the Virgin Mary; Sacrificed with nails, On the cross for us men, Cleanse us by the blood and water streaming from thy pierced side, Feed us with thy body broken, Now and in death's agony.] Once again I was singing and dancing for Balanchine.

Technically, this dance was short and simple, but it required a state of mind beyond anything I had ever attempted before. It was a hymn shared by George and me, an offering that could happen only in movement and music, not in words.

After the "Preghiera," the lights brighten and the ballet proceeds with a "Gigue" for a solo man in black, a "Menuet" for four tall girls dressed like the children from the opening, the variation and pas de deux for Ib and me, and a finale for the whole cast that culminates in some of the most brilliant, exultant dancing Balanchine ever devised. If *Davidsbündlertänze* ends on a note of ineffable sadness and desperation, *Mozartiana* ends on a note of superhuman joy. It was as if together these last ballets traced the progression of Balanchine's knowledge and feeling in the face of death—he saw not a blackness but rather a beginning, a lightness.

. . .

When the ballet was finally presented again in New York that fall, my costume had been redesigned into a longer, lighter version, and my foot was healed. After the performance Mr. B came back to my dressing room, and we sat looking at each other in silence for a while. Finally, I said to him, "You know, George, I think *Mozartiana* is what heaven must be like." He looked closely at me. "Oh really," he said, and nodded ever so slightly. There was a look of recognition and serenity on his face.

He had not just made a ballet with *Mozartiana*, he had altered and extended the spectrum of my life. Having danced it, I felt that I had just begun to dance, just been borne into life itself. In *Mozartiana* George and I were at peace with each other, and the pervasive calm and corresponding strength I felt while performing it were truly transcendent.

Balanchine at the age of seventy-seven had given us a vision of heaven as he interpreted it from the Lord's Prayer, "on earth as it is in heaven," and it was a very beautiful place indeed, a place past desire, where dancers perform for the glory of God. My dream of climbing spires was answered—*Mozartiana* was the light. It was because this ballet existed that I could survive the death of the man who made it.

CHAPTER SEVENTEEN

A Private Prayer

A fter Paul had been in Guatemala for a year the company's financial situation became impossible, and he flew home. In a few months, he departed again, this time to the job Mr. B had suggested he take several years earlier.

Chicago had a long history of struggling to establish and maintain a ballet company, and with Maria Tallchief at the helm, Balanchine was very keen to help the efforts. In late 1979 Maria, at Balanchine's suggestion, invited Paul to stage his *Romeo and Juliet* for the Chicago Lyric Ballet, and so began a collaboration that was to last for eight years.

For the fund-raising first performance by the newly independent Chicago City Ballet, George and I flew out to lend moral and artistic support. "Rubies" from *Jewels* was also on the program, but at the last minute the lead male dancer was injured, and without an understudy, there was considerable havoc backstage. The only person who knew the role was Paul, so after donning beige tights and red-jeweled vest, he leaped out onstage. Because his main interest had shifted to choreography, I knew that he was not in tip-top dancing shape, but he performed admirably.

Sitting in the audience with George, watching his ballet "Rubies" performed by my husband, turned out to be more entertaining than uncomfortable. Backstage we were all able to communicate with one another easily, our previous volatile personal emotions happily neutralized by our mutual belief in Balanchine.

Then George and I flew back to New York together in the private plane belonging to Maria's husband, Henry Paschen, leaving my husband and George's ex-wife in Chicago. It seemed quite normal to everyone.

Among other duties as associate artistic director, Paul became the company's chief choreographer. The most ambitious of his ballets was a full-length production of Prokofiev's *Cinderella*, which he made on me and which premièred in November 1981, only a few months after I had danced *Mozartiana*.

With a relatively small budget of $250,000, a company of only twenty dancers and one hundred children, Paul made *Cinderella* an extravagantly costumed two-act ballet that became a grand success for the company. Adam Lüders and I obtained permission from Balanchine to spend a few weeks in Chicago for this production. Having always felt that fairy tales were for adults as well as children, I relished the opportunity to play the title role with all its transitions—from humble, barefoot poverty by the hearth to slippered glory at the ball.

Preparations for costumes and scenery began on the island that summer, and Paul came to New York several times to choreograph the pas de deux for Adam, a very charming Prince Charming, and me. There were also numerous lengthy phone calls between Chicago and New York, not only to discuss the progress of the ballet generally but even to alter the choreography. Adam and I would try out Paul's alterations the next day in the studio to a cassette tape, and I would phone back with a report on the possibilities. Like George, Paul believed in his dancers.

He made several wonderful dramatic decisions in this ballet: the stepsisters were not men dressed as ugly women as they are in many productions, but beautiful girls whose personalities defined their mean natures; Cinderella was dressed for the ball by the four seasons, each giving her in succession a crown, a gown, a cape, until finally Winter, her fairy godmother in disguise, gave her the glass slippers, a poignant metaphor for her destiny—just as pointe shoes are for a dancer.

I had worked with Paul as a choreographer several times before, mostly in Belgium, but this production was on a larger scale, and we were happy to find that thanks to our mutual respect for each other and for our work, we functioned as a very professional team. I adored dancing *Cinderella*, and continued to return to Chicago for more performances over the next few years.

After many summers of work, Cedar Islands had finally become everything we had hoped for. After installing a diving board on the floating pier, a Jacuzzi, a gazebo, and a flagpole to fly the Stars and Stripes, there remained one last, all-important addition. In 1976 a glass-enclosed dance studio was completed, and by 1981 we had decided to open a small dance camp for young students, many of whom came from Chicago, who could enjoy nature, boating, and swimming while studying dancing.

With two classes a day, Paul and I alternated teaching, and for the first few years we experimented with different arrangements for food preparation. Mother was the cook one year, but she produced so much food that island life slowed to a crawl. Another year we hired one of my teenage nephews to oversee the island upkeep, but eventually we found that we were most efficient working alone, and developed a fine system of teaching and cooking together.

One year, in the hope of integrating pas de deux classes into the curriculum, we accepted, on scholarship, our first boy student—but he didn't last long. Distracted by all the girls, he ran over his foot with the lawnmower and spent the remainder of the summer being ministered to while we mowed the lawn.

As the camp became an annual event, the island became a point of interest for local tourist boats, which would announce with a megaphone as they sailed by, "And to your right lies Ballerina Island." One nearby couple on the mainland timed their dinner to coincide with our early evening ballet class and thanked us for the romantic accompaniment.

In the small nearby town of Inlet, where we shopped, the idea of ballet was a new one, and we were fascinated to overhear the following exchange in the grocery store: "Oh, she's a ballerina, and he's a choreographer," said the grocer. "Do you like choreography?" "No," replied the customer emphatically, "I don't look at dirty pictures."

The year 1982 was the hundredth anniversary of Stravinsky's birth, and despite an obvious decline in his physical strength, Balanchine once again announced a festival for the spring season. While he oversaw and planned the whole Stravinsky Centennial Celebration, and the week featured ten world premières, the shadow of his failing health hung over the entire enterprise.

Of the five works revived, revised, or choreographed by Mr. B, there were two solos for me, *Élégie* and *Variations*, both new versions of solos he had done with me sixteen years earlier. In rehearsals we found ourselves, as we had so often, alone in a small studio with Gordon Boelzner. We had always had an empty studio for our workroom, dance steps for our language, and music as our binding force. These three things were still as essential, stable, and comforting as ever. It took me back to *Meditation*. But now it was twenty years later; the music was Stravinsky, not Tschaikovsky; I no longer had chubby cheeks and wobbly bourrées; Gordon's temples were graying; and George was seventy-eight and moved with pain. Rehearsals were ad lib, depending on how Mr. B felt that day—a morning phone call determined whether or not we would work.

Because of the flurry of festival activity and Mr. B's modest demands, we had trouble on several occasions finding an empty studio. He was always gracious and uncomplaining, but the fact that he of all people did not have a place to work when he physically could made me sad and angry. I remember one day going with him from studio to studio, peeking in the doors, and George quickly withdrawing when he saw that the room was taken. Finally, we cleared the music stands from the center of an orchestra rehearsal room on the Lower Concourse and worked on the slippery waxed floor. He didn't mind, choosing, as always, to reserve his energies for dance, not temperament.

In 1966 I had been dressed in black for *Élégie*, but now that Balanchine was closer to death, he dressed me in white. It was the color I had first worn in *Meditation*. I was perhaps the same girl I had been in that ballet, but I was alone, and the spirit of mourning was tangible in my intimate, weighted gestures.

As the curtain rose I was kneeling, head lowered, in a pool of light, and while I ascended onto pointe, to reach for an absent one, I never strayed far from that solitary circle, ending as I began, kneeling, head bowed, in the warming but lonely light.

The dance was infinitely sad, given the circumstances, and I had great trepidation about being able to do it. But because the sadness was beautiful, it was bearable. Sixteen years earlier George had said he wanted me to dance *Élégie* at his funeral. Now he had rechoreographed it, and his wish, in effect, had come true—and he had been there to see it.

Because Mr. B's energies were required for several big Stravinsky productions, we didn't have a rehearsal for *Variations* until the day before it was scheduled. As a result, the première did not occur during the actual festival but on July 2, the last Friday of the New York season.

To try to ease an already very difficult situation, I tried to recall as much of the 1966 version as I could. I remembered some steps, but not all, and when I told George, he said, "Oh dear, it doesn't matter. I don't want to do the same thing. It was good, but I really didn't understand the music as well then. It was too musical, too clean." Balanchine never rested on his laurels; he was concerned to the end with righting all "wrongs"—musical, choreographic, and personal.

The final version of *Variations* began and ended as before, but much of the central activity was different, even less "choreographed" than previously. Despite Mr. B's steadily failing health, we managed to have a good time when we rehearsed. One day he said, "I don't know how much I can do today. I'm very dizzy." I said, "Well, just do what you want, and I'll be back here trying to get it." He proceeded to do some truly wild movement, and when I reproduced it for him, he looked at me and said, "Is that what I did?" and we both laughed so hard that we had to take a five-minute break to recover. The movement, of course, remained in the ballet.

After the première he came to my dressing room, as he had so many times before. His eyes gleamed with a familiar look of mischief, and he said with great satisfaction, "The music is a mess, and now, you're a mess. You look just like the music. It's wonderful." It was one more miraculous dance among many; I also think I knew that it was the last.

The company began its summer season in Saratoga less than a week after the première of *Variations*, but already Mr. B was absent. While he spent the month there, he never came to the theater. His balance had become very unpredictable.

No one knew exactly what was wrong with him. During the past few years he had undergone every kind of test to try to discover what was affecting his motor functions, an especially cruel affliction for a man who had dedicated his life to the movement of the human body. Without a diagnosis, no treatment could be prescribed, leaving everyone concerned, including Mr. B, frustrated and helpless.*

Following a six-week layoff after Saratoga, the company traveled to Washington, D.C., and it was there that Mr. B became suddenly so violently ill that he was rushed in an ambulance to the hospital. I danced *Mozartiana* that night and remember crying through the whole ballet—yet somehow I was carried along by the music, the steps, the prayer. After he had recovered enough to travel, George went back to New York, but in early November he was admitted to Roosevelt Hospital, which he was never to leave.

Because of his lifelong dislike of being seen at anything less than his best, I knew that visiting George in the hospital would be difficult for both of us. Still I went. I did not go every day, or even every week, but I went as often as I could bear to. It was cruelly sobering to walk down Columbus Avenue and pass first Lincoln Center and the New York State Theater, where I danced, then two blocks farther down St. Paul the Apostle, where I was married, and then on the next block arrive at Roosevelt Hospital, where George lay dying. My whole life was on that street.

Because so many miracles had happened in the theater, I hoped and prayed that one might transfer itself down the street to George. He had, after all, survived many serious illnesses in his life, including tuberculosis that left him with only one lung, and open-heart surgery; perhaps he could rally this one last time.

In the early months when I visited, he was often in fine spirits, and we had a good time talking about cats, food, something he had read, even ballet. On one occasion I told him a silly story about a cat I had seen on television that played Ping-Pong with its master, sitting on the end of the table and batting the ball back on each relay. George listened very quietly, then he smiled. Sometimes he talked about the past, about Russia, but we never talked about his imminent death; he had already addressed that issue onstage, and there were no words to add.

Other visits were sadder, like the time he asked me, as he had so many times before, "How are your knees?" My knees were fine, but for the first time I hesitated even to talk about them; my good health

---

*It was not until a year after he died that his illness was diagnosed as the rare Creutzfeldt-Jakob virus.

seemed so unimportant now. But remembering how happy it made him to know my knees were strong, I told him, "You know, my knees are great; I could do anything." He smiled and said, "Oh, I'm so glad, because I've been lying here praying for your knees."

I had a great deal of trouble admitting to myself that George was dying. As recently as September I had been to his apartment for dinner, and he had seemed fine. He had cooked wonderful Russian meatballs and noodles, opened a bottle of wine, and we had celebrated, belatedly, my birthday.

As the months went by, I could see him shaking, growing thinner, paler, reacting more slowly. Often we wouldn't talk at all. I would just sit on the bed, holding his hand while he slept, but as soon as I rose to go, his hand would grip mine more tightly. I would finally back out of the room—it was like the end of *Meditation.*

In December, my grandmother, with whom I had spent my childhood summers in the Adirondacks, also became ill, and after living with my mother for some time and then with me, she entered Roosevelt Hospital. Her room was on the floor below George, and I would sometimes visit them both. As Christmas approached, she voiced one last request, to spend it with her family, and she was released on Christmas Day. We all had a lovely time together, and three days later she died peacefully. But George, unlike Grandma, was not ready; he wanted to live, but he couldn't, and no one knew why.

For his seventy-ninth birthday on January 22, a party was arranged in his hospital room with the champagne, caviar, and other delicacies that he was so fond of. But he was too ill to enjoy it, and the atmosphere was heartbreaking. He began sleeping more and slipping in and out of lucidity, but when I held his hand I like to believe he knew my touch and recognized my voice.

During these very difficult months, dance was once more my salvation, while several extracurricular projects served as much needed distractions. I appeared in an episode of the situation comedy "Love, Sidney" with Tony Randall. Later, several episodes of "Sesame Street" added a whole new dimension to my performing experience. True glory came when my nieces and nephews saw the show and were finally impressed with Aunt Suzi. Throughout the experience I kept thinking how much George would have liked "Sesame Street" and its decision to highlight our profession.

One evening I received a midnight phone call from Peter. "I'll be blunt, Suzanne," he said abruptly. "I'm choreographing a ballet. I was planning to use Merrill [Ashley], but she has a bad foot. Would you do it?" I said yes. Mr. B was obviously not making any new ballets, and I still wanted to dance. I also wanted to support Peter. Although not officially named by Balanchine, Peter had, for the last year, been his obvious successor, and now he was overseeing, in consultation with Mr. B when possible, the daily responsibilities of company life—casting, programing, choreographing—in addition to performing himself.

Cast with Adam as my partner, *Rossini Quartets* was the first Martins ballet I danced (he had by now choreographed over fourteen works), and it was a very revealing experience to have the man who was usually my partner in front of me giving the directions, instead of behind me taking them. After hearing him repeat the phrase, "I don't want to see you . . . I don't want to see you, Adam," meaning that in partnering me Adam was not to be a distraction but to enhance our unified movement, I put my leg down from arabesque and burst out laughing. Looking rather worried Peter said, "What's so funny?" and I told him, "Peter, you're asking Adam to do everything that Mr. B always wanted you to do." His face relaxed, and he grinned, saying, "I know, I know, I can hear him now. He was so right."

It was through Peter's influence that I was to dance in a Paul Taylor work. At the time, Taylor, one of America's most innovative modern-dance choreographers, had his own highly acclaimed company performing at City Center, and he made a pas de deux entitled *Musette* to the music of Handel for Peter and me. It was the first time Taylor had choreographed for a dancer on pointe, an experiment in trying to marry his very modern, stark dance vision with classical dance. I had a thoroughly good time; I always valued experimentation far more than possible success or failure, and as it turned out the pas de deux was well received.

In early February, Balanchine was chosen to receive the nation's highest civilian honor, the Medal of Freedom. Because he was bedridden, it was decided that Lincoln Kirstein, as director of the New York City Ballet, Barbara Horgan, and I would fly to Washington to represent George. There was a luncheon at the White House with President Reagan and his wife, Nancy, followed by a simple ceremony of brief tributes and presentation of a small wooden box. Inside, resting on blue velvet was the Medal of Freedom, which actually consisted of three medals of varying sizes, each destined for different social occasions from the largest, intended for formal public functions, to a lapel pin for less momentous days.

I had very mixed feelings being at the White House for George— pleased that he was being acknowledged by the country he called his home, proud to be accepting for him, but most of all sad that he could not be there himself. I wondered why the recognition could not have come a little sooner. He would have enjoyed it.

When they told him in the hospital that he was to be honored by the President, his sense of humor was apparently intact, for he responded, "Of what country?"

In mid-April, just before the start of the spring season, Ib Andersen and I went to Chicago to guest for four performances with the Chicago City Ballet. I had obtained permission to perform *Tzigane* and *Mozartiana*. This was the first time *Mozartiana* was performed outside of the New York City Ballet—but Chicago was not to see it again. At the party after the first night, Ib started complaining of a stomachache. The next day, although he was still feeling ill, he insisted he could perform. By late afternoon he was rushed to the hospital for an emergency appendectomy, and at a moment's notice Paul had to climb out of his street clothes and into a pair of leather gypsy boots while I talked him through *Tzigane*. Once again, *Mozartiana* was canceled.

When I arrived home in New York, I was concerned not to find Bottom at the door to greet me. Although by now I had six other cats, she remained my link to the past and to Mr. B. She had proved a brave and noble traveler, spending four years eating Belgian cat food and summers on Cedar Islands hunting mice and taking swims, and had even learned to wiggle door handles which had opened yet more rooms for her exploration. She was the only cat I ever really confided in, and by now she knew everything about me.

I found her crouching in a corner; her appetite was gone, and she was noticeably uncomfortable. The next morning she was dead. She was as dignified in death as she had been in life. I lifted her little body and looked at the calendar. It was April 23. The cat who had lived through my whole career, whom I had acquired at Mr. B's suggestion, who had taught me to be a tender Titania, had died on George's name day. She was twenty.

Seven days later, I was awakened by a phone call at 4:00 A.M. and heard Eddie Bigelow's familiar voice: "George is dead." There was nothing more to say. The one thing I couldn't bear to hear had been said, and I hung up. Now I felt really alone—as I'd never felt in my whole life.

I got up, fed the cats, watered the plants, and walked around the apartment, watching the sun rise. The morning was bright, clear, and sunny. I called my mother to tell her the news. After that, my phone stayed quiet. At nine o'clock I locked my front door and walked over to the theater. I wasn't thinking clearly, I only knew that was where I had to be. I was drawn there as if by an invisible string.

I met Peter, and we sat in his office, mostly in silence, staring at each other. I was thirty-seven years old, but I felt like an orphan.

In the late morning we walked together to the Juilliard building to watch a final rehearsal of the annual School of American Ballet's Workshop. We sat in the audience while the young dancers performed *Western Symphony*. Fourteen-, fifteen- and sixteen-year-olds, already professionals, they, too, were orphans, the first young blood trained for Balanchine who would not know him. But watching them dance Balanchine, a miracle seemed to happen. Although Mr. B had died, the ballet still existed, and it took on a resonance, as did every Balanchine ballet after this day, not so much of being his work as of being him.

The company's spring season had opened four days earlier, and I was scheduled to perform the adagio of *Symphony in C* that evening. It was Saturday, April 30. Peter, rigid with grief, was now, together with Jerome Robbins, the company's new artistic director, and he asked me if I could dance that night. I was as close to hysterics as I had ever been, and it was apparent to him that I might not be able to put on makeup, a crown, a tutu, and bourrée onstage. I appreciated his concern, but I knew the answer to his question. "I'm going to dance tonight—he would want me to," I said with a calm that surprised even me. Then I asked Peter if he would dance with me. (Because of his new job as director he was not dancing as often as he had and was not scheduled for that performance.) "Absolutely," he said. "I'll do it with you."

I didn't know what would happen onstage. I knew only that if I didn't get out there that night, I might never get out there again. I would never again be understood the way Mr. B had understood me, I would never be used the way he had used me, I would never be loved the way he had loved me, but I had to get out there. In a very real sense, I was getting out there alone for the first time. If I had frequently been acclaimed for my "independence," "fearlessness," and "courage" onstage, it had always been because of the man in the front wing. Now, he wasn't there.

I sat in my dressing room and went through all the motions—sewing my toe shoes, gluing my false eyelashes, hoping they would conceal my red eyes, powdering my face, pinning on my tiara. I warmed up at the barre backstage, put on my tutu, tucked in my toe-shoe ribbons, and bourréed onstage with Peter.

Technically, the performance was smooth, thanks to years of discipline and familiarity. I certainly wasn't thinking about the steps as such; I wasn't "thinking" about anything. I was dancing for George.

For the first time that day I felt strangely strong and calm. Surrounding the strains of Bizet, there was a quiet in the audience that I had never heard before. It was like a church.

Standing in a wing with Peter afterward, watching the third movement of the ballet, I said to him, "Thank you for dancing with me. I really needed to be out there." Victor Castelli, a soloist in the company, was standing beside me, and he said, "We really needed to see you out there." My eyes filled with tears. Despite my deep daily involvement with the company, I did not have much personal contact with the other dancers. I never had had, and for whatever reasons, perhaps shyness on both sides, they didn't say much to me. So at Victor's words, I quietly lost my composure.

After the performance I went out and had a drink, and reality began to set in. I felt insecure in a way I never had before. The New York City Ballet was suddenly changed. The theater was filled with dancers walking around, taking class, rehearsing, doing silly things, none of which seemed to make sense anymore.

A few days later in class a young dancer in the company came over to stand next to me at the barre and said, "I'm going to stand here, Suzanne, and feed off your energy." I was touched, but I said, tongue-in-cheek, "You can feed off it—just leave some for me."

Balanchine was to be buried in the Russian Orthodox Church, and for the three days preceding the funeral, memorial services were held at the Cathedral of Our Lady of The Sign. Eddie Bigelow, dear, faithful Eddie, picked me up and took me up the little private elevator one flight into the church. I was being led; my peripheral vision was gone.

In the Russian tradition, everyone stood, hundreds of us, trailing out to the street, holding lighted candles, during a long, beautiful service of choral singing and chanting in Russian. The atmosphere was so heavy with grief, some people fainted. It had taken so little, perhaps only a nod or a single comment, to be touched and changed by Mr. B. Around the open casket four of his wives were grouped— Tamara Geva, Alexandra Danilova, Maria Tallchief, and Tanaquil Le Clercq (Vera Zorina was in Europe). All of them had outlived him.

One by one, we approached the coffin, and as I looked, with great difficulty, at his forehead covered by the Orthodox funerary band, I saw Don Quixote. The band was like the gauze he had worn as the Don when he, too, was on his deathbed. We had seen each other like this before, onstage; he had prepared me for this moment. I bent down, spoke to him, touched him, and put my face by his. I didn't say goodbye; I will never say that.

The actual funeral was on the following Tuesday and after the church service, he was driven out to be buried in Sag Harbor, Long

Island. The burial was officially "private." No one said anything to me about it; I was not invited or given directions; but I knew I had to be there. Eddie Bigelow drove me out, and we stopped briefly on the way at a restaurant that looked like *Western Symphony* with sawdust on the floor. George would have been amused. As we approached the cemetery, I saw a black limousine driving in the opposite direction. Because the windows were dark I couldn't see inside, but I said to Eddie, "That couldn't have been them, it couldn't be over."

We parked near the site of the grave. No one familiar was there, only the gravediggers. Eddie climbed out of the car and went over to find out what had happened. He came back and said, "Yes, that's George. It's over." I was shattered. The limousine had indeed been the funeral party.

I climbed out of Eddie's old car and went over to the grave. The coffin had already been lowered into the earth, but it was still visible. I said some prayers and threw on some soil. Just before the gravediggers covered the coffin, I threw in a white rose I had brought for him. He had so often sent me white roses.

When we arrived home, it was dark. I entered my apartment alone and went over to the kitchen window. I was looking out, wondering what was going to happen to me now, when suddenly my peripheral vision was lifted for the first time since George died and I felt a surge of blinding white light energizing me. It was like my dream of *Mozartiana*. Then I knew. I said to myself, "I'm going to be all right. I'm going to survive."

The funeral arrangements were only the first sign of the strange situation I found myself in after George's death. I had all the emotions, all the feelings of unparalleled loss, but because we had had no official ties as the world perceives them, I did not fit into any existing category to justify my grief. I was not his wife; I was his dancer.

As the weeks went by, I received an enormous number of letters, mostly from people I had never met, people who had only seen me dance. They were loving and beautiful letters, and they gave me great strength, but they were letters written to a widow.

A month or so after George's death I opened my mailbox to find an official letter from the Balanchine Estate informing me that he had left me two ballets in his will, *Tzigane* and *Don Quixote*. At the time, this served only to remind me in yet another way that he was gone. I tossed the letter into a desk drawer and tiptoed around it every day until I got used to its presence. But as my grief slowly lifted, my feelings changed. Like *Meditation*, these ballets were integral parts of my life, and I was moved that he entrusted them to me. Barbara

Horgan, who was the executrix of his estate, gave me his Medal of Freedom one day, saying, "Suzanne, I think you should have this." It was generous of her, and I was grateful.

CHAPTER EIGHTEEN

Rejoicing

❦

An early scene in the movie *The Red Shoes* has Moira Shearer as the aspiring ballet dancer at a party given by her rich aunt. She is talking to Lermontov, the ballet company director. Skeptically, he asks her the crucial question, "Why do you want to dance?" Without missing a beat, she gives him the answer, the only answer, "Why do you want to live?"

These lines had stuck in my mind, but now, with George gone, while I certainly didn't want to die, I did seriously wonder if I still wanted to dance. He, beyond all other incentives, had been my reason and my need to dance. It wasn't so much that we would no longer have the fun of experimenting on a new ballet; he had made enough beautiful ballets to fill and fulfill hundreds of dancers for hundreds of years. It was that he wouldn't be there to notice the little things, the small differences between performances, the personal things that had become a silent dialogue between us.

His was the omnipotent eye that saw everything and missed nothing. Dancing is hard, but Balanchine's energy, encouragement, and appreciation made it a joy, not an effort. I never thought or worried about the status of my career as such; dancing was simply something very special that I did every night.

As the days and weeks passed, the notion of not dancing anymore became increasingly remote. Discipline and habit were stronger than brooding, and I realized that despite the "thoughts" that grief sent through my mind, I was just as much a dancer now as I had been when George was alive. Balanchine, who he was and what he stood for, was in my body, and I could not forget it.

For the annual School Workshop performance Helgi Tomasson, an elegant principal dancer in the company, had choreographed his first ballet. *Ballet d'Isoline* to the music of André Messager was a lovely classical work, and Peter immediately suggested that Helgi stage it for the company. It had premièred at the School the day Balanchine died.

Peter and I were to dance the first performance on June 9, but because of his extra duties as company director, Peter was not available for all the rehearsals. As a result, the performance threatened to become a classical comedy, and my long experience at improvisation was put to good use. The music repeats in several sections and, confusing them, Peter ran offstage at the wrong time, leaving me leading an adagio section without a partner. I remained composed and tried to do some appropriate choreography by myself.

Peter, watching from a wing, said to the ballet mistress, "Doesn't Suzanne look great out there," to which she replied, "Yes, but you're supposed to be there with her." Aghast, he ran to the back wing and made an unexpected grand entrance down the center of the stage. By this time I had adjusted quite nicely to my new predicament, and when he started grabbing at my arms trying to lend support, it felt strangely awkward.

The incident was a sharp reminder of Peter's very difficult dual job as both dancer and director. He was now my partner and my boss, but this situation was not to last long. Within a month he telephoned me at home and said, "Suzanne, I want to tell you this before you read it in the paper. I'm going to retire in December."

I felt as if suddenly my partners were all leaving me at once. I tried to suggest something less drastic, that perhaps he could gradually dance less without retiring altogether. But he told me he had made up his mind. He had found he could not do what was required of him and dance at the same time. I understood the difficulty of his position, but it was nevertheless a blow to me. We had had eight years of dancing together, and now another curtain was lowering on my life. My only solace was that December was still six months away and he might change his mind. But he did not.

I could not help thinking that it would be better for him to keep dancing, at least for a while. Better for the company and better for his new job. He had great security as a dancer, but as a director he was a novice, and perhaps the security of one might shore up the insecurity of the other. Peter was only thirty-seven and in his prime as a dancer. Dancing is such a short life, at best, and I kept this in mind for my own future.

The Nutcracker was the first ballet we had danced together in New York in 1967, and now, on December 6, we danced it for the last time. It was the 1,000th performance of Balanchine's magical Christmas ballet, Peter's and my last official dance together with the company, and a very emotional evening.

In my dressing room I received a note and a little turquoise box from my retiring partner.

> My Dear Suzanne,
>
> There's very little to *say* at this point, other than *feeling* a lot. I'm not quite sure what I feel (shaky though)—and it's hard to try and express!! However, you gave me the most fulfilling thing one could ask for: *not to be alone* in one's career.
>
> For that I'm always grateful. And I know our friendship will carry us much further in the future!!
>
> This little thing is just a token for your dressing room table— because *you will dance more*—and it has turquoise which of course I love.
>
> So, tonight—just relax—try and enjoy—I'll do it all (at least I'll try) and let's get this thing over with.
>
> > *Much, much* love,
> > Peter

Part of me was retiring too, and again, in desperation, it flashed through my mind that I didn't want to dance anymore either. During the pas de deux that evening I looked down and saw my hand shaking in Peter's; it had never done that before. It was a year of final curtains. But my own hadn't come down quite yet, although I had already received the first signs that it would. But I refused to recognize them.

Immediately after the Saratoga season in 1983, Adam Lüders and I joined the Chicago City Ballet for a four-week European tour. I danced *Tzigane, Romeo and Juliet,* and *Tschaikovsky Pas de Deux.* We performed at many outdoor festivals—Rome, Ravenna, Naples, Bormio, Vaison-la-Romaine, Tunis, Lyon, and Milan. It was wonderfully reminiscent of Paul's and my Béjart touring days, but the frequent long bus trips between cities, the small makeshift stages, and the all-too-brief rehearsal time made it undeniably arduous. Normally, I would not have thought twice about the circumstances, but halfway through the tour I began feeling pain in my right hip that refused to respond to all the usual treatments of Ben-Gay, hot baths, and good warm-ups.

Initially, I suspected it was a pulled or strained muscle from doing a certain swiveling step in *Tzigane* so many times in succession, and I thought that once the tour was over it would heal of its own accord. On August 22 I departed for Europe with the New York City Ballet for a triumphant six-week tour to London, Copenhagen, and Paris. It was only three months after Balanchine's death, and the company was welcomed and applauded as never before; we probably also danced as never before. The pride we felt representing Mr. B pervaded the company, and the result was performance after performance of true exaltation. My hip continued to ache, but I kept on dancing; it didn't seem like the time to be out, the tour had a kind of epic memorial significance. We were Balanchine's children, and it was our chance to show our love and respect for him after receiving his for so many years.

By October my hip had been getting steadily worse for three months, and I decided I should get a professional opinion. I had always been skeptical of doctors in regard to dance injuries; too often they wanted to operate, something I had managed to avoid for twenty-two years. But I wasn't improving, and I feared something more serious. First, at Peter's suggestion, I tried a chiropractor on the chance that it was only a mechanical alignment problem. This was the first of many doctors I would visit over the next few years, all of whom, after taking X rays, gave me the same diagnosis—the very last one I wanted to hear.

I was unwilling even to say the word "arthritis" to myself, and I certainly did not admit it to anyone else for a very long time. For a dancer it is the equivalent of a death sentence, perhaps the only physical ailment that is deemed irreversible by everyone. I associated arthritis with old age, but I was only thirty-eight and at the height of my physical abilities as a dancer in every way—except for my right hip. That hip, the X rays showed, had cartilage erosion of someone twice my age.

Desperate, I made appointments with other specialists—osteopaths, homeopaths, internists, acupuncturists—hoping to hear a different diagnosis. The basic advice was always the same: stop dancing. When I said that this was not an option for me, the doctors shrugged and told me dancing might not increase the rate of erosion; it could be equally fast if I stayed in bed. That was enough for me to begin four years of dancing against time. The only thing no one could predict was just how fast or how much my hip would deteriorate. I preferred to find out while doing what I loved best rather than sitting at home, waiting.

Keeping my problem private as long as I could was very important to me. It was not the concern of the public or the critics, and I abhorred the idea that my dancing could or would be judged conditionally. Fortunately, the unhappy state of my X rays did not always coincide with my physical abilities, and often I danced completely oblivious to pain or restriction. Other days were not so good, but the fact that they varied enabled me to remain relatively optimistic.

I did, however, not only pray for help but also looked for it. There was not a prospective "cure" or alleviation that I didn't try. As if it weren't enough that George and Peter had both left me, my own body was now threatening desertion. If I had to stop dancing, I wanted it to be my choice, not my sentence.

I tried downing large amounts of cod liver oil capsules in the old-fashioned hope that they would oil my hip joint; I went on a macro-biotic diet of brown rice and green tea; I didn't touch meat or wine for a year and a half; I sent my X rays to a highly respected Parisian homeopathic doctor whose treatment involved large glass vials of various cartilage-regenerating minerals—gold, silver, copper—to be taken at very specific times of the day. When Paul saw all the labels, he teased, "Honey, you're worth almost as much inside as out." I also tried all the more conventional anti-inflammatory drugs, vitamins, massage, and hot baths.

As I tested each new approach I was optimistic, but eventually it became clear that while some symptoms—pain and reduced mobility—could be temporarily deflected, their source, deep in my hip joint, could not. The deterioration was relatively fast; I could feel it happening. I was truly living from day to day.

By 1985 I had tried every possible physical treatment, so when my mother suggested a faith healer, I thought, "Why not?" I was desperate, and I believe in miracles. I needed one.

There were many of us in an auditorium, and a lovely woman sang, spoke encouragingly, and went through her procedure. Finally she went up and gave a little tap on the forehead to each person. As I watched everyone collapse to the ground, I decided I was not going to, but when she touched me I sank instantly. Lying on the floor, I was hesitant to rise and prayed, "Dear God, please when I get up, let it be gone. Let me be well." When I finally rose, my hip was as sore as ever.

Throughout these adventures in self-healing I continued to dance, and the only cure I didn't try was taking time off. I knew two things: first, if I didn't keep performing, I would probably never dance again; it would be too difficult physically and emotionally, and second, it was only when the curtain rose that the pain abated. Undoubtedly endorphins, the body's naturally occurring opiate, which are released by physical activity, were in part responsible, but there was something else. Dancing was the only occupation where my mind was totally absorbed, where my responsibilities were all-consuming, where the world was truly transformed, and I think these concerns simply took priority over my otherwise very real joint problem. I invited one of my orthopedic doctors, who had said that according to my X rays I shouldn't be able to walk, to the ballet one night, and he sat in the audience with Mother, flabbergasted that I could dance.

But I was having increasing trouble walking—it was, curiously, more painful than dancing—and one day, despairing, I said to Paul, "I just don't know how I'm going to dance tomorrow. I can't even walk." "Oh, honey," he replied, "that's all right. You don't need to walk, you only need to dance." We both laughed when we realized what he had said, but it was strangely true. Perhaps this was my miracle—at least for the moment.

Despite Balanchine's absence there remained, mercifully, many challenges, old and new, onstage. A new production of *Liebeslieder Walzer* was mounted in 1984 after ten years out of the repertoire and became another revelation of Balanchine's genius for the many who had never before seen it. I danced the same role I had first performed in 1963, but by now I had had experiences enough for a lifetime, and the ballet's passions had a resonance for me that was not possible before. I have little doubt that my dancing also had a resonance not possible before. It was like revisiting the romantic mind of the man who had created it, and on the night of the first performance I felt his presence in the theater as if he were there watching. No doubt he was, but from a different location.

The fact that the company was created primarily as a workshop for new ballets did not change because of Balanchine's death, and revivals even of his ballets were not enough to keep the company vital. The press had already philosophized at great length about fears that the company might become a museum, albeit a Balanchine one; but this was not to be the case.

In becoming the company's administrative director Peter had inherited, alongside Jerome Robbins, the job of company choreographer, and in May of 1984 I premièred in a new ballet of his, entitled *Réjouissance,* to the music of Bach. I enjoyed working with Peter, as I had in *Rossini.* I had by now adjusted to his no longer dancing. The ballet had a huge cast, including two lead couples besides myself and Joseph Duell, a newly promoted principal dancer trained at the School of American Ballet. In Peter's desire not to produce "a conventional pas de deux" he used six leading dancers instead of two for the adagio music. It was an artistic choice about which I retained some reservations; a pas de deux between a man and a woman is one of the central elements in the classical dance idiom, and I didn't think it could be improved upon by a crowd. Peter's choice was indicative of the very real dilemma all choreographers faced in the aftermath of Balanchine. "Originality" became a passionate challenge—and a virtual impossibility. There was very little Balanchine himself hadn't tried, and if he hadn't, it probably wasn't worth doing. Still, I respected Peter's desire to experiment, and with a generous knowledge of steps and possibilities, he was equipped to attempt the task.

The following month, with the Pennsylvania Ballet, I did *Apollo* with someone I had never thought I would dance with. Rudolf Nureyev, whom I knew from my Béjart days, was, like Baryshnikov, somewhat too short for me as a partner, but his presence more than offset the height discrepancy. The Pennsylvania Ballet was offering a gala fund-raiser, and Peter, the company's artistic adviser, arranged this one-time performance.

Apollo was one of the few signature Balanchine ballets that were in the repertoire of companies all over the world, and while Nureyev had never danced the role in Balanchine's own company, he had done it many times elsewhere. Ballets have such a fragile form that they are easily altered in subtle ways, and this became very clear when Nureyev and I had our first rehearsal of the pas de deux. It felt, presumably to both of us, as if we were dancing two different ballets. A diagonal was not a diagonal, a normal arabesque was an exaggerated penché, a pirouette, a pose. Eventually we ironed out some of the discrepancies, and while the final version was still not the one danced at the New York City Ballet, it was a respectable compromise.

As we parted after the first rather difficult rehearsal, he said to me with a grin, "Oh, you made me have to work so hard and change this and change that." I replied with equal good humor, "I didn't change anything. Don't forget, Rudi, I was dancing *Apollo* before you even defected." We left the theater arm-in-arm. Despite our different ideas about the ballet, our relationship was both cordial and professional.

Shortly after this *Apollo* I learned that Nureyev also wanted to dance *Mozartiana*. This was not possible for several reasons, but he was always on the lookout for good roles, and he subsequently approached Paul in Chicago about dancing *Cinderella* with me. The three of us met in New York to discuss the idea, but while we were watching a video of the ballet it became apparent that Nureyev had his own very specific ideas about the role of Prince Charming, and the project was abandoned.

Meanwhile Paul had arranged a sequence of eight Richard Adler songs from the musicals *Pajama Game* and *Damn Yankees* into a ballet in which I danced with nine men. I loved the songs, and the jazzy rhythms provided a kind of movement that was easy on my hip. For the second section of the ballet I wore my old black *Slaughter on Tenth Avenue* costume and high heels and strutted through *8 By Adler* with all my "Broadway" savvy. Early the following year the ballet was filmed for television. Paul had tailor-made a ballet for me in which, to our pleasure, I won an Emmy Award, an honor rarely, if ever, bestowed on a ballet dancer.

By now my hip was limiting the times I was able to perform, but when I did, there was no slowing me down. Always hungry for something new, I danced "Élégie," the first section of *Tschaikovsky Suite No. 3*, for the first time. This was a ballet Balanchine had made in my absence in 1970, and I had always adored the loose-haired, high passion of the scenario where a young man is confronted by seven women. He chooses to dance with one, an obvious love, only to lose her again.

Many people wondered why I wanted to do the role considering my hip problem, but to me the reason was simple. I wanted to dance to that beautiful music. At one time Mr. B had even wanted me to dance both the first and last sections and without any new Balanchine ballets, doing one I hadn't done before still provided a challenge. I also knew that my time was growing short, and I suppose I felt a desperate need to dance everything I possibly could before it was too late.

One day in early 1985 I was standing near the water fountain outside the main hall after class when Jerry Robbins came up to me and said, "I have an idea for a new ballet, and I'd like to have you in it. What do you think?" This was the first time, except for *In G Major* ten years earlier, that Jerry had suggested using me in a new ballet. I was pleased but thought it only fair to warn him: "Well, Jerry, you know I have a bad hip, and I can't work five hours every day. I don't even know if I can work two. There will be days when I might not be able to work at all. I just can't predict, but if you can live with that, I'd love to do your ballet. I can promise you only one thing. I'll commit myself to getting out there and doing it onstage."

As a result of this conversation, Jerry was extraordinarily considerate of me, sometimes even choreographing my role on another dancer so as not to tax my hip, although most of that work was ultimately discarded. At one rehearsal, after he had choreographed a good deal of a pas de deux between Adam Lüders and me, he wasn't sure what he wanted next. "Isn't your hip bothering you yet?"

he asked hopefully, to which I responded with a smile, "No, Jerry, I'm having a good day."

The Alban Berg score of the ballet commemorated the death of a young girl, but although the final version depicted a life, death, and resurrection, Jerry never said that there was any specific story. Just before the première on June 13, the ballet was given the title *In Memory Of . . .* , which led to the speculation that it was a homage to Balanchine. But with true Balanchinian wisdom, Jerry refused to comment. I enjoyed dancing the evolution of my role from a young woman in love with a young man to a highly dramatic pas de deux with Death to a resurrection supported by both figures. In the aftermath of Balanchine, *In Memory Of . . .* was a ballet of welcome substance.

The role of Death was danced with great force and an eerie tenderness by Adam Lüders, the man who had become my most frequent partner since Peter's retirement. With his beautiful European manners, Adam was—and still is—a partner of great sensitivity, and we had by now danced together in many ballets including *Walpurgisnacht, Rossini Quartets, Cinderella, Chaconne, Meditation,* and *Vienna Waltzes.* I felt secure in his hands and identified with his passionate perfectionism about his work. During those last years, when my hip placed me in such a precarious position, I was especially grateful to have his uncompromising support.

I had begun to dance frequently with Joe Duell who also had the rare ability to be a highly self-effacing, strong, and unusually graceful partner. Like myself, Joe came from Ohio. He danced the part of the young man in *In Memory Of . . .* as well as Jacques' role in a revival of *Brahms-Schoenberg Quartet.* By mid-1985 I was dancing only about half my usual ballets, but I was adamant about revisiting the gypsy world of this one. My hip was extremely bad, however, by the time of the first performance, and I confided in Joe.

"I really don't know if I can go through with this," I said, and Joe replied, "Well then, do it for me." This echoed an exchange one night several months earlier before a performance of *In Memory Of . . .* when our roles were reversed; he was depressed and did not feel like dancing. "Oh, Joe, do it for me," I had said. So now, with *Brahms,* I returned the favor. At tenuous times I would frequently dance for other people, and Joe's request gave me the courage to override my physical pain.

Unknown to many, Joe was undergoing his own very deep emotional and spiritual pain, and on February 16, 1986, he committed suicide by jumping out of his apartment window. Again, as with George, I received an early morning phone call. Joe had become one of the company's much-needed moral forces since Balanchine's death, and his own death at the age of twenty-nine was a devastating shock for the company—only three weeks earlier I had danced with him in a very successful revival of *Slaughter on Tenth Avenue*. The tragedy was unexpected and seemingly unpreventable: it had been impossible to know the terror and despair that Joe was feeling, since he was himself always so charming, so supportive, so full of promise.

One week later, for the final night of the season in a performance for the Dancers' Emergency Fund, I danced, against all physical probability, *Mozartiana*, for Joe. I felt none of my own pain, and the performance somehow reached far beyond my capabilities. It was not only my last public prayer for Joe. It was also the last time I would dance *Mozartiana*.

I had turned forty in August 1985, but I had no emotional pangs about reaching any kind of dividing line in my life. Aside from my hip, I had never been stronger, more willing or more able. But my hip was taking over, and within a year I could no longer overcome its deterioration. I was of retirement age for a ballerina, but far from being bitter or bored by my profession, I still loved to dance as much as ever. It was fate, not choice, that determined my future.

On November 9, 1985, I danced with yet another new partner. A dinner in honor of Prince Charles and Princess Diana was being given at the White House, and I was invited as part of the celebrity contingent. Paul flew to Washington to meet me for an impressive evening of food and entertainment. After dinner the Reagans and the Royals took to the dance floor for the first dance. An envoy approached me and said, "Miss Farrell, His Royal Highness would like to dance with you." So, as John Travolta, the hip-swinging hero of *Saturday Night Fever*, whirled Diana around the floor, Charles and I took a more classical approach. He was charming and elegant, but we found little to say to each other. Suddenly we received a jolt from one side as John Travolta and Diana flew by in a flamboyant swing, and Charles broke the ice. "*They* bumped into *us*," he whispered conspiratorially, and I agreed.

After one last appearance in New York as the Siren in a revival of *Prodigal Son* with Ib Andersen, a most moving Prodigal, I traveled with the company to Saratoga for the 1986 summer season. There I danced a few performances of *In Memory Of . . . , Prodigal Son*, and a single performance of *Duo Concertant* with Sean Lavery. I didn't know at the time that this came close to being the last performance of my career.

Duo was one of the three Balanchine masterworks that remained in the repertoire from the 1972 Stravinsky Festival, but I did not dance it until ten years after its creation, first with Peter and then, that summer, with Sean. Two dancers share the stage with two musicians and their instruments, a piano and a violin. In simple practice clothes the dancers listen to the music from behind the piano before dancing together, often mirroring each other, and then individually, until just before the final movement of the music, when a love story unfolds. The stage is darkened except for a pool of light in which hands and faces are momentarily united before they separate again. *Duo Concertant* is one of Balanchine's most beautiful homages to fated love, and it has a strangely overt emotional tone not always found in Stravinsky ballets.

After Saratoga the company had the usual August layoff before embarking on a tour of the West Coast in October. I had now been dancing for three years with my bad hip, and I decided to take a few weeks off while I was on Cedar Islands. By September I was back in class trying to get in shape for Paul's production of *La Gioconda*, which I was scheduled to perform in Chicago, when disaster struck. I could hardly move. My hip was rigid. After my initial alarm, I decided it would simply need more time and coaxing than I had expected.

I was wrong. For the first time messages my brain sent to my foot and knee were blocked at my hip. I realized I had hit another level of degeneration, and this was one I could not overcome. With enormous emotional pain I canceled the Chicago engagement. I was scheduled for only a single performance of *Tzigane* with the New York City Ballet in Orange County, California. I could not rally even for that. It was the first time I had canceled a performance because of my hip, and it was a great blow to my physical pride.

I could find no relief. I could hear clicking and grinding inside my hip where the cartilage was completely gone. Bone was gnawing bone, and I was visibly limping. Although I was still unable to consider the obvious—an operation—I knew this was the beginning of the end and decided it was time to retire.

In consultation with me, the company issued a brief statement to the press on November 1 announcing that this would be my last season with the New York City Ballet and I would officially retire in February 1987. There was no mention of the reason for this decision, and I wanted none. At the time I was especially wary of the negative press, which, in the aftermath of Balanchine's death, was full of stories about the hardships and victimization of ballet dancers. I had no intention of adding fuel to this fire by being viewed as one wounded by my profession. Nothing, after all, could have been further from the truth.

I do not believe my Balanchine training in any way contributed to my hip problem. On the contrary, I think his technique preserved my body and its abilities far longer than might have been expected. It is to the speed, musicality, and consistency of his training and the freedom of adaptability it allows that I attribute my ability to dance for three years in spite of a deteriorating hip. His training in no way threatened or destroyed the human body, and I have never danced any other choreography that offered such natural transitions.

Despite my attempts to keep my physical problems private, it became known that I had a bad hip, and articles were written describing, often incorrectly, my situation and its causes. This upset me deeply. Balanchine had always had very strong feelings about the privacy of injuries; to him they were not a part of a dancer's life that should be open for public scrutiny. A dancer's purpose was to dance, and what happened offstage was not for public consumption. But along with the ever-growing audience for dance came a voracious curiosity about backstage life, and revelations were being offered on an almost daily basis, most of them negative. There were allegations of underpayment, overwork, undereducation, and even physical abuse. I had been dancing for over twenty years and had none of these complaints, only gratitude for all the beauty and opportunity in my life.

The backlash focused in great part on Balanchine, who was, of course, not present to defend himself, and one of its loudest voices was that of Gelsey Kirkland, a former New York City Ballet dancer. I saw her dance only once, in 1979 at a gala in West Palm Beach. She joined the corps of the New York City Ballet less than a year before I left in 1969 and had departed before I returned in 1975. Her bitterness about Balanchine I found most curious.

Balanchine had recognized her talent. He promoted her, choreographed for her, and encouraged her in every way, as he had many dancers over the years. But for her own reasons she obviously didn't want to accept the opportunities he offered her, and she seemed to resent him for it. Balanchine functioned on a plateau that, clearly, wasn't for everybody, but to abandon the challenge of Balanchine for an approach to dancing that seemed more like an act of defiance than an act of love and respect for one's craft was something I could not comprehend.

Another frequent allegation against Balanchine made him almost singlehandedly responsible for anorexia nervosa among young ballet dancers. I hope my own example proves that being bone-thin was not a prerequisite for his interest or attention. I asked George once half jokingly after I came back to the company in 1975—when, incidentally, he told me I was too thin—why he had presented me onstage so often in the 1960s when I still had the roundness of youth. "Oh, but, dear," he said, holding up his hands helplessly, "you were always heavy."

No one goes through life pain free, emotionally or physically, and I don't consider what happened to my hip a sacrifice I made to dance. My body allowed me more actual moments of dancing than most dancers ever have, given my huge repertoire and long seasons of dancing often two or three ballets a night, year after year, not to mention the fact that the speed of Balanchine's ballets condenses the number of steps in a three-act classical ballet into a twenty-minute neoclassical one.

I consider myself blessed by my profession. It gave me more beauty, joy, and wisdom than I could ever have imagined existed back in Cincinnati when I was a child. I had had the privilege of dancing with, and for, George Balanchine for the last and most triumphant years of his life. My career was a magical event, full of hard work and also all the luck of timing and circumstance.

By December of 1986 I realized that I was not even going to be able to retire. I couldn't reach down to put my shoes on, I couldn't sleep, and I was using a cane to walk around the house. The writing had been on the wall for some time, but now I looked up and read it. I needed a hip replacement, and I knew that if I had one I would probably never dance again. But by now I just wanted to walk like a normal person.

Once I had decided, things happened quickly. Dr. Hamilton recommended I see Dr. Philip Wilson, Jr., at The Hospital for Special Surgery. I liked him, and we immediately started arranging the operation. I had X rays, stood on wooden blocks to measure how much bone had deteriorated—I had lost an inch—and lay on the examining table to have my range of motion calculated with a tape measure. It all felt terribly invasive, as if I were divulging my deepest secrets. I was especially anguished to feel reduced to the limits of a tape measure, when I was so used to representing the outermost capabilities of human movement.

After I gave several pints of blood for the operation, I discussed with Dr. Wilson which kind of plastic hip to have—with or without cement. Cement was the older version and enabled a quicker recovery after surgery, while cementless required that the bone grow into the rough metal, anchoring the joint in a more natural manner, but it required several months of horizontal living. Because I was relatively young and my bones were healthy—so healthy that after the operation they kept what was removed for their bone bank—Dr. Wilson suggested I have a cementless replacement. Once healed it would offer better mobility, something clearly of great importance to me.

I hoped I could have my new hip within a week, but because of various hospital logistics I had to wait a month. It was a long four weeks. I wanted to get on with my life, and that wasn't going to happen while I was preoccupied with dragging around my right leg.

On February 5, one week before my operation was scheduled, *Sinfonia Mistica*, the first ballet choreographed by Paul for the New York City Ballet, premièred at the State Theater. Originally intended for me, the ballet did not turn out as he had envisioned it. Nevertheless, I wanted to be there for the performance, and so we hired a car to pick me up and drive me the four blocks to the theater. It was the first time in my life I hadn't walked that short distance. Paul had to return to Chicago immediately and then came back a few days later. It was a terribly stressful time.

I went into the hospital the evening before my operation. Later that night the anesthesiologist came into my room to discuss the anesthesia. Mother was with me and, being a nurse, knew something about the various procedures. We both had our minds set on my having sodium Pentothal, which I had had for the operation in Belgium, and we looked at the doctor aghast when he suggested a different drug. I had blissful memories of Pentothal's dreamy effects and was counting on having it again.

The doctor thought this would be risky because Pentothal slows down all one's vital functions, and since I would have to lie on my left side for many hours during the operation, it would be arduous on my heart. He wanted to give me an epidural in the spine, and after recovering from my disappointment, I told him to go ahead. I had to trust the doctors; they were all I had right now.

The next morning, February 11, I went singing into the operating theater; I was so glad the day had finally come. But throughout the whole ordeal no one, especially Dr. Wilson, had mentioned dancing to me. He had told Mother it would be impossible.

Before the operation I had been sent home with the standard tome of fine print about casualty rates, rejection statistics, and infection probabilities, all protecting the doctors and hospital in the case of an unpredictable outcome. I was not in a state of mind to want to read about such things and quickly signed on the dotted line. The risk for me was simple enough—I had no choice. It was only after the operation that I understood the complexities of it and felt a kind of strange fascination with what was now inside my body.

My femur was scraped smooth, and a four-inch canal was drilled in the thighbone, into which was inserted a rough-edged metal shaft as an anchor for the new hip. At the top of this shaft was the new joint, a steel ball which rotates inside a plastic-coated metal cup. It was all very smooth and high-tech, and there were six screws involved. The whole package weighed three pounds. The surgery took over six hours.

Awakening in intensive care, I briefly recognized Paul's and Mother's faces bending over me, telling me everything had gone well. I reached down to feel one leg and then the other and immediately panicked despite my heavily drugged state. My good leg, my left leg, felt enormous, while the bad one felt normal. The nurse explained that the good leg was swollen from so many hours spent lying on that side. I passed out again.

By the following morning I was up walking down the hallway with a walker and getting my toes pricked in bed, both circulation exercises. Although I was barely putting weight on my new hip, I felt instantly that my right leg was too long, and I envisioned limping for the rest of my life. My fears did not abate when the nurse nonchalantly suggested that I could always wear a lift in one shoe. I could only think, "Maybe, but I sure couldn't wear one in a toe shoe."

Later, I realized that in fact my hip had been measured to perfection and I was now, for the first time in many years, entirely symmetrical. The sensation was because I had compensated for my bad hip for so long that my spine had shifted over several inches, and true symmetry felt wrong. My new hip was to shift many things in my life besides my spine.

When Dr. Wilson came to check on me, I was in bed with my leg in a sling. I smiled at him when he asked how I felt and said enthusiastically, "I feel as if I could dance." He looked at me skeptically and said nothing. A few days later my blood count was still not in the "normal" range and I hadn't had an appetite for a week. A battle ensued when a transfusion was suggested. When I took my daily walks I was referred to as "the ghost in the hall," and I must have looked as if I needed a good dose of blood. Mother and I fended off the attendants each time they came into the room with someone else's blood, until Dr. Wilson was called in. I argued that I had always been pale, it was normal for me, I was not feeling as frail as I looked, and finally he capitulated and let me recover of my own accord, provided I promised to eat.

I received many cards, flowers, and phone calls in the hospital, but one call moved me more than any other. "Hello, Sue," I heard a man's voice say, and at once I knew. My father had always called me

Sue. Even now, after almost thirty years of near silence, his voice was familiar; it rang in my ears as if some long hibernating part of me had awakened.

For many years after leaving Cincinnati, we had no contact with him, but later, when my sisters had children of their own, they made an effort to find him. It wasn't hard; he still worked for the Kluener Packing Company, and he lived just across the river from Cincinnati in Kentucky. He had never remarried, and now, so many years later, he was happy to be a grandfather.

Mother was ambivalent about the renewed acquaintance with my father, but as they never visited their grandchildren simultaneously, outright conflict was avoided. During the 1970s I had had some sporadic contact with him via Donna and Beverly, but it was always tense, brief, and emotionally difficult, reminiscent of the visiting days when we were children. One year I received a birthday card from him, but the following year I didn't.

It was Mother who had called him upon learning that I was to have a hip operation. It was, no doubt, a very difficult call for her to make, and I am truly grateful to her. The situation was serious, and she wanted advice—my father had had not one but two hips replaced, one of them twice. This revelation put my own hip problem into a whole new perspective when I realized that I had inherited not only my father's height but his problematic hips!

Now I heard my father's voice on the telephone telling me everything would be fine, just follow the doctor's orders. Then he said, "I love you, Sue."

I had always thought that one could have everything in life, just not all at the same time, and now this was proving true. The fact that it took something as severe as major surgery for me to "find" my father was perhaps sad, but I felt no bitterness. I knew how hard it must have been for him to call me after lost decades, and I appreciated his effort. I had no interest in digging up the past or wasting energy on wishing my father could have been a father to me when I was a child and needed one. The saddest thing was that Dad had missed my whole career. It was too late now, but ultimately it didn't really matter.

As time went on, however, I discovered to my great surprise that my father had in fact been following my life—from a distance. He sent me a giant box of newspaper and magazine clippings that he had been collecting for the past twenty years, clippings I had not even seen. I went through the box in a flood of tears, realizing how much he must have loved me, while being literally incapable of actually talking to me or seeing me.

Now he was no longer a young man, and I was no longer a little girl, and we simply picked up where we were. He was reaching out, and I accepted it. We never talked about the past. I never even joked with him about his fight, more than thirty years ago, with Mother, over his girls' artistic talents. We were both vulnerable now, and that proved to be our meeting ground.

After nine days in the hospital I was well enough to convalesce at home and was loaded into an ambulance to take me to Mother's. (My apartment was a fifth-floor walkup, which made it off-limits.) Over the next few months she would care for me with all the love of a mother and all the knowledge of a nurse. Aside from very careful daily walks with crutches, I was basically bedridden for eight weeks, the time it took for my bone to grow into my new hip. I played endless games of cards, read, watched television, wrote thank-you notes, and tried to be a good patient. I thought only good thoughts. I wanted to give my hip the benefit of every doubt. Dr. Wilson, knowing I was young and a dancer, had taken special care with my incision, and the result is a truly beautiful, ruler-straight scar of which I am very proud.

On March 31 I made my first venture into the outside world despite the winter weather. I had been notified that I was to receive a Lion's Award from the New York Public Library, and I wanted to be there for the presentation. I had been indoors for four weeks, and I was facing a performance involving great preparation. It took me an hour just to put on clothes and another to hike myself down in the elevator. Paul came to town to escort me and hired a car for the occasion. It was the first time in a great while I had worn earrings, and the first big step to recovery.

Within a few weeks the doctor said I could go home to my own apartment, and I learned to negotiate the stairs, with both crutches and curious cats underfoot, with great dexterity. I began going each morning at seven o'clock to physical therapy at Eastside Sports Medicine where Marika Molnar, the company's physical therapist, worked. With the help of Marika's expert eye and indefatigable encouragement, I slowly began exercising to regain all the muscular control I had lost. I was like a baby learning to walk, retraining all my motor functions, and the process was frustrating and arduous but ultimately amazing. By the time I was standing and walking alone I felt reborn with a new body and could see light at the end of the tunnel. In my mind I was running toward it, and, miraculously, there was no pain.

Meanwhile a conflict which could not be resolved had arisen between Paul and the board of directors of the Chicago City Ballet, and he moved back to New York. It was a change in our lifestyles—with the exception of summers on Cedar Islands, we had been apart on and off now for almost ten years—but by June he had gone to Texas. The Fort Worth Ballet was undergoing management problems, and he was invited by Anne Bass, one of its most generous supporters, to help out in a precarious situation. The company was small and disorganized, but he saw great possibilities, and within a few months he was installed as the artistic director.

In early May, since both of us were without other commitments, Paul and I went up to Cedar Islands to enjoy the outdoors. By this time I was feeling very good and slightly bold, and again dancing entered my mind. My muscles were starting to twitch, and although I had been cautioned against any overt movements, Dr. Wilson had said I could do "little" things. One morning I got up early, climbed into my leotard and tights, and went up to the studio. The sun was just beginning to rise as I squeezed my feet into a pair of toe shoes, the first I had worn in seven months. Suddenly, everything felt right with the world; I had always thought best with those tight little satin shoes on my feet. I put my hand on the barre and executed a very pathetic little plié followed by a very pathetic little tendu. I had begun.

Day by day I plugged away, and very slowly my muscles fell into their familiar patterns and the plié and tendu became a little bigger. When the girls arrived in June for summer camp, I took a deep breath and joined them in class. It was very humbling. I could do less than they; when their legs were around their ears, mine were only a few inches off the floor. But I wasn't proud, and I knew that my progress was relative only to me, and by that standard I was improving. I let my body dictate how far I could go each day, and slowly, very slowly it responded. Paul believed in me and knew, as I did, that I would be miserable if I didn't at least try. I was, however, still a long way from being able to dance on a stage, and I still listed to the left.

My father came to the islands that summer to visit for a few weeks, and we had a lovely time getting to know each other. He liked to fish, and I would sometimes look out of the window and see him showing the students how to bait a line and throw it out. On another occasion I overheard him lecturing the girls before I taught them afternoon class, "Now you girls listen to Miss Farrell; she knows what she's talking about." In the space of just a few months he had become . . . well, a father, and when I heard him say this I thought, "Now, Sue, you know anything is possible." And I persisted in trying to dance.

Over the years Mother and I had also spent many happy times on

Cedar Islands, and, while my parents never visited together, I considered myself lucky to have this measure of peaceful resolve. Now when the tourist boat sailed by in the late afternoon pointing out "the home of ballerina Suzanne Farrell," I would sometimes see a small smile of pride on Mother's face. She, after all, was the first one who had helped me believe I could be a ballerina.

In late June I was to receive a Golden Plate Award from the Academy of Achievement, and Paul and I traveled to Scottsdale, Arizona, for the ceremony. I had rarely been free to attend such functions before because I was always dancing, and now this honor came at a crucial time in my life. I was determined to walk up to the podium alone, straight as an arrow in high heels. Once there, I gave a speech to the audience of young students about my profession, the freedom bequeathed by discipline, and how my operation had affected my life. I started to cry; it was the first time I had publicly talked about what happened to me. It was a great catharsis to have said it aloud, and another step had been taken.

Some time later my new hip got me through another ceremony, but this time more steps were required, though there were no tears and no speeches. Along with nine other recipients, including Paul Newman (fresh from his Indianapolis 500 race) and the president of Princeton University, I was awarded an honorary Doctorate of Fine Arts from Yale University. The grandeur—and paradox—of my position, as I promenaded through the enormous crowd of parents, graduates, and guests, was not lost on me: this was the graduation I never had. Dressed in a heavy black gown and a mortarboard with tassel, I was a ballerina, a high school dropout—and now, with the flip of a tassel, Dr. Farrell. I had not earned my degree conventionally, by any means, but I had been practicing a perfectly fine art all my life.

By September I was back in New York. After four months of work I had regained a great deal of facility. The company was beginning rehearsals, and I made up my mind to go to company class. Extremely nervous and knowing that despite everyone's good will I would be stared at, I resumed my usual place at the barre behind the piano. Within a few days my presence became normal to both me and the company, and another hurdle had been crossed. Within a few more days, everyone's greatest fear, that I might fall, came to pass.

Peter was teaching, and since I was feeling good that day, I decided to try more than the usual double pirouette. I slipped and was down with a crash. The whole room froze in horror. I sat motionless for a minute before standing. I was not hurt, and I remembered Dr. Wilson's comment when I asked him what might happen if I fell. I knew it was going to happen at some point, and I had told him I was taking class. He was greatly impressed with my progress and said, "Don't worry, you're not made of eggshells." Now I felt great relief not only that I was intact but that the inevitable had happened. To everyone's concerned questions I simply said, "I'm fine . . . I'm fine, however, I think I've had enough for today," and contentedly left the studio.

La Sonnambula, Balanchine's evocative ballet about a poet, a sleepwalker, her husband, and his mistress, was being revived for the fall season of 1987, and I wanted to dance the Sleepwalker. Having done it many times, I knew exactly what the part involved and went over it in the studio privately. I did not foresee any hazards. Peter did, and panicked.

I think he felt an enormous responsibility. Not knowing the workings of a plastic hip, he did all he could to discourage me. I repeatedly requested rehearsals, which were never scheduled. Finally Peter and I had a meeting. He had discussed the prospect with both Jerry Robbins and Dr. Hamilton, and they decided to send Dr. Wilson a videotape of the ballet. Peter, Dr. Hamilton, and I went to see him in his office. He and I disappeared so he could reevaluate my hip, and he told me he had seen the tape and didn't notice any apparent pitfalls. He left me in the examination room to get dressed while he went to confer with Peter and Dr. Hamilton.

When I returned to the round table I could see I was up against a wall; I couldn't fight three men. Suddenly, Dr. Wilson was talking to me about the additional rigors of class, rehearsal, and performance, and I knew he had been briefed. I was furious. I felt my own body, not to mention my career, was out of my control, and I wanted to dance in order to regain them. I wanted my retirement to be my decision and my choice, and I didn't want it to end with a physical infirmity. I wanted it to end with a dance.

I had lost this specific battle, but Peter was amenable to my dancing something else. I think his greatest trepidation was for me to dance on pointe, even though I had been up there all my life and it was—and still is—as natural to me as brushing my teeth. *Vienna Waltzes* was not on pointe, and it was agreed that this was the ballet in which I would appear . . . or reappear.

Vienna Waltzes, Mr. B's ode to the romance of the waltz, remained as popular and glittering an event at the New York State Theater as it had been at its unveiling ten years earlier. It was scheduled for five performances in January and February. I thought only of the first one. If I could survive that, the others would follow.

Because I danced the *Rosenkavalier* waltz in satin shoes and a very long, very heavy satin dress, I knew I would need some rehearsals to adjust my new hip to the pulls, sways, and tensions of the role. Already readjusted to pointe shoes, I found yet another enormous transition in lowering my body into low-heeled shoes, and then down farther to kneel and pick up the train of my gown. It felt more difficult than any pirouette combination on pointe. I remember one especially taxing walk home after a rehearsal. I felt like a wanderer in the desert dragging my body to a far-off oasis, and I thought to myself, "Oh dear God, I can't even do this." Exasperated, I realized that my body was not reacting as quickly or as precisely as before, that there was nothing there to make it happen except my desire. But desire can go a long way, and within a few days my body was responding to my determination. I felt that I was being reborn.

I ran into Peter in the hallway one evening just after I had had a rehearsal onstage alone, and he mentioned that he had been watching me on the television monitor in his fourth-floor office. After I recovered from the shock of learning that Peter resorted to such Big Brother tactics, he made an observation that impressed me enormously: "You move more easily backward than forward, don't you?" I did indeed, and I could get away with a multitude of sins moving backward with only Peter and me knowing why!

Several weeks before D day, I awoke on Christmas morning feeling paralyzed. I couldn't get out of bed, I couldn't breathe normally, my entire body ached, and all my joints were inflamed. Because of the holidays, all my doctors were unavailable. Paul finally carried me into a taxi and took me to the emergency room at New York Hospital. Doctors there were able to diagnose only a high fever, and they instructed me to take aspirin and stay in bed. It was truly frightening and mysterious, and the symptoms kept me in bed for almost four weeks. By the time I could walk around the house again, my other hip, my good hip, was aching. I was in despair, thinking, "I've survived Mr. B's death, I've survived a hip operation, and now my comeback is going to be canceled because of some bizarre virus."

Five days before the performance I gingerly walked over to the theater to take my first barre in four weeks. Not wanting anyone to know about my illness, I explained my absence by saying I'd had the flu. My trek back to the stage was proving to be a test of desire beyond anything I had ever known. Every possible obstacle seemed to be planted in my way, but one by one, I stepped around them until January 27 arrived.

Shortly after my operation "The MacNeil/Lehrer News Hour" had contacted me about doing a story on my operation and recovery. They considered a ballerina's undergoing such surgical invasion a newsworthy occasion and because I was impressed with the show's dignified approach I agreed to be filmed in all the various stages of my recovery. I had only one stipulation, to which they courteously agreed. If I didn't dance again, if I didn't get onstage on January 27, the segment would not be shown. I was adamant that my experience should not be viewed as a memorial service to a career or the martyrdom of a ballerina to her art. As a result the MacNeil/Lehrer cameras were now poised in the audience and backstage, awaiting the end of the story. They were not alone; I was waiting with them.

Physically I trusted my body to rally, but I had very little idea about how I would withstand the evening emotionally. Paul, Mother, my sisters, and their families were sitting anxiously in the audience along with thousands of others. No one knew what a cementless hip could do because it hadn't been tested before in this way—but I had a history of being an experimenter. Along with the fascination surrounding my proposed appearance, there was also an enormous amount of love. Alone as I was, I could feel the company and the audience were with me, wishing me well.

I arrived at the theater three hours before the performance and prepared as I had on hundreds of nights before. I hadn't danced for almost two years and I felt an overwhelming nervousness, but the prospect of being out there was so powerful that it pulled me forward until I was crowned and gowned and standing in the front wing awaiting my cue. I crossed myself and was suddenly calm as the music washed over me. I felt a little push from behind. No one was there; it was the familiar touch from George. I walked out into the mirrored ballroom to greet my phantom partner.

There was, I've been told, a burst of applause when I appeared, my back to the audience. But I did not hear it. Suddenly, I was kneeling, bowing, dancing, and waltzing as the music enveloped me. Adam's tender ministrations completed the sensation. I had never felt finer. My belief in miracles had received its ultimate affirmation. All the emotional fear and turmoil, all the physical struggle, all the risk were washed away in a moment. It was the only moment there was. MacNeil/Lehrer had an end to their story, and I had finished what I started—not only what I started by receiving a new body part a year earlier, but what I had started on the stage of the Cincinnati Music Hall thirty years before that.

CHAPTER NINETEEN

Beginning

❧

I 'm not dead," George said, looking up at me from his horizontal position, "I'm just laying low for a while." I was glad that, at least when he appeared in this dream, his sense of humor remained unchanged five years after he was buried. I had cause to think of his words more than once during the months that followed.

In 1986 Balanchine's alma mater, the famous Kirov (previously Maryinsky) Ballet, appeared in the United States for the first time in twenty-four years. At the time the company's enterprising director, Oleg Vinogradov, somewhat surprisingly approached Barbara Horgan about allowing the Kirov to dance some Balanchine ballets. She was interested, but it took two and a half years for arrangements to be worked out. One of her most important stipulations was that the two ballets chosen, *Scotch Symphony* and *Theme and Variations*, be taught, cast, rehearsed, and overseen by ballet masters or mistresses trained by Balanchine himself.

In the fall of 1988, Barbara asked me if I would go to Leningrad to stage *Scotch Symphony*. It was not the first time she had suggested that I stage a Balanchine ballet, but it was the first time I seriously considered the prospect. Until now dancing had been my priority and I always envisioned myself on that side of the footlights.

I had, however, done considerable teaching at the School of American Ballet at George's suggestion, both in the 1960s and later, after I returned from Europe. At first I had found this request rather strange, given how much I myself still needed to learn, but I now think that was one of George's intentions—I could learn by teaching, while the students were learning from my example. I had also frequently auditioned students around the country for the School's scholarship program, and as recently as 1987 I had overseen a production of *Agon* for Paul's company in Fort Worth.

By late 1988 I had a wonderful new hip, had performed again, and was ready to move on with my life. I immediately agreed to go to Russia. Since his death Balanchine's ballets had survived in performance—as they will continue to—but the survival of his philosophy was threatened without his actual presence there to enforce it. The prospect of teaching one of his ballets to dancers trained at the same school that had trained him almost seventy years before was irresistible.

I prepared for my job by learning *Scotch Symphony* as I had never learned a ballet before. Having danced the principal role many times, I was thoroughly familiar with it, but now I also had to learn every step of everyone else, all nineteen of them. With the help of a videotape, I wrote down the entire ballet, using the names of steps and stick-figure diagrams, in conjunction with the musical score. Although I don't read music, I knew enough to identify the phrases and climaxes. Without even putting on a pointe shoe, I felt a renewed fascination with Mr. B's three-dimensional mind as I saw how he combined the music, the corps, the soloist, and the principal couple into a single interwoven work. I smiled to myself at the simplicity, logic, and beauty of his machinations.

On December 18, armed with my sixty scribbled pages, the videotape, six cans of tunafish, boots, sweaters, and three pairs of toe shoes, I boarded the Finnair plane for Leningrad. I was ready for battle. I did not expect rebellion, but I was hoping for revolution (or revelation), and I knew strategy was everything. I had precisely ten days to teach the whole ballet to dancers I had never seen.

I arrived in Leningrad at four-thirty in the afternoon; there was fresh snow on the ground, and a few dim streetlights enabled me to make out the magnificent turquoise, blue, red, gold, green, and yellow buildings erected by Peter the Great. In contrast, my "deluxe" hotel room had a small, rickety refrigerator, a television set, and a lamp—but only one electrical socket. I chose the lamp; its amber shade managed to reflect only deep shadows on the small room's sparse furniture. The bed was the width of a folding camp cot, the heat was inadequate, and the red phone rang all night. (In all fairness, the hotel was about to close for renovations.) The yellow bathwater reeked of sulfur, but it was hot and the tub was deep and I was adaptable. For the next ten days I lived on tins of tuna and cans of Heineken beer—not a bad twist on the ballerina diet and more effective than most. I had not come to Russia for a vacation; I had come to work.

My first day in the theater was chaotic, and I thought of Barbara's warning: "Remember, George always said, 'There is no word in the Russian language for organization.'" The confusion began at ten-thirty, when I was not picked up as planned from my hotel. After waiting forty-five minutes, I found a very dilapidated taxi, and after a scenic tour of Leningrad arrived at the beautiful sea-green Kirov Theater, the historic site that saw the birth of so many ballets—*The Sleeping Beauty, Les Sylphides, The Nutcracker*—and the stage that launched the careers of Anna Pavlova, Tamara Karsavina, Vaslav Nijinsky, Rudolf Nureyev, Natalia Makarova, Mikhail Baryshnikov— and Georgi Balanchivadze.

Entering through one of the numerous stage doors, I found it hard to understand how all those illustrious dancers had even managed to find the stage which utterly eluded me. After painstaking verbal exchanges in our respective languages, I convinced the little old *babushka* who guarded the doorway that I was indeed the "Amerikanskaya" ballet mistress and should be allowed entry. I showed her my pointe shoes and demanded, "Take me to where I can use these." Once past this inspection point, it took me another twenty minutes to find an opera singer who guided me to the ballet offices on the third floor. Although I had already missed most of the class, from which I had hoped to do some preliminary casting, I was taken to the studio to observe the last fifteen minutes.

It was unbelievable. While my heart sank at finding so few dancers, many of whom didn't even look like dancers, I couldn't help being amused watching the male dancers taking turns executing the finales to one variation or another, each at his own prescribed tempo, complete with dramatic backbends and passionate chest-beating. The teacher stood quietly to one side, obviously used to this display of pyrotechnics.

I was informed that there would be a forty-minute rehearsal (from one-fifteen to one fifty-five) for the corps, followed by an hour and a half with the soloists. I was beginning to understand just how different a world I was entering, and I thought that if part of me was Russian, it certainly wasn't my work habits.

At precisely one-fifteen an array of dancers came into the studio accompanied by a woman dressed in a pink jogging outfit. She started calling out names from a typewritten sheet, and I realized that she was the ballet mistress and that I was not to have the choice I was supposed to have. The girls all had the same physique, small and thin with a pronounced muscularity that indicated their very different training. They also had the wonderfully expressive faces, high cheekbones, and soulful eyes associated with Russian dancers.

Because of the steeply raked studios and stages, they tended to settle their weight on their heels as a counterbalance. One of Balanchine's greatest innovations was to push the weight forward onto, and over, the balls of the feet—"like a pussycat"—enabling dancers to move with much greater speed and agility. This profound shift of the body's placement was to be one of the many challenges the Russian dancers were to encounter.

While I was making some rapid assessments, the dancers looked me up and down until I felt as if *I* were being auditioned. In a very real sense I was. They didn't know anything about me except that I was here from America to teach them a ballet by a man called Balanchine.

All they knew of him was that he was Georgian and had left Russia and founded a ballet company in America and, as one girl explained, "made several ballets." They had been young children in 1972 when he last brought his company to Russia. With the exception of a few pirated videotapes, none of them had seen any of his ballets. This was therefore an audition for Balanchine as well, and the crusader in me emerged full force. Here was a chance for dancers to meet him on their mutual turf of stage, steps, and music, without reputations intervening. For them, he had no reputation—but within ten days he did.

Meanwhile I started teaching the ballet. With no interpreter present, our only means of communication was through steps, and I started throwing sequences at them along with musical cues. I quickly realized that it was easier for me to adapt to their mysterious protocols than vice-versa, and as the ballet progressed, so did our rapport.

The ballet mistress, Gabriella, was a potential ally because she would be rehearsing some of the dancers after I left and before I returned in February for the première. A former ballerina with the Kirov, she had only recently retired, and after rehearsal she showed me several photographs of herself dancing in the adagio of *Symphony in C* in a skewed version that had been staged years ago in Moscow.

Later, a rehearsal came to a grinding halt when a British ballet book appeared, and I realized just how important and rare any information about Western dance was in Russia. Everyone gathered around to identify dancers they knew—but they knew them only from previous photos, not live performance. A photograph of myself in this book became my identification and credentials.

I had decided that I would not insist on casting the corps de ballet if I could choose the soloists. As it turned out, it was more a case of their choosing me. At the afternoon rehearsal, when I indicated to Gabriella that I was interested in one very young, very eager-looking girl, I was informed that I couldn't use her. Speaking fragmented French, I pretended that I didn't understand, and Gabriella pretended she didn't understand me. The language barrier was proving useful to both of us.

Frustrated, I left the studio to go upstairs to the offices to find some support. There was none to be found, so I decided not to fight the system but to work within it. When I went back to the studio, Gabriella remained insistent, but eventually did allow me to use the young girl, Larisa Lezhniná, for the solo girl. With only two boys in the room, I took the more promising-looking of the two, Yuri Zhukov; I had seen neither of them dance. I also chose another girl, Elena Pankova, as the ballerina. She was twenty-five and looked slim, fresh, feminine, and, best of all, interested. In the days that followed Elena and Yuri proved to be the only couple who consistently showed up for rehearsals, and I took their enthusiasm as *their* credentials. From my own experience, I knew that desire was the primary prerequisite for dancing Balanchine, especially here, where it would truly involve a leap of faith.

To my dismay, Elena, like all the girls, seemed to like learning the ballet on half-pointe, which, for whatever reason—saving their toes or their shoes—was to me a lost opportunity. It meant that a whole new level was added to the already complex job of learning, and later the entire ballet would have to be transposed onto pointe because it wasn't there to begin with. However, this was the way they did it in Russia, and it became one of many differences I noticed but decided not to challenge. I wanted to save my influence for the moments when it was essential. Acquiring mutual respect would be the key that might open all the other doors to Balanchine's world. Balletic *glasnost* was not going to happen in one day, much less one rehearsal, and meanwhile we were all learning.

Back at my hotel I spoke with Barbara on the phone and told her simply, "It was a disaster." The next day in the second rehearsal for the corps I told them the same. I had by now acquired an interpreter, Natasha, although she proved to have such extensive opinions of her own that I was never quite sure how my words were being edited. "Yesterday was not a good day for us," I said, "but today will be better." And it was. Much better. I said, "I trust you," and from then on there was a kind of *simpatico* that carried all of us forward into the land of *Scotch Symphony*.

Once there, the inevitable question arose: "What is the story? Who are we supposed to be?" Wary of any facile and misleading associations with Bournonville's *La Sylphide*, I explained only that Mr. B had been to Scotland and, impressed by its customs and kilts, had made a plotless ballet to Mendelssohn's "Scotch" symphony. The only similarity to the Bournonville was the setting. It was Balanchine's homage to Scotland in the form of a classic ballet. Its flavors, moods, dramas, and emotions are not prescribed; all are musical and flexible.

Elena and Yuri began to grasp the revolutionary and subtle concept that, even in an apparently very classical pas de deux, the woman can lead and the man can follow her lead. I told Elena that the girl in *Scotch* should be more expansive than a sylph, like a tiny flame that burns strong and clear, guiding the man from no matter how far away. She should be gentle yet strong, giving of herself, not keeping to herself. She is human but delicate, mortal, and yet, unlike the sylph, she doesn't die. There is not one drama but many choices for drama.

I suggested that Yuri not grab her hand in the usual partnering vise during the supported adagio but rather gently hold her wrist with only the tips of his fingers. It provides more than the necessary support, and a gesture of quiet grace replaces a smothering grip. It offers more freedom to both dancers and is Balanchine at his most feminist. It was one of the many small details that were important to him.

I had learned from Balanchine that suggestion has a far greater effect than demand, and as the days proceeded I suggested more details. Russian training emphasizes the climaxes, the big jumps, the multiple turns, and the grand finales, while the transition steps are treated as such and given little thought or value. But for Balanchine dancing did not reside in the pose but within the transitions themselves; the act of getting from one step to another, and one place to another, *is* the dancing.

On the second evening I was given a ticket to see the company's production of Petipa's *Don Quixote*. It was the first time I had sat in the audience of the beautiful gold-and-blue-velvet theater. I was in the Czar's box, an ornate little stage of its own, directly facing the larger stage. The performance brought back memories as I saw how Mr. B had used some of the effects—the windmill, the dummy Don Quixote, the horse and donkey, the oriental girl—in "our" *Don Quixote*.

I had been in Leningrad nine days before I met Oleg Vinogradov, the man whose persistence had made this whole project possible. He had been in Moscow on business, and by the time he arrived home, I had finished teaching the entire ballet. He came to watch an evening rehearsal. I had been informed by my interpreter that there had recently been a newspaper article that used the prospective Balanchine evening to oppose Vinogradov's methods and his desire to import ballets from the West. *Glasnost* had made things more possible for Russian ballet, but the road was still obstructed by prejudice and bureaucracy.

After introducing himself, he leaned back on the barre to watch *Scotch Symphony*. It was, aside from a version on videotape, the first time he had seen the ballet; it was his love of Scotland that had made him choose it. I used the opportunity to suggest to all the dancers that they rehearse on pointe; they knew the steps, now it was time to elaborate on them. It was the first complete run-through of the ballet, and as it proceeded I observed some new Soviet conventions.

The principals marked their parts rather than dancing them, and when I asked if they were feeling all right, they replied yes, and I realized that they weren't comfortable dancing anything less than a completely polished performance in front of their peers. Russian dancers are very proud, and I respected their position, although it seemed a sad waste of an opportunity. They preferred to work privately until every moment of the ballet was scientifically mastered. I, however, had no desire to see something finished, but rather something evolving. Dancing is a process, not a product.

I had grown accustomed to having the corps change faces and places each day of their own accord. They seemed to have some code of transmitting steps and positions between them, and there were never any vacancies. I told them that they all were important. So often in the old classical ballets the corps de ballet barely dances but acts largely as scenery for the central action, and I wanted them to know that this was not true for Balanchine. Every role, however big or small, long or short, is of vital importance, with each complementing, echoing, and enhancing the other. The corps was never an afterthought with Balanchine, and these dancers had already discovered that their parts in *Scotch* required as much actual movement, stamina, and technical prowess as the solo roles. Every now and then I saw a smile creep across a face as the dancing itself took precedence over other emotions.

Watching the rehearsal with Vinogradov, I noticed the dancers' strange tendency to avoid the center of the studio, which made the ballet look lopsided. Then I saw why: there was no mirror in the center of the studio, so no one ventured into that space of apparent oblivion. Devotion to one's mirror image is a habit that has crossed all political borders and is rampant on all continents. This reflection is not, however, a matter of vanity for a dancer; it is a useful tool for improvement.

When Vinogradov heard me giving directions and corrections, he said to me in a very matter-of-fact tone, "Just tell them what you want, and they will do it." His comment suggested a wonderful discipline, but it seemed to deny the possibility of difficulties and discoveries, as if the dancers were programmed to respond to any voice of authority. I didn't want to get results through oppression or fear; that would have nothing to do with Balanchine.

Dancing Balanchine gave the dancers a chance to rise above mere obedience. This could happen for them only if they found a reason to do it, and all the reasons were in the steps. By the same token, I was opposed to their watching or learning any of the ballet from a videotape. With their repertoire of old classics, these dancers had been surviving on imitation and reproduction for too long.

Knowing what a battle Vinogradov had waged to bring Balanchine to his country, I told him after rehearsal that I didn't care if we were booed off the stage when the ballet was performed in February. In the final analysis what mattered was that it happened at all; it was a beginning. I could see from his pale, tired face that this was something he knew all too well.

Early one morning I was taken to the Vaganova Academy, the official school of the Kirov, where Balanchine had trained as a little boy. The school was begun under the patronage of Empress Anna Ivanovna in 1738 and had just celebrated its 250th anniversary. It has the most impressive alumni list of any dance institution in the world, but that tradition can be a heavy weight for a young dancer to drag around.

I could imagine how a young man of George's vision and vitality would have felt artistically violated. True dance, music, and the energies they produce exist only in the moment in which they are spent. That was why Balanchine was determined to choreograph so far ahead of his time. He was not against many of the teachings of the past. He greatly admired Petipa and some of his old teachers. But he took what he liked from them and carried it forward. Here dance was frozen. Even the so-called new ballets that I saw on television looked old-fashioned. George would never have survived here.

Irina Kolpakova, a product of the school and, until her recent retirement, the company's beloved prima ballerina, now coaches the younger dancers, and she took a special interest in Balanchine. She came to all my rehearsals, dressed in her slim black pants, glittering sweaters, and lacy white bobby socks covered with red strawberries. I was impressed that this great ballerina, who exemplified the tradition of the Kirov, was so eager to learn still more about her craft, even though she would never dance Balanchine herself. She was more than curious, she was angry that it had taken so many years for this to happen. Although they had been shielded from Western ballet for decades, enough had seeped through for these dancers to know that their profession had progressed without them, and now there were only a few days in which to catch up.

Kolpakova invited me to watch her rehearse a young dancer as Princess Aurora in *The Sleeping Beauty*. After I had watched the variation, which was highly polished but very labored in tempo, she asked me what I thought, and I replied noncommittally, "It's very lovely." She peered at me closely and said, "Yes, yes, but what do you think?" She was a sly one—like George.

We proceeded to discuss a basic difference between Balanchine and the Russian school that we had both observed. The Russian training split the body horizontally at the waist, meaning the upper body worked separately from the legs. The expression and emotion was conveyed on top, where the heart resides, while the technical steps were executed below, a separate event. Balanchine had extended what the legs could do and might do by envisioning the body vertically. He would often close one eye and optically split the body down the center, leaving each half with all the necessary components—head, arm, body, leg, and foot. To him, the lower body was as capable of expression as the upper. It was a profoundly revolutionary image.

The Kirov's extensive coaching system, whereby former dancers take on younger dancers and become their personal teachers, often threatened to confuse rehearsals more than ever when three opinions, instead of one, were being voiced simultaneously. Balanchine had a very strict policy toward private coaching and never allowed it at the New York City Ballet. The kind of dependence generated by such day-to-day one-on-one interaction interfered with personal experimentation and freedom. He taught class for everyone and believed in self-discovery—he could only offer, he could not force. I had not realized until now just how much latitude and responsibility he offered.

During one rehearsal Yuri and Elena conversed together for a few moments after I had told them to run from one corner to another. Yuri, as spokesman, asked if they could change this run, perhaps put in some actual ballet steps. I said, "Running *is* the step." Because so much of the Kirov's repertoire is very old, they are in the habit of changing small things to accommodate themselves, but this was something I did not feel was appropriate for Balanchine. Every step and movement was made on purpose and therefore has a specific reason. It was curious that they requested changing such an "easy" step as running, but to them it wasn't a step, and they felt uncomfortable with the various possibilities.

"But it's so pretty," I said. "It conveys the thrust of what is happening. You can't go somewhere and not go there at the same time. Just try it, and we'll see . . . we have time." They thought about what I said and tried it again . . . and again, and it was beautiful. I could see that they had felt freedom and were ready to run—and run fast. With so much discipline no one was more ready for a little freedom and yet had so little idea what to do with it. Their "run" was not just a beautiful visual image; to me it became a poignant metaphor for the whole endeavor, as if Yuri and Elena were daring to push open the closed doors of the last seventy years and were running through to Balanchine. They never asked to change another thing. It was a victory for them, for me, for Balanchine.

This was only the first of many movements that became emotional experiences in and of themselves. These two dancers were hungry and ready to feast; the more they tasted, the more they wanted. Elena was learning rapidly, absorbing like a sponge, and asking questions. "What should I feel?" she asked one day. "It doesn't matter what you feel, it matters what you do and what it looks like," I answered. She looked relieved. Her feelings were her own business, and she seemed to like that.

"Just listen to the music—it will dance for you," I suggested and gave her a tape recording. During the following week I kept hearing the distant sounds of *Scotch Symphony* echoing through the cavernous halls of the Kirov backstage. They were emanating from Elena's dance bag.

On another occasion, following a pirouette sequence, I told her she could hold her arms any way she wanted. Her eyes opened wide, and she asked the interpreter, "What did she say?" "Yes, you can do whatever you like," I repeated, and she smiled as if I were joking. I wasn't, and later she stopped me in the hall, raised her arms up in a triumphant halo about her head, and said, "Can I do this?" I nodded, and she looked gloriously happy and continued down the hallway, arms in a halo.

We worked right through December 25, as there is no Christmas in the Soviet Union. But I spent Christmas Eve at the American Consulate where a cassette of Christmas carols and a buffet table of food that looked and tasted familiar were somber reminders of home. I had gone to Russia thinking how lovely it would be to spend Christmas there with George—but he was not to be found. He was definitely back in America.

By the time I was ready to leave on December 30, not only had the whole ballet been taught, it had started to take on shapes and nuances beyond just the steps. Despite the language barrier, it was amazing how close I had become to the Russian dancers. Although I felt the desperate need for a warm bed and a good meal, I was sad to leave. In just ten days a new world had been opened up to all of us.

We exchanged New Year gifts. I gave bottles of French champagne, a much desired item available only to foreigners with hard currency. Kolpakova gave me a book commemorating the Vaganova Academy's 250th anniversary, and the dancers gave me a little stuffed "Father Frost," who looks suspiciously like the forbidden Santa Claus, chocolates, and a Russian calendar of icon prints. A photographer took Polaroids of Elena, Yuri, and Larisa with myself, and as we parted in tears, we each clutched our blurry photos. One can never leave Russia knowing with certainty one will return. The flight is only ten hours, but the distance cannot be measured.

On the morning of my departure there was a knock at my hotel door. I opened it, and to my great surprise there stood the company's director. We, too, had become friends, and he had come to assure himself of my return. My suitcase had ripped, so he ran down to his car to fetch a length of rope and proceeded to tie it up in a most professional manner; it was obviously not the first suitcase he had repaired. The hotel porter came to take the luggage, but as I was about to follow him, Vinogradov stopped me. "Suzi, come back. Sit down," he said and beckoned toward the luggage rack. Obediently, I perched on the wooden slats. "Now," he said after a long, ritualistic pause, "I know you will come back."

The Leningrad première of "An Evening of Balanchine" consisted of *Scotch Symphony* and *Theme and Variations,* which was staged by Francia Russell, a director of the Pacific Northwest Ballet and a former dancer and ballet mistress with Balanchine's company. It was scheduled for February 18, and then, in typical Russian confusion, changed at the last minute to the twenty-first. But, as the dancers were fond of saying in English, "No problem."

When I returned on February 10 to oversee the final production, there were, however, problems. Despite all the promises the ballet did not look as if it had been rehearsed since I left six weeks earlier. Many faces were unfamiliar, and the whole thing was frantic and sloppy. Vinogradov apologized profusely, explaining that a severe flu epidemic had depleted the ranks, so he had had "everyone" learn the ballet. I appreciated the problem, but with the première only eleven days away I suggested it was time to establish one cast that could proceed with security. He nodded in agreement as yet another unfamiliar set of principal dancers came bounding out of the wings. Doubts about the potential success of the project floated through my mind.

As before, I began the second day by saying, "Yesterday was not a good day, today will be better." Again I said, "I trust you." I could see that everyone was tired from performing each night, and I didn't want to alienate them by being a wicked ballet mistress. Eventually a single cast—more or less—was established, and the ballet came together rather quickly.

I was somewhat disconcerted when Elena and then Larisa both came up holding three fingers across their stomachs to announce that their monthly three-day vacation was due. In America I had never encountered such a situation, and three days were a long time when time was short. When I learned that tampons don't exist in the Soviet Union, my worry turned to sympathetic horror. The deprivation this reveals—and the social consequences for women—are hard for a Westerner to comprehend.

During the week I began to notice that a small, quiet older man, who looked not unlike Stravinsky, was regularly attending the rehearsals for *Scotch*. It was Dzhemal Dalgat, the conductor for the Balanchine program. During one onstage orchestra rehearsal just before the première I became aware that Larisa's solo was being played more slowly than it should have been, and I asked him why. He shook his head sadly and confessed that Larisa had asked for it slower. When I said, "It's not Larisa's decision, it's Mendelssohn's," I thought he was going to burst into tears.

In Russia the dancer dictates the tempo he or she wants. In Balanchine's world, as I told Dalgat, the music is king; the dancers follow the conductor's baton. His face lit up, then darkened again. "Yes, but what will I do when you are gone?" I smiled and said, "Don't worry, I'm not gone yet."

On Valentine's Day the scenery for the two Balanchine ballets appeared. For *Theme* there was a truly gorgeous backdrop of the Maryinsky as it had been when Balanchine was a boy. Hung at the back of the present stage, it completed a circle of time, as if the theater, despite the huge bust of Lenin that dominated the lobby, was being redecorated with a semblance of freedom and joy for the return of Balanchine.

The set for *Scotch*, a dusky brown and green highland scene, was equally tasteful, although initially I had misgivings about the two sets of "ruins" on either side of the stage. I had previously suggested to Vinogradov that we didn't need a little hut à la *Giselle*, and these ivy-covered stairs to nowhere were the substitute. The stage was so deep, however, that the ruins blended nicely and did not interfere with the dancing.

Costumes also appeared, beautifully designed and crafted. Vinogradov's enthusiasm for Scotland went so far as to provide a different plaid on every pair of men's knee socks. The idea was touching, but the visual effect was jarring, and finally one plaid was chosen for all.

With orchestra, costumes, scenery, pointe shoes, and a consistent cast all in place, I decided to say very little in rehearsals and let the dancers go straight through the ballet and discover it for themselves. I had told them everything I knew, now my role was, in effect, over. My faith in them became their responsibility.

In the usual Russian tradition, there were two formal dress rehearsals for an audience before the actual première. Because tickets are so difficult for the ordinary citizen to obtain—many are reserved for dignitaries, politburo members, and tourists who pay in dollars with American Express cards—these extra performances were crowded with children, who are not permitted at evening performances, and Vinogradov's "friends." The rehearsals went well; the audiences were full and enthusiastic, and aside from fallen knee socks, the look of Balanchine was there.

The morning of the première I visited the Alexander Nevsky monastery across the street from my hotel. Though the temperature was relatively warm, a light covering of snow had fallen the night before and the graves of some of Russia's greatest artists were veiled in quiet splendor; here was the final resting place of Dostoyevsky, Glazunov, Rimsky-Korsakov, Moussorgsky, and Borodin, whose glorious tombstone was engraved with musical notes, inlaid with glittering gold. Ironically the cemetery, like the theater, felt strangely fresh and alive in a city of gray faces and emotions.

Slightly to one side, enclosed by a low iron fence, lay the most magnificent grave of all, Tschaikovsky's. His proud likeness carved in stone was protected by two angels, one sitting and reading with a look of great calm and sweetness, the other towering statuesquely behind him, holding a cross, its majestic wings rising defiantly upward over the city. I thought of George as a young man standing before this monument, perhaps anticipating that he and Tschaikovsky would travel a life together. The angel's soaring wings are to be found in many of Balanchine's ballets, most explicitly in his wrenching 1981 rendition of the "Adagio Lamentoso" from Tschaikovsky's *Pathétique Symphony*, music written by the composer as his own requiem.

Later that afternoon, I was rehearsing an alternate principal couple when Kolpakova came running into the studio waving a copy of the evening's program in the air, her eyes blazing. Apparently it contained an essay by a young Leningrad dance historian about the "meanings" of the two Balanchine ballets. *Scotch Symphony* was declared to be not only Balanchine's *Sylphide* but also a testament to her survival in the twentieth century. Poor George, he had been fleeing from her dusty wings all his life, but she was, and is, persistent.

Kolpakova suspected that this was wrong. She grabbed my hand and led me into Vinogradov's office to explain the problem. When I told him, as Balanchine had often said, "You don't ask a rose to explain itself," he made an angry phone call, tore the offending sheet in half, and announced, "There will be no programs tonight." This episode heralded a bizarre reversal of history. Here, in the theater where he was educated and then for most of his life ignored, Balanchine now had some of his most outspoken disciples. Kolpakova was a rebel in strawberry socks.

I went backstage to wish the dancers good luck, and we exchanged gifts; for Dalgat, a bottle of Scotch; for the dancers, champagne and peanut M&M's brought especially from America. To Larisa, Yuri, and Elena I gave flowers and little lapel pins, the Noguchi lyre from Balanchine's *Orpheus* which has become a symbol of the New York City Ballet. They didn't know its precise significance, but later I saw each of them wearing the pin proudly; its meaning needed no explanation. Indeed, never before had that lyre signified so much; as students at the Vaganova Academy they had worn a similar gold pin—only it was of Lenin.

I had asked Natasha to translate a note to them into Russian: "February 21, 1989. Thank you for coming with me on this very special dancing journey. It is fun to learn through work the joys of adventure, discovery and friendship. Mr. Balanchine will be happy. In strength and love, Suzanne."

Taking my seat in the Czar's box, I was calm. I was proud of them, and I knew they would do well. As the curtain rose, I held concealed in my palm a wooden cross that had belonged to George. Onstage Elena was wearing my own *Scotch Symphony* costume, which I had brought from America. The performance was beautiful—fast, exciting, and alive—but to my surprise I did not sit there wishing it was I who was dancing. My joy was for the dancers and the audience, who were responding with uncharacteristic spontaneity, and I knew that this event was not only historic on a grand scale but for me represented a new path.

As the curtain fell to resounding applause, I was ushered backstage and onstage for a bow. It was the first time I had ever been up there not in a costume and toe shoes but in my street clothes, as the enabler, not the enabled. As I tried to exit, Elena suddenly broke rank and rushed over to me in her Karinska tutu. She grasped my hand, lunged onto one knee, bowed her beautiful head, and thrust her huge bouquet of flowers into my arms. Tears blurred my vision as Yuri and Larisa followed suit.

Only moments before, Elena Pankova had established herself as a Russian Balanchine ballerina, a contradiction in terms. Who would have imagined that the circle would be joined so neatly on the stage of the Maryinsky Theater? Perhaps George.

Immediately following the performance, Vinogradov hosted a banquet for everyone involved. In typical Russian fashion, he tapped his knife on his vodka glass at periodic intervals and ordered various people to stand and make a speech. For the Americans it was nerve-racking, but for the poised Russian dancers it was normal. "Balanchine was a man of few words," I said when called upon, "and he was, as you know, very quick. I learned this from him and will also be quick. I feel that I am a better person for having come here and worked with you. Thank you." As I sat down, Vinogradov looked astonished and announced, "No one has given such a toast to us before."

Yuri's speech was also brief and to the point. He held up his shot glass, grinned, and dedicated his toast to "fast tempos." After initial resistance, he was now an enthusiastic convert—because he had felt Balanchine's energy in his own muscles. Elena stood with her soft, serious face and said that she had learned, "I can dance as I honestly wish." *Scotch Symphony*, she confessed, was now her favorite ballet.

Following the festivities, Elena and her husband insisted on driving me back to my hotel in their car. As a leading dancer, she was now in the position to possess such a luxury, but was terribly embarrassed when one of its doors jammed. She gave me an inscribed picture book of Leningrad, knowing that I had not had time to visit her beautiful city properly. She also gave me a stone copy of the "Primavera," saying that I reminded her of Botticelli's creation. George had said the same thing many years before.

She insisted that I sit in the front of the car, and I looked at her scrunched in the back seat, a scarf around her head, her overflowing dance bag on her lap, her face ineffably sad. "I'm not dying, you know," I said. "I'll be back." She squeezed out an unconvinced smile, and I saw she was clutching in her hand a photo of me.

The next morning my eyes were swollen, and not from too much champagne. As I waited in the hotel lobby for the taxi to take me to the airport, a handsome, sunny face appeared suddenly on the other side of the cavernous hall. It was Yuri. He had brought me a watercolor of the Neva and insisted on accompanying me to the airport. As we drove across a bridge, he ordered the car to stop in mid-traffic and pull over to one side. He told me I must throw a silver ruble into the Neva; it would guarantee my return. Presumably, like the luggage rack, this was another old Russian tradition.

At the airport, Yuri carried my bags through the various stages of customs, but when it was time to go through the final metal detector he was stopped. My last image of Russia was of his unhappy face as we waved goodbye through the narrow door.

There was one day in the studio when Elena stayed behind after rehearsal and we worked on pirouettes. Like most dancers, she had been trained to take off from a small fourth position with both legs bent. As I watched her take a wide fourth position, back leg straight, arm extended in front, I suddenly saw myself in class with Balanchine. It was 1964, and he was saying, "Wider, dear . . . wider . . . bigger . . . bigger . . . now turn."

As I watched Elena pirouette out of her proud, wide fourth position I saw for myself, for the first time, what Balanchine had, perhaps, seen in me. Having a small head, long neck, and long limbs was not enough. Being feminine and beautiful was not enough. Being technically masterful and musical was not enough. It was when I saw Elena dancing Balanchine for the first time—when I witnessed her willingness to take a chance—that finally I understood.

Entr'acte

∼⌒∼

R ussia provided the spiritual resolve I needed to move on with my life, but there was one last piece of unfinished business. I had had every experience a professional dancer could have except one. It was the hardest, and I didn't know how to do it. I had never retired before, and because I didn't know what lay beyond that last step—I feared oblivion—I thought I might just fade from public view. Then I realized that I could leave the stage only on the stage.

It was decided that my farewell would be on November 26, 1989. I was to perform two ballets, *Vienna Waltzes* and *Sophisticated Lady*. After my hip operation, Peter had choreographed two ballets on me— *Echo*, in which I danced on pointe again, and *Sophisticated Lady*. Taking its title from one of the Duke Ellington songs that comprised the ten-minute *pièce d'occasion*, this dance was a sweet, lighthearted, senti-mental journey for Peter and me.

Dressed in a glittering black gown and Van Cleef & Arpels jewels, I entered escorted by a diagonal of sixteen men in black tie. The lineup broke to reveal Peter, in an unprecedented return to the stage, also in black tie. Our last onstage tryst together was, appropriately, a jazzy dance to "Don't Get Around Much Anymore."

We were both uncharacteristically nervous. Peter even came to my dressing room at intermission and suggested we run up to the studio and rehearse one last time. Although we did, in performance we still made several mistakes—but only we knew it.

At the end of *Vienna Waltzes* I stood in my white satin gown on the center of the stage while Lincoln Kirstein and Peter each gave me roses, some red, some white. As the curtain lowered, Lincoln, ever-present and ever-absent in his omniscient way, tried to leave the stage, but I held his arm and pleaded with him, "Don't leave me now." It was only then, when the curtain rose again and we were standing alone together, that I thought emotion would overwhelm me, but I held on to him and did not fall.

The curtain rose again and again, and I was showered with white roses, over five thousand of them, tied in little bouquets with silver streamers. The volunteers of the New York City Ballet had removed every thorn from every rose. As if in a choreographed dream, none hit me.

People have asked me what it was like to be on that stage, where I had lived so many lives, knowing it was the last time. Did my whole career pass through my mind in a flash? No, it didn't. It was not a memorial, it was a celebration. I felt like Cinderella at the ball, and I had been there all my life. It was roses without thorns.

Dancing the *Rosenkavalier* waltz that night, I did, of course, think of Mr. B, the little push, the absent partner, the silver rose under my gown. As I said at the time, my last bow will always be to him.

Source Notes

Chapter 1 CINCINNATI

"Donna Ficker, well-known Hilltop dancer. . . ." Cincinnati newspaper, 1954.

"Tale of Three Sisters. . . ." *Cincinnati Post and Times Star*, December 12, 1958.

Chapter 4 MOVEMENTS

"Young Suzanne Farrell, a member. . . ." Joseph Gale, *Newark Evening News*, March 29, 1963.

"It may well go down in history. . . ." Allen Hughes, *The New York Times*, April 10, 1963.

"As for Miss Farrell, she is the ideal. . . ." Walter Terry, *New York Herald Tribune*, April 10, 1963.

"In its [*Movements*] first performance a week. . . ." Allen Hughes, *The New York Times*, April 21, 1963.

"It was in *Concerto Barocco* that the greatest solo delight. . . ." Allen Hughes, *The New York Times*, August 28, 1963.

Chapter 5 CRASH COURSE

". . . probably Balanchine's first excursion. . . ." Lillian Moore, *New York Herald Tribune*, January 4, 1964.

"... nøt being sufficiently authoritative. . . ." Allen Hughes, *The New York Times*, October 16, 1964.

"She is an alabaster princess. . . ." *Time*, October 30, 1964.

Chapter 6   THE DON AND DULCINEA

"... a knight-errant without love. . . ." *Don Quixote de la Mancha*, Miguel de Cervantes, Part 1, Chapter 1.

"... her name is Dulcinea, her country. . . ." *Don Quixote de la Mancha*, Miguel de Cervantes, Part I, Chapter 13.

"Woman is the goddess, the poetess, the muse. . . ." George Balanchine, *Life* magazine (international edition), August 1965.

Chapter 7   EUROPEAN DINING

"Suzanne has a phenomenal presence. . . ." George Balanchine, *Life* magazine (international edition), August 1965.

"How can you praise her? She has speed. . . ." Earl Wilson, syndicated columnist.

Chapter 8   PEARLS

"I don't mind being listed alphabetically. . . ." *Newsweek*, October 25, 1965.

"... casualties of Balanchine's emphasis on youth. . . ." *Newsweek*, October 25, 1965.

"... the young, brave and heartless." Clive Barnes, *The New York Times*, November 1965.

"... simmering discontent within the. . . ." *Newsweek*, October 25, 1965.

"For Pygmalion Balanchine. . . ." *Newsweek*, October 25, 1965.

"I disagree with everybody and I don't want to argue. . . ." George Balanchine, *Life* magazine (international edition), August 1965.

"When we married it was as if I were. . . ." Maria Tallchief, *Dancing for Mr. B: Six Balanchine Ballerinas*, a film by Anne Belle and Deborah Dickson, 1989.

Chapter 9   DIAMONDS

"Without her there would be no *Variations*. . . ." *Newsweek*, May 2, 1966.

"... all the innocent musicality. . . ." Clive Barnes, *The New York Times*, April 1, 1966.

"If George Balanchine were a novelist. . . ." Arlene Croce, *The New Yorker*, February 24, 1975.

Chapter 10   TRAVELING STEPS

"Miss Farrell, who dances the role of. . . ." Irv Kupcinet, *Chicago Sun-Times*, November 2, 1967.

"George Balanchine, choreographer of the New York. . . ." Irv Kupcinet, *Chicago Sun-Times*, November 2, 1967.

Chapter 12   EXILE

"Could anyone really think I would change. . . ." *Newsweek*, May 26, 1969.

Chapter 13   THROUGH THE LOOKING GLASS

". . . never before has a rejection of my work. . . ." *The New York Times*, February 1971.

"Folies Béjart . . . squanders the talents of some. . . ." Neil Goodwin, *Daily Express*, May 4, 1972.

Chapter 14   BACK TO THE FUTURE

"No words, not even those by Cervantes. . . ." Anna Kisselgoff, *The New York Times*, February 18, 1978.

"It isn't amusing to speculate. . . ." Arlene Croce, *The New Yorker*, February 3, 1975.

". . . five years in an alien and diseased repertory. . . ." Arlene Croce, *The New Yorker*, February 3, 1975.

"The music is not exactly a Hungarian cousin. . . ." Lincoln Kirstein, *Thirty Years of the New York City Ballet*, Alfred A. Knopf, 1978.

INDEX

Acknowledgments

We would like to thank the following for their help with this book:
Diana Adams, Ellen Alderman, Edward Bigelow, Betty Cage, Donna
Coessens, Lucia Davidova, Robert Ficker, Lloyd Fonvielle, Celia Franca,
Nathalie Gleboff and the School of American Ballet, Maxine Groffsky,
Dr. William Hamilton, Donna Holly, Barbara Horgan and the Balanchine
Estate, Kate Kahn, Paul Kolnik, Beverly Leeson, Peter Martins, Paul Mejia,
Arthur Mitchell, Vernon Rader, the Santa Fe Restaurant, Perry Silvey, J. B.
White—and, nonalphabetically, our editor, Anne Freedgood.

Suzanne Farrell
Toni Bentley
1990

Suzanne Farrell joined the New York City Ballet in 1961 and went on to become one of George Balanchine's most celebrated muses. By the time she retired from performing in 1989, she had achieved a career without precedent in the history of ballet. She danced over one hundred ballets, a third of which were composed expressly for her by Balanchine, Jerome Robbins, and Maurice Béjart, including masterpieces in which the limits of ballet technique were expanded to a degree not seen before. As a *répétiteur* for the George Balanchine Trust, she has staged Balanchine ballets for companies throughout the United States, as well as for the Royal Danish Ballet, the Kirov Ballet, and the Bolshoi Ballet. In 1999 she staged a week-long season of Balanchine for the Kennedy Center for the Performing Arts in Washington, D.C., which led to the creation of the Suzanne Farrell Ballet as an ongoing partnership with the Center. Farrell joined the faculty of the Department of Dance at Florida State University as a Francis Eppes Professor in 2000. She is the recipient of honorary degrees from several universities, including Yale, Georgetown, and Notre Dame.

Toni Bentley, a former member of the New York City Ballet, is the author of the books *Winter Season: A Dancer's Journal*, *Costumes by Karinska*, and *Sisters of Salome*, and of many articles on dance.